FOR GOOD MEASURE

AN AGENDA FOR MOVING BEYOND GDP

EDITED BY

JOSEPH E. STIGLITZ,
JEAN-PAUL FITOUSSI, AND
MARTINE DURAND

THE
NEW
PRESS

NEW YORK
LONDON

The use of this work, whether digital or print, is governed by the Terms and Conditions to be found at
http://www.oecd.org/termsandconditions. Requests for permission to reproduce selections from the
Introduction should be made through The New Press website: https://thenewpress.com/contact.

A version of this book was first published as Stiglitz, J., J. Fitoussi, and M. Durand (eds.) (2018), *For Good Measure: Advancing Research on Well-being Metrics Beyond GDP*, OECD Publishing, Paris, https://doi.org/10.1787/9789264307278-en.

Published in the United States by The New Press, New York, 2019
Distributed by Two Rivers Distribution

The opinions expressed and arguments employed herein do not necessarily reflect the official views of OECD member countries.

This document, as well as any data and any map included herein, are without prejudice to the status of or sovereignty over any territory, to the delimitation of international frontiers and boundaries and to the name of any territory, city or area.

The statistical data for Israel are supplied by and under the responsibility of the relevant Israeli authorities. The use of such data by the OECD is without prejudice to the status of the Golan Heights, East Jerusalem and Israeli settlements in the West Bank under the terms of international law.

ISBN 978-1-62097-571-8 (hc)
ISBN 978-1-62097-572-5 (ebook)
CIP data is available

The New Press publishes books that promote and enrich public discussion and understanding of the issues vital to our democracy and to a more equitable world. These books are made possible by the enthusiasm of our readers; the support of a committed group of donors, large and small; the collaboration of our many partners in the independent media and the not-for-profit sector; booksellers, who often hand-sell New Press books; librarians; and above all by our authors.

www.thenewpress.com

Book design and composition by Bookbright Media
This book was set in Adobe Garamond and Avenir

Printed in the United States of America

10 9 8 7 6 5 4 3 2 1

This report is dedicated to the memory of Alan B. Krueger.

Alan played a central role in the Commission on the Measurement of Economic Performance and Social Progress and in the High-Level Expert Group, especially through his work on subjective well-being and the ways it links to other life domains.

Brilliant academic, dedicated public servant, valued colleague, and dear friend, he helped transform the understanding of labor markets, showing (with David Card) that an increase in minimum wage does not have the adverse employment effects previously claimed. He brought his deep economic insights, combined with his strong focus on data, into the realm of policy when he served as Chairman of President Obama's Council of Economic Advisers, where he advocated for policies that promote equality and opportunity.

Alan understood the power of economics to transform our society—to reduce human suffering and to improve societal well-being. He dedicated his life to these lofty goals.

We will sorely miss him. He was more than a brilliant mind; he was above all a good person who sincerely cared for people.

CONTENTS

INTRODUCTION

While news media constantly report on what's happening to GDP—the measure of the total value of the goods and services produced within a country—few today believe that number provides an adequate picture of how well an economy or society is doing. In the aftermath of the Great Recession of 2007 to 2009, as the upbeat GDP numbers reported by the US government seemed to show a recovery, some suggested that government employees *must* be lying. If only a tiny part of society benefits from growth while the vast majority sees conditions worsen, people are not going to believe triumphant reports on the economic situation. But the government *was* accurately reporting what the measure said. The problem was with the measure itself. In the US, a closer look at the numbers showed that some 91% of the increase in national income went to the top 1% in the years between 2009 and 2012, so for nearly all Americans, there was no recovery. That's why the GDP number was misleading—and it misled some policy-makers into thinking the economy was well on the mend.

Even before the Great Recession and the euro crisis, some economists, politicians, and policy-makers were not happy with GDP as a measure of economic performance. That's what motivated President Nicolas Sarkozy of France in 2008 to organize an international Commission on the Measurement of Economic Performance and Social Progress, which I co-chaired with Jean-Paul Fitoussi, a distinguished economist at Sciences-Po Paris. Nobel Prize winner Amartya Sen served as an advisor. The Commission's report, issued in 2009 and published in 2010 in the US under the title *Mismeasuring Our Lives: Why GDP Doesn't Add Up*, had enormous impact (including thousands of academic citations). It also strengthened a global academic and civil society movement sometimes referred to as the *beyond GDP* movement that focuses on *all* the dimensions of well-being, including inequality, insecurity, and sustainability, which are largely ignored by GDP metrics.

The OECD had long tried to improve our statistical base for assessing economic performance. Indeed, in 2004, well before the formation of the Commission on the Measurement of Economic Performance and Social Progress, the OECD held its first World Forum on Statistics, Knowledge and Policy in Palermo, Italy, which focused on key indicators of success. Enrico Giovannini, then Chief Statistician for the OECD and a member of both the Commission and, later, the High-Level Expert Group hosted by the OECD, was the driving force behind the conference.

In 2011, under the leadership of its new Chief Statistician, Martine Durand, the OECD launched its Better Living Initiative, presenting in a flagship report entitled *How's Life? Measuring Well-Being*, a much broader set of indicators of economic performance and social progress, and enabling individuals to build an index of economic and social performance (the Better Life Index) based on their own values, weighing different dimensions of what makes for a good economy and society.

Then, in 2013, the High-Level Expert Group (HLEG) hosted at the OECD was established to continue the work of the Commission—in particular, to pick up on some of the many important subjects the Commission had suggested required more work. The OECD provided enormous institutional and intellectual support, without constraining in any way the work of the Commission, and for that we are very grateful. The group was chaired by Martine Durand, the chief statistician of the OECD, Jean-Paul Fitoussi, and me.

We decided to expand our membership beyond the distinguished group of academics that had constituted the Commission to include heads of some of the key national statistical offices around the world, to increase the chance that our ideas would be both implementable and implemented.

And rather than attempt to write a consensus report, we decided to publish our results in two forms, a chair's summary (in a companion volume entitled *Measuring What Counts: The Global Movement for Well-Being*[1]) and the chapters of this volume, which present research results in some of the key areas discussed by the HLEG and written by one or more members of the group, often together with some of their colleagues.

The importance of the areas explored by the HLEG, and the deficiencies in GDP, should be obvious. Four of the chapters deal with different aspects of inequality, a key issue of the day. My earlier remarks highlighted the importance inequality plays in assessing economic performance: GDP can be going up even while most individuals in society can see their incomes stagnating or declining. This kind of economy is not a well-performing economy, and unfortunately it didn't just happen in the aftermath of the Great Recession. In the US, it's been the case for more than a quarter century.

Agreeing on precisely what's going on turns out to be difficult, partly because of the kind of measurement problems the HLEG focused on. Measuring income is difficult enough, but any assessment of well-being needs to take into account goods and services received from the government (health and education benefits, for example), often received in kind. These are hard to value. For instance, because prices in health care in some countries (such as the US) have, over long intervals, gone up far faster than prices in general, government spending on health benefits for the poor, for example, could have gone up significantly and yet the *real* benefits received decreased.

Chapter 3 tackles some key aspects of measuring the distribution of household income, consumption, and wealth; Chapter 4 focuses on what are called "horizontal inequalities," that is, inequalities among different groups in society or within families; while Chapter 5 centers on the challenges in measuring inequalities of opportunity, which many have argued should be of more concern than inequalities in outcomes. Chapter 6 addresses the difficult issue of reconciling data on the distribution of income with standard data on national incomes through what are called distributional national accounts. A variety of advances in both methodology and technology have provided us with better tools with which to do this. Most importantly, we have been able to collate data from different sources, including administrative data (such as tax records) and from surveys.

The Great Recession and the euro crisis highlighted another critical issue that had been festering for years: economic insecurity. The austerity that followed in many countries led to cutbacks in systems of social protection, including pensions and government expenditures, leaving many feeling far more vulnerable. The measures were supposed to aid in economic recovery. Even conventional GDP measures suggested they did not. But many of the costs of austerity were not well captured in GDP statistics, most importantly the increase in economic insecurity. There can be no reasonable policy analysis of "reforms" in social protection that do not assess the consequences for economic security. That's why developing metrics for insecurity is so important—the subject of Chapter 8.

Still another consequence of the Great Recession was the erosion of trust, both in our institutions and in our political leaders. It wasn't just that the economic system was not as robust as its advocates had claimed and that the media did less than they might have to warn us of an impending disaster (most of the talk was about the wonders of the New Economy and the Great Moderation, suggesting business cycles were a thing of the past); but in the aftermath of the crisis political leaders seemed to pay more attention to rescuing the banks than to anything else. Little of the hundreds of billions of dollars that were spent went to those losing their jobs and homes. Survey data reflected what many people intuitively felt: a growing weakening of trust, which may help to explain the results of several political elections since the crisis on both sides of the Atlantic. This ebbing trust engendered a robust research agenda. Were there different kinds of trust, each of which could be affected differently, and each of which might have different effects on multiple dimensions of economic performance? Trust was important for itself—there is a difference between living in a society in which there is generalized trust and in which there is not—but a lack of trust also undermines economic performance. Chapter 10 illuminates the key issues surrounding the measurement of trust and its economic consequences.

Since the publication of the Commission's report there have been two important developments. One is the global agreement in September 2015 on a set of norms for what the world should strive for, in the form of the Sustainable Development Goals (SDGs), applicable to all countries, developed and less developed. These goals were accompanied by a large set of metrics—in the view of the authors of Chapter 2, too many metrics—of how we might assess performance in achieving them. The Commission had earlier addressed the question of achieving a balance between simplicity and comprehensiveness—no single number could adequately reflect the many dimensions of concern in assessing even narrowly defined economic performance; but too many numbers could be perplexing, making it difficult to identify important deficiencies or strengths. That's why the Commission had recommended a dashboard of indicators—a small number to be chosen carefully, perhaps differing across societies depending on their circumstances and their stage of development. Chapter 2 extends these insights into a discussion of how the SDGs can best be incorporated in a system of judging national performance.

The second important development is climate change. It has been three decades since the threat of climate change was first widely recognized. Matters have grown worse faster than was initially thought. There have been more extreme events, greater melting of glaciers, and greater destruction of natural habitats. Again, in response, the world came together in Copenhagen in 2009 and then in Paris in 2015 to commit to limit the extent of global warming. The goal was to keep temperature increases to no more than 2 degrees Celsius in comparison to pre-industrial levels. This has highlighted the broader issue of assessing the sustainability of economic policies, and Chapter 9 provides a framework for measuring sustainability, with an emphasis on the need for a "systems approach" and for identifying the important role of capital accounts in assessing sustainability.

All of these efforts are directed at trying to derive better assessments of societal well-being. An important contribution of the earlier Commission report was to provide impetus for ongoing research by economists, psychologists, and other social scientists into measures of *subjective well-being*: how individuals perceive their own state of well-being. As in many of the other advanced areas explored in this volume, like security and trust, it turns out that there are replicable ways to assess subjective well-being, metrics that can be explained in part by objective indicators and can themselves help explain other objective indicators. As Chapter 7 notes, since the earlier report of the Commission, there have been significant advances both in methodology and in the general acceptance of the importance, relevance, and use of such metrics.

Angel Gurría, Secretary-General of the OECD, wrote in his foreword to the companion volume to this book: "It is only by having better metrics that truly reflect people's lives and aspirations that we will be able to design and implement 'better policies for better lives.'"

He also wrote: "I very much hope that the views expressed in this book, and in the companion volume [the volume being published here] . . . will have the same significant influence in the economic and statistical community as those of the 2009 Stiglitz-Sen-Fitoussi Commission."

This has been the inspiration of the work of the High-Level Expert Group on the Measurement of Economic Performance and Social Progress and the two volumes that reflect its deliberations.

In concluding, a few acknowledgments: I want to add my personal thanks to the members of the High-Level Expert Group for their hard work and deep intellectual contributions, which should be evident in the following pages; and to those who made the work of the HLEG possible (listed in the Editors' Note below). To these, I need to add a few more: to Andrea Gurwitt, Debarati Ghosh, Sarah Thomas, and Caleb Oldham, who helped manage my own contributions to this effort; and to Marc Favreau and Emily Albarillo of The New Press. The New Press's publication of the Commission's report under the title of *Mismeasuring Our Lives: Why GDP Doesn't Add Up*, played an important role in disseminating the ideas of the Commission,[2] and I am confident that its publication of this and the companion volume will play a similarly important role in disseminating the work of the High-Level Expert Group on the Measurement of Economic Performance and Social Progress.

Joseph E. Stiglitz

Notes

1. Published originally as Stiglitz, J., J. Fitoussi and M. Durand (2018), *Beyond GDP: Measuring What Counts for Economic and Social Performance*, OECD Publishing, Paris, https://doi.org/10.1787/9789264307292-en.

2. I should also acknowledge those who have published the Commission's report in other languages, in particular Odile Jacob in French, Xinhua in simplified Chinese, Etas in Italian, Dongnyok in Korean, and RBA in Spanish.

EDITORS' NOTE

The OECD-hosted High-Level Expert Group on the Measurement of Economic Performance and Social Progress (HLEG) was created in 2013 to pursue the work of the Commission on the Measurement of Economic Performance and Social Progress convened by former French President Nicolas Sarkozy in 2008, the so-called Stiglitz-Sen-Fitoussi Commission, whose final report was published in September 2009. This book contains a collection of chapters written by members of the HLEG on topics that were the focus of the Group's work. A companion volume, *Measuring What Counts: A New Dashboard for Well-Being*, presents the Chairs' overview of the issues discussed by the HLEG over the past five years and sets out a number of recommendations on what needs to be done next.

Significant progress has been achieved in the agenda of "going beyond GDP" since the 2009 Stiglitz-Sen-Fitoussi Commission's report. This is the case, in particular, of subjective well-being and of different kinds of inequality measures. In a broader context, the Paris COP21 climate agreement and the UN 2030 Agenda (with its 16 Sustainable Development Goals, SDGs) demonstrate the extent to which the 2009 report's call to go "beyond GDP" when assessing progress has influenced the international policy agenda. At the same time, the SDGs' 169 targets and over 200 indicators illustrate the difficulties in balancing completeness and clarity. The HLEG recommends using a more limited dashboard of indicators that countries can design to suit their own priorities.

The authors of the ten chapters collected here provide an in-depth overview of the thinking that should underpin new approaches to measurement in a crucial set of fields, as well as the technical and organizational questions that have to be answered. These contributions underline the importance of integrating different scales of analysis (that of the individual, the household, the country, and the world) to produce a realistic picture of how societies are doing, and highlight the centrality of aspects that traditional approaches have neglected because of conceptual limitations, technical difficulties, or lack of data. Sustainability, for example, is a systemic global issue, but many of the actions that influence it happen at the level of each community. The health of a community is itself determined by the objective conditions and subjective experiences of all its individual members. The life chances of these individuals, in turn, are shaped not just by their personal attributes, but also by the different socio-economic groups they belong to, their ethnicity, gender, and so on.

We need to develop data sets and tools to examine the factors that determine outcomes for people and for the places where they live. The economy is, of course, a major influence, but the most used economic indicators concentrate on averages, and give little or no information on well-being at a more detailed level, for instance, how income is distributed within households and not just among them. One overall conclusion from this report is that we need more granular data. We also need to complete and make more timely the data sets we do have, both by integrating administrative and other types of data that already exist and by redesigning national accounts to incorporate distributional aspects.

It is often easier to measure outcomes than the factors that contributed to producing those outcomes. The Group devoted considerable effort to circumstances outside the control of individuals, such as ethnicity or gender, that can have a significant impact on inequality and access to opportunities. The HLEG also looked at factors that can be both a cause and consequence of particular outcomes such as trust: subjective well-being is influenced by trust, while countries with higher levels of trust tend to have higher income. Interactions between the objective conditions and subjective assessments are also important in domains such as economic insecurity, and this book discusses the need to consider both observed and perceived security. The book also suggests that one way to integrate these multiple strands into a holistic approach to the measurement of economic performance and social progress is to adopt a systems viewpoint to complement the capital approach and deal with the many interactions at play.

We hope that the present publication and its companion volume (*Measuring What Counts: A New Dashboard for Well-Being*) will provide useful elements to further the Beyond GDP agenda. In our companion volume, we highlight why we believe this agenda is even more important today than it was when the Stiglitz-Sen-Fitoussi Commission began its work a decade ago.

We recognize that we could not have got this far without the hard work and devotion of HLEG members and our partners. Over the course of this work, HLEG members periodically convened to discuss many of the issues that are reflected in this book. The HLEG also organized a number of thematic workshops, which were hosted and supported by various foundations and attended by dozens of researchers. We are grateful to them all for their help and support.

These workshops focused on:

- **"Intra-generational and Inter-generational Sustainability"** (September 22–23, 2014), Rome, hosted by the Einaudi Institute for Economics and Finance and the Bank of Italy and sponsored by SAS;
- **"Multi-dimensional Subjective Well-Being"** (October 30–31, 2014), Turin, Italy, organized in collaboration with the International Herbert A. Simon Society and the Collegio Carlo Alberto, and with the support of Compagnia di San Paolo;
- **"Inequality of Opportunity"** (January 14, 2015), Paris, hosted by the Gulbenkian Foundation in collaboration with Sciences-Po Paris and the CEPREMAP;
- **"Measuring Inequalities of Income and Wealth"** (September 15–16, 2015), Berlin, organized in collaboration with Bertelsmann Stiftung;
- **"Measurement of Well-Being and Development in Africa"** (November 12–14, 2015), Durban, South Africa, organized in collaboration with the Government of South Africa, the Japanese International Cooperation Agency, Columbia University, and Cornell University;
- **"Measuring Economic, Social and Environmental Resilience"** (November 25–26, 2015), Rome, hosted by the Einaudi Institute for Economics and Finance, supported by the Bank of Italy and the Italian statistical office (ISTAT), and sponsored by SAS;
- **"Economic Insecurity: Forging an Agenda for Measurement and Analysis"** (March 4, 2016), New York, organized in collaboration with the Washington Center for Equitable Growth, the Yale Institution for Social and Policy Studies, and the Ford Foundation; and
- **"Measuring Trust and Social Capital"** (June 10, 2016), Paris,

organized in collaboration with Science-Po Paris and the European Research Council.

Finally, we would like to thank a number of colleagues who have supported our work throughout this period: Marco Mira d'Ercole, for his many valuable inputs to the substance and organization of this book; Elizabeth Beasley, for acting as rapporteur of the present volume; Martine Zaïda, for coordinating the HLEG and organizing all the thematic workshops and plenary meetings; Patrick Love, for editing support; Christine Le, Thi for statistical assistance; Robert Akam, for communications support; and Anne-Lise Faron, for preparing this book for publication.

Joseph E. Stiglitz
Jean-Paul Fitoussi
Martine Durand
Chairs of the High-Level Expert Group on the Measurement of
Economic Performance and Social Progress

PREFACE

Assessing the progress of society presents a range of challenges: conceptual challenges (e.g., the inevitable trade-off between trying to be comprehensive and the limits in people's capacity to deal with too much information); technical challenges (e.g., how to combine information across micro-data sets dealing with different issues, how to integrate micro-data informing on inequalities with macro-economic accounts dealing with averages); and organizational (e.g., how to improve coordination among different data-collectors, how to balance international harmonization and local accountability, how to improve timeliness of existing data). The High-Level Expert Group on the Measurement of Economic Performance and Social Progress (HLEG), hosted by the OECD from 2013 to 2018, addressed some of these challenges, building on the report of the Stiglitz-Sen-Fitoussi Commission published in 2009. The aim remains the same—help to develop the means to describe progress and, in this way, contribute to better policies. This book consists of a collection of authored chapters dealing with those issues that the HLEG felt deserved further attention and have thus been at the core of the Group's deliberations over the past few years. A complementary volume by the HLEG Chairs (J.E. Stiglitz, J.-P. Fitoussi, and M. Durand, *Measuring What Counts: A New Dashboard for Well-Being*) provides a broader overview of the issues discussed by the Group.

The Sustainable Development Goals and the Measurement of Human Progress

The adoption of the Sustainable Development Goals (SDGs) by the UN General Assembly in 2015 is the most visible manifestation of how the Beyond GDP agenda has influenced policy discussions. But the SDGs also highlight the inevitable tension between the pull to broaden the set of measures used for monitoring progress and the imperative to focus on a small number of top-level indicators—a tension that can only be solved through prioritization of the UN goals and targets at the national level. National Statistical Offices should be given the governance independence and financial resources they need to fulfill their obligations on monitoring the SDGs, while the international community should support statistical offices in less developed countries starting from those global phenomena requiring good metrics for all countries.

Measuring the Distribution of Household Income, Consumption, and Wealth

The way household income, consumption, and wealth are distributed is important in relation to fairness, but an unequal distribution of economic resources also lessens the impact of economic growth on reducing extreme poverty. Unfortunately, analyses in this field often use databases that not only show different levels of inequality from one database to another but also, for some countries, diverging trends. Data in this field suffer from under-coverage and under-reporting at both ends of the distribution, from limited information on wealth distribution, and from the difficulty in linking information among data sets to know what is happening to the joint distribution of economic resources. More work is also needed to reflect the value of in-kind benefits such as education and health care services in a broader income concept, and to assess the distributive impact of consumption taxes and subsidies.

Horizontal Inequality, Intra-household Inequality, and the Gender Wealth Gap

Inequality in income, consumption, and wealth among individuals ("vertical inequality") ignores systematic inequities among population groups, omits important nonincome dimensions, and assumes that each individual in a household receives the household's mean income. Horizontal inequalities (inequalities among groups with shared characteristics, both in income and nonincome dimensions), intra-household inequality, and the gender wealth gap are important in their own right, but they also link with each other in important ways (for example, a key aspect of intra-household inequality is inequality between the genders). Progress in all these fields should be a priority for future research.

Inequality of Opportunity

Inequalities in income and wealth are more acceptable to individuals and more sustainable for society when people feel they have a fair chance to improve their situation. Inequality of opportunity—that is, in the circumstances involuntarily inherited or faced by individuals (such as gender or ethnicity) that affect their economic achievements—also matters: beyond contributing to outcomes inequality, it reduces the efficiency of an economy by weakening incentives for those who think they can never succeed. While it will never be possible to observe differences among individuals across all the circumstances that shape their economic success independently of their will and effort, data on some aspects are available, and should be monitored regularly. But more is needed—for example, developing long-term panels linking parents and offspring, and including retrospective questions in surveys.

Distributional National Accounts and the World Inequality Database

The World Inequality Database (WID.world), which was originally called the World Wealth and Income Database, project provides annual estimates of the distribution of income and wealth using concepts that are consistent with national accounts, which allows for policy questions to be addressed that could not be answered through other data sets. These data highlight substantial variations in the magnitude of rising inequality across countries, suggesting that country-specific policies and institutions matter considerably. High growth rates in emerging countries reduce between-country inequality but do not guarantee low within-country inequality levels nor ensure the social sustainability of globalization. Access to more and better data (administrative records, surveys, more detailed national accounts, etc.) is critical to monitor global inequality and to get a better picture of how the benefits of growth are distributed.

Understanding Subjective Well-Being

Subjective well-being has great potential as an indicator of the "health" of a community and of individuals. Measures of societal progress should take into account how people feel about and experience their own lives, alongside information about their objective conditions. At a societal level, subjective well-being measures can signal wider problems in people's lives, capture prevailing sentiment, and predict behavior in ways that complement more traditional measures. Deepening the measurement initiatives undertaken in this field as a response to the recommendation of the 2009 Stiglitz-Sen-Fitoussi Commission is a necessary step toward providing responses to the many research questions that are still open.

Economic (In)security

People's confidence in the economic and political system is destroyed quickly when there is a sentiment that economic security is declining. Economic insecurity captures individuals' (or households') degree of vulnerability to an economic loss. Three elements are inherent in this definition: some probability of an adverse event; some negative economic consequence if this event occurs; and some protection (from formal insurance to informal risk-sharing, self-insurance through savings, and the like) that could potentially offset or prevent these losses. Measures are needed for each of these elements and for their combined effects. It is also important to distinguish between *observed* security, which can be measured using economic data, and *perceived* security, where people themselves reveal their subjective appreciation of their economic situation.

Capital and Systems Approaches to Measuring Sustainability

The SDG framework recognizes that progress has to be considered holistically and in a long-term perspective, taking account of trade-offs, spill-overs, and unintended consequences of policy and investment decisions. Capturing the inter-temporal consequences of today's decisions requires measures of the various types of resources that will sustain future well-being, i.e., natural, human, social, and economic capital. Complex systems theory provides a complementary approach for integrating the analysis of the different types of capital by dealing with the many interactions that shape sustainability. A systems approach could also more adequately capture the extent to which a production and consumption path is sustainable, safe, and resilient.

Trust, Social Progress, and Well-Being

People's trust in others and in institutions is a key determinant of economic growth, social cohesion, and subjective well-being. While most of the research on the role of trust and cooperation draws on survey data, this type of information requires caution in use and interpretation. One way forward is to combine surveys with experiments asking participants to make decisions under circumstances where their degree of trust influences their behavior. Evidence of this type, based on representative samples of the population for several countries, is now starting to become available. It has the potential to deepen our understanding of trust, its causes as well as its consequences.

1.

Overview

Elizabeth Beasley

This chapter provides a high-level overview of the themes discussed in more detail in the subsequent chapters. It walks through each issue, spelling out the reasons for its importance, the measurement challenges it raises, and the steps that should be taken to improve statistics in the related fields.

Elizabeth Beasley is currently a Researcher at CEPREMAP, Paris. The author wishes to thank Marco Mira d'Ercole and Patrick Love for their inputs, as well as all HLEG members for their comments on the previous draft of this chapter. The opinions expressed and arguments employed in the contributions below are those of the author and do not necessarily reflect the official views of the OECD or of the governments of its member countries.

Introduction

The Commission on the Measurement of Economic Performance and Social Progress—also known as the Stiglitz-Sen-Fitoussi Commission—concluded its work in 2009 with the hope that the report it produced would start a debate over the adequacy of current ways of measuring economic performance and social progress, and motivate further research on developing better metrics.

The Commission's 12 recommendations (see sidebar below) have been met with a high level of enthusiasm from the statistical community, civil society, international organizations, governments, and researchers. Their efforts are transforming the landscape of measurement.

The present volume does not replace the 2009 report. It focuses on a selection of topics that the report covered, rather than carrying out a complete review. In addition, several new topics are discussed in this volume that did not feature in the report, in part because of the way the world has changed since 2009. For example, the financial crisis highlighted the importance of economic (in)security, and thus the need to develop metrics of it. In evaluating economic performance, such metrics need to be considered alongside more conventional indicators.

The overall message of these chapters is one of tempered optimism: there has been rapid progress in several areas, bolstered by input from multiple stakeholders, while other areas continue to face conceptual or practical hurdles. Our understanding of subjective well-being, for example, has greatly evolved, as has our ability to measure some types of inequality.

The environment and sustainability were central to the Stiglitz, Sen, and Fitoussi report, and despite the fallout from the financial crisis and the Great Recession that followed, the international community negotiated major agreements in both of these domains. In 2015, it signed the COP21 (Paris Agreement) on climate and the UN 2030 Agenda (United Nations, 2015), consisting of the 17 Sustainable Development Goals (SDGs) and their 169 targets. The latter agreement in particular demonstrates the extent to which the "Beyond GDP" message of Stiglitz, Sen, and Fitoussi has been incorporated into the international policy agenda. The SDGs, which are applicable to all countries, try to capture multiple dimensions of social and economic progress.

Key messages from each of the chapters included in this volume are summarized below.

RECOMMENDATIONS OF THE COMMISSION ON THE MEASUREMENT OF ECONOMIC PERFORMANCE AND SOCIAL PROGRESS (2009)

- Recommendation 1: When evaluating material well-being, look at income and consumption rather than production, as conflating GDP and economic well-being can lead to misleading indications about how well off people are and entail the wrong policy decisions.
- Recommendation 2: Emphasize the household perspective, as citizens' material living standards are followed better through measures of household income and consumption.
- Recommendation 3: Consider income and consumption jointly with wealth, which requires information on balance sheets and proper valuation of these stocks.
- Recommendation 4: Give more prominence to the distribution of income, consumption, and wealth, which requires that measures of average income, consumption, and wealth should be accompanied by indicators of their distribution.

- Recommendation 5: Broaden income measures to nonmarket activities, such as the services people received from other family members as well as leisure time.
- Recommendation 6: Quality of life depends on people's objective conditions and capabilities, such as people's health, education, personal activities, and environmental conditions but also their social connections, political voice, and insecurity.
- Recommendation 7: Quality-of-life indicators in all the dimensions covered should assess inequalities in a comprehensive way, taking into account linkages and correlations.
- Recommendation 8: Surveys should be designed to assess the links between various quality-of-life domains for each person, and this information should be used when designing policies.
- Recommendation 9: Statistical offices should provide the information needed to aggregate across quality-of-life dimensions, allowing the construction of different indexes.
- Recommendation 10: Measures of both objective and subjective well-being provide key information about people's quality of life, and statistical offices should incorporate questions to capture people's life evaluations, hedonic experiences, and priorities in their own survey.
- Recommendation 11: Sustainability assessment requires a well-identified dashboard of indicators, whose elements should be interpretable as variations of some underlying "stocks."
- Recommendation 12: The environmental aspects of sustainability deserve a separate follow-up based on a well-chosen set of physical indicators.

Source: Stiglitz, J.E., A. Sen, and J.-P. Fitoussi (2009), *Report by the Commission on the Measurement of Economic and Social Progress*, http://ec.europa.eu/eurostat /documents/118025/118123/Fitoussi+Commission+report.

Sustainable Development Goals and the Measurement of Economic and Social Progress

As Ravi Kanbur, Ebrahim Patel, and Joseph Stiglitz argue in Chapter 2, the process leading to the SDGs reveals the tension between the desire for completeness and thoroughness on one side, and the need for clarity on the other. This was a central tension discussed in the Stiglitz, Sen, and Fitoussi report. Obviously, the more that detailed information and data are disaggregated, the more complete picture one has of what is going on. The 169 SDG targets and 232 indicators provide a useful platform and have the virtue that they are agreed to internationally. But their implementation will need to be sensitive to national needs and priorities, as well as limited resources. Accountability and sovereignty lead to the recommendation that this streamlining and selection of indicators takes place in the context of a national dialogue informed by international frameworks. The international dimension is important because there is a trade-off with comparability across countries; countries themselves need to be mindful of comparability as, to know how well one is doing, one needs to know how well other similarly situated countries are performing.

In order to pursue the agenda of the SDGs, and the larger agenda of measuring social and economic progress, National Statistical Offices (NSOs) must have the governance and financial resources necessary to provide an independent and credible statistics to nourish the national policy dialogue and enable accountability. In low-income countries, statisticians have to have the means to resist not only the political pressures any NSO is subject to, but also pressures coming from powerful international organizations that may inadvertently harm the autonomy of NSOs by imposing an agenda that takes insufficient account of national needs and capacities.

When considering global and transnational issues, such as world inequality and poverty or climate change, harmonization of measurement over countries is of key importance. International organizations have a large and important role to play to support such harmonization, and the international community should commit resources to supporting the production of those national statistics that are critical for assessing global issues.

Measuring the Distribution of Household Income, Consumption, and Wealth

Stiglitz, Sen, and Fitoussi emphasized the importance of inequality. Even if average income per capita was increasing, a majority of citizens could be experiencing a decline. One of the original motivations for the Commission was the concern, expressed by President Sarkozy, that our indicators were presenting a picture that was inconsistent with individuals' own perceptions. Even though the government could boast that GDP was increasing, most individuals could still feel worse off.

In Chapter 3, Nora Lustig addresses the challenges posed by measuring vertical inequalities in household income, consumption, and wealth. The issue is important from a normative standpoint in relation to social justice, but there are instrumental reasons to care about these inequalities too. Inequality in the distribution of household resources has come to the fore of the political debate in recent years, partly as it has become more extreme and partly as the economic, social, and political costs have become clearer.

While there have been notable improvements in the availability of data (including more extensive use of administrative data), substantial challenges remain in measuring inequality in economic circumstances through the joint analysis of income, consumption, and wealth. These analyses are often based on databases relying on household surveys: micro-based data sets, which calculate inequality measures directly from these surveys; secondary sources data sets, which combine inequality indicators from a variety of other sources; data sets that generate inequality measures through a variety of imputation and statistical inference methods instead of relying directly on unit-record data sets; and WID.world, described below. Unfortunately, different international databases show not only different levels of inequality but also, for some countries (especially in sub-Saharan Africa), diverging trends.

These different data sets all suffer from the fact that household surveys suffer from under-coverage and under-reporting of incomes at both ends of the distribution. The under-reported top incomes are sometimes referred to as "the missing rich" problem. The factors embedded in the data collection process that may explain the missing rich problem in household surveys are many, ranging from under-reporting of their income or a refusal to answer by very rich people, to the fact that very few rich people are likely to be included in the sampling frame of the survey. Approaches to address the missing rich problem can be classified into three broad groups: using alternate data (such as using tax records instead of surveys); operating within survey, making inferences about the missing data using parametric and nonparametric methods; and correcting survey data (or inequality estimates) by combining surveys and administrative data.

The bottom incomes are not being covered sufficiently either—for example, the incomes of the homeless or others with no fixed address. And many low-income people often report levels of consumption expenditures well in excess of their declared income, suggesting that they are consuming out of savings or experiencing a temporary drop in income or that they may be simply under-reporting their material living standards. This underscores the importance of joint analysis of income, consumption, and wealth; such an analysis would enable us to ascertain the extent to which the poor are "eating up" their assets.

There are also large differences in the nature of data sets between advanced and developing countries, and the extent to which the data provided correspond to appropriate definitions of income or consumption. For advanced economies, economic inequality is typically measured based on equivalized income (where adjustments are made for family size) while in the rest of the world, per capita consumption or income is used. While in principle the income variable that should be the focus of attention is disposable income—what individuals can spend, after paying their taxes and receiving any transfer—the income concept used in developing countries' data is often not clear. Likewise, while many argue that income or consumption should include consumption of own production (goods and services produced within the household) and imputed rent of owner-occupied housing (the rent that individuals would have had to pay if they were renting their house), in practice this is generally not the case.

Moreover, the analysis of the "true" level of economic inequality is typically hindered by the fact that standard measures of income exclude free in-kind services (especially, education and health care) provided by governments and nonprofit institutions. Valuing social transfers in kind raises both conceptual and measurement challenges. There are difficulties in ascertaining the appropriate range of services to be considered; the monetary valuation of the services provided; and their allocation to various beneficiaries. In practice, the most frequently used approach is to value in-kind transfers at the costs incurred by the government in producing them. This approach, however, does not take into account variations in needs across income or age groups, nor does it consider service quality, and may not reflect the actual valuation by beneficiaries. Imputation to individual users is particularly complex in the case of health care. The allocation of benefits is done following either the "actual consumption approach" or the "insurance value approach"—which assigns the same per capita spending to everybody sharing the same characteristic such as age or gender, irrespectively of their actual use of these services. The choice of methods has a large influence on the results obtained.

The impacts of consumption taxes and subsidies on household resources are often neglected too. While it is acknowledged that household consumption possibilities are reduced or increased by, respectively, consumption taxes or production subsidies passed on to the prices that households pay for goods and services, taking this impact into account has not been part of the conventions typically used for analyzing disparities in households' economic well-being.

In addition, there are many technical issues affecting the comparability of data, which in turn affect the ability to make cross-country comparisons. Databases differ on whether adjustments (and which ones) are made to the micro-data to correct for under-reporting, to eliminate outliers, or to address missing responses. Inconsistencies mean that different data sets frequently produce different results about the level of inequality and whether there is convergence in levels of inequality among countries, and this is so even when the same metric is employed.

Timeliness is another problem, with estimates of economic inequalities in many countries lagging behind GDP data by years.

A further issue is that, with exceptions, household surveys collect data on only income or only consumption, which significantly limits the possibility of undertaking the joint analysis of both variables and rigorous cross-country comparisons. Even when measures exist on the distribution of household income, consumption, and wealth, very few countries collect data in ways that would allow the joint distribution of household income, consumption, and wealth to be analyzed in a coherent way; doing so was one of the key recommendations of the Stiglitz-Sen-Fitoussi report.

An additional challenge is that, for most countries in the world, totals for house-

hold income and consumption from surveys do not match the equivalent totals from national accounts; not even their growth rates match. (This is a topic discussed more extensively in Chapter 6.)

As in other areas of the measurement of economic performance, greater international efforts should be devoted to assess the availability and quality of data on wealth distribution, and to ensure that the data collected provides information that is comparable across countries and over time.[1] Accurate measurement of economic inequality will require a political commitment. Governments, international organizations, and the academic community need to be committed to transparency and to make information publicly available in ways that facilitate the measurement and analysis of economic inequality while protecting the identity of respondents to preserve confidentiality.

Horizontal Inequalities

Inequality in income, consumption, and wealth among individuals, sometimes called "vertical inequality," ignores systematic inequities among population groups, leaves out nonincome dimensions of inequality, and assumes that each individual in a household receives the mean income of that household. In Chapter 4, Carmen Diana Deere, Ravi Kanbur, and Frances Stewart discuss the importance of "horizontal inequalities," inequalities among groups with shared characteristics in both income and nonincome dimensions, intra-household inequality, and the gender wealth gap. The three issues are important in their own right, but they also link with each other in important ways. For example, a key aspect of intra-household inequality is inequality between men and women within the household, and this relates to the broader question of horizontal inequality in society.

While these inequalities are of great policy relevance, notably because of their implications for justice and social stability, there are no systematic efforts to collect the necessary data and publish the appropriate indicators. This is due, in part, to the conceptual and practical challenges that their measurement entails. However, much more could be done to standardize the practice of collecting the relevant information and broadening the diagnostic indicators used for social progress assessments.

People are members of many groups (age, gender, ethnicity, religion, etc.) so multi-dimensionality is an essential feature of horizontal inequality and its measurement. Three prime dimensions are socio-economic, political, and cultural recognition, each with an array of elements. For example, socio-economic inequalities include inequalities in access to basic services and inequalities in economic resources, including income, assets, employment, and so on. In the political dimension, it is a matter of representation in government, the upper levels of the bureaucracy, the military, the police, and local administrations. On the cultural side, relevant inequalities include those in recognition, use of, and respect for language, religion, and cultural practices.

The measurement of horizontal inequalities raises the question of which group classification to adopt. And given that group size varies, it may be desirable to weight any aggregate measure by the size of each group.

An inequality measure that is silent as to the relationship of inequality to the overall structure of a society (for example, economic inequality between ethnic groups or between men and women) is of limited value, since a concern about inequality is rooted in a concern for justice and overall societal health.

In addition, when intra-household inequality is ignored, overall inequality will be underestimated. Quantifying intra-household inequality is a first step toward getting a more accurate measure of the overall level of inequality in society and of the responsiveness of poverty reduction to economic growth. It can also be an important part of an investigation of inequality across gender and across age groups, both of which are aspects of horizontal inequality. But, as we have seen, so far as the headline money-metric measures of inequality are concerned, most household surveys collect information only at the household level, so that understatement of inequality is endemic to official statistics.

It is unlikely that all official household surveys can be turned to collecting individual-level information. But there are alternatives. Structural econometric methods can be used to estimate intra-household inequality parameters by modeling distribution at the household level. Systematic investigation of other indicators available at the individual level in some surveys (for example, individual earnings, or individual anthropometrics) could be analyzed to develop a sense of the understatement of overall inequality in situations where individual information is not available. Finally, small specialized surveys can also be mounted.

The level of detail of traditional surveys is usually not sufficient to explore certain types of inequalities. A case in point is that of within-household inequalities in terms of wealth. When data on asset ownership is collected in household surveys, for example, it has tended to be at the household rather than the individual level, constraining gender analysis; some assets may also be held in joint ownership, and in some cases this may not be well defined and depend on the specific legal provisions of each country. Methodological constraints are one of the reasons that progress on measuring individual level wealth has been slow, such as whether reliable data on the valuation of assets can be elicited from respondents. Other issues include the questions of who should be interviewed in an asset survey, how ownership should be defined, how the value of assets should be measured, and whether all assets need to be included in wealth estimates.

Several questions could be added to household surveys to help in this respect, such as those seeking to understand the relevant marital regime and those collecting data on who in the household owns its immovable property.

Inequality of Opportunity

One key dimension of inequality is inequality of opportunity. While the Stiglitz, Sen, and Fitoussi report emphasized the difficulties in measuring inequalities of income and wealth, those presented by inequality of opportunity are far greater.

In Chapter 5, François Bourguignon looks at how the circumstances involuntarily inherited or faced by individuals (such as gender or ethnicity, or the income or education of one's parents) affect their economic chances, opportunities, and achievements. Inequality of opportunity is often presented as the truly unfair part of the inequality of income, as opposed to that part of income inequality that results from free individual decisions. Apart from this basic question of fairness, inequality of opportunity matters because it is a key determinant of inequality of income and also because it may reduce the aggregate efficiency of an economy, or the average outcome, by weakening incentives. People who get off to a bad start in life due to circumstances beyond their control, or face discrimination in the economic system because of particular personal traits, may see little point in trying hard since they will be left behind anyway. Likewise, those who are favored have less incentive too, since they know they are more likely to succeed. Moreover, inequalities of opportunity imply that many individuals will not be able to live up to their potential.

Measuring the inequality of opportunity is practically and conceptually challenging. It will never be possible to observe differences among individuals across all the circumstances that may shape their economic success independently of their will. Besides, the distinction between what is not under the control of individuals, i.e., circumstances, and what is, often referred to as "efforts," may often be extremely ambiguous. However, it is possible to measure some observable dimensions of inequality of opportunity and, most importantly, their impact on inequality of outcomes. Data on specific outcomes, some circumstances, and, possibly, some types of efforts are available in household surveys or from administrative sources. It is also possible to measure directly some dimensions of inequality of opportunity independently of their impact on economic outcomes—for example, cognitive ability or health status. The most obvious example of inequality of opportunity in a specific dimension is inter-generational mobility of earnings, i.e., the relationship between the earnings of the parent and those of the child.

If progress has been made lately in measuring some aspects of the inequality of opportunity and in making international comparisons, monitoring them over time at the country level is still infrequent and often imprecise. Few consensual estimates are available about whether inter-generational mobility has increased, remained the same, or decreased in recent decades. Progress has been made in monitoring mean educational achievements in many countries, most notably under the OECD PISA initiative, but no systematic reporting or discussion takes place on the evolution of their dispersion. Also, if the mean earnings gap across gender is reported regularly in most advanced economies, the same cannot always be said of the earnings gap adjusted for changes in the educational attainment of women and men (a measure which suggests that most of the narrowing in the gender wage gap observed in recent years mainly reflects higher education of women, rather than lower gender gaps between women and men of similar education); or the gap across ethnic groups or between natives and first- and second-generation migrants. Yet, in most countries, data to evaluate these and other indicators on a regular basis either are available, or could often be made available at little cost.

The data required to improve the situation and monitor observable dimensions of inequality of opportunity in a systematic way include data on family background, wealth, and students' skills. Three basic statistics should receive priority attention and should be harmonized as much as possible across countries and over time: inequality of economic outcomes (earnings, income) arising from parental background and its share in total inequality of outcome; variance analysis of scores in PISA and analogous surveys at earlier ages, including pre-school, the share of that variance explained by parental/social background, or the gaps in scores between students from different families; and gender inequality in earnings, unadjusted and adjusted for differences in education, age, job experience, types of occupation, etc.

Distributional National Accounts

In Chapter 6, Facundo Alvaredo, Lucas Chancel, Thomas Piketty, Emmanuel Saez, and Gabriel Zucman discuss the limits of the System of National Accounts (SNA) for looking at disparities within the household sector. The focus of the SNA has been on the main sectors in the economy, only distinguishing results for the household sector as a whole. Partly as a result, the discrepancies between income levels and growth rates displayed in national accounts and the ones displayed in microstatistics and underlying distributional data have been growing in all dimensions: income, consumption, wealth. Scholars have been aware of the discrepancies for some time (see, for instance, Anand, Segal, and Stiglitz, 2010), and have proposed ideas to explain the reasons behind them, but systematic and coordinated action to put national accounts and micro-economic data in a consistent framework started only in 2011, when the OECD and Eurostat launched a joint Expert Group to carry out a feasibility study on compiling distributional measures of household income, consumption, and saving within the framework of national accounts, on the basis of micro-data.

The World Inequality Database (WID.world) project presents a renovated approach to the measurement of economic inequality consistent with macro aggregates, aiming to rebuild the bridges between distributional data available from micro sources and national accounts aggregates in a systematic way through Distributional National Accounts (DINA). In some cases, this may require revising central aspects of key national accounts concepts and estimates. The two main data sources used in DINA income series are income tax data and national accounts, as in earlier versions of the approach. However, these two core data sources are now used in a more systematic and consistent manner, with fully harmonized definitions and methods, and together with other sources such as household income and wealth surveys, inheritance, estate, and wealth tax data, as well as wealth measures for those at the top of the distribution provided by "rich lists" compiled by the press.

The DINA initiative aims to provide annual estimates of the distribution of income and wealth using concepts that are consistent with the macro-economic national accounts. In this way, the analysis of GDP growth and economic inequality can be carried over in a coherent framework. The long-run goal of DINA is to release income and wealth synthetic micro-files for many countries on an annual basis. Such data can play a critical role in the public debate, and can be used as a resource for further analysis by various actors in civil society and the academic, business, and political communities.

A comparison between the United States, China, and France (broadly representative of Western Europe) illustrates how DINA can be used to analyze the distribution of economic growth across income groups. National income per adult increased in the three countries between 1978 and 2015: by 811% in China, 59% in the United States, and 39% in France.[2] In China, the top earners experienced very high growth rates, but average growth was so large that the average income of the bottom 50% also grew markedly, by around 400%. In contrast, the bottom 50% of adults in the United States experienced a small drop. In France, very high incomes grew more than average, but their numbers are too small to affect the overall average, while the bottom 50% income group enjoyed the same growth as average growth (39%).

Statistics on the distribution of wealth are highly imperfect, but they show substantial variations in their size and trends across countries, suggesting that country-specific policies and institutions matter considerably. High GDP growth rates in emerging countries reduce between-country inequality, but this in itself does not guarantee acceptable within-country inequality levels and ensure the social sustainability of globalization. Access to more and better data (administrative records, surveys, more detailed and explicit national accounts, etc.) is critical to monitor global inequality dynamics, as this is a key building block both to properly understand the present as well as the forces that will dominate in the future, and to design potential policy responses.

Understanding Subjective Well-Being

Stiglitz, Sen, and Fitoussi argued that traditional metrics need to be supplemented with indicators of subjective well-being, i.e., measures of how people perceive their own well-being and experience their life. Advances in psychology have led to the development of replicable indicators that are systematically related to other aspects of economic performance and social conditions, and which themselves could be at least partially explained by other objective indicators. In Chapter 7 Alan B. Krueger and Arthur A. Stone discuss the potential of subjective well-being as an indicator of the "health" of a community and the individuals that compose it. There is an increasing consensus that broader measures of societal progress should take into account how people feel about and experience their own lives, alongside information about their objective conditions. At a social level, subjective well-being measures are powerful indicators that can signal wider problems in people's lives, capture prevailing sentiment, and predict their behavior.

The availability of survey data on subjective well-being, including panel data, has increased rapidly since the 2009 Stiglitz, Sen, and Fitoussi report. National Statistical Offices are increasingly including subjective well-being questions in their surveys, and a majority of OECD countries now collect at least some subjective well-being data. Continued methodological progress would be facilitated by the collection and dissemination of long time series in large, high-quality data sets. Collection of such data will also facilitate the generation of policy-relevant insights.

Advances have been made on many of the methodological and interpretive issues that caused concern about using subjective well-being measures in 2009. While a deep examination of these issues is important to improving the measurement of subjective well-being, it is equally important to avoid setting a uniquely high standard for subjective well-being in contrast to other indicators, such as income, consumption, or wealth inequality, which can also be difficult to calculate or are similarly derived from self-reported measures that are equally sensitive to survey methodology. We have come to accept these other measures, and gloss over their methodological problems, simply because they have been used for so long.

There have also been other advances, such as the wider implementation of time-use surveys for collecting detailed information on subjective well-being connected to daily activities.

Applications of subjective well-being have also begun to appear—for example, in assessing the impact of the global financial crisis. Other innovative but early work is experimenting with the incorporation of subjective well-being into standard cost-benefit analysis. Several harmonized international data sets now exist, allowing comparison of subjective well-being levels over time.

An area with great potential for development is the examination of different types of subjective well-being. Existing research generally focuses on life evaluation (how satisfied one is with one's life) but less on emotion (happiness or depression) and eudaemonia (meaning and purpose in one's life). While these types of subjective well-being are related, they are not the same, and each yields different insights that can be helpful for policies and research.

Achieving a better understanding of the direction of causality between subjective well-being and people's objective circumstances (e.g., does better health increase happiness, or does happiness help people engage in healthier behaviors?) is one of the issues that needs to be explored further for a more complete understanding of subjective well-being. It is difficult to reach strong conclusions about causality on the basis of on much of the subjective well-being research that is currently available, which relies mainly on observational and self-reported data. Heterogeneity across individuals also needs to be addressed: just as focusing on the simple average income gives an incomplete picture, so too does focusing on the average level of subjective well-being. For example, life-cycle patterns of income are important to understand, and the same applies for subjective well-being. One wants to understand inequalities in subjective well-being—what drives them and how they are related to inequalities in income.

Although data collection on subjective well-being has expanded enormously, there remain two important areas where there is still a lack of data, and where the inclusion of subjective well-being questions in surveys is likely to be relatively low cost. The first is to expand high-quality data collection on subjective well-being to less developed countries—for example, by including a life satisfaction and experiential well-being module in household surveys. Second, in order to increase our understanding of experiential well-being, subjective well-being measures should be included in official time-use surveys.

Economic Security

People's economic security has both observed (objective) and perceived (subjective) dimensions. In Chapter 8, Jacob S. Hacker reminds us that even before the financial crisis, citizens of advanced democracies and their leaders perceived that economic security was declining. Various observed measures provide an indication of the likely scale of the problem. For example, while around 12% of people in developed countries are classified by the OECD as "income poor," the share of those having financial assets insufficient to cover more than 3 months of (poverty level) living standards is typically three times as high. Similarly, around 12% of adults will typically experience an income loss of 25% or greater in any given year.

In developing countries, governments have also grappled with economic insecurity, as citizens move into wage labor, health care grows more costly, and the traditional risk-spreading role of the family declines. In both developed and developing countries, public debate has centered on the changing character of the economy and society, and on the relative roles of governments, markets, and households in coping with the related economic risks.

Still, the definition and measurement of economic security have continued to pose serious difficulties. This is in part because of the multiplicity of definitions and measures proposed; indeed, even the boundary between economic security and other forms of security remains hazy. It is also because of the relative scarcity of high-quality data, particularly panel data in comparable form across a significant number of countries. Despite the difficulties, it is possible to identify a common definition of economic security that is implicit or explicit in much existing literature: individuals' (or households') degree of vulnerability to economic loss. Three elements are inherent in this definition: some probability of an adverse event; some negative economic consequence if this event in fact occurs; and some set of protections (from formal insurance to informal risk-sharing, self-insurance through savings, and the like) that potentially offset or prevent these losses.

Within that definition, two distinctions are important when talking about economic security. The first is between observed security and perceived security. Observed security describes measures that use economic data to determine whether an individual or household is insecure (for example, because they are at risk of a large reduction in income or consumption). Perceived security describes measures based on individuals' own reports of their subjective response to their economic situation (whether through surveys, experiments, or some other revelation technique).

The second distinction is between scoreboards or indices of economic security based on (weighted) multiple measures, and integrated measures, which try to capture individual or household security in a single statistic. The main class of integrated measures looks at income volatility in some form, particularly large drops in income from one period to the next. For many reasons, integrated measures are preferable to weighted indices measures, which are less transparent and more sensitive to analysts' choice of components and weights.

Since 2009, thinking has greatly advanced on how to conceptualize a lack of economic security as distinct from (but related to) poverty, as well as how to understand the role of psychology, the voluntary or nonvoluntary nature of income losses, and the role of buffers that reduce those losses. The development of new indices, as well as new and improved measures, has expanded our understanding of how these metrics perform.

Considerable additional work is required, however, to select the best types of measure and understand their properties. The availability of reliable and cross-nationally comparable data has been a crucial constraint on the development of improved measures of economic security. Three shortcomings of existing statistics stand out: the limited pool of long-term and cross-nationally comparable panel data; the weaknesses of most administrative data for tracing individuals over time; and the lack of regular questions about perceived security in conventional random-sample surveys, much less in panel data.

Nonetheless, these data have been rapidly improving, catalyzed by the extensive and increasingly sophisticated literature on volatility. In addition to offering crucial conceptual and methodological guidance, the literature on volatility also provides many valuable clues about the evolution of citizens' economic security. It is increasingly clear, for example, that volatility is particularly high in the United States. Moreover, high volatility suggests that, since an individual's circumstances change often over time, many more people turn to social benefits to cushion them from shocks at some point over their lives than a survey at one point in time would suggest. This was particularly true during the crisis, which not only directly reduced economic security in many countries, but also created pressures for policy changes that could further reduce the risk-protecting role of government.

Measuring Sustainability

The SDGs framework recognizes that progress has to be considered in a holistic manner to take account of the inevitable trade-offs, spill-overs, and possible unintended consequences of policy and investment decisions. In Chapter 9, Enrico Giovannini, Marleen De Smedt, and Walter J. Radermacher argue that complex systems theory provides a powerful complement to the capital approach for integrating the analysis of the different types of capital involved in sustainability, and for dealing with the many interactions that determine sustainability. A systems approach could also more adequately capture the extent to which a production and consumption path is sustainable, safe, and resilient.

The capital approach implies that a sustainable community should keep capital intact for the next generation. It will not consume more than it can produce, so that the level of capital that it leaves for the future is greater than that which it inherited. Sustainability requires taking a broad view of capital, including economic, natural, human, and social capital. Measuring changes in capital thus requires adopting a balance sheet to record changes in each of the components. In such a framework, extraction of natural resources is not counted only as a gain (due to the revenue from selling the resources) but also as a loss (since the natural resources have been depleted).

Although it is difficult in practice to build such a measurement framework, there have been substantial advances in advancing our understandings of different elements of the capital approach since 2009. For example, the System of Environmental-Economic Accounting—Central Framework (United Nations et al., 2014), formally adopted in 2012, extends standardized national accounting practices to include a broader set of environmental assets such as fish stocks.

The G20 Data Gaps Initiative[3] is working toward comprehensive measures of economic sustainability, and the *Guide on Measuring Human Capital* (UNECE, 2017) provides a systematic overview of methods for measuring human capital.

At the same time, many issues remain open, with unresolved controversies over the best way, for instance, of accounting for the depletion of natural resources, the degradation of the environment, and the loss of biodiversity. There are also disputes on the best way of improving and expanding measures of human and social capital.

Measuring the sustainability of the *systems* (sets of processes working together and interacting) that contribute to human society—including our eco-system in particular—also requires accounting for transboundary issues, uncertainties, instabilities, tipping points, and other issues related to complexity. For example, our eco-system clearly interacts with our economic system, stretches across international boundaries, and is likely to be vulnerable to tipping points that we do not yet understand well. Indeed, a common flaw of economic analysis is that it does not take into account the planetary boundaries within which our economic system operates. While some progress has been achieved on the environmental aspects of our overall global "system," notably with respect to emissions of greenhouse gases (through global input-output tables), the quantification of uncertainties, instabilities, and tipping points has mostly remained confined to scientific journals and has not yet translated into statistical practice or even standard economic analysis.

Risk and resilience are other important aspects of complex systems. The repercussions of the financial crisis apart from the financial sphere have intensified interest in measuring the interactions of different sectors to quantify sustainability and systemic risk, as well as raising issues about accurate measurement of the value added by the financial sector. The G20 Data Gaps Initiative, which is working toward comprehensive measures of economic risk, is an important part of this analysis. Bringing different sectors together in the systems approach is a new idea, and substantial work will be required to make it operational, requiring inputs from across disciplines. An international task force would be important to move this agenda forward.

Trust and Social Capital

A key component of social capital is trust, the topic discussed by Yann Algan in Chapter 10 on the basis of the OECD's definition of trust: "a person's belief that another person or institution will act consistently with their expectations of positive behaviour." Trust between individuals (inter-personal trust) and trust in institutions (institutional trust) are a key determinant of economic growth, social cohesion, and subjective well-being. Higher levels of inter-personal trust at the country level are associated with higher GDP per capita and lower income inequality (as measured by Gini coefficients). Having cooperative social relationships with others affects people's health and happiness above and beyond the monetary gains derived from cooperation. Institutional trust is a key element of a resilient society and is critical for implementing effective policies, since public programs, regulations, and reforms depend on the cooperation and compliance of citizens. Trust is therefore a crucial component for policy reform and for the legitimacy and sustainability of any political system.

Most of the research on the role of trust and cooperation draws on answers from survey questions. Survey data supply subjective information, which requires caution in use and interpretation. Issues include how individuals interpret the question they are asked, and whether there are systematic differences between groups in their interpretations that might be misread as differences in the underlying level of trust. Surveys are generally unable to disentangle the variety of social preferences that can be involved in inter-personal trust such as altruism, reciprocity, social desirability, and reputation. In some cases there is insufficient data coverage to fully analyze differences across people or countries, or over time.

Experimental measures of trust are a promising tool for improving our grasp of these issues, especially when implemented in conjunction with surveys. Experimental measures ask participants to make decisions under uncertainty, with their degree of trust influencing their decision, allowing for a measure of trust that may be more reliable than responses to survey questions. There have been significant advances in experimental measures since 2009, including the development of online platforms that permit data collection based on representative samples at low cost. The relationship between lab-based experimental measures and field outcomes, however, has to be investigated more thoroughly if we are to rely on the experimental method to make inferences about the real world. In addition, identical experiments are generally not repeated in different countries, so it is difficult to understand if there is cross-country variation in the underlying mechanisms of trust.

One solution is to combine surveys with experiments. Experiments carried out on representative samples could also shed light on the nature of social attitudes and on the extent of bilateral cooperation between individuals in the larger population.

Both generalized trust and trust in institutions are higher among higher-income groups and among more highly educated people, and they are lower among unemployed people and single-person households with at least one dependent child. While these patterns hold true across the majority of OECD countries, it is important to study the drivers of trust in the context of countries' specific circumstances so as to shed light on how policy-makers could develop such an important type of social capital. If trust plays a key role in explaining economic and social outcomes, it becomes urgent to identify the institutions and public policies needed for it to develop.

Notes

1. Similarly, those producing the data sets should document all assumptions clearly and thoroughly; make the data, programs, and results publicly available to allow for replicability whenever it applies; compare their methods and results with one another; and, eventually, agree on conventions and best practice when calculating inequality indicators from micro-data, secondary, and imputation-based sources.

2. The DINA data are compiled based on tax records; as these records do not always allow combining information on individuals belonging to the same household, the national income data mentioned in the text are expressed on a "per adult" basis (with no adjustment for family size). This concept differs from the "per consumption unit" basis (with adjustment for family size) used for the income data discussed in Chapter 3.

3. www.imf.org/external/np/seminars/eng/dgi/index.htm.

References

Anand, S., P. Segal and J.E. Stiglitz (eds.) (2010), *Debates on the Measurement of Global Poverty*, Oxford University Press, New York.

Stiglitz, J.E., A. Sen, and J.-P. Fitoussi (2009), *Report by the Commission on the Measurement of Economic and Social Progress*, http://ec.europa.eu/eurostat/documents/118025 /118123/Fitoussi+Commission+report.

UNECE (2017), *Guide on Measuring Human Capital*, United Nations, New York, http:// dx.doi.org/10.18356/c136-en.

United Nations (2015), "Transforming our world: The 2030 agenda for sustainable development," Resolution 70/1 of the UN General Assembly, www.un.org/ga/search/view _doc.asp?symbol=A/RES/70/1&Lang=E.

United Nations et al. (2014), System of Environmental-Economic Accounting 2012—Experimental Ecosystem Accounting, https://unstats.un.org/unsd/envaccount ing/seeaRev/eea_final_en.pdf.

2.

Sustainable Development Goals and the Measurement of Economic and Social Progress

Ravi Kanbur, Ebrahim Patel, and Joseph E. Stiglitz

The report by the Stiglitz-Sen-Fitoussi Commission raised fundamental questions about GDP as a measure of economic performance and social progress. The Sustainable Development Goals (SDGs) process put in train by the UN system proposes a number of goals and targets going beyond GDP that apply universally, to developing and developed countries alike. This chapter takes stock of the SDG process in relation to the general movement toward a broader perspective on the measurement of economic performance and social progress. Three central themes emerge. First, the inevitable and enduring tension between the pull to broaden and expand indicators for assessing and monitoring economic and social progress in development on the one hand, and the imperative to keep a relatively small number of top-level indicators, in order to facilitate national discourse and policy-making, on the other. The SDG list of 17 goals and 169 targets is useful as a platform from which to choose and narrow down, but choose we must at the national level. Second, National Statistical Offices must be given the governance independence and the financial resources with which to provide the framework for a data-based dialogue on economic and social progress at the national level. Third, some aspects of the measurement of progress and development are global and beyond the sole remit of any one National Statistical Office. For these exercises, and as a conduit for providing support to National Statistical Offices, the international community needs to commit resources for the provision of this global public good.

Ravi Kanbur is T.H. Lee Professor of World Affairs, International Professor of Applied Economics and Management, and Professor of Economics at Cornell University; Ebrahim Patel is Minister of Economic Development in South Africa; and Joseph E. Stiglitz is University Professor at Columbia University. This chapter draws on the outcomes of an HLEG workshop on "Measurement of Well-Being and Development in Africa," sponsored by the Government of South Africa, the Japanese International Cooperation Agency, Columbia University, and Cornell University, and held in Durban, South Africa, on November 12–14, 2015. The authors wish to thank those who participated in this workshop for their contributions. The section titled "The Rationale of Goal Setting" draws on the section "Conceptual Foundations of the MDG Process" in Bourguignon et al. (2010). The opinions expressed and arguments employed in the contributions below are those of the authors and do not necessarily reflect the official views of the OECD or of the governments of its member countries.

Introduction

The report by the Stiglitz-Sen-Fitoussi Commission raised fundamental questions about GDP as a measure of economic performance and social progress (Stiglitz, Sen, and Fitoussi, 2009, 2010). The critique included GDP's neglect of (1) nonmarket and social transactions; (2) stocks and flows of physical, natural, and human capital; and (3) broad distributional issues. It also highlighted that GDP has many shortcomings even as a measure of market production. The OECD-hosted High-Level Expert Group on the Measurement of Economic and Social Progress (HLEG) has been working on developing further the recommendations of the report by the Stiglitz-Sen-Fitoussi Commission. This chapter focuses, in particular, on the suitability of GDP, and alternatives to it, for developing countries. At the same time, the SDG process has been put in train by the UN system and has proposed a number of goals and targets as successors to the Millennium Development Goals (MDGs) after 2015, the MDG target date. It is thus becoming increasingly clear that the international community views progress in broader terms than just an increase in

GDP. All of this links to, and feeds into, ongoing processes in developing countries to develop robust indicators of human, social, and economic development.

This chapter takes stock of the SDG process in relation to the general movement toward a broader perspective on the measurement of economic performance and social progress. We begin with a brief history of the MDGs and their transformation into the SDGs. Then, we consider the rationale for global targeting of the type found in the MDGs and SDGs in terms of their potential for setting norms. After that, we translate this global norm setting into the national context and take up, in particular, the "dashboard versus single index" question, as well as the question of how large a dashboard should be. We follow up with implications for statistics and statistical processes within countries. Next, we address the question of global level monitoring, beyond a primarily national perspective, before sharing our concluding thoughts.

MDGs and SDGs: A Brief History

The push to take a broad perspective on well-being, and especially in the measurement of development progress, goes back at least as far as the basic needs indicators and physical quality-of-life indexes in the 1970s. Both of these reflected the dissatisfaction with standard GDP as a measure of well-being. Basic needs went further than income and included access to food, water, shelter, clothing, sanitation, education, and health care. Richard Jolly (1976) spoke of the "enthronement of basic needs." In 1980, Morris (1980) proposed his Physical Quality of Life Index (PQLI) by taking a simple average of measures of literacy, infant mortality, and life expectancy. And in the 1980s Amartya Sen developed his capability theory, which broadened the basis of social evaluation beyond income to "functionings and capabilities," defined as aspects of what human beings could be and do, whether they are in good health and can perform paid work in safe conditions (see, for example, Sen, 1985).

Agencies like the World Bank still gave primacy to national income per capita as a measure of development, but this began to change during the 1980s. The 1990 *World Development Report* (World Bank, 1990) was on poverty. It introduced the famous "dollar a day" poverty line, and the iconic figure of "one billion people around the world" who "live below one dollar a day." But the move toward broader perspectives was given a big push by the launch of the Human Development Index (HDI) in UNDP's first *Human Development Report* in 1990 (UNDP, 1990). This index was a simple average of per capita income and measures of literacy and longevity. Although criticized for various technical reasons at the time of its release (Kanbur, 1990), the HDI proved to be enormously useful in (1) shifting attention to other development outcomes beyond income, such as health and education; and (2) setting up a competition between countries on their HDI rank. The HDI has been modified and improved over the years to take account of the criticisms, incorporating, in particular, concerns about inequality. But the core index still elicits great attention when it is published, and leads to national and international press coverage comparing different countries, which in turn can be used by civil society as a lever to pressure their governments in areas like health and education.

The move toward multi-dimensional evaluation continued with a series of United Nations conferences throughout the 1980s and 1990s that emphasized gender, children, environment, food, and so on. This move was combined with the norm-setting potential of the HDI and culminated in the MDGs, which derived from the Millennium Declaration, proclaimed by over 150 world leaders at the Millennium Summit in September 2000. The MDGs set out eight goals, and targets within each goal, to be achieved by 2015. The eight goals were (1) eradicate extreme poverty and hunger; (2) achieve universal primary education; (3) promote gender equality and empower women; (4) reduce child mortality; (5) improve maternal health; 6) combat HIV/AIDS, malaria, and other diseases; 7) ensure environmental sustainability; and 8) create a global partnership for development. Specific targets were put forward under each goal, including, for example, the iconic target 1A: "Halve, between 1990 and 2015, the proportion of people whose income is less than $1.25 a day."

As 2015 approached, progress was gauged relative to these targets. Perhaps not surprisingly, United Nations Secretary General Ban Ki-moon proclaimed success and attributed it to the MDGs:

> The MDGs helped to lift more than one billion people out of extreme poverty, to make inroads against hunger, to enable more girls to attend

school than ever before and to protect our planet. They generated new
and innovative partnerships, galvanized public opinion and showed
the immense value of setting ambitious goals. By putting people and
their immediate needs at the forefront, the MDGs reshaped decision-
making in developed and developing countries alike. (United Nations,
2015a, p. 3)

Whatever the truth of the causal link (considered in the next section), the scope
of the goals was bound to be broadened when considering what to do after 2015,
as interested parties brought to the fore key elements they considered were left out
of the MDGs. In September 2015, the United Nations General Assembly adopted
Resolution 70/1, entitled "Transforming Our World: the 2030 Agenda for Sustainable Development," which stated:

The new Agenda builds on the Millennium Development Goals and
seeks to complete what they did not achieve, particularly in reaching
the most vulnerable. . . . In its scope, however, the framework we are
announcing today goes far beyond the Millennium Development Goals.
Alongside continuing development priorities such as poverty eradica-
tion, health, education and food security and nutrition, it sets out a
wide range of economic, social and environmental objectives. It also
promises more peaceful and inclusive societies. . . . We are announcing
today 17 Sustainable Development Goals with 169 associated targets
which are integrated and indivisible. Never before have world leaders
pledged common action and endeavour across such a broad and universal policy agenda. (United Nations, 2015b)

These seventeen goals are now under the following headings: (1) no poverty;
(2) no hunger; (3) good health and well-being; (4) quality education; (5) gender equality; (6) clean water and sanitation; (7) affordable and clean energy; (8)
decent work and economic growth; (9) industry innovation and infrastructure;
(10) reduced inequalities; (11) sustainable cities and communities; (12) responsible
consumption and production; (13) climate action; (14) life below water; (15) life on

land; (16) peace, justice, and strong institutions; and (17) partnership. Compared to the eight MDGs listed above, the SDGs represent some constants (e.g., poverty) and some bundling together (e.g., child mortality and maternal health) but mainly unbundling (e.g., poverty and hunger are separated out) and the addition of new dimensions (i.e., a full range of environmental goals, as well as goals on inequalities, on peace, on urbanization, on employment, etc.).

The politics and pressures that led to an expansion of the scope of the eight MDGs to 17 SDGs (with its associated 169 targets and 232 indicators for these targets) are clear. Each constituency argued for its own particular goal to be represented in the overall list. Thus, for example, Doyle and Stiglitz (2014) argued, with success, for inequality reduction to be an explicit goal. Climate change was introduced as a separate goal but so, for example, was the goal to "conserve and sustainably use the oceans, seas and marine resources for sustainable development." The urban constituency got its goal, to "make cities and human settlements inclusive, safe, resilient and sustainable," and so on. The fact that everyone wanted the focal point of their concern (e.g., rule of law, inequality, urban issues, etc.) to be included in the list of SDGs is testimony to at least the belief in the power of these goals. Advocates believed that inclusion increased the chance of progress in their area of concern. But is 17 goals and 169 targets just too much, as some have argued? The answer to this depends on the objective of the exercise, i.e., the "goal" of goal-setting.

The Rationale of Goal Setting

There are at least two questions we can ask about the SDGs (as indeed about the MDGs). First, in what sense are they goals of the development process? Second, how, if at all, does goal setting aid the development process? Let us take these questions in turn.

Are the SDGs truly the goals of development? Following Bourguignon et al. (2010), we can translate their questions on the MDGs to questions for the SDGs: (1) Do the SDGs command (close to) universal agreement? (2) Are the SDGs the final goals of development? Are they inputs, outcomes, or outputs (intermediate variables of interest mainly because of their relationship to some ultimate objective)?[1] (3) How are we to weigh the SDGs relative to each other?

The first issue is perhaps easiest to answer in a formal and substantive sense. In a formal sense, the SDGs have been signed off on by political leaders of almost all of the countries in the world, and are encapsulated in a resolution of the United Nations General Assembly. Agreement does not get much more universal than that in an international setting. In a substantive sense, the SDGs as a package are likely to command consensus precisely because they are so wide ranging, so that many perspectives on development and well-being are brought into the 17 goals and 169 targets. But it is this comprehensiveness that leads to the next question, on what exactly they represent.

On the second issue, the 17 SDGs (both in the general pronouncement of them, and in their further specification into detailed targets) are a mixture of the causal chain from inputs to outputs to outcomes. Take, for example, Goal 8: "Promote sustained, inclusive and sustainable economic growth, full and productive employment and decent work for all." This goal, and its associated targets, mixes up inputs, outputs, and outcomes, especially if we think back to the literature that took us away from GDP in the first place. Following Sen (1985) and Stiglitz, Sen, and Fitoussi (2009), GDP is seen as an input, a means to an end rather than an end in itself. Yet target 8.1 is "Sustain per capita economic growth in accordance with national circumstances and, in particular, at least 7% gross domestic product growth per annum in the least developed countries." Target 8.5 comes much closer to a final outcome variable in specifying employment and pay equality as objectives: "By 2030, achieve full and productive employment and decent work for all women and men, including for young people and persons with disabilities, and equal pay for work of equal value."

In the MDGs, Goal 8 on partnerships was often criticized for being a catchall with little structure. In the SDGs, perhaps Goal 17, "Strengthen the means of implementation and revitalize the global partnership for sustainable development," takes on that role. This goal has no fewer than 19 targets, grouped under the subheadings of Finance, Technology, Capacity Building, Trade, and Systemic Issues. Specific targets include such disparate components as, "Mobilize additional financial resources for developing countries from multiple sources"; "Significantly increase the exports of developing countries, in particular with a view to doubling the least developed countries' share of global exports by 2020"; and "By 2030, build on existing initiatives to develop measurements of progress on sustainable development that complement gross domestic product, and support statistical capacity-building in developing countries." The last of these is relevant to our discussion below, in the section "Measurement at the Global Level," but the sheer complexity of Goal 17 is a testament to how the SDG process has catered to a very wide range of constituencies who have focused on their goal or target (be it inequality reduction, or primary education, or employment generation, or water and sanitation, etc.) and claim some legitimacy from it being present in the list of SDGs, whether it is as input, output, or outcome.

On the third issue raised by Bourguignon et al. (2010), the large number of goals and targets, spread out along the input-output-outcome chain, raises obvious questions of evaluation and assessment. Supposing even that we were to agree on genuine outcome variables focused on human well-being, how are we to address the inevitable trade-offs? In their discussion of the MDGs, Bourguignon et al. pose the issue as follows: "In a world of limited resources, it is likely that often progress on one MDG will have to be at the expense or postponement of another. Suppose country A rushes ahead on MDGx but falls behind on MDGy, whereas for country B the reverse is true. How is the MDG performance of the two countries to be assessed? Whose trade-off weights are to be used—country A's, country B's, or a universal trade-off determined internationally?"

The same questions can be asked with "SDG" substituted for "MDG." The issue has become, if anything, even sharper with the broadening of the scope from the 8 MDGs to the 17 SDGs and associated targets. As argued in the next section, the issue is perhaps best resolved at the national level, by selecting which of the SDG targets and goals is most relevant in the specific country context, but this does not, of course, avoid the problem of trade-offs.

The second major question posed at the start of this section is how, if at all, does goal setting aid the development process? The answers to this question can be given at both the international level and the national level (Bourguignon et al., 2010). At the international level, goal setting can be useful from the technical point of view, quantifying the resources needed to achieve the selected goals. Thus, for example, Sachs (2005) used the MDG targets to estimate that, in order to achieve those goals, development assistance would have needed to increase to around $200 billion annually (compared with its level of around $65 billion in the early 2000s). Detailed sector-by-sector technical calculations underlie this overall figure, and the sector-specific goals and targets again play a role in guiding and focusing these technical calculations.

UN Secretary General Ban Ki-moon set out a second use of goal setting in the international context when, as quoted earlier, he said: "[The MDGs] generated new and innovative partnerships, galvanized public opinion and showed the immense value of setting ambitious goals." They do this, for instance, through the norm-setting role noted earlier. Given the difficulties of attribution, quantitative assessment of such claims is not easy. The assessments tend to be more qualitative in nature, as in McCarthy (2013):

> The greatest MDG successes undoubtedly concern health. The MDGs have invigorated multilateral institutions, such as the GAVI Alliance (formerly called the Global Alliance for Vaccines and Immunization), which seeks to achieve MDGs "by focusing on performance, outcomes and results." The goals have also inspired a huge increase in private-sector aid. Ray Chambers, a respected philanthropist and co-founder of a New York private equity firm, first learned of the goals in 2005. Since then, working with Sachs and others, Chambers has co-ordinated a worldwide coalition of policy, business, and NGO leaders in an effort to help the developing world meet the goal for malarial treatment and prevention. Thanks in part to this global effort, malaria-related mortality has dropped by approximately 25 percent since 2000, with most of those gains probably occurring since 2005. Many pharmaceutical companies have also put forth major efforts to make their medicines more widely available in poor countries, and new initiatives are continuing to take shape. The MDG Health Alliance, founded in 2011, is comprised of business and NGO leaders around the world working toward the MDG health targets, including the elimination of mother-to-child HIV transmission.

Many sectors can no doubt claim successes of this type, which might help explain the dramatic increases in goals and targets by the time the MDGs were transformed into the SDGs.

Other reasons for the dramatic increase in goals and targets in the SDGs are (1) the inclusive process used to develop the SDGs; and (2) the SDGs' broadening of perspective to include the environment and human rights agendas. Perhaps the appropriate way to think about the SDGs is indeed in a broad perspective, as a platform that provides global civil society with a base from which to organize around one of the many issues in the SDGs. It also provides national civil society organizations an entry point in the dialogue with their own governments. The fact that the SDGs are sanctioned, after a fashion, by the community of world leaders gives national civil society a starting point in their national organizing, if organizations care to use them in that way, although one danger is that the discussion focuses so much on measurement that discussion on how to actually achieve the goals gets drowned out. But what this highlights is that, ultimately, the SDGs have to be brought to the national level, and be translated into specific goals and targets as a compact between governments and their populations. Here, technical operationalization and political salience are both needed to go from 17 goals and 169 targets to a dashboard that can capture key national political concerns and can be monitored and communicated easily.

Implications for National Policy

A heterogeneous mixture of 17 goals and 169 targets, negotiated between and balancing the interests of a wide range of global groups, cannot provide specific guidance for national policy. That guidance has to come from national concerns and national processes, although the SDGs can provide a useful frame of reference as needed. In the opening statement to the HLEG workshop on "Measurement of Well-Being and Development in Africa,"[2] Ebrahim Patel, South Africa's Minister of Economic Development and one of the co-authors of this chapter, posed two questions as a national policy-maker, recognizing both the centrality of GDP and the depth of its problems:

- Can we find a single composite index to replace GDP?

- If not, how big should the dashboard of indicators be and what should be on it (apart from GDP or, as alternatives, measures of household income or consumption)?

As argued in Stiglitz, Sen, and Fitoussi (2009), GDP has been misused. In his presentation to the HLEG workshop, Lorenzo Fioramonti presented several directions in which GDP could be modified and supplemented, or even supplanted, from an African perspective.[3] As he argued, GDP has become a "proxy for everything." However, this could be because, in effect, GDP has stepped into a vacuum because of its simplicity and its correlation with at least some other dimensions of well-being. Despite its weaknesses, GDP has proved useful as a practical tool to policy-makers. While the critiques of GDP have been sharp, proposals to replace it have been less sharp—as reflected perhaps in the 17 goals and 169 targets that have emerged from the SDG process. This broad a range of goals and targets cannot make for practical policy-making.

So, should GDP be replaced by an alternative composite index? There are, of course, many possible candidates. Sticking initially to the income sphere, we could consider measures of national poverty, although there are many possible poverty indices that can be presented, ranging from absolute poverty to relative poverty. Or we could, still in the income domain, rely on a measure of per capita national income corrected for income inequality (e.g., we could use, as our composite index, per capita income multiplied by one minus the Gini coefficient); then if income inequality rises holding GDP constant, "corrected" GDP would fall. But even here, Joseph Stiglitz argued, in his presentation to the HLEG workshop, the Gini coefficient may be too simple a measure of inequality, hiding important movements within the income distribution (for example, changes in the income shares at the very top of the income distribution).[4]

But all of this is still in the income domain. Various versions of the HDI—starting from the basic one that takes a simple average of per capita income, literacy, and life expectancy—have attempted to move beyond the income space. As noted earlier, the HDI proved quite successful in the international domain in setting up comparisons across countries and giving ammunition to each country's civil society to spur healthy competition between governments to advance on the components of the HDI. Of course, the components in the basic HDI are national averages and do not take into account the distribution around the average. To address this issue, more sophisticated and distribution-sensitive component values can be developed before averaging across the three dimensions. The "inequality-adjusted HDI" (UNDP, 2016) can give markedly different rankings and, for some purposes, can become a focal point of norm setting. However, the greater the sophistication of each sub-index, and thus of the index as a whole, the more the index is likely to lose its power as a tool of communication.

An example of an index that combines multi-dimensionality of components with a focus on poverty or deprivation is the Multidimensional Poverty Index (MPI), developed by Alkire and Foster (Alkire et al., 2015) and presented by Sabina Alkire at the same HLEG workshop.[5] Here the issues are the selection of dimensions, the specification of the cut-off in each dimension to identify deprivation, and then the normative choice of the number of dimensions in which an individual must be deprived in order for that individual to count as deprived overall. Such reduction of complex multi-dimensionality into a single index has elicited critiques, which can be interpreted more generally as critiques of any composite index and as support for a dashboard of indicators:

> Recognizing that poverty is not just about lack of household command over market goods does not imply that one needs to collapse the multiple dimensions into one (uni-dimensional) index. It is not credible to contend that any single index could capture all that matters in all settings. . . . But when one faces a trade-off, because a policy spans more than one dimension, those with a stake in the outcomes will almost certainly be in a better position to determine what weights to apply than the analyst calibrating a measure of poverty. (Ravallion, 2011, p. 247)

In his presentation at the HLEG workshop, Stiglitz also argued that a dashboard was preferable to a composite index. Different numbers are useful for different purposes, and local context is important in selecting which numbers matter for what.

This then leads to Ebrahim Patel's second question: How big should the dashboard be, and what should be on it? On the number of goals and targets, the answer is, of course, country specific, but there may be some consensus developing on how many. It is generally agreed, and it was the view expressed by all participants at the HLEG workshop, that the SDGs are good as a platform, but 169 targets is way too large a number of indicators to be useful as a "top of the dashboard" list in a national dialogue. The Genuine Progress Indicator (Talberth, Cobb, and Slattery, 2006), for example, has not really taken off—is it because it has 26 component parts? The Mexican government uses income poverty as well as deprivation on seven other dimensions to monitor national well-being (CONEVAL, 2010). The case for a limited number of indicators is also made in the report of the Atkinson Commission on Global Poverty (Atkinson, 2016). The general point is that the number of top-level entries on a dashboard for measuring and monitoring well-being and development should not be too large, and there is a case to be made for the number to be below 10 and perhaps around 7, depending on country context, although some would argue that even that may be too many.

What should be on the dashboard is also, of course, a country-specific question. For South Africa, for example, key well-being indicators apart from GDP would have to include the employment dimension. Throughout Africa, the use of unemployment as an indicator is fraught with problems, as argued by Baah-Boateng at the HLEG workshop.[6] The high levels of informality mean that the standard International Labour Organization (ILO) measurement of unemployment does not capture the essence of lack of productive work. In South Africa there has been an argument for using employment rather than unemployment as a lead indicator.[7] Again in South Africa, the issue of income inequality is also front and center in policy debates and in the national consciousness. But which measure of inequality—the Gini coefficient, or the income share of the top X%? And which metric of household material conditions, e.g., household consumption or income, net or gross of taxes, per capita or equivalized? Access to basic services is yet another leading issue in South Africa, but here we risk getting into a proliferation of dimensions including education (different levels), health care, and housing. Perhaps for these social dimensions one could have a multi-dimensional deprivation index as suggested by Alkire et al. (2015). And none of this touches on longer-term environmental degradation concerns. Further, in South Africa, the metric of disaggregation by race is central to the policy dialogue, as is disaggregation by gender.

Ultimately the choice of what should figure on a dashboard is a national policy decision with no simple technical methodology to the rescue. But if, following Ebrahim Patel's question, we were forced to prioritize to, say, five indicators, what would they be? For a country like South Africa, and other countries in Africa, perhaps the following indicators would be prominent:

- per capita income
- income inequality and poverty
- employment
- Multidimensional Deprivation Index based on access to basic public services
- long-term environmental degradation

Throughout, these indicators would need to be disaggregated by race (and often ethnicity) and by gender, and perhaps by other categories such as age; so, because there would be several of these breakdowns by population groups, the sense of a small number of entries on the dashboard may be somewhat illusory. Furthermore, there are sub-indicators behind these key indicators, such as wages, under-employment, or individual dimensions of poverty in the Multidimensional Deprivation Index, or various aspects of long-term environmental degradation. And there may well be disagreements even on the selection of the top 5 key indicators. What is needed is a national-level discourse that takes the SDGs as a platform and then fashions a dashboard that meets national needs and priorities, as well as the statistical capacity of each country to generate the data needed.[8]

The Role of Statistics at the National Level

Statistics have power, and are political. In his presentation to the HLEG workshop, Ravi Kanbur discussed the role that statistics had played in colonial rule, in the struggle for independence, and in post-independence governance in India.[9] In the 19th and early 20th centuries, the India Office—the British government department administering Indian affairs—was required to present an annual report to Parliament on the "Moral and Material Progress and Condition of India." Indeed,

John Maynard Keynes, in his first job out of university, served in the India Office and edited the report for 1906–07.

But the same device that was used by the colonizers to convince themselves of their *mission civilisatrice* was turned on them by those struggling for independence. The National Planning Committee of the Indian National Congress, headed by India's future Prime Minister Jawaharlal Nehru, produced a report in 1936, the findings of which Nehru referred to in his book *Discovery of India*: "There was lack of food, of clothing, of housing and of every other essential requirement of human existence." Independence was needed "to ensure an adequate standard of living for the masses, in other words, to get rid of the appalling poverty of the people." Nehru wrote these words in prison, having been put there by the British authorities for his role in the Quit India movement of 1942. But a generation of Indian analysts had been using official statistics and doing their own surveys to bolster, in effect, the empirical case for independence.

Given this role of statistics in the Indian independence struggle, and especially the role played by statistics on well-being of the population, it is perhaps not surprising that special attention was paid in India after independence to data on the distribution of consumption and poverty, and on access to public services. The Indian National Sample Survey is the longest-running household survey in developing countries, stretching back to the 1950s. Each release of data is accompanied by lively debate and discussion, with the key statistics providing an assessment of policy outcomes and directions for the future (Deaton and Kozel, 2005).

The SDG process, and the emphasis given to goals, targets, and indicators in that process, has thrown into sharp relief the generation and use of statistics in developing countries, particularly in Africa. This includes the accessibility and availability of data to researchers and the population at large. In his presentation to the HLEG workshop, Pali Lehohla, former Statistician General of South Africa and head of Statistics South Africa, emphasized that GDP provided a good framework for what it intended to measure, but that it was badly used. In principle, for example, a Social Accounting Matrix (SAM) framework could be used to enrich distributional discussions anchored on GDP. These sentiments were echoed by Rashad Cassim, now Deputy Governor of the South African Reserve Bank and former Head of National Accounts in Statistics South Africa: "Getting GDP measures and its components right is not trivial and there are many challenges that a middle-income country like South Africa, let alone developing countries, face in getting a set of conventional economic indicators right. . . . Tensions are not only between social and economic data but between high frequency economic data and structural long term economic data. Put differently, should we gear up our statistical infrastructure to track, as accurately as we can, the business cycle or sacrifice this for something else—like putting more resources into estimating the value added of the informal sector, conduct area sampling to better understand small enterprises?"[10]

Cassim went on to elaborate upon a number of trade-offs faced in practice by National Statistical Offices, including those involving quality of data, even in the relatively standard area of national accounts, let alone in expanding their remit as seemingly required by the SDG process so as to track and monitor a vast number of indicators.

These concerns were further underlined by Daniel Masolwa of Tanzania's National Bureau of Statistics, who emphasized the cost of running regular establishment and household surveys, as well as specialized surveys on informal transactions such as unrecorded cross-border trade.[11] Chukwudozie Ezigbalike, Chief of the Data Technology Section of the UN Economic Commission for Africa, estimated that, in 2005, the cost of running a survey of 3,000 households exceeded $500,000.[12] However, he also argued for using new technology, the benefits of which included, along with improving and expanding administrative data, the opportunity to initiate an African data revolution in which agricultural and other data could be collected rapidly and at low cost.

For many low-income countries, these financing needs have driven their statistical offices into the hands of donors who have their own—and often shifting—priorities. The entire statistical system of some low-income countries is geared to the statistics that donors wish to collect. This may be no bad thing if the government is encouraged, for example, to collect gender-disaggregated data on well-being. But, as a general rule, statistics in democracies should be driven by data the government has to collect to satisfy the monitoring and planning needs on behalf of the population.

The data revolution and the use of new technology emphasized by Ezigbalike is not simply a technical fix to collect relevant data more cheaply. It also highlights the role that civil society and the population at large can play in the statistical discourse, taking it beyond the preserve of technical experts. A key requirement is, of course, the independence of statistical systems from partisan politics. But, beyond this basic governance requirement, we are back again to the question of how many top-level indicators there should be in a national dashboard. It can be argued that too many and too complex a set of indicators would actually be deleterious to an informed debate in society, including the vigorous participation of civil society.

There can be, and there always will be, specialized interactions on specific sectors, and resources will move back and forth to assess and monitor progress and prospects in these areas to reflect the ebb and flow of political interest. But if a relatively small number of top-level indicators can be agreed upon—for example, the five outlined in the previous section—national discourse can focus on these, and adequate resources can be made available to the National Statistical Office to provide the database for such discussion. The provision of additional resources for data collection is, along with helping develop tools and methodologies, an essential contribution needed from the international community.[13]

Measurement at the Global Level

Although the major significance of SDGs lies at the national level, as laid out in the previous sections, the goals are developed at the global level. The national discourse is, of course, central to the development process, but there are also uniquely global dimensions to key elements of the SDGs, for which we have to take a perspective that goes beyond the national. This triggers the need for establishing internationally agreed statistical standards, for which global and regional organizations such as the ILO, the OECD, or Eurostat (at the European level) have a major role to play.[14] We consider three such examples—global poverty, global inequalities, and global climate change.

SDG 1.1, the first quantitative target of the first SDG is: "By 2030, eradicate extreme poverty for all people everywhere, currently measured as people living on less than $1.25 a day." This is also the first of the new "twin goals" of the World Bank. The usual operational definition of "eradicate" is to reduce something down to 3%. But note that this is a *global goal*; in other words, it is a goal for a global measure of poverty. This immediately raises the question of how global poverty is to be measured. Dean Jolliffe's presentation at the HLEG workshop set out the World Bank's current thinking and the dilemmas it raises.[15] The report of the Atkinson Commission on the Measurement of Global Poverty (Atkinson, 2016) also takes up the issue in more detail.

Focusing on monetary measures, two questions arise in getting a global count of poverty. First, how are nominal incomes and consumption around the world to be turned into comparable real-income measures? Converting local currency values into a common currency globally by using official exchange rates (say to the US dollar) opens up the question of whether these exchange rates measure true cost-of-living differences between different countries. In general they do not, because market exchange rates reflect only traded commodities and may also reflect financial flows and government interference in market exchange rates. To overcome these problems, the World Bank and others use Purchasing Power Parity (PPP) exchange rates, the use of which is itself steeped in controversy (Deaton, 2010; Ravallion, 2014), one that reignites every time a new set of PPP exchange rates is published. The issue is not whether to use PPPs or not, but the methodology underlying their calculation. And, of course, PPPs are meant to be conversion factors for some aggregate basket of goods and services, rather than being representatives of what the poor consume.

The second question arises even if we were to successfully arrive at a true distribution of real income in the world as a whole. Where then do we draw the poverty line? There are various conceptual bases—for example, starting from basic capabilities inspired by Sen and working down from those to a line in the income space (e.g., Reddy and Pogge, 2010). But, as a practical matter, the World Bank has constructed its global poverty line using as inputs various national poverty lines (Ferreira et al., 2015), presuming that these national poverty lines reflect a range of actual normative perspectives. This method led to one poverty line of $1.25 per person per day at 2005 PPP, which is the line stated in SDG 1.1, and another poverty line of $1.90 at 2011 PPPs, as set out in Ferreira et al. (2015). The two lines do not lead to a big difference in the global poverty count (just over 14% of the world's population).

Turning now to inequality, SDG 10 is, "Reduce inequality within and among countries," which actually raises an interesting set of issues that go beyond statistics and measurement, to the conceptual. Take, for example, the case of income inequality. Overall inequality among all individuals in the world can be decomposed into inequality between countries and inequality within countries.[16] Inequality between countries is the inequality of the world distribution of income if each person in a country was given that country's average income—in other words, it is the inequality that would be left if within-country inequality were eliminated in each country. The difference between this inequality and total inequality is then the contribution of within-country inequality to total world inequality.

What do the numbers look like on this decomposition of global inequality into between-country and within-country components? For the "mean log deviation" measure of inequality (which takes a value of zero when everyone has the same income, rising as incomes become more unequal), Lakner and Milanovic (2015) find that the between-country contribution was 77% in 2008, down from 83% in 1988. The overall global inequality index fell by 10% over this same 20-year period. These trends capture broadly what we know about global inequality trends. Within-country inequalities have been rising in the large countries of Asia (Kanbur and Zhuang, 2012) and, because of their population size, this effect dominated the falling within-country inequality in Latin America. However, low-income countries have grown much faster than high-income countries, with the result that between-country inequality has fallen. The overall combination of these effects has been a fall in global income inequality by this measure.

These patterns—rising within-country inequality but falling between-country inequality—raise the conceptual question of how, if at all, we weight these components of inequality. The between-country component is numerically much larger— the well-being chances of an individual are predominantly determined by the probability that they are born in this or that country. Thus from this perspective it is important to monitor both between-country inequality and within-country inequality, and SDG 10 recognizes this imperative, although, perhaps surprisingly, no indicators in the "global list" agreed by the UN Statistics Division refer to this between-country element.

Our third example of global measurement is the most obvious case of why monitoring and assessment at a global level is crucial, and that is climate change and its determinants. Although the short-term consequences of climate change can vary by locality—rising sea levels will devastate small island states, but rising tempera-tures may be beneficial to some temperate zones—the long-term consequences pose an existential threat to humanity, especially if certain tipping points are reached. These global tipping points are precisely that—global. The extent to which we are approaching them is determined not just by greenhouse gas emission by this or that country, but by global emissions in total. Similarly, the carbon sequestration potential of the planet is determined by total forest cover in the world, and weather systems around the world are linked to each other.

Thus while action on adaptation and mitigation in response to climate change will necessarily have a national component, the monitoring and assessment is equally necessarily global in nature. Such global monitoring is not as prominent as it should be in the SDG platform. Under SDG 13, it can be glimpsed in the target SDG 13.3, "Improve education, awareness-raising and human and institu-tional capacity on climate change mitigation, adaptation, impact reduction and early warning," or perhaps in target 17.19, the last target of the 17th and last SDG, on partnership for sustainable development: "By 2030, build on existing initiatives to develop measurements of progress on sustainable development . . . However stated, global monitoring of global climate change is surely a key component of the measurement of economic and social progress, and common global measure-ment instruments and accounting systems such as the System of Environmental-Economic Accounting (SEEA) are crucial in developing common indicators. It is indeed the classic public good, like measuring and monitoring global poverty or global inequality.

Conclusions

The Stiglitz, Sen, and Fitoussi (2009) report came after the MDGs, but well before the SDG process got under way. The authors' insistence on going beyond GDP meshed well with, and greatly contributed to, the broadening of the agenda on the measurement of economic and social progress. But that report did not give as much emphasis as is appropriate to issues that arise in developing countries. The SDG process does indeed have a focus on development, although, of course, it is meant to encompass developed countries as well, and the time is right for us to take stock of where we have come and where we need to go in measuring economic and social progress in developing countries and globally. This chapter attempted such an exercise.

Three central themes emerge from our discussion, and from the HLEG workshop on which our discussion is based.

First is the inevitable and enduring tension between the pull to broaden and expand our indicators for assessing and monitoring economic and social progress in development, on the one hand, and on the other, the imperative to keep a relatively small number of indicators at the "top level of the dashboard," in order to facilitate national discourse and policy-making. The first pull is what explains the expansion of goals from the 8 MDGs to the 17 SDGs and 169 targets. This list is useful as a platform from which to choose and narrow down, but choose we must at the national level.

Second, National Statistical Offices must be given the governance independence and the financial resources with which to provide the framework for a data-based dialogue on economic and social progress at the national level.

Third, some aspects of the measurement of progress and development are truly global and beyond the remit of any National Statistical Office. For these exercises, and as a conduit for providing support to National Statistical Offices, the international community needs to commit resources to regional statistical offices and to multilateral agencies for the provision of this global public good.

Notes

1. The spectrum of inputs-outputs-outcomes is familiar in the evaluation literature. Of course, any classification of a continuum into three categories is bound to be problematic, but is useful as an analytical device. To use an example from infrastructure, in a road-building project concrete is an input, miles of road built an output, and "travel time saved" an outcome. An example from education would be school expenditure as an input, number of students enrolled as an output, and test scores measuring learning as an outcome.

2. www.oecd.org/statistics/measuring-economic-social-progress/HLEG%20 workshop%20on%20measurement%20of%20well%20being%20and%20 development%20in%20Africa%20agenda.pdf.

3. https://www.slideshare.net/StatsCommunications/hleg-thematic-workshop-on -measurement-of-well-being-and-development-in-africa-lorenzo-fioramonti.

4. https://www.slideshare.net/StatsCommunications/hleg-thematic-workshop-on-measurement-of-well-being-and-development-in-africa-joseph-stiglitz. At a more technical level, only if the Lorenz curves of two distributions do not cross can one say that one distribution is unambiguously more or less equal than the other.

5. https://www.slideshare.net/StatsCommunications/hleg-thematic-workshop-on-measurement-of-well-being-and-development-in-africa-sabina-alkire.

6. https://www.slideshare.net/StatsCommunications/hleg-thematic-workshop-on-measurement-of-well-being-and-development-in-africa-william-baahboateng.

7. But that view seems to privilege formal jobs over productive informal work. The problem is that it is hard to distinguish from the available data truly productive informal sector work that increases the size of the national income pie from work that mostly entails getting a large share of some commons rents.

8. As an intermediate step between the setting of indicators at the global level and at the national level, initiatives have been launched in different regions in the world. A set of more than 100 sustainable development indicators—structured around ten themes—has been defined at the level of the European Union for over a decade. Two-year monitoring reports (http://ec.europa.eu/eurostat/web/sdi/indicators) are compiled and published by the statistical office of the EU (Eurostat). These reports evaluate progress on the long term (since the year 2000) and on the short term (looking at the last 5 years). Eurostat is currently reflecting on how to adapt its monitoring activity on sustainable development to the SDGs. In 2013, the Conference of European Statisticians also agreed on a set of recommendations on measuring sustainable development. Drawing on their experience gained in the European region, the UN Economic Commission for Europe (UNECE), OECD, and Eurostat are now developing a road map on statistics for the SDGs, which will help to structure the statistical reporting in the UNECE region.

9. https://www.slideshare.net/StatsCommunications/hleg-thematic-workshop-on-measuring-inequalities-of-income-and-wealth-ravi-kanbur.

10. https://www.slideshare.net/StatsCommunications/hleg-thematic-workshop-on-measurement-of-well-being-and-development-in-africa-rashad-cassim.

11. https://www.slideshare.net/StatsCommunications/hleg-thematic-workshop-on-measurement-of-well-being-and-development-in-africa-daniel-masolwa.

12. https://www.slideshare.net/StatsCommunications/hleg-thematic-workshop-on-measurement-of-well-being-and-development-in-africa-chukwudozie-ezigbalike.

13. On tools, see OECD (2017) for development and application of SDG measurement tools to OECD countries.

14. The need for internationally agreed statistical standards also applies to indicators for monitoring targets that are primarily under the responsibility of the individual countries. Comparing countries and, above all, combining country information to obtain a global picture requires comparable data.

15. https://www.slideshare.net/StatsCommunications/hleg-thematic-workshop-on -measurement-of-well-being-and-development-in-africa-dean-jolliffe.

16. For an introduction to decomposition methodology, see Kanbur (2007).

References

Alkire, S. and J.E. Foster (2011), "Understandings and misunderstandings of multidimensional poverty measurement," *Journal of Economic Inequality*, Vol. 9, pp. 289–314.

Alkire, S. et al. (2015), *Multidimensional Poverty Measurement and Analysis*, Oxford University Press, Oxford.

Atkinson, A.B. (2016), *Monitoring Global Poverty: Report of the Commission on Global Poverty*, World Bank, Washington, DC.

Bourguignon, F. et al. (2010), "Millennium Development Goals at Midpoint: Where Do We Stand?," in Kanbur, R. and A.M. Spence (eds.), *Equity in a Globalizing World*, World Bank for the Commission on Growth and Development, pp. 17–40.

CONEVAL (2010), *Methodology for Multidimensional Poverty Measurement in Mexico*, www.3ieimpact.org/media/filer_public/2014/02/19/methodology_poverty_measurement_mexico.pdf.

Deaton, A. (2010), "Price indexes, inequality, and the measurement of world poverty," *American Economic Review*, Vol. 100, pp. 5–34.

Deaton, A. and V. Kozel (2005), "Data and dogma: The great Indian poverty debate," *World Bank Research Observer*, Vol. 20(2), pp. 177–200.

Doyle, M.W. and J.E. Stiglitz (2014), "Eliminating extreme inequality: A sustainable development goal, 2015–2030," *Ethics and International Affairs*, Carnegie Council, www.ethicsandinternationalaffairs.org/2014/eliminating-extreme-inequality-a-sustainable-development-goal-2015-2030/.

Ferreira, F. et al. (2015), "A global count of the extreme poor in 2012: Data issues, methodology and initial results," *Policy Research Working Paper*, No. 7432.

Guio, A.C. and E. Marlier (2016), "Amending the EU material deprivation indicator: Impact on the size and composition of the deprived population," in Atkinson, A.B., A.C. Guio, and E. Marlier (eds.), *Monitoring Social Europe*, Publications Office of the European Union, Luxembourg.

Jolly, R. (1976), "The world employment conference: The enthronement of basic needs," *Development Policy Review*, Vol. A9(2), pp. 31–44.

Kanbur, R. (2007), "The policy significance of inequality decompositions," *Journal of Economic Inequality*, Vol. 4(3), pp. 367–374.

Kanbur, R. (1990), "Poverty and development: The Human Development Report and the World Development Report, 1990," in van der Hoeven, R. and R. Anker (eds.), *Poverty Monitoring: An International Concern*, St. Martin's Press, New York.

Kanbur, R. and J. Zhuang (2012), "Confronting rising inequality in Asia," in *Asian Development Outlook 2012*, Asian Development Bank.

Lakner, C. and B. Milanovic (2015), "Global income distribution: From the fall of the Berlin wall to the Great Recession," *World Bank Economic Review*, Advanced Access, www.gc.cuny.edu/CUNY_GC/media/LISCenter/brankoData/wber_final.pdf.

McCarthy, J. (2013), "Own the goals: What the Millennium Development Goals have accomplished," Brookings Institution, www.brookings.edu/research/articles/2013/02/21-millennium-dev-goals-mcarthur.

Morris, M.D. (1980), "The physical quality of life index (PQLI)," *Development Digest*, Vol. 18(1), pp. 95–109.

OECD (2017), *Measuring Distance to the SDG Targets: An Assessment of Where OECD Countries Stand*, OECD, Paris, www.oecd.org/std/OECD-Measuring-Distance-to-SDG-Targets.pdf.

Ravallion, M. (2014), "An exploration of the international comparison program's new global economic landscape," *NBER Working Paper*, No. 20338, National Bureau of Economic Research.

Ravallion, M. (2011), "On multidimensional indices of poverty," *Journal of Economic Inequality*, Vol. 9(2), pp. 235–248.

Reddy, S.G. and T.W. Pogge (2010), "How not to count the poor," in Anand S., P. Segal, and J.E. Stiglitz (eds.), *Debates on the Measurement of Global Poverty*, Oxford University Press, Oxford, pp. 42–85.

Sachs, J.D. (2005), *The End of Poverty: Economic Possibilities for Our Time*, Penguin Press, New York.

Sen, A. (1985), *Commodities and Capabilities*, Elsevier, North-Holland, Amsterdam.

Stiglitz, J.E., A. Sen, and J.-P. Fitoussi (2010), *Mismeasuring Our Lives: Why GDP Doesn't Add Up*, The New Press, New York.

Stiglitz, J.E., A. Sen, and J.-P. Fitoussi (2009), *Report by the Commission on the Measurement of Economic and Social Progress*, http://ec.europa.eu/eurostat/documents/118025/118123/Fitoussi+Commission+report.

Talberth J., C. Cobb, and N. Slattery (2006), *The Genuine Progress Indicator 2006—A Tool for Sustainable Development*, Redefining Progress, Oakland, CA, http://rprogress.org/publications/2007/GPI%202006.pdf.

UNDP (2016), *Human Development Report 2016—Human Development for Everyone*,

United Nations Development Programme, New York, http://hdr.undp.org/sites /default/files/2016_human_development_report.pdf.

UNDP (1990), *Human Development Report 1990*, United Nations Development Programme, New York, http://hdr.undp.org/sites/default/files/reports/219/hdr_1990_en _complete_nostats.pdf.

United Nations (2015a), *The Millennium Development Goals Report 2015*, https://www .un.org/millenniumgoals/2015_MDG_Report/pdf/MDG%202015%20rev%20 (July%201).pdf.

United Nations (2015b), "Transforming our world: The 2030 agenda for sustainable development," Resolution 70/1 of the UN General Assembly, www.un.org/ga/search /view_doc.asp?symbol=A/RES/70/1&Lang=E.

World Bank (1990), *World Development Report 1990: Poverty*, Oxford University Press, New York, https://openknowledge.worldbank.org/handle/10986/5973.

3.

Measuring the Distribution of Household Income, Consumption, and Wealth

Nora Lustig

This chapter addresses the challenges posed by measuring vertical inequalities in household income, consumption, and wealth. It takes stock of international databases on economic inequality, highlighting the fact that they often display not only different levels of inequality but, for some countries, diverging trends as well. The chapter also discusses the challenges in measuring inequality because of under-coverage and under-reporting of top incomes (the "missing rich") and approaches to correct for the problem. The shortcomings of typical welfare metrics used to measure economic inequality in international databases (disposable income and/or consumption expenditures) are also discussed, stressing the need of a more comprehensive metric, using an income variable that includes social transfers in kind (especially for education and health care) and adds the effect of consumption taxes and subsidies. The chapter makes several recommendations to address the existing shortcomings in the measurement of income and wealth inequality.

Nora Lustig is Samuel Z. Stone Professor of Latin American Economics at Tulane University. The author is very grateful to members of the High-Level Expert Group on the Measurement of Economic Performance and Social Progress (HLEG) for their comments and suggestions. In particular, the author wishes to acknowledge Facundo Alvaredo for invaluable discussions and inputs throughout the preparation of this text, as well as François Bourguignon, Marco Mira d'Ercole, and Sharon Christ for their comments on a previous draft. The author is also grateful to Angus Deaton, Jacob Hacker, Joseph E. Stiglitz, Jean-Paul Fitoussi, and Martine Durand for their comments on earlier versions of this chapter, and to the participants of the Workshop on Measuring Inequalities of Income and Wealth, hosted by the Bertelsmann Foundation in Berlin on September 15–16, 2015. Last but not least, the author is grateful to Xavi Recchi for his research assistance. The section titled "Measuring Economic Inequality: Scope and Limitations of International Databases" draws largely on Ferreira, Lustig, and Teles (2015). "The 'Missing Rich' in Household Surveys" is based on Lustig's "The 'missing rich' in household surveys: Causes and correction methods," CEQ Working Paper (forthcoming), Tulane University. The opinions expressed and arguments employed in the contributions below are those of the author and do not necessarily reflect the official views of the OECD or of the governments of its member countries.

Introduction

After decades of relative neglect, the issue of how household economic resources (income, consumption, and wealth) are distributed is back on the agenda. We have moved from "bringing distribution in from the cold," as Tony Atkinson wrote in 1997, to putting it in the political and research spotlight.[1] The rising prominence of distribution can be readily observed in the UN Sustainable Development Goals, which, in contrast to the previous Millennium Development Goals, now include a specific goal—Goal 10—to reduce inequality within and among countries. Similarly, multilateral organizations such as the IMF, the OECD, UN agencies, and the World Bank as well as global nongovernmental groups have been paying unprecedented attention to the causes and consequences of economic inequality.[2] This growing prominence is, in large measure, the product of significant changes in the distribution of income and wealth—in particular, rising inequality in advanced countries—and their implications for political outcomes.[3] It is also the consequence of developments in economic theory and improvements in the available data.[4]

Why do we care about the distribution of economic resources across individuals and households? This is an issue charged with value judgments, where different authors have arrived at very different conclusions. A conventional view in economics has long argued that incentives are needed to promote economic growth, and that these incentives imply some degree of inequality in material rewards (Mirrlees, 1971). Higher inequalities may also result from a historical process whereby some people escape from destitution before others, as the benefits from improved technologies, higher living standards, and better policies reach some people and communities first before spreading elsewhere (Deaton, 2013).

From a normative standpoint, the interest in inequality is related to considerations about justice and, as emphasized by Rawls (1971), about fairness. Rawls suggested that citizens blocked by a "veil of ignorance"—unknowing about their lot in life—would choose a social arrangement that maximizes the level of welfare achieved by the less well-off person (the maximin principle) as the accepted social contract. This principle sets up the basic notion of justice as equality of *ex ante* opportunity (World Bank, 2006). Equality of opportunities, in this way, entails that individuals' achievements in life—including their income—are independent from initial circumstances (see the discussion by François Bourguignon in the present volume). However, inequality of outcomes may be unpalatable as such, too. High inequality in both opportunities and outcomes are perceived to be problematic in most societies.[5]

In addition to normative concerns, there are instrumental reasons to care about inequality. A more unequal distribution of economic resources lowers the impact of economic growth on reducing absolute poverty (Bourguignon, 2003; Ravallion, 2001). Economic inequalities may also translate into inequalities in health and education, which, by lowering productive opportunities, may dampen the overall productivity of the economy and economic growth. Economic inequality manifests itself also as misallocation and inefficiency in the use of resources. Since some economic disparities arise from market failures, reducing them can have important payoffs in terms of productivity and efficiency, boosting individuals' capacity to generate income and contribute to aggregate economic growth.

Economic inequalities may also promote social and political inequality and breed social conflict, disaffection, and violence. Very high levels of wealth and income concentration at the top are associated with a disproportionate amount of influence by certain actors and lead to state capture and policy distortions, whereby the interests of those at the top are systematically favored (Esteban and Ray, 2006). Inequality, in this way, can shape not only the bargaining power of actors today, but those of the next generation as well. In sum, high inequality may be associated with lower inter-generational mobility, in which the poor are trapped in a state of permanent deprivation. High concentration of capital is also likely to generate persistent inequalities of income in a vicious circle (Piketty, 2014). Finally, the distribution of household economic resources has implications for macro-economic policies (Alvaredo, Atkinson, and Morelli, 2017). For example, the size and distribution of assets and liabilities has implications for macro-economic stability, while differences in household savings rates and wealth-to-income ratios across the distribution have implications for demand management, and may explain the weakness of the recovery from the global financial crisis.

Given its prominence and far-reaching consequences, measuring the level and evolution of economic inequality accurately is of utmost importance. This chapter focuses on the data challenges encountered while measuring vertical economic inequality, i.e., inequality of income and consumption, and—whenever feasible—wealth among households or individuals ranked by the level of their economic resources.[6] The World Bank's *Monitoring Global Poverty: Report of the Commission on Global Poverty* (Atkinson, 2016) complements the issues discussed here in a number of ways—for instance, on how to tackle under-reporting and noncoverage at the bottom of the distribution; on the limitations of available data on purchasing power parities; and on how to address the shortcomings of price indexes. This chapter is not meant to be exhaustive concerning all topics relevant to economic inequality: it focuses on some of the areas that, in the view of the author, require greater investment by the statistical and research communities. In particular, the chapter does not present an overview of inequality trends or discuss the advantages and disadvantages of specific summary inequality indicators. These topics have been thoroughly covered elsewhere.[7]

The chapter is organized as follows. The next section presents a critical assessment of international databases on inequality. As we shall see, among the worrisome facts is that international databases not only show different levels of inequality but also, for some countries (especially in sub-Saharan Africa), diverging trends. A key factor behind the limitations of these databases is the quality of the underlying data: that is, of the household surveys (micro-data) used as inputs for their construction. The challenges encountered when running household surveys are the topic of the third section. Among the salient challenges is that household surveys suffer from undercoverage and under-reporting of top incomes, i.e., the "missing rich." Given its importance for inequality measurement, the missing rich problem is taken up in the fourth section, which presents an analytical taxonomy of approaches to correct for this population. As discussed in the section immediately following this, the typical welfare metrics used to measure inequality in international databases are disposable income and consumption expenditures; these, however, take into account only part of the effect that taxes and transfers have on people's economic well-being. The fifth section suggests that a more comprehensive assessment needs to use an income or consumption variable, or a pairing of both, that includes social transfers in kind (especially for education and health care) and adds the effect of consumption taxes and subsidies as well. The concluding section presents a number of recommendations to improve the quality of statistics in this field.

Measuring Economic Inequality: Scope and Limitations of International Databases

As a result of multiple efforts by academics, statistical offices, and international organizations to improve and harmonize inequality data, there has been an increase in the number of publicly available databases providing measures of economic inequality covering a broad range of countries, ranging from specific world regions (e.g., Latin America, OECD countries) to the world as a whole. All these databases contain summary statistics (the most common being the Gini coefficient) that describe (with very few exceptions) national-level inequality in incomes or consumption expenditures in multiple countries over multiple years. These cross-national inequality databases are being used by researchers, with increasing frequency, to document global or regional inequality trends (e.g., Atkinson and Bourguignon, 2015a; Atkinson, 2015; Bourguignon, 2015a; and Piketty, 2014), as well as by scholars interested in including inequality measures in cross-country regression analyses, either as dependent or independent variables (e.g., Acemoglu et al., 2015; Ostry, Berg, and Tsangarides, 2014). Yet these different databases are often designed for different purposes, and constructed in very different ways. Given that results could be sensitive to the choice of data set, a special issue of the *Journal of Economic Inequality*, edited by Ferreira and Lustig (2015), was devoted to an assessment of the merits and shortcomings of eight such databases. Some of its conclusions are summarized below.

Depending on the source of the summary inequality statistics they report, there are four types of databases among those that rely directly or indirectly on household surveys.[8]

- *Micro-based data sets*, which calculate inequality measures directly from household surveys.[9] These include: CEPALSTAT, by the UN Economic Commission for Latin America and the Caribbean (ECLAC), which provides income distribution estimates for Latin American countries and is computed by ECLAC based on the micro-data transmitted by statistical offices in the region; the Standard Indicators of the Commitment to Equity (CEQ) Institute, Tulane University; the income distribution estimates underpinning the EUROMOD microsimulation model (developed by the University of Essex); the OECD Income Distribution Database (IDD), which provides indicators and semi-aggregated tables computed by national contact points in member countries based on common definitions and treatments; the micro-data files on the distribution of income and wealth provided by the Luxembourg Income Study (LIS); the Socio-Economic Database for Latin America and the Caribbean (SEDLAC), compiled by the Center of Distributive, Labor and Social Studies at Universidad Nacional de La Plata and the World Bank; and PovcalNet (World Development Indicators, World Bank).[10]

- *Secondary Sources Data Sets*, which combine inequality indicators from a variety of other sources, typically from household surveys: these include the All the Ginis (ATG); the GINI Project; and the World Income Inequality Database (WIID, UNU-WIDER) (see Atkinson and Brandolini, 2001).

- *Imputation and Statistical Inference-Based Data Sets*. This type of data set generates inequality measures through a variety of imputation and statistical inference methods instead of relying directly on household surveys or unit-record data sets. These include the Global Consumption and Income Project (GCIP); the Standardized World Income Inequality Database (SWIID);[11] and the University of Texas Income Inequality Project (UTIP).

- Finally, there is the World Inequality Database (WID.world) launched in January 2017, whose precursor was the World Top Incomes Database (WTID) (Alvaredo et al., 2015a). Unlike the other data sets, WID.world uses information from tax returns (mainly) to estimate the share of income earned by certain groups at the top of the distribution (such as the richest 1% or 0.5% of the population) and gross up the income totals to match their equivalent to National Accounts. WID.world includes series on income inequality for more than 30 countries, spanning most of the 20th and early 21st centuries, with over 40 additional countries now under study. The database was recently extended to study the long-run evolution of top wealth shares (Saez and Zucman, 2016; Alvaredo, Atkinson, and Morelli, 2016; and Garbinti, Goupille-Lebret, and Piketty, 2017). The key feature of WID.world is to combine fiscal data (tax data, in particular), survey data, and national accounts data in a systematic manner. This characteristic sets it apart from the other data sets that rely on survey data almost exclusively, and from the data sets that rely on imputations or statistical inference. As stated on its website: "The overall long-run objective of WID.world is to be able to produce Distributional National Accounts (DINA), that is, to provide annual estimates of the distribution of income and wealth using concepts of income and wealth that are consistent with the macro-economic national accounts."[12]

Chapter 6 of this volume discusses in detail the proposed methodology to accomplish this objective.

The above data sets differ in a number of ways. First, and most obviously, they differ in their geographical coverage, hence on the quality of the underlying national data feeding them. Second, they differ in the nature of the individual welfare metric used: given that in most of the developing world household surveys are consumption-based, the existing data sets that are global in reach report consumption inequality for most developing and emerging countries, and income inequality for advanced countries and Latin America. Third, for advanced countries, economic inequality is typically measured based on equivalized income (i.e., household income is measured by pooling the income streams of each household member and then, attributing this to each member, based on an "adjustment" to reflect differences in needs across households of different size and structure) while in the rest of the world, per capita consumption or income is used. Fourth, while in principle the income variable should be disposable income (i.e., income after direct taxes and current transfers), this is often not clear when it comes to developing countries' data, where it is often difficult to establish whether the reported income is net or gross of direct taxes, or pre- or post-transfers. Likewise, while income or consumption should include consumption of goods produced for own production and imputed rent of owner's occupied housing, in practice this is not the case in general and, in some cases, it is hard to tell.

Lastly, the databases differ on whether adjustments (and which ones) are made to the micro-data to correct for under-reporting, to eliminate outliers, or to address missing responses.[13] While in most OECD countries such adjustments and data cleaning are performed by the statistical offices themselves, before making the data available to users, such practice is far less common in low- and middle-income countries, implying that the international data sets with broad geographic coverage often rely on adjustments implemented by the agency responsible for the secondary data, or on data nonadjusted for item nonresponse. For the data sets that use imputation methods or statistical inference, results are sensitive to the methods utilized, and one often does not have the full information on the characteristics of the underlying data even if the methods are described with care (which is also not always the case).

Given the differences in definitions and methods across data sets, the analyses can therefore yield conflicting pictures of economic inequality, both in terms of levels and trends, depending on the data set used (see Bourguignon, 2015b; Ferreira, Lustig, and Teles, 2015; Gasparini and Tornarolli, 2015; Jenkins, 2015; Ravallion, 2015; Smeeding and Latner, 2015; and Wittenberg, 2015). For example, in the case of sub-Saharan Africa (SSA) and its inequality dynamics over the 1990s and 2000s, the IMF *Fiscal Monitor* (2012, p. 51) suggests that in 11 out of 16 SSA countries inequality had fallen between 1985–95 and 2000–10. However, as shown in Table 3.1, when compared with the World Bank PovcalNet inequality trends for the same countries, not only levels but, more importantly, also the direction of change is sensitive to the choice of data set. Matters get even more complicated if we draw on other data sets as well.

Furthermore, important questions such as whether or not economic inequality has converged across countries in the world—the finding that income inequality has fallen in what had been highly unequal countries, and risen in countries that

Table 3.1. Change in Inequality 1985–95 to 2000–10

Country	IMF Fiscal Monitor	PovcalNet Average
Côte d'Ivoire	5.0	6.5
Ghana	2.4	6.3
Kenya	-6.2	-2.1
Madagascar	-1.0	0.2
Niger	-6.2	0.4
Senegal	-7.8	-7.6
Tanzania	-3.1	2.3
Zambia	-13.5	-3.5

Note: Change in inequality is measured as the percent change in the Gini coefficient between two points in time.
Source: Author, based on Table 5 in Ferreira, F.H.G., N. Lustig, and D. Teles (2015), "Appraising cross-national income inequality databases: An introduction," in Ferreira, F.H.G. and N. Lustig, "Appraising cross-national income inequality databases," special issue, *Journal of Economic Inequality*, Vol. 13(4), pp. 497–526. StatLink 2 http://dx.doi.org/10.1787/888933839506.

had been more egalitarian (Benabou, 1996; Bleaney and Nishiyama, 2003; and Ravallion, 2003)—are affected by the choice of data set. As shown in Lustig and Teles (2016), different data sets frequently produce different results in terms of inequality convergence, even when the countries, welfare concept, inequality metric, and time period are the same.

Assessments of fiscal redistribution are also sensitive to the choice of data sets. Figure 3.1 shows the difference between the Gini coefficients for disposable (i.e., net) incomes and for market incomes for the same survey and country, as estimated both by CEQ (which calculates them through a detailed fiscal incidence analysis, validated by local experts and through a series of robustness checks) and SWIID (where all data points are estimated through multiple imputation meth-

Figure 3.1. Fiscal Redistribution: Change in Gini from Two Databases

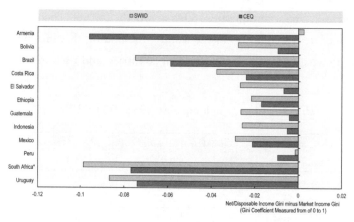

Note: Difference in Gini points. CEQ's Disposable Income is equivalent to SWIID's Net Income, e.g., market income after taxes and government cash transfers for the scenario that considers contributory pensions as government transfers. Based on Younger and Khachatryan (2014) in the case of Armenia; Paz Arauco et al. (2014) for Bolivia; Higgins and Pereira (2014) for Brazil; Sauma and Trejos (2014) for Costa Rica; Beneke, Lustig, and Oliva (2018) for El Salvador; Hill et al. (2017) for Ethiopia; Cabrera, Lustig, and Moran (2015) for Guatemala; Afkar, Jellema, and Wai-Poi (2017) for Indonesia; Scott (2014) for Mexico; Jaramillo (2014) for Peru; Inchauste et al. (2017) for South Africa; and Bucheli et al. (2014) for Uruguay. For both data sources, contributory pensions were classified as a government transfer (CEQ has estimates for pensions as deferred income—part of market income—as well). Comparisons for Bolivia, Brazil, Peru, and Uruguay refer to data collected in 2009; for Costa Rica, Guatemala, Mexico, and South Africa to 2010; for Armenia and El Salvador to 2011; for Indonesia to 2012. The comparison for Ethiopia is made with the CEQ estimate for 2011 and the SWIID estimate for 2010.
Source: CEQ Institute Data Center on Fiscal Redistribution (http://commitmentoequity.org/datacenter) and SWIID: V 5.0 database. StatLink 2 http://dx.doi.org/10.1787/888933839487.

ods using whichever data are available from other sources as the basis for the "rectangularization"). While discrepancies between the two sources are not systematic (i.e., sometimes SWIID's estimate of redistribution is higher and sometimes lower than CEQ's), they can be quite large (e.g., Guatemala and Indonesia) or contradictory (e.g., Armenia, where taxes and benefits are unequalizing according to SWIID—i.e., net income inequality is higher than market income inequality—and equalizing in CEQ).[14]

The above discussion makes clear that, basically, many of the limitations of the international databases are due to the limitations of their main input: country-level household surveys. We turn to this issue in the next section.

Household Surveys: Data Challenges

The overwhelming majority of analysis on income, consumption, and wealth inequality over the last four decades has been based (directly or indirectly) on household surveys, the main data source for research on distribution. While data availability, coverage, and quality have improved relative to 2009 when the Stiglitz-Sen-Fitoussi report was released, there are still a number of important issues to be resolved. Furthermore, the problems faced by high-income countries in measuring distribution of economic well-being are orders of magnitude larger in poorer and middle-income countries, where surveys are undertaken infrequently (if at all), generally based on different welfare metrics (either income or consumption), with potentially inadequate and outdated sampling frames, and often with large rates of nonresponse (see, for instance, Ferreira, Lustig, and Teles, 2015).

Most OECD countries undertake regular (annual, sometimes every 2 or 3 years) collections of income distribution data, based on household surveys or registers that started in the 1980s or 1990s. Household budget surveys are undertaken in OECD countries around every 5 years, typically based on diaries that households use to record the value of their consumption expenditures.[15] Even in advanced OECD countries, however, there are important challenges in terms of coverage of various income streams (e.g., imputed rents) or asset types (e.g., pension wealth or the stock of consumer durables), of frequency of data collections, and of timeliness of the resulting estimates, which in many countries lag by *years* the timing of releases of GDP data. In these areas, despite the many initiatives that have been taken by statistical offices since 2009, we are still far from the objective of feeding policy discussion with income distribution data that are as timely as conventional measures of quarterly GDP growth.

The picture of data availability is different in the developing countries. The number of low- and middle-income countries with household surveys has increased dramatically since 1990. For instance, the World Bank estimate of extreme poverty in 1990 was based on data for only 22 countries. The data in the World Bank's PovcalNet presently cover 153 countries, of which 34, as of July 2013, are classified as High Income (Atkinson, 2016).[16] However, lack of data is still a problem. In the Middle East and North Africa region, where there are 19 countries, only around half are covered by PovcalNet. Furthermore, according to World Bank (2016), the largest possible set of countries for which at least two comparable data points are available between 2008 and 2013 was 83 countries. This set covered 75% of the world's population but fewer than half of the world's countries; population coverage was 94% in the East Asia and Pacific region but only 23% in sub-Saharan Africa.[17,18] Even if surveys exist, in many countries governments still restrict access to the micro-data, a factor that limits the ability of independent researchers to carry out an analysis of their own.

A second problem is that, with exceptions, household surveys collect data on either income or consumption, which significantly limits the possibility of undertaking the joint analysis of both variables and rigorous cross-country comparisons. Of the 83 countries included in World Bank (2016), for example, 34 contained consumption data and 49 contained income data. The latter included primarily OECD countries and Latin America. If OECD high-income countries are excluded, of the 1,165 data sets included in the World Bank's PovcalNet database, 41% (59%) were income- (consumption-) based (Table 3.2). While the distribution of income—if income is properly measured—may closely mirror that of consumption expenditures in countries at low levels of economic development, that assumption becomes less tenable as countries develop and household saving rates increase, casting doubts on the practice of combining measures of income and consumption inequalities as if they were describing the same underlying phenomenon.[19]

While there are international conventions and standards for measuring *income* dis-

Table 3.2. Income and Consumption Distributions in PovcalNet

Number of datasets

	Micro data	Grouped data	Total (in %)
Income	399	79	478 (41%)
Consumption	563	124	687 (59%)
Total	962	203	1165 (100%)

Note: This table excludes distributions from high-income countries available in the LIS and/or other databases.
Source: Ferreira, F.H.G. et al. (2016), "A global count of the extreme poor in 2012: Data issues, methodology and initial results," *Journal of Economic Inequality*, Vol. 14(2), pp. 141–172. StatLink 2 http://dx.doi.org/10.1787/888933839525.

tribution (first articulated in the 2001 *Canberra Group Handbook*, codified in the 2003 standards adopted by the International Conference of Labour Statisticians, and brought up to date with the 2011 revision of the *Canberra Handbook*), important issues—such as the systematic under-reporting of incomes at both extremes—subsist.

Second, while the World Bank's Living Standards Measurement Surveys (LSMS) use a series of guidelines to measure household *consumption*, no international conventions or guidelines exist in this field. Frequently, the instruments that are used to collect micro-level data on consumption expenditures (household budget surveys) are conducted with the main goal of deriving average weights for the consumer price index rather than to assess household economic well-being. While deemed easier to implement than income surveys in less developed countries where informality is widespread, the comparability of these estimates is affected by factors such as the length of the reference period considered, and the length of the list of items that households are asked to report (Beegle et al., 2012). These deficiencies led the Commission on Global Poverty to include developing a set of statistical standards for household consumption as one of its key recommendations (Atkinson, 2016).

Third, international guidelines on measuring the distribution of household *wealth* have yet to go through a similar process of convention-setting by an international body in charge of setting standards globally.[20]

Finally, even when measures exist on the distribution of household income, consumption, and wealth, very few countries undertake these data collections in ways that would allow the joint distribution of household income, consumption, and wealth to be analyzed in a coherent way, one of the key recommendations of the Stiglitz-Sen-Fitoussi report.[21]

Even when international standards and guidelines exist, however, countries' data collections may adhere to them to different degrees, implying that some items are available and included in measured household income and consumption for some countries (e.g., imputed rents, taxes paid, and agricultural goods produced for own consumption) but not for others.[22] In the best of cases, the income or consumption concept reported in household surveys corresponds to what the Canberra convention would describe as "disposable income" and "final consumption expenditures," but not all countries are able to adequately measure these concepts.[23] Additionally, there is evidence that the problems related to unit nonresponse, item nonresponse, and measurement errors in household surveys have increased over time (Groves et al., 2009; Meyer, Mok, and Sullivan, 2015).

Although there are countries for which long historical series on the distribution of wealth from a variety of administrative registries exist, survey-based data collections on the distribution of household wealth are much more recent than those for income, and the available data are significantly less comparable across countries than income data, mainly on account of the different capacity of surveys to capture developments at the top end of the distribution. Wealth distribution data are available, with varying degrees of quality, for the United States (based on the Survey of Consumer Finances), the United Kingdom (based on the Wealth and Asset Survey), countries in the euro area (through the Household Finance and Consumption Survey coordinated by the European Central Bank), as well as for Australia, New Zealand, Canada, China, Indonesia, Norway, Korea, Japan, and Chile.[24] As discussed in Chapter 4 of this volume, there are also a series of new initiatives to measure the distribution of wealth by gender. In the case of the distribution of wealth, survey estimates are even more likely to go wrong, simply because wealth is much more unequally shared than income, so that all the problems associated with the estimation of the shares of small groups of top wealth holders are exacerbated.

As stated, the overwhelming majority of inequality data has been based on household surveys. The Nordic countries, however, stand apart from other countries, due to their reliance on a well-developed system of registers that allow statistical offices to get information on personal income (and sometimes wealth) from various personal records, which are then combined into household files. While administrative records allow more precise information on people's economic resources to be obtained, and to link these resources for the same individual and sometimes across generations, these registers are far from perfect. An important downside is that they may only imperfectly match people belonging to the same household, and record members of the same household as separate households (e.g., students living away from the parental home for part of the year).

The distinction between survey-based and record-based methods is, moreover, becoming increasingly blurred, as several statistical offices in advanced countries have come to rely on mixed methods of data collection, whereby some of the information required by the survey is retrieved from administrative records (in most cases with the prior consent of the person being interviewed), or information from administrative records is used to identify groups of individuals that should be oversampled in the survey (as done by the Survey of Consumer Finances in the United States). While these mixed methods of data collection have proved effective in delivering higher-quality information, their use is sometimes limited by statistical laws and administrative constraints. Obviously, the quality of statistical information provided by administrative registers depends on the quality of the registers (e.g., on how widespread tax evasion is), on the capacity of various administrations to link their records, and so on.

An additional challenge for data on the distribution of household economic resources refers to the problems in reconciling the totals from micro-data—i.e., consumption, income, and wealth totals from household surveys and administrative records—with those available through macro-data—i.e., totals for the (supposedly) same variables in the System of National Accounts. For most countries in the world, totals for household income and consumption from surveys do not match the equivalent totals from national accounts. These differences can be very large in some countries, as illustrated by Table 3.3 for a sample of Latin American countries.[25] Also, discrepancies are not limited to levels of different types of household economic resources but extend, more importantly, to their growth rates (Deaton, 2005). Gaps between macro- and micro-statistics have been widening in many countries. While the causes of this pattern are not all well understood—and some of the discrepancy is probably due to the same problem of under-coverage and under-reporting of top incomes mentioned above—its very existence casts doubts on efforts to disentangle the relation between GDP growth and income distribution on the basis of metrics that rely not only on different definitions of household income, but which may also suffer from a series of measurement errors themselves. Diverging trends in income and consumption growth between household surveys and national accounts have led to the creation of the OECD-Eurostat Expert Group on Integrating Disparities in National Accounts in Europe. The US Census Bureau and others in the United States are also trying to address this challenge.

One of the most important limitations of household surveys is that they underrepresent the rich and the poor, and under-report incomes at both ends of the distribution. Much of the current attention of researchers and statisticians has focused on the top end of the distribution. While this issue will be taken up in more detail in a later section of this chapter, it should be stressed here that—as emphasized by Deaton (2005)—there can be no general supposition that estimated inequality will be biased either up or down in the case of "selective under-sampling."[26] Issues of noncoverage, underrepresentation, and under-reporting of the richest households become particularly relevant whenever much of the action concerning changes in the distribution is taking place at the top (as has been the case in many countries over the last decades) and is particularly problematic in very unequal societies, characterized by income and wealth being highly concentrated in the hands of a small number of families.

The potential for mismeasurement is, however, not limited to the top end of the distribution but extends to the bottom end, as discussed in Atkinson (2016). Many poor people may not be adequately covered by existing measures, due to lack of a permanent address (e.g., the homeless), because they live in collective living quarters (e.g., slum-dwellers), or because they are recent arrivals in the country (e.g., refugees). Because of the undeclared and sometimes illegal nature of their activities, very poor people may also be unwilling to fully declare their income when asked in surveys. Many low-income people often report levels of consumption expenditures well in excess of their declared income, a factor that underscores the importance of joint analysis of income, consumption, and wealth to assess, for instance, whether the poor are "eating up" their assets.

While problems of underrepresentation and under-reporting exist at both ends

Table 3.3. Ratio of Mean Income in Household Survey to Mean Household Final Consumption Expenditure per Capita in National Accounts, Selected Latin American Countries

Country	1997	1998	1999	2000	2001	2002	2003	2004	2005	2006	2007	2008	2009	2010	2011	2012
Bolivia	1.26		1.07	1.01	1.08	1.08			1.17	1.19	1.17	1.21	1.27		1.26	1.27
Brazil				0.84	0.84	0.85	0.82	0.82	0.84	0.86	0.83	0.84	0.82		0.78	0.81
Colombia					0.50	0.67	0.60	0.63	0.66			0.65	0.68	0.71	0.71	0.67
Costa-Rica					0.80	0.79	0.80	0.75	0.76	0.75	0.80	0.80	0.90			
Dominican Republic				0.92	0.88	0.82	0.69	0.58	0.60	0.57	0.59	0.48	0.55	0.49	0.47	0.50
Ecuador							0.66	0.87	0.70	0.75	0.75	0.66	0.66	0.70	0.69	0.71
El Salvador								0.57	0.56	0.53	0.54	0.49	0.55	0.52	0.50	0.51
Honduras					1.13	0.93	0.95	0.96	0.91	0.92	0.98	1.03	1.03	1.01	0.98	
Mexico		0.44		0.49		0.47		0.43	0.43	0.43		0.43		0.42		0.44
Paraguay	1.44		1.34		1.32	1.22	1.26	1.15	1.18	1.08	1.07	0.98	1.10	1.06	1.06	0.00
Peru		0.81	0.81	0.70	0.67	0.76	0.71	0.72	0.67	0.72	0.75	0.73	1.77	0.78	0.76	0.77
Uruguay		0.80		0.83	0.82	0.76	0.71	0.70	0.70	0.69	0.69	0.71	0.82	0.74	0.73	0.70

Source: Bourguignon, F. (2015b), "Appraising income inequality databases in Latin America," in Ferreira, F.H.G. and N. Lustig (eds.), "Appraising cross-national income inequality databases," special issue, Journal of Economic Inequality, Vol. 13(4), pp. 557–578. StatLink 2 http://dx.doi.org/10.1787/888933839544.

of the distribution, for inequality measures it is particularly relevant to correct the data for the missing rich, a topic that is discussed in the next section.

The "Missing Rich" in Household Surveys

Whether they collect data on income, consumption, or wealth, there is reason to believe that household surveys do not capture the rich well. How do we know that very high incomes are not captured in household surveys? Why is this issue important? What are its causes? What can be done to address the problem? Here I present a synthesis of the factors that give rise to the "missing rich" problem in household surveys, and review the approaches that have been proposed to deal with the problem.[27]

By inspection, one can observe that the top incomes as measured by surveys are at most close to the earnings of a well-paid manager; additionally, capital incomes as measured by surveys are a tiny fraction of what national accounts identify as the amounts accrued to the household sector.[28] The fact that rich individuals are large-ly missing and that their income is frequently under-reported in household surveys may explain in part the worrisome result that, especially in middle- and low-income countries, the survey-based measure of per capita household income (or some of its components) or consumption frequently show levels substantially lower than the per capita household income or consumption from either national accounts[29] or tax records.[30] The missing rich problem may explain as well why there are striking discrepancies in inequality levels and trends, depending on the source of the data (e.g., surveys versus tax records) (see Alvaredo and Londoño-Velez, 2013; Alvaredo et al., 2015; and Belfield et al., 2015). If the rich are missing, the survey-based distributions of income, consumption, or wealth, and the concomitant inequality measures should be viewed with caution: actual inequality may be considerably different than that recorded by survey estimates.[31] As discussed below, however, it is not necessarily true that correcting the information for the rich that are missing will necessarily result in higher inequality.

The most obvious reason why the rich, especially the ultra-rich, are missing in household surveys is because there are very few of them in the target population; thus, the probability of including one of these individuals in a survey (sample) is rather low. As discussed in Lustig (forthcoming) there are, essentially, five additional factors embedded in the data collection process that may give rise to the missing rich problem in household surveys: (1) frame or noncoverage error; (2) unit nonresponse; (3) item (income) nonresponse; (4) under-reporting; and (5) top coding and trimming. Surveys may suffer from one or any combination of problems 1–5, and any one of them can potentially result in an underestimation of the income share of the top income fractile. In addition, as mentioned above, even if there is full coverage and response rate, no under-reporting and no top coding or trimming, rich individuals may not appear in household surveys due to sparseness: i.e., there is no density mass at all points of the upper tail of the true distribution's support, especially for extreme values.[32] Sparseness or low frequency of observations at the top will result in a frequent underestimation of the income share of rich individuals but, on occasion, the income share may be overestimated.

In the presence of any of the sampling and nonsampling problems described above, survey-based inequality measures will be biased. The direction of the bias in inequality measures can be positive or negative, as use of the corrected data will affect both what happens at the top but also on how correcting for the missing rich problem affects the mean (Deaton, 2005).[33] Even if there are no errors in the achieved sample that led to biased inequality estimates, sparseness in the upper tail can result in volatile inequality estimates. If the rich are selected in the sample with a very low frequency, the survey-based inequality measures will frequently be below the true inequality measure and above it on occasion (Higgins, Lustig, and Vigorito, 2017).

As described in Lustig (forthcoming), a variety of approaches have been proposed in statistics and in the measurement of inequality literature to address the missing rich problem.[34] In terms of the data sources used, these can be classified into three broad groups: alternate data (i.e., relying on alternative data such as tax records instead of surveys); within-survey corrections (i.e., correcting top incomes in surveys using parametric and nonparametric methods); and survey-cum-external data (i.e., correcting survey data or inequality estimates by combining surveys, administrative data, and national accounts using parametric and nonparametric methods).

A key distinction among existing methods is whether they correct the data by *replacing* incomes at the top by a parametric distribution (e.g., Pareto) or using external information (e.g., tax records); or by changing the weights of the "rich" and "nonrich" population, i.e., *reweighting* or poststratification. The first approach assumes that the population shares of top incomes (the rich) and the rest (the non-rich) in the achieved sample survey are correct, and that the problem lies in that the incomes captured at the top are incorrect. This can occur either because the incomes in the survey are under-reported or because the individuals captured by the survey are not really representative of the rich (due to undercoverage, under-representation, top coding, and/or sparseness). The second approach assumes that the population weights for the rich and nonrich in the sample are incorrect: one must "add people" at the top either by increasing the weights of rich individuals in the survey or generating the upper tail through some parametric or nonparametric method. Under the replacing and reweighting approaches, there exist a variety of methods. Table 3.4, drawn from Lustig (forthcoming), presents a summary of the correction approaches and refers the reader to a sample of their applications.

Broadening the Indicators of Households' Economic Well-Being

There is a long-standing discussion, among economists and statisticians, about the best metric to describe people's economic well-being. One perspective, articulated by Stiglitz, Sen, and Fitoussi (2009), is that, ideally, one would like to focus on the distribution of consumption *possibilities* across people, socio-economic groups, and generations. While income flows and wealth holdings are an important gauge for assessing power relations within a community, a narrower economic view is that what really matters for people's economic well-being is what they are potentially able to consume over time—including across generations.

Consumption possibilities are determined not only by current earned income but also by accumulated wealth and by the ability to borrow against existing wealth or future savings. Wealth is an important indicator of the sustainability of observed consumption: for a given income, consumption can be raised by running down assets or by increasing debt. Similarly, savings and additions to assets reduce consumption for a given level of income. In addition to earned income flows and wealth, consumption possibilities are determined by transfers between households

Table 3.4. Approaches to Address the Missing Rich Problem in Household Surveys

Approach	Survey Data	Administrative Data	References
Panel A: TAX DATA ONLY			
Tax data from individual records or tabulations are used to calculate the income shares of top incomes (e.g. the 1%)	Not used	Yes: Tax Records (individual records and tabulations)	Atkinson and Harrison (1978); Atkinson and Piketty (2007, 2010); Kuznets (1953); Piketty (2001); Piketty and Saez (2003)
PANEL B: WITHIN SURVEY CORRECTION METHODS			
B.i REPLACING TOP INCOMES: POPULATION SHARES (WEIGHTS) OF TOP INCOMES (b100%) AND NONTOP INCOMES [(1 - β)100%] UNCHANGED			
Semiparametric methods: Pareto distribution (or other models) for top (b100%) incomes and survey data for nontop [(1 - β)100%]	Yes	Not used	Methodology: Cowell and Victoria-Feser (1996); Cowell and Flachaire (2015) Application: Alfons, Templ and Filzmoser (2013); Burkhauser et al. (2012); Cowell and Flachaire (2007); Hlasny and Verme (2017); Ruiz and Woloszko (2016)
Imputation methods: parametric (regression imputation) and nonparametric (e.g. hot deck)	Yes	Not used	Methodology: Little and Rubin (2014) Application: Autor, Katz and Kearney (2008); Burkhauser, Feng and Larrimore (2010); Campos-Vazquez and Lustig (2017); Jenkins et al. (2011); Lemieux (2006)
B.ii REWEIGHTING: POPULATION SHARES (WEIGHTS) OF TOP INCOMES (b100%) AND NONTOP INCOMES ((1 - β)100%) CHANGE			
Poststratification: replace the expansion factors in sample by new weights generated with information on respondents obtained from survey producers.	Yes	Not used	Methodology: Atkinson and Micklewright (1983); Biemer and Christ (2008); Korinek, Mistiaen and Ravallion (2006); Mistieaen and Ravallion (2003) Application: Hlasny and Verme (2017)

Approach	Survey Data	Administrative Data	References
PANEL C: COMBINING SURVEY AND ADMINISTRATIVE DATA			
C.i REPLACING TOP INCOMES: POPULATION SHARES (WEIGHTS) OF TOP INCOMES (b100%) AND NONTOP INCOMES [(1 - β)100%] UNCHANGED			
C.i.a Combining Data			
Nonparametric			
Replace the survey-based mean incomes for pre-specified fractiles (e.g. percentiles) by tax data cell-specified fractiles (e.g., percentiles) by tax data cell-means; cut-off at which replacement takes place varies	Yes	Yes: Tax Records	Alvaredo et al. (2017a); Bach, Corneo and Steiner (2009); Burkhauser, Larrimore and Lyons (2016); Campos-Vazquez and Lustig (2017); Department for Work & Pensions (2015)
Adjust to National Accounts: capital incomes of top β% in survey grossed-up to match total income from capital in National Accounts. (Method also grosses up labor income)	Yes	Yes: National (Household Income) Accounts	Methodology: Altimir (1987) Application: CEPALStat (UN Economic Commission for LAC) until 2016
WID.World Approach: Assume survey below percentile β' (e.g. 0.9) is reliable; replace by tax data above percentile β (e.g. 0.995 percentile); assume quantile ratio upgrade factor rises linearly in between β' and β (interpolation to "join" both distributions); if data comes in form of tabulations, apply generalized Pareto (Blanchet, Fournier and Piketty, 2017); add tax-exempt capital income (undistributed profits); gross-up to national accounts totals.	Yes	Yes: Tax Records (tabulations) and National Accounts	Methodology: Alvaredo et al. (2017b and 2017c) Applications: Garbinti, Goupille and Piketty (2016); Novokmet, Piketty and Zucman (2017); Piketty, Saez and Zucman (2016); Piketty, Yang and Zucman (2016)
C.i.b Combining Inequality Estimates			
Calculate total inequality using inequality decomposition formula: sum of inequality within top, inequality within bottom, and inequality between. That is, estimate Gini for top (b100%) with tax data; estimate Gini for bottom (1 - β)100% based on survey; apply decomposition formula (Atkinson, 2007 and Alvaredo, 2011) to estimate total Gini	Yes	Yes: Tax Records	Alvaredo (2011); Alvaredo and Londoño-Velez (2013); Atkinson (2007); Atkinson, Piketty and Saez (2011); Diaz-Bazan (2015); Jenkins (2017), Lakner and Milanovic (2015)

Approach	Survey Data	Administrative Data	References
C.ii: REWEIGHTING: POPULATION SHARES (WEIGHTS) OF TOP INCOMES (b100%) AND NONTOP INCOMES ((1 - β)100%) CHANGE			
C.ii.a Combining Data			
Poststratification: replace the expansion factors in sample by new weights from administrative sources (e.g. social security records). Use information from external "donors" to generate new weights	Yes	Yes: Tax Records	Methodology: Biemer and Christ (2008) Application: Campos and Lustig (2017)
Poststratification: reweight so as to be "close" to survey-based distribution below a certain income threshold and "close" to tax-based distribution above that threshold	Yes	Yes: Tax Records	Bourguignon (2017b)
C.ii.b Combining Inequality Estimates			
Poststratification: Calculate total inequality using inequality decomposition formula: sum of inequality within top, inequality within bottom, and inequality between, but assume survey represents only bottom share of population. That is, assume survey data is the (1 - β)100% instead of 100%; estimate the Gini for top redefined bottom (1 - β)100%; estimate Gini for top (b100%) with tax data; and apply Atkinson (2007) and Alvaredo (2011) formula to estimate total Gini	Yes	Yes: Tax Records; rich lists (e.g. Forbes)	Methodology: Atkinson and Bourguignon (2000) Applications: Anand and Segal (2015)

Note: The "mapping" of studies to methods under the "References" column should be viewed as an approximation because studies frequently apply more than one method.

Source: Lustig, N. (forthcoming), "The missing rich in household surveys: Causes and correction methods," *CEQ Working Paper,* No. 75, Commitment to Equity Institute, Tulane University, Table 1. StatLink 2 http://dx.doi.org/10.1787/888933839563.

(e.g., gifts, remittances, and inheritance) and within them (e.g., from income earners to other members).

Consumption possibilities are also determined by state action. Subtracting direct taxes (e.g., personal income and wealth taxes) and social security contributions paid by workers, and adding current transfers provided by governments and nonprofit institutions (e.g., cash transfers to the poor or to people unable to work) to earned and unearned income yields *disposable income*. Disposable income at any point in time, however, does not capture consumption possibilities accurately. A better indicator of the latter is *final consumption expenditures*, equal to disposable income plus consumption financed by borrowing or by drawing down assets and less saving. In practice, however, measured *final consumption expenditures* do not capture consumption possibilities accurately either. For example, the benefits from consumer durables other than housing are typically recorded when expenditures are incurred, rather than over the longer period when these benefits are provided. In some instance, to avoid distortionary spikes in consumption expenditures, spending on consumer durables other than housing is not included at all. Additional limitations occur with the exclusion of specific types of difficult-to-measure flows (such as imputed rents, i.e., the income that accrues to property owners from the dwellings that they own; or the value of goods produced by households for own consumption, which are important in countries with large subsistence farming).

In this section, however, we would like to draw attention to two elements that are typically excluded from the conceptual definitions of household income and expenditures that are conventionally used in analysis of economic inequalities: free in-kind services (especially, education and health care) provided to households by governments and nonprofit institutions; and consumption taxes and subsidies.[35]

Social Transfers in Kind

In addition to earned income and cash transfers, households receive benefits in kind such as education, health care, and social housing that governments provide to households for free (or at highly subsidized prices) and whose provision is financed out of taxes (and often user fees or other forms of direct payments made by the user of such services). Including these in-kind benefits in measures of household income and consumption is important, for example, to avoid that reductions in direct taxes, offset by lower provision of these government services, lead to higher measures of people's economic welfare simply because the concomitant reduction in public services has not been recorded. Adding the value of those services—also called "social transfers in kind"—to household income and consumption provides, in theory, a better measure of households' consumption possibilities. However, there is no consensus on how to make these imputations; there are also concerns that such imputations may lead to metrics that are further away from what people actually experience (UNECE, 2011).

Valuing social transfers in kind raises both conceptual and measurement challenges. Decisions are needed in terms of the range of services to be considered (ideally, all types of individualized services provided by governments and nonprofit institutions, excluding public goods such as defense or law and order); the monetary valuation of the services provided; and their allocation to various beneficiaries.[36]

In practice, the most frequently used approach is to value in-kind transfers at the production costs incurred by the government in producing them (Lustig, 2018a). For education, the method most commonly used consists of attributing a value to an individual who attends public school, using values equal to the per-beneficiary input costs obtained from administrative data, and adding this value to the household's income. For example, average government expenditure per primary school student obtained from administrative data is allocated to households based on how many children are reported attending public school at the primary level (the same method applies to other levels of schooling). Information on whether school-age children are attending public or private school, or whether they are in school at all, may not be collected in income and consumption surveys, so that general allocation based on the age of children may fail to identify the true beneficiaries or allocate to them a benefit that they never received.

Imputation to individual service users is even more complex in the case of health care. In this case, the allocation of benefits is done following either the "actual consumption approach" or the "insurance value approach." As described in Higgins and Lustig (2018), the first approach allocates the value of public services to the individuals who are actually using the service. The second approach assigns the same per capita spending to everybody sharing the same characteristic such as age or gender, irrespectively of their actual use of these services, based on the principle that all people with the same demographic characteristics are entitled to these public benefits. The reliance on one approach over the other depends, often, on data availability, but the choice, along with leading to very different empirical results, raises conceptual problems. To impute the value received from public health services on the basis of actual consumption, the household survey must provide information about the use of health services, and distinguish between public care (which is usually received from the public health system or paid for by public health insurance schemes) and private care. In the absence of information about whether the care received was subsidized by government, a survey may ask about whether the patient is covered by private insurance. Patients who received health care and report having private health insurance are considered to have received private care, and thus received no in-kind transfer, while patients who report not having private health insurance are considered to have received public care. Ideally, the survey should also contain one or more questions about the type of service received (for more details, see Higgins and Lustig, 2018). Attributing health care services to users also implies making sick people "richer" than they would otherwise have been, while also raising the issue of whether allowance should be made for their higher needs, which are ignored by the equivalence scales typically used in analysis.

In sum, the approach to valuing the benefits of public education and health care services amounts to asking the following question: How much would the income of a household have to be increased if it had to pay for the free or subsidized public service (or the insurance value in the cases in which this applies to health care benefits) at the full cost to the government? The conventional answer to this question is to look at production costs. This approach, however, raises a number of issues: it does not take into account variations in needs across income or age groups, nor does it consider service quality, and may not reflect the actual valuation by beneficiaries.[37] Teachers may not show up at local schools, and the quality of the schooling services provided may be a fraction of what households would deem as adequate given the amount of taxes that they have paid. Distributional analysis of in-kind transfers may reveal that poorer households gain larger shares of particular categories of public spending than higher-income households. However, this result may owe to the fact that the middle classes and the rich opt out of public education and health care because of their poor quality. Given the limitations of available data, however, the cost-of-provision method is the best one can do for now.[38]

Consumption Taxes and Subsidies

A second element that is typically excluded from assessments of people's consumption possibilities is the impact that consumption taxes and production subsidies have on what—following the naming convention established in the Commitment to Equity project—we can call "consumable income," i.e., the *actual* consumption of goods and services by people.[39] To illustrate this point, let's consider two countries (or the same country but at two points in time) and assume that final consumption expenditures are the same in the two cases, but that in one the value added tax (VAT) is 10% while in the other it equals 20%. Obviously, for a given amount of money income, what households can actually consume will be higher in the first case than in the second.

Consumption taxes can increase poverty. In a sample of 28 low- and middle-income countries, the Commitment to Equity project found that for Armenia, Bolivia, Ethiopia, Ghana, Guatemala, Honduras, Nicaragua, Sri Lanka, and Tanzania, the headcount poverty for consumable income, based on a poverty line of $2.50 per day (in 2005 PPP), is *higher* than the headcount for market income (before personal income and consumption taxes, cash transfers, and consumption subsidies), i.e., consumption taxes increase the prevalence of income poverty. In Ghana, Nicaragua, and Tanzania, net payers to the fiscal system begin in the income range $0–1.25/day in purchasing power parity (i.e., the ultra-poor) when consumption taxes are included. In Guatemala, Ethiopia, and Armenia, net tax payers begin in the income group of extreme poor with $1.25–2.50/day. In Sri Lanka, Peru, El Salvador, Dominican Republic, Honduras, and Bolivia, net payers to the fiscal system begin in the income category $2.50–4/day, i.e., in the group classified as moderately poor.[40]

Beyond these effects on the absolute level of consumption, consumption taxes may also impact on distribution. When annual income is used as a measure of economic well-being, consumption taxes are regressive, i.e., relatively more of them are paid by low-income groups of the population, as poor people spend a greater share of their income on consumption than rich people. Conversely, when lifetime income is used as a metric of economic well-being, consumption taxes could be proportional (or even progressive), under the assumption that today's savings will be spent on consumption goods in the future. Even in a life-course perspective, however, consumption taxes may have regressive effects when considering that accumulated savings may be used to finance the future purchase of capital goods (e.g., housing) rather than consumption goods; that this purchase may be effected abroad rather than domestically; that different consumption goods may be subject to different levies; and that the structure of consumption may differ across the income distribution. In all these cases, consumption taxes will have redistributive effects that are generally ignored by studies of fiscal redistribution, in addition to those operating through the general level of prices.

While it is acknowledged that household consumption possibilities are reduced and increased by, respectively, consumption taxes and production subsidies passed on to the prices households pay for goods and services, taking this impact into account has not been part of the conventions typically used for analyzing disparities in households' economic well-being.[41]

Conclusions

Since the turn of the 21st century, both policy-makers and the public at large have paid growing attention to the distribution of household economic resources. This has been accompanied by a growing number of micro-data sets becoming available in individual countries (notably on wealth), a growing focus on the top end of the distributions, the mobilization of additional data sources such as tax records, steps to bring closer together macro- and micro-data streams, and a growing attention to the "global distribution of income," which has led to the construction of large international data sets combining information from different national sources. These developments have changed significantly the landscape since as recently as 2009, when the report of the Stiglitz-Sen-Fitoussi Commission was published. In particular, returning to the use of tax data and, especially, combining them with data from (income and wealth) surveys and from national accounts has generated a number of seminal contributions, and helped focus attention on top incomes in an unprecedented manner.[42]

While there has been progress, major issues remain in achieving the goal of measuring the distribution of household economic resources across countries and over time. Different international data sets feature important discrepancies in terms of both levels and changes of inequality for the same country and time period; inconsistent narratives on inequality levels and trends among micro- and macro-sources are notable and, in some cases, have become larger over time; inequality indicators tend to reflect only partially the true extent of inequality due to the underreporting and noncoverage of rich individuals in household surveys; measuring the correct income concept is still challenging; international conventions remain incomplete; and data on wealth inequality, while more common than before, still remain scarce.

In this context, a number of recommendations are put forward:

- *Defining and measuring a more comprehensive income concept.* As discussed above, more analytical and empirical work is needed to accurately reflect in a broader income concept the value of in-kind benefits such as education and health care services provided to households by governments and nonprofit institutions. In addition, the measurement of consumption possibilities must consider the impact of the services that households produce for their own consumption as well as the impact of consumption taxes and subsidies. The international convention proposed by the *Canberra Group Handbook* acknowledges the need to broaden the conceptual definition of household income to consider benefits in-kind, but remains silent on how to achieve this in practice, while excluding both household services produced for own use and consumption taxes and subsidies. This needs to change, in ways that do not compromise the quality and comparability of existing measures of other income streams. This could be achieved by complementing existing measures of household disposable income (which largely follow international guidelines) with experimental measures based on broader concepts (e.g., measures that integrate the value of benefits in kind, services produced by households for their own use, and consumption taxes). Clearly, consumption possibilities are different depending on, for example, VAT rates: two individuals with the same disposable income (or adjusted final income, for that matter) but with different structure of their consumption expenditure would have different consumption possibilities when the VAT rates applied to goods and services differ.

• *Correcting for under-reporting and noncoverage of the rich.* Assessing the extent to which there is under-reporting at the top (and bottom) end of the distribution and whether rich (and poor) people are "missing" from income, consumption, and wealth distributions should be a common practice in the measurement of economic inequality. "Rich lists" (reporting the number and the income/wealth values of very wealthy individuals and households) exist for many countries, and tax records (when of good quality) provide an important resource for implementing that correction. Proposals for adjustments, where appropriate at the national level, for underrepresentation and noncoverage by surveys should be made. All of this will require considerable investment in improving and developing statistics. Of prime importance is for governments to make the information from (anonymized) tax records available and allow for the linking through personal identification numbers between surveys and registries.[43] The scholarly community working on inequality should undertake a thorough and systematic assessment of the various methods to contend with under-reporting and noncoverage, and come up with recommendations of best practices, including some key robustness checks.

• *Increasing the availability of data on the distribution of wealth.* There are a series of sources to obtain information on the distribution of wealth: dedicated household surveys on wealth; administrative data on investment income, capitalized to yield estimates of the underlying wealth; lists of large wealth-holders, such as the annual *Forbes Richest People in America List*, or the *Sunday Times Rich List for the UK*; population censuses, which in some cases and years included questions on household wealth; administrative data on individual estates at death, multiplied-up to yield estimates of the wealth of the living; and administrative data on the wealth of the living derived from annual wealth taxes. Greater international efforts should be devoted to assess the availability and quality of data on wealth distribution and make recommendations so that the necessary data are periodically collected in as many countries as possible, and in ways that make the information comparable across countries and over time.

• *Addressing inconsistencies in international data sets.* Growing interest in the "global distribution" of income or wealth (i.e., the distribution that would obtain when all people of the world are considered as citizens of the same country) has recently led to the proliferation of international data sets combining information from a large array of national sources. While the quality of these data sets is generally a function of the underlying national data, the agencies and researchers initiating these data sets often make various assumptions to fill data gaps or to increase the *ex post* comparability of these estimates. Even when these international data sets are limited to parts of the world where country-level data are more readily available, different data treatments applied to national data, and differences in data collections (across countries and over time), may not be visible to users. Given that global inequality analyses are so sensitive to the choice of database, data set users should acquire a thorough understanding of the assumptions and methodological choices embodied in the data they are about to use, and undertake systematic robustness checks to determine if their results are sensitive to the use of a particular data set. Data set producers should document all assumptions clearly and thoroughly; make the data, programs, and results publicly available to allow for replicability whenever it applies; compare their methods and results with one another; and, eventually, agree on conventions and best practice when calculating inequality indicators from micro-data, secondary, and imputation-based sources. Finally, the international community should devote greater financial resources to allow poorer countries to put in place the statistical infrastructure that is needed to fill the gaps and provide the information needed to gain a better understanding of national and global inequalities. Providing a better picture of the global income distribution is a global public good (needed, for example, to assess the impact of globalization on people in all countries of the world), and the onus is on rich countries to provide part of the necessary resources for this to happen.

• In line with one of the main recommendations of the *Monitoring Global Poverty* report, an international organization should take the lead in setting up a standing Statistical Working Group on economic inequality, with a remit to set guidelines for the measurement of household income, consumption, and wealth; to examine the relation between the three; to investigate the relation between household survey, national accounts, tax records, and other data sources; and to make proposals on how consistency among them can be enhanced. The latter would be important to address the issue of sometimes inconsistent narratives among sources on inequality levels and trends.

• *To integrate or not to integrate?* Undoubtedly, the life of users of economic inequality data would be made much easier by the existence of one integrated data source on the distribution of household income, consumption, and wealth, compiled from various sources: household surveys, administrative registries, statements provided by financial institutions, and national accounts. However, we are still far away from this ideal: individual data sources are compiled with different goals, according to different conventions and definitions. The assumptions made by national accounts statisticians when integrating counterpart information from various institutional sectors may be less palatable to survey statisticians. While several initiatives are currently underway in developed countries (both to integrate micro- and macro-statistics for the household sector, and to integrate various types of micro-statistics), in low- and middle-income countries the questions about the quality of data makes integration exceedingly difficult. When survey income aggregates are between 40% and 60% of national accounts aggregates, for instance, one wonders whether the problem is really the existence of under-reporting and noncoverage in the surveys or rather with the accuracy of national accounts. In such a context, there is considerable value in a multi-source approach to investigate the distribution of income, consumption, and wealth. No single method is sufficient on its own, and it is necessary to draw attention to their strengths and weaknesses (Alvaredo, Atkinson, and Morelli, 2016). In these situations, rather than choosing one alternative, one should probably pursue both the integrated data approach as well as the dashboard approach (Bourguignon, 2016). The dashboard approach would entail reporting estimates from household surveys and tax data (and possibly other distribution data) separately as they describe different segments of the distribution; integrating both through, for example, the DINA (Distributional National Accounts) methodology described in Chapter 6, as well as other methods described above; and using national accounts and administrative data to investigate sources of inconsistency and to assess their implications for inequality results.

Addressing all these issues will require more investment of resources (both financial and intellectual) on the part of governments, statistical offices, multilateral organizations, philanthropic foundations, and researchers alike. It will also require cooperation among these constituencies to generate international conventions where they are lacking, and implementation guidelines where needed. Finally, accurate measurement of economic inequality will require a political commitment. Governments, international organizations, and the scholarly community need to be committed to transparency and to make information publicly available in ways that facilitate the measurement and analysis of economic inequality while protecting the identity of respondents to preserve confidentiality.

One final word: While the discussion here has emphasized the shortcomings, problems, and limitations of existing statistics on economic inequality, we have adopted in this chapter the same view underpinning the *Report of the Commission on Global Poverty* (Atkinson, 2016). We should be aware of the uncertainty that surrounds inequality indicators, and be conscious that both levels and changes in inequality are measured with a considerable margin of error. Different sources are, however, affected by different problems and biases, and by crossing different perspectives and information sources we can get a better and richer understanding of the underlying reality. Hence, rather than taking the position that nothing can be said, we want to encourage the research and statistical communities to identify different potential sources of error, to develop methodologies to address these problems, and to attach an indication of their possible size, as well as propose ways to introduce more robustness in measuring such a crucial indicator as the extent of economic inequality and how it changes over time (Atkinson [2016], p. 15).

Notes

1. See, for example, Alvaredo and Gasparini (2015), Anand and Segal (2015), Atkinson (2015), Bourguignon (2015a), Bourguignon and Morrisson (2002), Bourguignon, Ferreira, and Lustig (2005), Cornia (2014), Deaton (2013), Ferreira et al. (2012), Ferreira et al.

(2016), Lopez-Calva and Lustig (2010), Milanovic (2016), Piketty (2014), and Stiglitz (2012). See also Klasen et al. (2018) and other chapters of the report by the *International Panel on Social Progress* (2018).

2. See, for example, Dabla-Norris et al. (2015); Gurría (2011), ILO (2015); ISSC, IDS, and UNESCO (2016); Love (2016), OECD (2011, 2015); Ostry, Berg, and Tsangarides (2014); Oxfam (2016); Save the Children (2012); UNDESA (2011); UNDP (2014); UNICEF (2011); and World Bank (2016).

3. See, for example, https://www.nytimes.com/2016/10/16/upshot/whats-behind-a-rise -in-ethnic-nationalism-maybe-the-economy.html.

4. One of the key developments in economic theory has been the demonstration that, once the Arrow-Debreu conditions (no increasing returns, no monopolies, a complete set of markets for present and future goods, complete insurance markets, fully available and symmetric information, and available lump sum transfer instruments) are relaxed, there is no separation of efficiency and equity. With imperfect information, lump sum redistribution of endowments can improve efficiency (in the sense of making at least one person better off without making anyone else worse off) under certain conditions, or worsen it under others. In the absence of lump sum instruments, market interventions may reduce efficiency, but improve equity. Efficiency and equity have to be taken together, i.e., they are not separable.

5. See, for example, the Pew Research Global Attitudes Project. See also the discussion on the subject in World Bank (2017).

6. Measuring inequality of opportunity, horizontal inequality—that is, inequality among socio-economic and demographic groups—and intra-household inequality are discussed in other chapters of this volume.

7. For trends, see citations in endnote 2. For the properties and advantages and disadvantages of indicators, see, for example, Atkinson and Bourguignon (2000 and 2015a), Cowell (2009), Duclos and Araar (2006), and Jenkins and Van Kerm (2009). For discussions on inequality beyond the income dimensions, see Sen's pioneering article "Equality of what?" (Sen, 1980) and the pertinent chapters in Atkinson and Bourguignon's *Handbook of Income Distribution* (2015a) such as those by Aaberge and Brandolini (2015) on multi-dimensional inequality; Koen, Fleurbaey, and Schokkaert (2015) on inequality and well-being; and Roemer and Trannoy (2015) on inequality of opportunity. Also, on the latter, see Aaberge, Mogstad, and Peragine (2011). Also, see Akerlof and Kranton (2000) on identity-driven inequality. On measures of polarization, see Chakravarty (2009). For an overview of gender inequality, horizontal inequality, and inequality within the household, see the chapter by Deere, Kanbur, and Stewart in the present volume.

8. Atkinson et al. (2010) discuss a hierarchy of methodologies employed in the standardization of income inequality data sets. "In short," they write, "we have a 'hierarchy' of degrees of standardization: (1) Common survey instrument (European Community

Household Panel, ECHP); (2) *Ex ante* harmonized framework (EU-SILC); (3) *Ex post* standardized microdata (LIS); (4) *Ex post* customized results (OECD); 5) Meta-analyses of results (Kuznets)" (p. 103).

9. By "directly" here it is meant that indicators were calculated directly by the organization or by the National Statistical Office but following specific guidelines that ensure comparability. For details on each data set, see Table 2 in Ferreira, Lustig, and Teles (2015).

10. It should be noted that the inequality measures are not always produced directly from the micro-data, because in a number of countries, only grouped data is available.

11. For a discussion of the limitations of SWIID, see Jenkins (2015).

12. The first series from the DINA project are available on WID.world for the United States and France.

13. For a summary of how international data sets differ, see Table 2 in Ferreira, Lustig, and Teles 2015.

14. Such discrepancies suggest that caution is needed when interpreting the results of cross-country regression analysis based on the SWIID imputation-based data, such as those of Acemoglu et al. (2013) and Ostry, Berg, and Tsangarides (2014).

15. See the section on the limitations and shortcomings of international data sets below. Also see Ferreira, Lustig, and Teles (2015).

16. To put this number in perspective, in January 2016, the United Nations had 193 members and 2 permanent observers (the Vatican and Palestine).

17. "The geographical coverage across regions was not uniform. Of the 83 countries, 24 belonged to a single region, eastern Europe and central Asia, while East Asia and Pacific, Latin America and the Caribbean, and sub-Saharan Africa contributed 8, 16, and 9 countries, respectively. In South Asia, 4 countries were covered, and, in the Middle East and North Africa, 2." (World Bank, 2016, p. 53).

18. The World Bank's PovcalNet indicates the policy regarding public access in each country contained in their database, http://iresearch.worldbank.org/PovcalNet/data.aspx.

19. The GCIP database described above standardizes across the welfare concepts measured in surveys to supply income-based estimates of global inequality (Jayadev, Lahoti, and Reddy, 2015).

20. The OECD produced guidelines on how to measure wealth distribution in 2013 (OECD, 2013a), in response to the recommendations of the Stiglitz-Sen-Fitoussi Commission. The European Central Bank has also produced guidelines for members of the euro area in the context of the implementation of the Euro System Household Finance and Consumption Survey.

21. A framework for the joint analysis of micro-statistics on household income, consumption, and wealth was released by the OECD in 2013 (OECD, 2013b). An example of

analysis of the joint distribution of income, consumption, and wealth for the United States is provided by Fisher et al. (2016). An OECD-Eurostat Expert Group is currently working to develop experimental measures of inequality in the joint distribution on household income, consumption, and wealth for around 25 countries.

22. Beyond OECD countries, most income surveys do not report data on direct taxes paid by households. Around one-third of all OECD countries lack micro-data on wealth distribution, a proportion that is much higher for developing countries. Micro-data on consumption expenditures in OECD countries are rarely used for distributive analysis.

23. See the proposed checklist to assess quality and comparability of data in Atkinson and Bourguignon (2015b).

24. Data on the distribution of household wealth, for 28 countries, are available through the OECD Wealth Distribution Database released in 2015. These data are sourced from national surveys, which may differ in significant aspects, and from register data from some Nordic countries.

25. For example, according to Fesseau and Mattonetti (2013), in the case of Mexico, the adjusted national accounts total was more than seven times higher than the micro total from the income and expenditures household survey.

26. For a formal discussion, see Deaton (2005) p. 11. Also see Alvaredo, Atkinson, and Morelli (2017), in the case of wealth. Deaton uses the term "selective under-sampling" while Jenkins (2015) calls it "underrepresentation."

27. Regardless of its cause, I will call the issue at hand the "missing rich" problem. Other terminology has been used. Jenkins (2015), for example, refers to the problem as "under-coverage" of the rich.

28. See Alvaredo and Londoño-Velez (2013) for Colombia; Jenkins (2015) for the United Kingdom; Székely and Hilgert (1999) for Latin American countries.

29. See the pioneering work on this by Altimir (1987).

30. See, for example, the chapter by Alvaredo et al. in this volume.

31. The *Report of the Commission on Global Poverty* (Atkinson, 2016) includes a thorough discussion of these problems at the bottom of the distribution and recommendations on how to deal with them. Here we shall concentrate on the various approaches that have been proposed to address similar problems but at the other end of the distribution, i.e., the high incomes group or the so-called rich.

32. Put differently, the probability that Warren Buffett or Bill Gates are selected in a sample in US household surveys, or Carlos Slim in a Mexican household survey, is negligible.

33. As Deaton (2005) puts it "With greater nonresponse by the rich, there can be no general supposition that estimated inequality will be biased either up or down by the selec-

tive undersampling of richer households. (The intuition that selective removal of the rich should reduce measured inequality, which is sometimes stated as obvious in the literature, is false, perhaps because it takes no account of reduction in the mean from the selection)" (p. 11). A simple example can illustrate this point. Let's assume that we observe a population of 4 people, with the first three having $0 income and the fourth $1 (0, 0, 0, 1). The coefficient of variation for this distribution is 2 and the share of income of the richest person is 100%. Let's now assume that one "rich" person is missing, so that the true distribution is (0, 0, 0, 1, 1): in this case, the coefficient of variation is 1.37 and the income share of the richest person is 50%, i.e., inequality is lower when the sample is corrected to fully capture the top end of the distribution.

34. Cowell and Flachaire (2015), classify the (right-) tail errors into two main types of "data problems": (1) measurement error and data contamination; and (2) incomplete data. Their paper discusses a variety of methods to address them.

35. These concepts and how they affect households' incomes are discussed in detail in Lustig (2018a).

36. The options are summarized by Bastagli (2015), p.12.

37. Atkinson and Bourguignon (1990); OECD (2015); Sahn and Younger (2000). By using averages, this approach ignores differences across income groups and regions. For example, governments may spend less (or more) per pupil on poorer students. We recommend averaging at as disaggregated a level as possible (not only by education level but also by state and rural/urban area within states, for example). The level at which it is possible to disaggregate will depend on data from national accounts. Data obtained from the education ministry is likely to be more disaggregated than that obtained from national accounts.

38. Barofsky and Younger (2018) describe the pros and cons of three methods that can be used to value the distributional impact of health care spending: average cost, behavioral-outcome approach, and willingness to pay. Their conclusion is that all the methods have their pros and cons: they provide different types of information and, as such, should be used as complements rather than substitutes.

39. See Lustig (2016). "Consumable income" in the CEQ project is defined as disposable income net of indirect taxes and subsidies. In other contexts, "consumable" has been referred to the income subject to consumption taxes (Ebel and Petersen, 2012). For more on the CEQ project, visit www.commitmentoequity.org.

40. These results are based on the CEQ Institute studies and are summarized in Lustig (2018b). Also, see Higgins and Lustig (2016) for estimates of the extent of fiscal impoverishment that taxes (net of transfers and subsidies) can generate and how to measure this phenomenon formally. Consumption subsidies work in the opposite direction.

41. The 2011 *Canberra Group Handbook* states that "ideally all indirect taxes that can be attributed in some way to individual households should be included in any comprehensive

analysis of the effects of government benefits and taxes on the distribution of household income. This includes not only consumption taxes on final expenditure of households, but also taxes on inputs into the production process of goods and services" (UNECE [2011], pp. 47–48). See also Table 2.1 (p. 18) of the same report as well as Zwijnenburg, Bournot, and Giovannelli (2017).

42. See the fairly long list of finished and ongoing studies featured in the WID.world website and the studies they cite in turn.

43. The Uruguayan government has taken such a step and shared this type of information with academics. See Higgins, Lustig, and Vigorito (2017).

References

Aaberge, R. and A. Brandolini (2015), "Multidimensional poverty and inequality," in Atkinson, A.B. and F. Bourguignon (eds.), *Handbook of Income Distribution*, Vol. 2, Elsevier, North-Holland, Amsterdam.

Aaberge, R., M. Mogstad, and V. Peragine (2011), "Measuring long-term inequality of opportunity," *Journal of Public Economics*, Vol. 95(3), pp. 193–204.

Acemoglu, D. et al. (2015), "Democracy, Redistribution, and Inequality," in Atkinson, A. and F. Bourguignon (eds.), *Handbook of Income Distribution*, Vol. 2, Elsevier, North-Holland, Amsterdam.

Acemoglu, D. et al. (2013), "Democracy, redistribution and inequality," *National Bureau of Economic Research Working Paper*, No. 19746, December.

Afkar, R., J. Jellema, and M. Wai-Poi (2017), "The distributional impact of fiscal policy in Indonesia," in Inchauste, G. and N. Lustig (eds.), *The Distributional Impact of Taxes and Transfers: Evidence from Eight Low- and Middle-Income Countries*, World Bank, Washington, DC.

Akerlof, G.A. and R.E. Kranton (2000), "Economics and identity," *Quarterly Journal of Economics*, Vol. 115(3), pp. 715–753, https://doi.org/10.1162/003355300554881.

Alfons, A., M. Templ, and P. Filzmoser (2013), "Robust estimation of economic indicators from survey samples based on Pareto tail modelling," *Journal of the Royal Statistical Society*, Vol. 62(C), pp. 271–86.

Altimir, O. (1987), "Income distribution statistics in Latin America and their reliability," *Review of Income and Wealth*, Vol. 33(2), pp. 111–155.

Alvaredo, F. (2011), "A note on the relationship between top income shares and the Gini coefficient," *Economics Letters*, Vol. 110(3), pp. 274–277.

Alvaredo, F. et al. (2018), "Distributional national accounts," in Stiglitz J.E., J.-P. Fitoussi, and M. Durand (eds.), *For Good Measure: Advancing Research on Well-Being Metrics Beyond GDP*, OECD Publishing, Paris.

Alvaredo, F. et al. (2017a), "Household surveys, administrative records and national accounts in Mexico 2009–2014. Is a reconciliation possible?," PowerPoint presentation, LACEA Annual Meeting, Buenos Aires, November 11.

Alvaredo, F. et al. (2017b), "Distributional national accounts (DINA) guidelines: Concepts and methods used in WID.world," *WID.world Working Paper*, June, http://wid.world/document/dinaguidelines-v1.

Alvaredo, F. et al. (2013), "The top 1% in international and historical perspective," *Journal of Economic Perspectives*, Vol. 27(3), pp. 3–20.

Alvaredo, F. and L. Gasparini (2015), "Recent trends in inequality and poverty in developing and emerging countries," in Atkinson, A. B. and F. Bourguignon (eds.), *Handbook of Income Distribution*, Vol. 2, Elsevier, North-Holland, Amsterdam.

Alvaredo, F., A.B. Atkinson, and S. Morelli (2017), "Top wealth shares in the UK over more than a century," *Research Paper Series 01*, Department of Economics, University Ca' Foscari of Venice, Italy, January, https://ssrn.com/abstract=2903853.

Alvaredo, F., A.B. Atkinson, and S. Morelli (2016), "The challenge of measuring UK wealth inequality in the 2000s," *Fiscal Studies*, Vol. 37(1), pp. 13–33.

Alvaredo, F. and J. Londoño-Velez (2013), "High incomes and personal taxation in a developing economy: Colombia 1993–2010," *CEQ Working Paper 12*, Center for Inter-American Policy and Research and Department of Economics, Tulane University and Inter-American Dialogue, March, www.commitmentoequity.org/publications_files/CEQWPNo12%20HighTaxationDevEconColombia1993-2010_19March2013.pdf.

Anand, S. and P. Segal (2015), "The global distribution of income," in Atkinson, A.B. and F. Bourguignon (eds.), *Handbook of Income Distribution*, Vol. 2, Elsevier, North-Holland, Amsterdam, pp. 937–979.

Atkinson, A.B. (2016), *Monitoring Global Poverty: Report of the Commission on Global Poverty*, World Bank, Washington, DC.

Atkinson, A.B. (2015), *Inequality: What Can Be Done?*, Harvard University Press, Cambridge, MA.

Atkinson, A.B. (2007), "Measuring top incomes: Methodological issues," in Atkinson, A.B. and T. Piketty (eds.), *Top Incomes over the 20th Century: A Contrast Between Continental European and English-Speaking Countries*, Oxford University Press, Oxford, pp. 18–43.

Atkinson, A.B. (1997), "Bringing income distribution in from the cold," *Economic Journal*, Vol. 107(441), pp. 297–321.

Atkinson, A.B. and F. Bourguignon (2015a), *Handbook of Income Distribution*, Vol. 2, Elsevier, North-Holland, Amsterdam.

Atkinson, A.B. and F. Bourguignon (2015b), "Introduction: Income distribution today," in Atkinson, A.B. and F. Bourguignon (eds.), *Handbook of Income Distribution*, Vol. 2, Elsevier, North-Holland, Amsterdam.

Atkinson, A.B. and F. Bourguignon (2000), *Handbook of Income Distribution*, Vol. 1, Elsevier, North-Holland, Amsterdam.

Atkinson, A.B. and F. Bourguignon (1990), "Tax-benefit models for developing countries: Lessons from developed countries," in Khalilzadeh-Shirazi, J. and A. Shah (eds.), *Tax Policy in Developing Countries: A World Bank Symposium*, World Bank, Washington, DC.

Atkinson, A.B. and A. Brandolini (2001), "Promise and pitfalls in the use of secondary data-sets: Income inequality in OECD countries as a case study," *Journal of Economic Literature*, Vol. 39(3), pp. 771–799.

Atkinson, A.B. et al. (2010), "Income poverty and income inequality," in Atkinson, A.B. and E. Marlier (eds.), *Income and Living Conditions in Europe*, Eurostat, Publications Office of the EU, Luxembourg.

Atkinson, A.B. and A.J. Harrison (1978), *Distribution of Personal Wealth in Britain*, Cambridge University Press, Cambridge.

Atkinson, A.B. and J. Micklewright (1983), "On the reliability of income data in the family expenditure survey 1970–1977," *Journal of the Royal Statistical Society, Series A*, Vol. 146(1), pp. 33–61.

Atkinson, A.B. and T. Piketty (2010), *Top Incomes: A Global Perspective*, Oxford University Press, Oxford.

Atkinson, A.B. and T. Piketty (2007), *Top Incomes over the 20th Century: A Contrast Between Continental European and English-Speaking Countries*, Oxford University Press, Oxford.

Atkinson, A.B., T. Piketty, and E. Saez (2011), "Top incomes in the long run of history," *Journal of Economic Literature*, Vol. 49(1), pp. 3–71.

Autor, D.H., L.F. Katz, and M.S. Kearney (2008), "Trends in U.S. wage inequality: Revising the revisionists," *Review of Economics and Statistics*, Vol. 90(2), pp. 300–323.

Bach, S., G. Corneo, and V. Steiner (2009), "From bottom to top: The entire income distribution in Germany, 1992–2003," *Review of Income and Wealth*, Vol. 55(2), pp. 303–330.

Banerjee, A. and T. Piketty (2010), "Top Indian incomes, 1922–2000," in Atkinson, A.B. and T. Piketty (eds.), *Top Incomes: A Global Perspective*, Oxford University Press, Oxford.

Barofsky, J. and S. Younger (2018), "Appendix 6F. Comparison of methods to value the distributional impact of health spending," in Lustig, N. (ed.), *Commitment to Equity Handbook: Estimating the Impact of Fiscal Policy on Inequality and Poverty*, Brookings Institution Press and CEQ Institute, Tulane University, www.commitmentoequity.org.

Bastagli, F. (2015), "Bringing taxation into social protection analysis and planning," *ODI Working Paper*, No. 421, Overseas Development Institute, London, www.odi.org/sites /odi.org.uk//odi-assets/publications-opinion-files/9700.pdf.

Beegle, K. et al. (2012), "Methods of household consumption measurement through surveys: Experimental results from Tanzania," *Journal of Development Economics*, Vol 98(1), pp. 3–18.

Belfield, C. et al. (2015), *Living Standards, Poverty and Inequality in the UK: 2015*, Report no. R107, London, www.ifs.org.uk/publications/7878.

Benabou, R. (1996), "Inequality and growth," *NBER Macroeconomics Annual 1996*, Vol. 11, MIT Press, Cambridge, MA.

Beneke, M., N. Lustig, and J.A. Oliva (2018), "The impact of taxes and social spending on inequality and poverty in El Salvador," in Lustig, N. (ed.), *Commitment to Equity Handbook: Estimating the Impact of Fiscal Policy on Inequality and Poverty*, Brookings Institution and CEQ Institute, www.commitmentoequity.org/publications/handbook .php.

Biemer, P. and S. Christ (2008), "Weighting survey data," in De Leeuw, E., J. Hox, and D. Dillman (eds.), *International Handbook of Survey Methodology*, Psychology Press, New York.

Blanchet, T., J. Fournier, and T. Piketty (2017), "Generalized Pareto curves: Theory and applications," *WID.world Working Paper, No. 2017/3*.

Bleaney, M. and A. Nishiyama (2003), "Convergence in income inequality: Differences between advanced and developing countries," *Economics Bulletin*, Vol. 4(22), pp. 1–10.

Bourguignon, F. (2017a), "Equivalence Between Adjusting Income Levels and Sample Weights in Correcting Income Distributions," unpublished document, Paris School of Economics, June.

Bourguignon, F. (2017b), "Correcting Survey Data for Top Incomes," PowerPoint presentation, Methodological Advances in Fiscal Incidence Analysis, Commitment to Equity Institute (Tulane University), Universidad de San Andrés, Buenos Aires, November 7–8.

Bourguignon, F. (2016), "Issues in the Measurement of Income Inequality," keynote lecture at the conference on the Measurement of Income Distribution and Inequality, PUED-UNAM and INEGI, Mexico City, November 16.

Bourguignon, F. (2015a), *The Globalization of Inequality*, Princeton University Press, New Jersey.

Bourguignon, F. (2015b), "Appraising income inequality databases in Latin America," in Ferreira, F.H.G. and N. Lustig (eds.), "Appraising cross-national income inequality databases," special issue, *Journal of Economic Inequality*, Vol. 13(4), pp. 557–578.

Bourguignon, F. (2003), "The growth elasticity of poverty reduction: Explaining heterogeneity across countries and time periods" in Eicher, T. and S. Turnovsky (eds.), *Inequality and Growth: Theory and Policy Implications*, MIT Press, Cambridge, MA.

Bourguignon, F. and C. Morrisson (2002), "Inequality among world citizens: 1820–1992," *American Economic Review*, Vol. 92(4), pp. 727–744.

Bourguignon, F., H.G. Ferreira, and N. Lustig (eds.) (2005), *The Microeconomics of Income Distribution Dynamics in East Asia and Latin America*, World Bank and Oxford University Press, Washington, DC.

Bucheli, M. et al. (2014), "Social spending, taxes and income redistribution in Uruguay," in Lustig, N., C. Pessino, and J. Scott (eds.), "The redistributive impact of taxes and social spending in Latin America," special issue, *Public Finance Review*, Vol. 42(3), pp. 413–433.

Burkhauser, R.V., S. Feng, and J. Larrimore (2010), "Improving imputations of top incomes in the public-use current population survey by using both cell-means and variances," *Economic Letters*, Vol. 108(1), pp. 69–72.

Burkhauser, R.V., J. Larrimore, and S. Lyons (2016), "Measuring health insurance benefits: The case of people with disabilities," *Contemporary Economic Policy*, Vol. 35(3), pp. 439–456.

Burkhauser, R.V. et al. (2012), "Recent trends in top income shares in the USA: Reconciling estimates from March CPS and IRS tax return data," *Review of Economics and Statistics*, Vol. 94, pp. 371–88.

Cabrera, M., N. Lustig, and H.E. Moran (2015), "Fiscal policy, inequality, and the ethnic divide in Guatemala," *World Development*, Vol. 76, pp. 263–279.

Campos-Vazquez, R. and N. Lustig (2017), "Labour income inequality in Mexico: Puzzles solved and unsolved," *UNU-WIDER Working Paper*, No. 2017/186.

Capgemini and Merrill Lynch (2011), *World Wealth Report*, New York.

Chakravarty, S.R. (2009), *Inequality, Polarization and Poverty: Advances in Distributional Analysis*, Springer, New York.

Cornia, G.A. (ed.) (2014), *Falling Inequality in Latin America: Policy Changes and Lessons*, UNU-WIDER, Studies in Development Economics, Oxford University Press, Oxford.

Cowell, F.A. (2009), *Measuring Inequality*, London School of Economics Perspectives in Economic Analysis, Oxford University Press, Oxford.

Cowell, F.A. and E. Flachaire (2015), "Statistical methods for distributional analysis," in Atkinson, A.B. and F. Bourguignon (eds.), *Handbook of Income Distribution*, Vol. 2, Elsevier, North-Holland, Amsterdam.

Cowell, F.A. and E. Flachaire (2007), "Income distribution and inequality measurement: The problem of extreme values," *Journal of Econometrics*, Vol. 141(2), pp. 1044–1072.

Cowell, F.A. and Victoria-Feser, M.-P. (1996), "Robustness properties of inequality measures," *Econometrica*, Vol. 64, pp. 77–101.

Dabla-Norris, E. et al. (2015), *Causes and Consequences of Income Inequality: A Global Perspective*, International Monetary Fund, Washington, DC, www.imf.org/external/pubs /ft/sdn/2015/sdn1513.pdf.

Deaton, A. (2015), "On tyrannical experts and expert tyrants," *Review of Austrian Economics*, Vol. 28(4), pp. 407–412.

Deaton, A. (2013), *The Great Escape: Health, Wealth and the Origins of Inequality*, Princeton University Press, Princeton.

Deaton, A. (2005), "Measuring poverty in a growing world (or Measuring growth in a poor world)," *Review of Economics and Statistics*, Vol. 87(1), pp. 1–19.

Deere, C.D., R. Kanbur, and F. Stewart (2018), "Horizontal inequalities," in Stiglitz J.E., J.-P. Fitoussi, and M. Durand (eds.), *For Good Measure: Advancing Research on Well-Being Metrics Beyond GDP*, OECD Publishing, Paris.

DeNavas-Walt, C. and B.D. Proctor (2015), *Income and Poverty in the United States: 2014*, US Bureau of the Census, Washington, DC.

Department for Work and Pensions (2015), *Households Below Average Income: An Analysis of the Income Distribution 1994/95–2013/14*, London.

Diaz-Bazan, T. (2015), "Measuring inequality from top to bottom," *World Bank Policy Research Paper*, No. 7237, World Bank, Washington, DC.

Duclos, J. and A. Araar (2006), *Poverty and Equity: Measurement, Policy and Estimation with DAD*, International Development Research Centre, Springer, New York.

Ebel, R.D. and J.E. Petersen (eds.) (2012), *Oxford Handbook of State and Local Government Finance*, Oxford University Press, Oxford.

Esteban, J. and D. Ray (2006), "Inequality, lobbying and resource allocation," *American Economic Review*, Vol. 96(1), pp. 257–279.

EUROMOD, "Statistics on the Distribution and Decomposition of Disposable Income," www.iser.essex.ac.uk/euromod/statistics/.

Ferreira F.H.G. et al. (2016), "A global count of the extreme poor in 2012: Data issues, methodology and initial results," *Journal of Economic Inequality*, Vol. 14(2), pp. 141–172.

Ferreira, F.H.G. et al. (2012), "Economic mobility and the rise of the Latin American middle class," *Latin America and Caribbean Studies*, World Bank, Washington, DC.

Ferreira, F.H.G. and N. Lustig (2015), "Appraising cross-national income inequality databases," special issue, *Journal of Economic Inequality*, Vol. 13(4).

Ferreira, F.H.G., N. Lustig, and D. Teles (2015), "Appraising cross-national income inequality databases: An introduction," in Ferreira, F.H.G. and N. Lustig, "Appraising cross-national income inequality databases," special issue, *Journal of Economic Inequality*, Vol. 13(4), pp. 497–526.

Fesseau, M. and M. Mattonetti (2013), "Distributional measures across household groups in a national accounts framework: Results from an experimental cross-country exercise on household income, consumption and saving," *OECD Statistics Working Papers*, No. 2013/04, OECD Publishing, Paris, http://dx.doi.org/10.1787/k3wdjqr775f-en.

Fisher, J. et al. (2016), "Inequality in 3D: Income, consumption and wealth," *Working Paper Series*, No. 2016-09, Washington Center for Equitable Growth, Washington, DC, http://cdn.equitablegrowth.org/wp-content/uploads/2017/12/21123945/12211 7-WP-Inequality-in-3D.pdf.

Fishlow, A. (1973), "Some reflections on post-1964 Brazilian economic policy," in Stepan, A. (ed.), *Authoritarian Brazil*, Yale University Press, New Haven.

Garbinti, B., J. Goupille-Lebret, and T. Piketty (2017), "Income inequality in France, 1900–2014: Evidence from Distributional National Accounts (DINA)," *WID.world Working Paper*, No. 2017/4.

Gasparini, L. and L. Tornarolli (2015), "A review of the OECD income distribution database," in Ferreira, F.H.G. and N. Lustig, "Appraising cross-national income inequality databases," special issue, *Journal of Economic Inequality*, Vol. 13(4), pp. 479–602.

Groves, R.M. et al. (2009), *Survey Methodology*, John Wiley & Sons, Hoboken, New Jersey.

Gurría, A. (2011), "Tackling inequality," *OECD Observer*, http://oecdobserver.org/news /fullstory.php//3717/Tackling_inequality.html.

Higgins, S. and C. Pereira (2014), "The effects of Brazil's high taxation and social spending on the distribution of household income," in Lustig, N., C. Pessino, and J. Scott (eds.), "The redistributive impact of taxes and social spending in Latin America," special issue, *Public Finance Review*, Vol. 42(3), pp. 346–367.

Higgins, S. and N. Lustig (2018), "Allocating taxes and transfers, constructing income concepts, and completing sections A, B, and C of CEQ master workbook," in Lustig, N. (ed.), *Commitment to Equity Handbook: Estimating the Impact of Fiscal Policy on Inequality and Poverty*, Brookings Institution Press and CEQ Institute, Washington, DC, and Tulane University, advance online version available at www.commitmentoequity.org /publications/handbook.php.

Higgins, S. and N. Lustig (2016), "Can a poverty-reducing and progressive tax and transfer system hurt the poor?," *Journal of Development Economics*, Vol. 122, pp. 63–75.

Higgins, S., N. Lustig, and A. Vigorito (2017), "Top incomes, issues with survey data, and inequality: Evidence from simulations and linked income and tax return data," Power-Point presentation, LACEA Annual Meeting, Buenos Aires, November 9.

Hill, R. et al. (2017), "A fiscal incidence analysis for Ethiopia," in Inchauste, G. and N.

Lustig (eds.), *The Distributional Impact of Taxes and Transfers: Evidence from Eight Low- and Middle-Income Countries*, World Bank, Washington, DC.

Hlasny, V. and P. Verme (2017), "The impact of top incomes biases on the measurement of inequality in the United States," *ECINEQ Working Paper*, No. 452.

ILO (2015), *Global Wage Report 2014/15: Wages and Income Inequality*, International Labour Organization, Geneva, https://euro.indiana.edu/doc/archive/past-events /wcms_324678.pdf.

IMF (2012), *Fiscal Monitor October 2012: Taking Stock A Progress Report on Fiscal Adjustment*, Washington, DC.

IPSP (2018), *Rethinking Society for the 21th Century: Report of the International Panel on Social Progress*, Cambridge University Press, Cambridge.

ISSC, IDS, and UNESCO (2016), *World Social Science Report 2016, Challenging Inequalities: Pathways to a Just World*, UNESCO Publishing, Paris, http://unesdoc.unesco.org /images/0024/002458/245825e.pdf.

Inchauste G. et al. (2017), "The distributional impact of fiscal policy in South Africa," in Inchauste, G. and N. Lustig (eds.), *The Distributional Impact of Taxes and Transfers: Evidence from Eight Low- and Middle-Income Countries*, World Bank, Washington, DC.

Jaramillo, M. (2014), "The incidence of social spending and taxes in Peru," in Lustig, N., C. Pessino, and J. Scott (eds.), "The redistributive impact of taxes and social spending in Latin America," special issue, *Public Finance Review*, Vol. 42.(3), pp. 391–412.

Jayadev, A., R. Lahoti, and S.G. Reddy (2015), "Who got what, then and now? A fifty-year overview from the Global Consumption and Income Project," *Social Science Research Network*, https://dx.doi.org/10.2139/ssrn.2602268.

Jenkins, S.P. (2017), "Pareto models, top incomes and recent trends in UK income inequality," *Economica*, Vol. 84(334), pp. 261–289.

Jenkins, S.P. (2015), "World income inequality databases: An assessment of WIID and SWIID," in Ferreira, F.H.G. and N. Lustig, "Appraising cross-national income inequality databases," special issue, *Journal of Economic Inequality*, Vol. 13(4), pp. 629–671.

Jenkins, S.P. et al. (2011), "Measuring inequality using censored data: A multiple-imputation approach to estimation and inference," *Journal of the Royal Statistical Society, Series A*, Vol. 174(1), pp. 63–81.

Jenkins, S.P. and P. Van Kerm (2009), "The measurement of economic inequality," in Salverda, W., B. Nolan, and T. M. Smeeding (eds.), *The Oxford Handbook of Economic Inequality*, Oxford University Press, Oxford.

Klasen, S. et al. (2018), "Economic inequality and social progress," in IPSP, *Rethinking Society for the 21th Century: Report of the International Panel on Social Progress*, Cambridge University Press.

Koen, D., M. Fleurbaey, and E. Schokkaert (2015), "Inequality, income and well-being," in Atkinson, A. B. and F. Bourguignon (eds.), *Handbook of Income Distribution*, Vol. 2, Elsevier, North-Holland, Amsterdam.

Korinek, A., J.A. Mistiaen, and M. Ravallion (2006), "Survey nonresponse and the distribution of income," *Journal of Economic Inequality*, Vol. 4, pp. 33–55.

Kuznets, S. (1953), *Economic Change*, Norton, New York.

Lakner, C. and B. Milanovic (2015), "Global income distribution: From the fall of the Berlin wall to the Great Recession," *World Bank Economic Review*, Vol. 30(2), pp. 203–232, http://dx.doi.org/10.1093//lhv039.

Lemieux, T. (2006), "Increasing residual wage inequality: Composition effects, noisy data, or rising demand for skill?," *American Economic Review*, Vol. 96(3), pp. 462–498.

Little, R.J.A. and D.B. Rubin. (2014), *Statistical Analysis with Missing Data* (2nd ed.), Wiley Series in Probability and Statistics, John Wiley and Sons, Hoboken, New Jersey.

Lopez-Calva, L.F. and N. Lustig (eds.) (2010), *Declining Inequality in Latin America: A Decade of Progress?*, Brookings Institution Press and UNDP, Washington, DC.

Love, J. (2016), "Christine Lagarde on income inequality, Brexit and the power of M&Ms," *Kellogg Insight, Policy*, October 10, https://insight.kellogg.northwestern.edu/article /christine-lagarde-on-income-inequality-brexit-and-the-power-of-mms.

Lustig, N. (forthcoming), "The 'missing rich' in household surveys: Causes and correction methods," *CEQ Working Paper*, No. 75, Commitment to Equity Institute, Tulane University.

Lustig, N. (ed.) (2018a), *Commitment to Equity Handbook: Estimating the Impact of Fiscal Policy on Inequality and Poverty*, Brookings Institution Press and CEQ Institute, Tulane University, advance online version available at www.commitmentoequity.org /publications/handbook.php.

Lustig, N. (2018b), "Fiscal policy, income redistribution and poverty reduction in low- and middle-income countries," in Lustig, N. (ed.), *Commitment to Equity Handbook: Estimating the Impact of Fiscal Policy on Inequality and Poverty*, Brookings Institution Press and CEQ Institute, Tulane University, advance online version available at www .commitmentoequity.org/publications/handbook.php.

Lustig, N. (2018c), "The sustainable development goals, domestic resource mobilization, and the poor," in Ocampo, J.A. and J.E. Stiglitz, (eds.), *The Welfare State Revisited*, Columbia University Press, New York.

Lustig, N. (2016), "Inequality and fiscal redistribution in middle income countries: Brazil, Chile, Colombia, Indonesia, Mexico, Peru and South Africa," *Journal of Globalization and Development*, Vol. 7(1), pp. 17–60.

Lustig, N. and D. Teles (2016), "Inequality convergence: How sensitive are results to the choice of underlying data?," *Department of Economics Working Paper*, No. 1613, Tulane University, October.

Meyer, B.D., W.K.C. Mok, and J.X. Sullivan (2015), "Household surveys in crisis," *Journal of Economic Perspectives*, Vol. 29(4), pp. 199–226.

Milanovic, B. (2016), *Global Inequality: A New Approach for the Age of Globalization*, Harvard University Press, Cambridge, MA.

Mirrlees, J.A. (1971), "The theory of optimum income taxation," *Review of Economic Studies*, Vol. 38(2), pp. 175–208.

Mistiaen, J.A. and M. Ravallion (2003), "Survey compliance and the distribution of income," *Policy Research Working Paper*, No. 2956, World Bank.

Novokmet F., T. Piketty, and G. Zucman (2017), "From Soviets to Oligarchs: Inequality and property in Russia 1905–2016," *WID.world Working Paper Series*, No. 2017/09, Paris School of Economics.

OECD (2015), *In It Together: Why Less Inequality Benefits All*, OECD Publishing, Paris, http://dx.doi.org/10.1787/9789264235120-en.

OECD (2013a), *OECD Guidelines for Micro Statistics on Household Wealth*, OECD Publishing, Paris, http://dx.doi.org/10.1787/9789264194878-en.

OECD (2013b), *OECD Framework for Statistics on the Distribution of Household Income, Consumption and Wealth*, OECD Publishing, Paris, http://dx.doi.org/10.1787/9789264194830-en.

OECD (2011), *Divided We Stand: Why Inequality Keeps Rising*, OECD Publishing, Paris, http://dx.doi.org/10.1787/9789264119536-en.

OECD (2008), *Growing Unequal? Income Distribution and Poverty in OECD Countries*, OECD Publishing, Paris, http://dx.doi.org/10.1787/9789264044197-en.

Ostry, J., A. Berg, and C.G. Tsangarides (2014), "Redistribution, inequality, and growth," IMF Staff Discussion Note 14/02, www.imf.org/external/pubs/ft/sdn/2014/sdn1402.pdf.

Oxfam (2016), "An economy for the 1%," *210 Oxfam Briefing Paper*, January, https://www.oxfamamerica.org/static/media/files/bp210-economy-one-percent-tax-havens-180116-en_0.pdf.

Paz Arauco, V. et al. (2014), "Explaining low redistributive impact in Bolivia," in Lustig, N., C. Pessino, and J. Scott, "The redistributive impact of taxes and social spending in Latin America," special issue, *Public Finance Review*, Vol. 42(3), pp. 326–345.

Piketty, T. (2014), *Capital in the 21st Century*, Harvard University Press, Cambridge, MA.

Piketty, T. (2001), *Les Hauts revenus en France au 20e siècle : inégalités et redistribution*, 1901–1998, Éditions Grasset, Paris.

Piketty, T. and E. Saez (2003), "Income inequality in the United States, 1913–1998," *Quarterly Journal of Economics*, Vol. 118(1), pp. 1–39.

Piketty, T., E. Saez, and G. Zucman (2016), "Distributional national accounts: Methods and estimates for the United States," *NBER Working Paper*, No. 22945.

Piketty, T., L. Yang, and G. Zucman (2016), "Capital accumulation, private property and rising inequality in China, 1978–2015," *WID.world Working Paper*, No. 2017/6.

Ravallion, M. (2015), "The Luxembourg Income Study," in Ferreira, F.H.G. and N. Lustig, "Appraising cross-national income inequality databases," special issue, *Journal of Economic Inequality*, Vol. 13(4), pp. 527–547.

Ravallion, M. (2003), "Inequality convergence," *Economics Letters*, Vol. 80(3), pp. 351–356.

Ravallion, M. (2001), "Growth, inequality and poverty: Looking beyond averages," *World Development* Vol. 29(11), pp. 1803–1815.

Rawls, J. (1971), *A Theory of Justice*, Harvard University Press, Cambridge, MA.

Roemer, J. and A. Trannoy (2015), "Equality of opportunity," in Atkinson, A.B. and F. Bourguignon (eds.), *Handbook of Income Distribution*, Vol. 2, Elsevier, North-Holland, Amsterdam, pp. 217–296.

Ruiz, N. and N. Woloszko (2016), "What do household surveys suggest about the top 1% incomes and inequality in OECD countries?," *OECD Economics Department Working Papers*, No. 1265, OECD Publishing, Paris, http://dx.doi.org/10.1787/jrs556f36zt-en.

Saez, E. (2003), "The effect of marginal tax rates on income: A panel study of 'bracket creep'," *Journal of Public Economics*, Vol. 87(5), pp. 329–347.

Saez, E. and G. Zucman (2016), "Wealth inequality in the United States since 1913: Evidence from capitalized income tax data," *Quarterly Journal of Economics*, Vol. 131(2), pp. 519–578.

Sahn, D.E. and S. Younger (2000), "Expenditure incidence in Africa: Microeconomic evidence," *Fiscal Studies*, Vol. 21(3), pp. 329–347.

Sauma, P. and J.D. Trejos (2014), "Social public spending, taxes, redistribution of income, and poverty in Costa Rica," *CEQ Working Paper*, Vol. 18, Center for Inter-American Policy and Research and Department of Economics, Tulane University and Inter-American Dialogue, March.

Save the Children (2012), *Annual Report 2012*, Save the Children Fund, London.

Scott, J. (2014), "Redistributive impact and efficiency of Mexico's fiscal system," in Lustig, N., C. Pessino, and J. Scott, "The redistributive impact of taxes and social spending in Latin America," special issue, *Public Finance Review*, Vol. 42(3), pp. 368–390.

Sen, A. (1980), "Equality of what?," in McMurrin, S. (ed.), *Tanner Lectures on Human Values*, Vol. 1, Cambridge University Press, Cambridge.

Smeeding, T. and J.P. Latner (2015), "PovcalNet, WDI and all the Ginis: A critical review," in Ferreira, F.H.G. and N. Lustig, "Appraising cross-national income inequality databases," special issue, *Journal of Economic Inequality*, Vol. 13(4), pp. 603–628.

Solt, F. (2009), "The standardized world income inequality database," *Social Science Quarterly*, Vol. 90(2), pp. 231–460.

Stiglitz, J.E. (2012), *The Price of Inequality: How Today's Divided Society Endangers Our Future*, W.W. Norton, New York.

Stiglitz, J.E., A. Sen, and J.-P. Fitoussi (2009), *Report by the Commission on the Measurement of Economic and Social Progress*, http://ec.europa.eu/eurostat/documents/118025/118123 /Fitoussi+Commission+report.

Székely, M. and M. Hilgert (1999), "What's behind the inequality we measure: An investigation using Latin American data," *Research Department Working Paper*, Inter-American Development Bank.

The Canberra Group (2001), *Expert Group on Household Income Statistics: Final Report and Recommendations*, United Nations, Ottawa.

UNDESA (2011), *Social Inequalities Concern Us All*, UN, New York, www.un.org/en /development/desa/news/social/social-inequalities.html.

UNDP (2014), *Annual Report 2013–2014: New Partnerships for Development*, New York, www.undp.org/content/undp/en/home/librarypage/corporate/annual-report-2014. html.

UNECE (2011), *The Canberra Group Handbook on Household Income Statistics* (2nd ed.), Geneva, United Nations, www.unece.org/fileadmin/DAM/stats/groups/cgh /Canbera_Handbook_2011_WEB.pdf.

UNICEF (2011), *Annual Report 2010*, UN, New York, www.unicef.org/publications /index_59002.html.

Wittenberg, M. (2015), "Problems with SWIID: The case of South Africa," in Ferreira, F.H.G. and N. Lustig, "Appraising cross-national income inequality databases," special issue, *Journal of Economic Inequality*, Vol. 13(4), pp. 673–677.

World Bank (2017), *World Development Report 2017: Governance and the Law*, World Bank, Washington, DC, www.worldbank.org/en/publication/wdr2017.

World Bank (2016), *Poverty and Shared Prosperity 2016: Taking on Inequality*, World Bank, Washington, DC, https://openknowledge.worldbank.org/handle/10986/25078.

World Bank (2006), *World Development Report 2006: Equity and Development*, World Bank and Oxford University Press, Washington, DC, http://documents.worldbank .org/curated/en/435331468127174418/pdf/322040World0Development0Report 02006.pdf.

Younger, S.D. and A. Khachatryan (2017), "Fiscal incidence in Armenia," in Inchauste, G.

and N. Lustig (eds.), *The Distributional Impact of Taxes and Transfers: Evidence from Eight Low- and Middle-Income Countries*, World Bank, Washington, DC.

Younger, S.D. and A. Khachatryan (2014), *CEQ Master Workbook: Armenia; Version: May 31, 2014*, CEQ Data Center on Fiscal Redistribution, CEQ Institute, Tulane University.

Zucman, G. (2015), *The Hidden Wealth of Nations: The Scourge of Tax Havens*, University of Chicago Press, London.

Zwijnenburg, J., S. Bournot, and F. Giovannelli (2017), "Expert group on disparities in a national accounts framework: Results from the 2015 exercise," *OECD Statistics Working Papers*, No. 2016/10, OECD Publishing, Paris, http://dx.doi.org/10.1787/daa921e -en.

Databases

Alvaredo, F. et al. (2015a), "The World Top Incomes Database," online between January 2011 and December 2015, http://wid.world/wid-world/.

Alvaredo, F. et al. (2015b), "The World Wealth and Income Database-WID," https://www .parisschoolofeconomics.eu/en/research/data-production-and-diffusion/the-world -inequality-database/.

Branko L. Milanovic, All the Ginis Dataset, World Bank Group, http://data.worldbank .org/data-catalog/all-the-ginis (accessed on May 16, 2018).

Global Consumption and Income Project (GCIP), http://gcip.info (accessed on May 16, 2018).

The GINI Project, www.gini-research.org/articles/data_2 (accessed on May 16, 2018).

LIS, The Luxembourg Wealth Study Database (LWS), www.lisdatacenter.org/our-data/lws -database (accessed on May 16, 2018).

OECD, Income Distribution Database (IDD), www.oecd.org/social/income-distribution -database.htm (accessed on 16, 2018).

Pew Research Center, Global Attitudes Project, www.pewglobal.org (accessed on May 16, 2018).

Socio-Economic Database for Latin America and the Caribbean (SEDLAC/CEDLAS at Universidad Nacional de La Plata and World Bank), http://sedlac.econo.unlp.edu.ar (accessed on May 16, 2018).

Solt, F. (2016), The Standardized World Income Inequality Database, *Social Science Quarterly* 97, SWIID Version 6.2, March 2018, http://fsolt.org/swiid/ http://fsolt.org /swiid/ (accessed on May 16, 2018).

Tulane University, Commitment to Equity Institute (CEQ) Standard Indicators, www
.commitmentoequity.org/indicators.php (accessed on May 16, 2018).

UN Economic Commission for Latin America and the Caribbean, CEPALSTAT, http://
estadisticas.cepal.org/cepalstat/WEB_CEPALSTAT/Portada.asp (accessed on May 16,
2018).

University of Essex, EUROMOD, www.euromod.ac.uk (accessed on May 16, 2018).

University of Texas Income Inequality Project (UTIP), http://utip.lbj.utexas.edu/ (accessed
on May 16, 2018).

UNU-WIDER, World Income Inequality Database (WIID), www.wider.unu.edu/project
/wiid-world-income-inequality-database (accessed on May 16, 2018).

World Bank, PovcalNet (World Development Indicators), http://iresearch.worldbank.org
/PovcalNet/povOnDemand.aspx (accessed on May 16, 2018).

World Inequality Database (WID.world), http://wid.world (accessed on May 16, 2018).

4.

Horizontal Inequalities

Carmen Diana Deere, Ravi Kanbur, and Frances Stewart

This chapter discusses the importance of horizontal inequalities, i.e., inequalities in both the income and nonincome dimensions among groups of people with shared characteristics; of intra-household inequality; and of gender inequalities in the distribution of wealth (the gender wealth gap). Measurement of horizontal inequalities raises the question of which group classification to adopt, whether to weight measures for each group by its population size in order to obtain an aggregate measure, and how to take into account intra-group distribution. The chapter then considers how estimates of overall inequality might be impacted by the neglect of intra-household inequality, highlighting the difference between household and individual welfare, and how to obtain better estimates of the gender wealth gap.

Carmen Diana Deere is Distinguished Professor Emerita of Latin American Studies and Food & Resource Economics, University of Florida; Ravi Kanbur is T.H. Lee Professor of World Affairs, International Professor of Applied Economics and Management, and Professor of Economics, Cornell University; Frances Stewart is Emeritus Professor of Development Economics, University of Oxford. Although the three themes have been integrated in a single chapter because of their substantive inter-relatedness, Frances Stewart is the author of the section on Horizontal Inequalities, Ravi Kanbur on Intra-household Inequality, and Carmen Diana Deere on the Gender Wealth Gap. The authors wish to thank Nora Lustig for bringing them together for this exercise, and Marco Mira D'Ercole and Joe Stiglitz for their comments. "Horizontal Inequalities" was prepared by Frances Stewart and draws on Stewart (2016). "Intra-household Inequality" was prepared by Ravi Kanbur and extracted from Kanbur (2018). "The Gender Wealth Gap" was prepared by Carmen Diana Deere. The opinions expressed and arguments employed in the contributions below are those of the authors and do not necessarily reflect the official views of the OECD or of the governments of its member countries.

Introduction

A major concern of this volume is inequality of income, consumption, and wealth among individuals. This type of inequality (also called vertical inequality), while important in many contexts, ignores systematic inequities among population groups, is often restricted to the "economic" dimensions of inequality, and assumes that each individual in a household receives the mean income of that household. This chapter discusses the importance of horizontal inequalities (i.e., inequalities among groups of people with shared characteristics), both in the income and non-income dimensions, of intra-household inequality, and of gender inequalities in the distribution of wealth (i.e., the gender wealth gap). The three sections of this chapter, while covering topics which are important in their own right, also link with each other in important ways. For example, a key aspect of intra-household inequality is inequality between women and men within the household, and this relates to the broader question of horizontal inequality in society; in turn, gender inequalities are especially important in the case of wealth inequality, an issue that this chapter explores through a focus on a specific measurement initiative.

While, as argued below, these inequalities are of great importance and policy relevance, there are no systematic efforts to collect the necessary data and publish the appropriate indicators. This is due, in part, to the conceptual and practical challenges that their measurement entails. However, as explained below, much more could be done to standardize the practice of collecting the relevant information and broadening the diagnostic indicators used for social progress assessments.

Horizontal Inequalities
Why Horizontal Inequalities Matter

Horizontal inequalities constitute one of the most important types of inequality, notably because of their implications for justice and social stability. Relevant group categories include race, ethnicity, religion, gender, and age. Despite their importance, much more attention is normally given to vertical inequalities (or inequalities among individuals generally, whatever groups they belong to) in analysis and policy.

Most people are members of many groups and, in assessing horizontal inequalities within any society, the first issue to address is which group classification to adopt. The appropriate classification(s) will reflect felt identity distinctions, not only in relation to people's own perceived identity but also to how they perceive others. Some group categories may be transient or unimportant—for example, membership of a particular club. But other categorizations shape the way people see themselves and how they are treated and behave. Age and gender distinctions are universally important, but societies differ as to what the other salient identities are, and there can be changes in their importance over time. For example, race has been an important identity distinction in South Africa, yet it is possibly of lesser importance today than previously. Ethnicity is a highly relevant category within many Latin American and African countries, associated with discrimination, grievance, and sometimes mass violence. Religion constitutes a critical dividing line between people the world over today, but in Europe it no longer leads to the wars it once did.

Group categorizations are fluid and may be blurred at the edges but nonetheless are keenly felt, are often a source of discrimination, and are typically associated with low levels of inter-group trust and weak social interactions. Identity differences are particularly significant in relation to social and political stability when categories overlap—e.g., when members of different ethnic groups also adhere to different religions.

Distributional issues are most often considered along a single dimension—notably in the income space—although the need for multi-dimensional measures has been strongly advocated (Sen, 1980). Multi-dimensionality is an essential feature of horizontal inequality. Three prime dimensions are socio-economic, political, and cultural. For each of these there is an array of elements. For example, socio-economic inequalities include inequalities in access to basic services—e.g., education, health care, water—and inequalities in economic resources, including income, assets, employment, and so on. In the political dimension, relevant inequalities include those in representation in government, the upper levels of the bureaucracy, the military and the police, and in local administrations. On the cultural side, relevant inequalities include those in recognition, use, and respect for language, religion, and cultural practices.

There are many causal connections across various dimensions and elements. For example, educational inequalities may be responsible for a range of economic inequalities, with reverse causality present such that low incomes tend to be associated with low education of children. Inequalities in cultural recognition can lead to educational and economic inequalities if, for example, a group's language is not used in government business or the education system. The tighter the causal connections, the more consequential these inequalities are. As with group classification, the relevant dimensions vary across societies. While land inequalities are of major significance in agrarian societies, for example, they matter little in economies where agriculture is relatively insignificant and where inequalities in financial asset ownership and skills determine life chances.

Horizontal inequalities are important both in themselves and instrumentally, since they affect other objectives (Loury, 1988). Above all, any significant horizontal inequality is unjust since there is no reason why people should receive unequal rewards or have unequal political power merely because they are black rather than white, women rather than men, or of one ethnicity rather than another. Anti-discrimination law is justified on this principle. Another intrinsic reason for concern with horizontal inequalities is that they can have a direct impact on well-being. Individual well-being can be affected not only by a person's own circumstances, but also by how well their group is doing, since membership of certain groups can form an integral part of a person's identity. Likewise, relative group poverty contributes to the perception that an individual may be trapped permanently in a poor position. Psychologists have shown, for example, that psychological ills of African Americans are sometimes associated with the position of their group (Broman, 1997). Hence, it has been argued that the relative position of the group should enter into an individual's welfare function (Akerlof and Kranton, 2000).

Besides these intrinsic reasons for concern, horizontal inequality affects the achievement of other objectives. The most powerful instrumental reason is that horizontal inequalities have been shown to raise the risk of violent conflict significantly (Stewart, 2008; Cederman, Weidmann, and Gleditsch, 2011). Group inequalities provide powerful grievances that leaders can use to mobilize political protest, by calling on cultural markers (e.g., a common history or language or religion) and pointing to group exploitation. This type of mobilization is especially likely to occur where there is political as well as economic inequality, such that the leaders of the more deprived groups are excluded from political power and therefore have a motive for mobilizing. Examples where group inequalities have been a factor in provoking conflicts include Côte d'Ivoire, Rwanda, Northern Ireland, Chiapas, and Sudan (Gurr, 1993; Langer, 2005; Stewart, 2002; Murshed and Gates, 2005). Sharp horizontal inequalities within countries (and between them) are an important source of grievance and of political instability, independently of the extent of vertical inequality. Indeed, most econometric investigations have shown little connection between vertical inequality and conflict (Fearon and Laitin, 2000; Collier and Hoeffler, 2004).

Another instrumental reason for concern with horizontal inequalities is that they are often an outcome of historical and current discrimination against people because of their identity, which is likely to lead to inefficiency when talented people fail to realize their potential. For example, most studies show that affirmative action for African Americans in the United States had a positive impact on economic efficiency (Badgett and Hartmann, 1995).

Finally, it may be difficult to attain certain targets, such as poverty elimination or universal education, without tackling horizontal inequality and the overall position of a deprived group, because deprived groups often find it particularly difficult to access state services.

Measuring Horizontal Inequalities

Given their significance, there is a need for systematic measurement and monitoring of horizontal inequalities. There is a lack of systematic data by group, though economic data by group is increasingly collected by national governments as well as through some global surveys such as the Demographic and Health Surveys (DHS) Program and the Living Standard Measurement Study (LSMS). The collection of data on inequalities in political power or cultural recognition is very rare, undertaken only by some individual scholars (e.g., Gurr, 1993; Langer, 2005; Wimmer, Cederman, and Min, 2009).

The measurement of horizontal inequalities raises particular issues, beyond those involved in measuring vertical inequalities (Mancini, Stewart, and Brown, 2008). First, there is the question of which group classification to adopt. Second, group size varies, and hence it may be desirable to weight any aggregate measure by the population of each group. Third, it may also be important to take into account intra-group distribution, since the political and policy implications of inequalities between groups can differ according to whether the differences arise at the top of the distribution of each group, or at the bottom, or because of uniform differences throughout the distribution of each group. A common measure of aggregate horizontal inequality in a country is a population-weighted coefficient of variation of average group performance on any indicator. Foster's general-means approach shows how group differences vary along the distribution (Foster, Lopez-Calva, and Székely, 2003). This involves estimating parametric means for each group at different points in the group distribution. An aggregate measure of horizontal inequalities for a country as a whole is helpful for comparisons across countries and over time, but for domestic policy purposes simple comparisons of each group with the country average are often sufficient.

What to Do?

Goal 10 of the UN's Sustainable Development Goals calls for the reduction of inequalities between and within countries, and makes explicit reference to inequalities based on "age, sex, disability, race, ethnicity, origin, religion or economic or other status." It is emphasized that no goal should be considered as attained by a country if it is not met for significant groups. This has clear relevance for measurement, monitoring, and policy. This is an issue that applies worldwide. In the European Union, for example, there has been a long process aimed at defining a set of "core social variables," to be included in all official surveys, that would allow common breakdowns of the population across various well-being dimensions.[1] For monitoring, there is a need to develop a common set of group categories and dimensions of opportunities and outcomes across countries, with common standards and definitions, particularly for some horizontal breakdowns such as disability, race, and ethnicity. Given the differences in salient groups and dimensions of deprivation across countries, however, only a minimal or core set of indicators are likely to be applicable worldwide. There is a need for flexibility in monitoring so as to fit the particular context.

A wide range of policies for tackling horizontal inequalities has been adopted in different countries (Stewart, Brown, and Langer, 2008). The first requirement is to identify which groups are particularly deprived and which dimensions of deprivation are most prevalent. Policies can be universal or targeted. Universal policies provide benefits or impose taxes according to universal categories, applicable equally to everyone in society. Generally, these benefits, such as universal access to health care services, are likely to benefit deprived groups most, and consequently to reduce horizontal inequalities. Targeted policies identify particular groups and grant their members particular favors, such as access to government employment or educational scholarships. Such targeted policies are often known as "affirmative action." Affirmative action can be effective, but the policies can also have undesirable side-effects, in some circumstances changing behavior, encouraging strong identification with the favored identity ("ethnicization"), and provoking opposition among the nonfavored groups (Hoff and Stiglitz, 1974; Harrison et al., 2006; Brown, Langer, and Stewart, 2012). Yet, in some situations, the visibility and rapidity of affirmative action is desirable to reduce resentment among deprived groups. Anti-discrimination law can be an effective policy when discrimination is at the root of inequalities, but it needs to be enforced and backed up by universal legal access. However, many horizontal inequalities arise from historical reasons, and consequently, anti-discrimination law will only be effective in reducing such inequalities if discrimination is interpreted very broadly, recognizing the historical origin. The most effective approach is to combine universal and targeted policies, as was successfully adopted in Northern Ireland and Malaysia (Faaland, Parkinson, and Saniman, 2003; Todd and Ruane, 2012). But in both cases, while horizontal inequalities were greatly reduced, societal cohesion remained fragile, pointing to the need for complementary policies to promote societal integration.

As noted earlier, horizontal inequalities affecting people's well-being go well beyond the strictly economic realm and include cultural discrimination, official and nonofficial behavior (e.g., by the police or the media), and political discrimination, all of which can affect economic opportunities as well as well-being. Consequently, the policy arena needs to be correspondingly extensive.

Intra-household Inequality and the Measurement of Money-Metric Inequality
Why Intra-household Inequality Matters

Consider any indicator of economic or social well-being, such as consumption, education, or health. Our normative frameworks are typically built on realizations of such indicators for each individual. When the value of an indicator falls below a normatively determined critical value, that individual is identified as being in deprivation. This critical value can be the poverty line for consumption, or other similar lines such as an adequate level of nutrition. The variation in the indicator across individuals in the population under consideration is the basis of inequality measurement. An important strand of the literature then begins with accounting for this variation along different dimensions. For example, how much of this variation is due to variations by caste, race, or ethnicity is often the starting point for a deeper investigation of the role of these factors in inequality. Similarly, variation accounted for by gender is a key element of discussion of gender inequality in a society. Indeed, as discussed in the previous section, inequality across groups with shared characteristics is the basis for analysis of horizontal inequality.

Gender inequality raises a troubling question: Could it be that boys and girls, and men and women, are treated so differently within the household that their well-being differs from each other? In other words, is there intra-household inequality? Intra-household inequality would lead us to question many normative frameworks where the household is meant to be an institution for cooperation and equity. If intra-household inequality exists, it contributes to overall inequality, and its patterns can in turn shed light on inequality across genders, and across age groups, in the population as a whole.

Measuring Intra-household Inequality

The standard instrument for measuring individual well-being is the household survey, which collects a mixture of individual- and household-level information. A key piece of information collected at the household level is data on household income and consumption (or, more accurately, on consumption expenditure). This is the central data source for generating headline poverty and inequality measures in a large number of countries. In the case of consumption data, leaving to one side a number of well-discussed issues such as the length of the recall period for expenditures, allowing for home-produced consumption, housing services, and price variations, the question arises as to how to go from household-level consumption to information on individual-level consumption, which is needed to generate inequality and poverty measures.

The answer for official figures for most countries is straightforward and somewhat disconcerting. Total household expenditure is typically divided by the number of members of the household, and each individual is allocated the per capita consumption of the household. In other words, it is assumed that there is no intra-household inequality. This is also the implicit assumption when adult equivalent scales are used to allow for different consumption needs by demographic characteristics. There is assumed to be no inequality across equivalized individuals. Put another way, our standard method of generating headline inequality and poverty measures systematically suppresses intra-household inequality. It therefore understates overall inequality, focusing only on inequality in household per capita consumption.

Before turning to empirical studies that try to establish the magnitude of intra-household inequality, it is as well to take up the argument that an understatement of inequality levels is not necessarily important when the focus is on *changes* in inequality over time, as a constant understatement will not affect the trend as such. This is of course true, but the following points should also be considered. First, if we are interested in overall inequality, surely the level matters as well—at the very least, a constant understatement may matter very differently at different levels of inequality. Second, how do we know that the understatement is constant? We will not know this unless we explore the matter empirically, and allow at least for the possibility of understatement.

How much understatement of inequality is there as the result of the neglect of intra-household inequality? The question is not easy to answer given the nature of standard data sources. If we had true individual-level consumption, which we do not measure in standard household surveys, the question would be irrelevant since we could observe the true overall inequality. There are two possible strategies we can follow.

The first is to use structural econometrics. In this approach, you start with a model of intra-household allocation, with a free parameter from which intra-household inequality can be inferred; then you estimate this parameter from observed patterns of household level consumption. This is the approach followed by Lise and Seitz (2011), who conclude that "previous work underestimates the level of individual consumption inequality by between 25% and 50%" (p. 352).

The second approach is to use indicators for which we do have individual-level data, either in the standard household surveys or in especially collected data sets. Since in these cases we do indeed have the "true" distribution of the indicator across all individuals, we can construct the hypothetical distribution where each individual in a household is allocated the household's per capita value of that indicator. The difference between inequality in the true distribution and the synthetic distribution gives us an estimate of how far wrong we would have gone had we not had individual level data on the indicator.

In a large number of surveys in the Luxembourg Income Study, Malghan and Swaminathan (2016) find that, for two-earner households, within-household inequality accounts for 30% or more of total inequality. Ponthieux (2015) uses a question in the EU-SILC 2010 thematic module ("What proportion of your personal income do you keep separate from the common household budget?") to construct a "modified equivalised income" measure. The author finds that "departing from the assumption of full income pooling within couples results in increased levels of various indicators of inequality." For calorie intake, in one of the first studies to quantify intra-household inequality, Haddad and Kanbur (1990) use a specially designed survey of a small number of households in the Philippines that collected information on nutritional intake of each individual. Using calorie adequacy as the well-being indicator, they find that possible errors in inequality could be of the order of 30%.

These are all, of necessity, indirect approaches to estimating the understatement of inequality when intra-household inequality is suppressed as in our standard headline measures. But they all indicate a significant scaling up of standard measures of overall inequality that neglect intra-household inequality.

Intra-household Inequality and the Growth Elasticity of Poverty Reduction

Clearly, the estimated level of overall inequality is significantly affected by the neglect of intra-household inequality. This understatement must surely affect the assessment of well-being in a society for any given level of per capita income. Empirical work is not sufficiently advanced to test if the understatement is constant or not but, in terms of changes over time, a constant understatement will obviously not affect trends. But are there other aspects of the development discourse, and indeed the discourse in developed countries, that are affected by the understatement of true inequality?

A key concept introduced in development economics in the last quarter century is that of the "growth elasticity of poverty reduction." The basic idea behind this notion stems from the argument that the reduction of absolute poverty between two periods can be broken down into a "growth component" and an "inequality change component." To derive the first component, analysts construct a distribution where all incomes grow at the growth rate of per capita income between the two periods. Then, by construction, inequality is unchanged since each income has grown in the same proportion. You can compute the poverty in the synthetic distribution, and label the change in poverty the "growth component" of poverty change, since it is the result of this "distribution neutral" growth. The remaining part of the actual poverty change can then be attributed to inequality change.

The percentage change in the "growth component" of poverty divided by the growth rate of the economy (which is, of course, the percentage change in per capita income) is designated the "growth elasticity of poverty reduction," measuring the responsiveness of poverty to distribution-neutral economic growth. However, the "growth elasticity of poverty reduction" is itself a function of the level of inequality. While the general case is technically ambiguous, Bourguignon (2003) has shown that, for specified functional forms and empirical simulations, the growth elasticity is lower the higher is the level of income inequality. This finding has been interpreted as implying that reducing inequality could not only have a direct level effect on poverty, for a given per capita income, but also have an indirect effect by increasing the responsiveness of poverty reduction to economic growth. For his specific parametrizations, Bourguignon (2003) finds that when the Gini coefficient rises by a third, the elasticity falls by a third.

One implication of the above discussion is that the true level of inequality is understated because standard methods suppress intra-household inequality. This must mean, by the Bourguignon (2003) argument, that the true growth elasticity of poverty reduction is overstated in standard calculations, since they rely on measures that understate true inequality. And the quantitative magnitudes are significant.

Estimating the "True" Levels of Inequality

Quantifying intra-household inequality is a first step toward getting a more accurate measure of the level of inequality, and of the responsiveness of poverty reduction to economic growth. It can also provide a platform for investigating inequality across gender and age groups, both of which are aspects of horizontal inequality. But, as we have seen, so far as the headline money-metric measures of inequality are concerned, standard national household surveys collect consumption information only at the household level, so that understatement of inequality is endemic to official statistics.

It is unlikely that official national household surveys can be turned to collecting individual-level consumption information, especially in developing countries. But there are alternatives, following the small empirical literature that exists. First, structural econometric methods can be used to estimate intra-household inequality parameters. Second, systematic investigation of other indicators available at the individual level in standard household surveys can be analyzed to develop a sense of the understatement in these cases if individual information is not available. Thus information on personal income streams and questions on the extent of income pooling can be used creatively by researchers to explore and estimate intra-household inequality. Third, small specialized surveys, like the one in Haddad and Kanbur (1990), can be mounted. As more data is collected we will get a sharper sense of the understatement of inequality as the result of suppressing intra-household inequality.

The Gender Wealth Gap
Why the Gender Wealth Gap Matters

As seen in the previous section, a growing literature has demonstrated that household and individual welfare are not necessarily the same, and that intra-household inequality may condition economic outcomes. What has been of much interest, specifically, is how a woman's fallback position (those resources she controls should the household dissolve) conditions her bargaining power within the household (Deere and Doss, 2006). To test this proposition, much of the literature on bargaining power has focused either on nonlabor income (data on which is readily available in household income surveys and can be derived from either asset ownership or public or private transfers) or on the ownership of particular assets, such as land or financial assets.

While much is known about the gender wage gap,[2] comparatively little is known about the gender asset or wealth gap, whether among couples (i.e., the intra-household distribution of wealth) or for the population as a whole. This is largely because data on asset ownership collected through household surveys—including in large-scale wealth surveys—have tended to be at the household rather than the individual level, constraining gender analysis. Analyses concerned with gender inequality have been limited to the study of household types, i.e., male or female sole-headed households in comparison to married couples.[3] Gender analyses of households composed of couples are sometimes attempted by focusing on the sex of the respondent, who is typically the best informed on financial matters;[4] but since wealth data is collected at the household rather than the individual level, such analyses do not shed light on the intra-household distribution of assets. The assumption that, in married couples, all assets are pooled and the benefits shared among all household members—i.e., the assumption of a unitary household—has prevailed for too long. However, in most legal systems, property rights are ceded to individuals, not households. As Doss, Grown, and Deere (2008) argue, analyses of "household wealth" ignore institutional frameworks governing individual property rights, as defined by marital regimes, inheritance laws, and social norms.

Whether asset ownership is in fact pooled in marriage (and consensual unions) largely depends on a country's default marital regime—the rules governing how property acquired prior to and during the marriage and how inheritances are treated should the union be dissolved (Deere and Doss, 2006). For example, under the prevailing separation of property regime in many African, Middle Eastern, and South Asian countries,[5] all property acquired by individuals prior to or after marriage, including any inheritances received, are considered to be their own individual property, i.e., should a union dissolve, each person leaves with only their own personal property. In some countries that have traditionally had this default marital regime, such as the United Kingdom, divorce legislation reform has subsequently modified this outcome, so that property acquired during the marriage with the earnings of either spouse is pooled and divided equally. In this case, the outcome resembles partial community property, under which property acquired prior to marriage and any inheritances are considered individual property, while property acquired during the marriage is split equally among the spouses upon its dissolution.

The main point is that institutional parameters shape the accumulation of wealth by individuals, and must be duly accounted for in data collection efforts and economic analysis. As an illustration, in Ecuador—where partial community property prevails and inheritance norms and practices are equitable—married women own 44% of couple wealth; conversely, in both Ghana and Karnataka, India—characterized by the separation of property marital regime as well as by male bias in inheritance—married women own only 19% and 9%, respectively, of couple wealth (Deere et al., 2013).

Measuring the Gender Wealth Gap

As mentioned above, when data on asset ownership is collected in household surveys, it has tended to be at the household rather than the individual level, constraining gender analysis. Among the large-scale wealth surveys included in the Luxembourg Wealth Study, for example, only the German Socio-Economic Panel collects data on individual ownership of a broad range of physical and financial assets, allowing analysis of the intra-household distribution of wealth (Grabka, Marcus, and Sierminska, 2015). Two other surveys collect partial data on what belongs to individuals: the United Kingdom Wealth and Assets Survey (on financial assets and liabilities, pension wealth, and real estate) and the Italian Survey of Household Income and Wealth (on real estate).[6]

The multi-purpose surveys most frequently carried out in developing countries are the Living Standard Measurement Study (LSMS) and the Demographic and Health Surveys (DHS) Program. An analysis of a sample of 72 LSMS questionnaires across six world regions for the mid-2000s revealed that the great majority of countries collected data on household ownership of housing, land, livestock, and major consumer durables. Only 21% of these, however, collected data on who in the household owned the residence, 17% on who owned the land, and 14% on who owned nonagricultural businesses (Doss, Grown, and Deere, 2008). A subsequent analysis of 167 household survey questionnaires for 23 Latin American and Caribbean countries found that only 23 questionnaires, for 11 countries, collected gender-disaggregated ownership information on at least one asset, most frequently for the main residence (Deere, Alvarado, and Twyman, 2012). Since 2009, the DHS has included questions asking surveyed individuals whether they are owners or co-owners of the main residence and land.[7] Thus, while it is increasingly possible to measure gender gaps with regard to specific assets, large lacunas remain in terms of being able to estimate total individual wealth and the gender wealth gap.

One of the reasons why progress on measuring individual level wealth has been slow has been because of methodological concerns, such as whether reliable data on the valuation of assets can be elicited from respondents. Other issues include who should be interviewed in an asset survey, how ownership should be defined, how the value of assets should be measured, and whether all assets need be included in wealth estimates.[8] The Gender Asset Gap Project was launched in 2009 to explore whether it was feasible to collect detailed, gender-disaggregated wealth data in developing countries, and to study the potential gender biases in the methods employed to do so. For this purpose, national-level household surveys were carried out in 2010 in Ecuador and Ghana and at the state level in India (Doss et al., 2011 and 2014). Two other projects are currently investigating some of these questions: the Methodological Experiment on Measuring Asset Ownership from a Gender Perspective (MEXA),[9] and Evidence and Data for Gender Equality (EDGE).[10]

The issue of who should be interviewed in a household wealth survey aiming to collect individual-level data has also been raised with respect to household income surveys. There is growing consensus that direct reporting is superior to reporting by proxy (where one household member reports on the income or assets of all other household members rather than just on their own resources).[11] The MEXA report, for example, recommends that household surveys move beyond their reliance on asking a single respondent (whether the household head or "the most knowledgeable" person in the household) to include multiple respondents, beginning with the members of the main couple, if not all adults (Kilic and Moylan, 2016).

The issue of how ownership should be defined has been raised primarily in the context of asset information,[12] since there are various ways that it can be measured: reported ownership, documented ownership, or one or several of the components of the bundle of property rights. Documented ownership (having a deed or other form of documentation) tends to be the most secure form of ownership. However, housing and land titles are not always widely available in developing countries. To mitigate this problem, many recent wealth surveys first ask about reported ownership and then ask about documentation and, if available, whose names are on the document. In contexts where private property rights are not well defined, it may be useful to ask about the full range of rights separately (i.e., to use, to lease, to use as collateral, to sell or bequeath) to explore "effective rights."[13]

The valuation of assets is commonly measured by asking respondents what an asset could be sold for today in its present condition (potential sales price or realization value) and/or its replacement cost. Household income surveys often ask about the rental value of immovable property, whereby the present value of the asset can be estimated. All of these measures assume the existence of rental or sales markets for assets, although in developing countries some of these may be particularly thin. The Gender Asset Project, nonetheless, found that the incidence of nonreporting on these different value measures was relatively low (Doss et al., 2013). Another concern is whether knowledge about asset markets and hence values is gender biased, leading to over- or under-reporting depending on who is interviewed. Nevertheless, this is difficult to determine in the absence of a benchmark such as administrative data on immovable property, which is rarely available in most developing countries (Doss et al., 2013; Deere and Catanzarite, 2016).

What Can Be Done to Obtain Better Estimates of the Gender Wealth Gap?

Collecting data on the ownership and value of all assets is a time-consuming process, leading to the question of whether there are any short cuts, particularly if an asset module is to be added to a multi-purpose household survey. The Gender Asset Gap Project, which collected data on ownership and value down to the last chicken in three developing countries, suggests that, as a minimum, data should be collected on all immovable property (i.e., the main residence, agricultural land, and other real estate), businesses, and financial assets. In the three countries covered by the project, immovable property and businesses ranged from 82% (Ghana) to 93% (India) of total household physical wealth.[14] Nonetheless, the composition of wealth may vary across the wealth distribution, with consumer durables making up a large share of wealth among the poorest quintile. Thus, the range and number of assets that need to be included in a wealth survey depend on its specific objectives.

Finally, for comparative purposes it is important for household wealth surveys to collect data on the marital regime—i.e., whether couples were married under civil, religious, or community law; and if the former, under what particular option if various are available. Moreover, to enrich gender analysis, it is important to collect data on how assets were acquired, who decides on their use, and—for potential use as an instrumental variable—on whether a respondent's parents owned immovable property.

Besides allowing analysis of the intra-household distribution of resources, the questions that gender-disaggregated wealth data could answer are many. Examples of the types of questions that could be analyzed include: How large is the gender wealth gap? Does it vary by countries' level of economic development or across the distribution in any systematic way? To what extent is the gender wealth gap conditioned by the institutional framework of each country, specifically marital and inheritance regimes? Are there differences in magnitude between the gender wealth gap among couples and the population as a whole, and how does this relate to increases in the divorce rate and specific divorce legislation? Does the composition of assets owned by men and women differ? What are the sources of the gender wealth gap and how much of it is explained by the observable characteristics of men and women?

Conclusions

The different aspects of inequality discussed in this chapter have clear implications for measurement and statistics, and these have been highlighted in each of the sections. But they also raise important policy questions. For example, in arguing for the need to have measures of intra-household inequality with respect to income, consumption, and wealth, one might mention that in many countries social assistance is based on various kinds of household means tests, excluding from support those members of nonpoor households who are individually poor and get a small share of the household income and wealth.

At the same time, an exclusive focus on vertical inequality, to the exclusion of inequalities across broadly defined groups based on, for example, ethnicity could mislead policy-makers in situations where vertical inequality is falling but horizontal inequality is rising, thus stoking social instability.

As a final example (linking the gender wealth gap with intra-household allocation, since wealth affects bargaining power within the household), neglect of gender-specific wealth inequalities will mislead policy-makers on the final beneficiaries of transfer and other schemes targeted at the household level. Particularly in developing countries, but also in developed countries, a focus on horizontal inequality, intra-household inequality, and the gender wealth gap will pay policy dividends.

Notes

1. http://ec.europa.eu/eurostat/documents/3859598/5901513/KS-RA-07-006-EN .PDF.

2. See Weichselbaumer and Winter-Ebmer (2005) for a meta-analysis of the gender wage gap internationally; World Bank (2012) for a good summary of findings for developing countries; and the discussion in Chapter 5.

3. See Schmidt and Sevak (2006) for such an analysis with the US Panel Study of Income Dynamics; and Yamokoski and Keister (2006) for an analysis utilizing the US National Longitudinal Survey of Youth.

4. See Neelakantan and Chang (2010) for such an analysis with the US Health and Retirement Survey and Ruel and Hauser (2013) for a similar study utilizing the Wisconsin Longitudinal Study.

5. World Bank (2012, p. 162) provides a summary of the default marital regimes in many developed and developing countries.

6. The content of these wealth surveys is described in www.lisdatacenter.org/frontend# /home.

7. See https://dhsprogram.com/.

8. OECD (2013) discusses some of the general issues. See Doss, Grown, and Deere (2008) and Doss et al. (2011) for some of the initial discussions of these issues from a gender perspective.

9. MEXA was implemented in Uganda by the Development Data Group of the World Bank, with support from EDGE and the World Bank Living Standard Measurement Study–Integrated Surveys on Agriculture. See Kilic and Moylan (2016) for preliminary results on the experiment, which featured 5 survey treatments over 13 asset groups.

10. EDGE is a project of the UN Statistical Division and UN Women in collaboration with the African Development Bank, the Asian Development Bank, FAO, the OECD, and the World Bank. It aims to develop guidelines for the collection of individual-level data on asset ownership and entrepreneurship, and is piloting data collection in seven countries.

11. See Fisher, Reimer, and Carr (2010) on how men tend to understate the income of their wives compared with wives' reports, hence potentially underestimating household income.

12. In household income or employment surveys, it is usually assumed that the person who earns the income "owns" it in the sense of controlling its use. However, there is growing evidence from developing countries that women, in particular, may not always control the income they earn. See World Bank (2012), Fig. 2.9.

13. On measuring land ownership in Africa, see Doss et al. (2015). An alternative, pursued in the MEXA experiment in Uganda, is to focus on economic ownership, defined as who keeps the proceeds of a sale should an asset be sold.

14. The remaining share corresponds to livestock, agricultural equipment, and a broad range of consumer durables, including vehicles. Financial assets range from 2% (Ecuador) to 5% (Ghana) of gross household wealth (Doss et al., 2013).

References

Akerlof, G.A. and R.E. Kranton (2000), "Economics and identity," *Quarterly Journal of Economics*, Vol. 115(3), pp. 715–753, https://doi.org/10.1162/003355300554881.

Alderman, H. et al. (1995), "Unitary versus collective models of the household: Is it time to shift the burden of proof?," *World Bank Research Observer*, Vol. 10(1), pp. 1–19.

Badgett, M.V.L. and H.L. Hartmann (1995), "The effectiveness of equal employment opportunity policies," in Simms, M.C. (ed.), *Economic Perspectives on Affirmative Action*, University Press of America, Washington, DC.

Bourguignon, F. (2003), "The growth elasticity of poverty reduction: Explaining heterogeneity across countries and time periods," in Eicher, T.S. and S.J. Turnovsky (eds.), *Inequality and Growth: Theory and Policy Implications*, The MIT Press, Cambridge, MA.

Broman, C. (1997), "Race-related factors and life satisfaction among African Americans," *Journal of Black Psychology*, Vol. 23(1), pp. 36–49.

Brown, G., A. Langer, and F. Stewart (eds.) (2012), *Affirmative Action in Plural Societies: International Experiences*, Palgrave, London.

Cederman, L.E., N.B. Weidmann, and K.S. Gleditsch (2011), "Horizontal inequalities and ethno-nationalist civil war: a global comparison," *American Political Science Review*, Vol. 105(3), pp. 478–495.

Collier, P. and A. Hoeffler (2004), "Greed and grievance in civil war," *Oxford Economic Papers*, Vol. 56(4).

Deere, C.D., G. Alvarado, and J. Twyman (2012), "Gender inequality in asset ownership in Latin America: Female owners versus household heads," *Development and Change*, Vol. 43(2), pp. 505–530.

Deere, C.D. and Z. Catanzarite (2016), "Measuring the intra-household distribution of wealth in Ecuador: Qualitative insights and quantitative outcomes," in Lee, F. and B. Conin (eds.), *Handbook of Research Methods and Applications in Heterodox Economics*, Edward Elgar Publishing, Cheltenham, pp. 512–534.

Deere, C.D. and C. Doss (2006), "The gender asset gap: What do we know and why does it matter?," *Feminist Economics*, Vol. 12(1&2), pp. 1–50.

Deere, C.D. et al. (2013), "Property rights and the gender distribution of wealth in Ecuador, Ghana and India," *Journal of Economic Inequality*, Vol. 11(2), pp. 249–265.

Doss, C. et al. (2015), "Gender inequality in ownership and control of land in Africa: Myth and reality," *Agricultural Economics*, Vol. 46(3), pp. 403–434.

Doss, C. et al. (2014), "The gender asset and wealth gaps," *Development*, Vol. 57(3–4), pp. 400–409.

Doss, C. et al. (2013), "Measuring personal wealth in developing countries: Interviewing men and women about asset values," *Gender Asset Gap Project Working Paper*, No. 15, November, https://sites.google.com/view/genderassetgap.

Doss, C. et al. (2011), *Lessons from the Field: Implementing Individual Asset Surveys in Ecuador, Ghana, India and Uganda*, Indian Institute of Management, Bangalore, https://sites.google.com/view/genderassetgap.

Doss, C., C. Grown, and C.D. Deere (2008), "Gender and asset ownership: A guide to collecting individual-level data," *World Bank Policy Research Working Paper*, No. WPS4704, World Bank, Washington, DC, https://openknowledge.worldbank.org/bitstream/handle/10986/3468/WPS4704.pdf?sequence=6.

Faaland, J., J.R. Parkinson, and R. Saniman (2003), *Growth and Ethnic Inequality: Malaysia's New Economic Policy*, Utusan Publications & Distributors, Kuala Lumpur.

Fearon, J.D. and D.D. Laitin (2000), *Ethnicity, Insurgency and Civil War*, Stanford University Department of Political Science, Stanford, CA.

Fisher, M., J.J. Reimer and E.R. Carr (2010), "Who should be interviewed in surveys of household income?," *World Development*, Vol. 38(7), pp. 966–973.

Foster, J.E., L.F. Lopez-Calva, and M. Székely (2003), "Measuring the distribution of human development: Methodology and an application to Mexico," *Estudios Sobre Desarrollo Humano*, PNUD Mexico, Mexico.

Grabka, M.M., J. Marcus, and E. Sierminska (2015), "Wealth distribution within couples," *Review of Economics of the Household*, Vol. 13, pp. 459–486.

Gurr, T.R. (1993), *Minorities at Risk: A Global View of Ethnopolitical Conflicts*, Institute of Peace Press, Washington, DC.

Haddad, L. and R. Kanbur (1990),"How serious is the neglect of intra-household inequality?," *Economic Journal*, Vol. 100, pp. 866–881.

Harrison, D.A. et al. (2006), "Understanding attitudes toward affirmative action programs in employment: Summary and meta-analysis of 35 years of research," *Journal of Applied Psychology*, Vol. 91(5), pp. 1013–1036.

Hoff, K. and J.E. Stiglitz (1974), "Theories of discrimination and economic policy," in von Furstenberg, G., B. Harrison and A.R. Horowitz, *Patterns of Racial Discrimination*, Lexington Books, Lexington, Mass, pp. 5–26.

Islam, M. and J. Hoddinott (2009), "Evidence of intra-household flypaper effects from a nutrition intervention in rural Guatemala," *Economic Development and Cultural Change*, Vol. 57(2), pp. 215–238.

Kanbur, R. (2018), "Intrahousehold inequality and overall inequality," in Ocampo, J.A. and J.E. Stiglitz (eds.), *The Welfare State Revisited*, Columbia University Press, pp. 147–164.

Kilic, T. and H. Moylan (2016), "Methodological experiment on measuring asset ownership from a gender perspective," *MEXA Technical Report*, World Bank, Washington, DC.

Langer, A. (2005), "Horizontal inequalities and violent group mobilisation in Côte d'Ivoire," *Oxford Development Studies*, Vol. 33(1), pp. 25–45.

Lise, J. and S. Seitz (2011), "Consumption inequality and intra-household allocations," *Review of Economic Studies*, Vol. 78(1), pp. 328–355.

Loury, G.C. (1988), "Why we should care about group equality," *Social Philosophy and Policy*, Vol. 5(1), pp. 249–271.

Malghan, D.V. and H. Swaminathan (2016), "What is the contribution of intra-household inequality to overall income inequality? Evidence from global data, 1973–2013," *IIM Bangalore Research Paper*, No. 522, http://dx.doi.org/10.2139/.2835276.

Mancini, L., F. Stewart, and G. Brown (2008), "Approaches to the measurement of horizontal inequalities," in Stewart, F. (ed.), *Horizontal Inequalities and Conflict: Understanding Group Violence in Multiethnic Societies*, Palgrave, London.

Murshed, S.M. and S. Gates (2005), "Spatial-horizontal inequality and the maoist insurgency in Nepal" *Review of Development Economics*, Vol. 9(1), pp. 121–134.

Neelakantan, U. and Y. Chang (2010), "Gender differences in wealth at retirement," *American Economic Review*, Vol. 100(2), pp. 362–367.

OECD (2013), *OECD Guidelines for Micro Statistics on Household Wealth*, OECD Publishing, Paris, http://dx.doi.org/10.1787/9789264194878-en.

Ponthieux, S. (2015), "Intra-household sharing of resources: A tentative "modified" equivalised income," in Atkinson A.B., A.-C. Guio and E. Marlier (eds.), *Monitoring Social Inclusion in Europe—2017 Edition*, Statistical book, Eurostat, Publication Office of the European Union, Luxembourg, www.researchgate.net/publication/284725525.

Ruel, E. and R.M. Hauser (2013), "Explaining the gender wealth gap," *Demography*, Vol. 50, pp. 1155–1176.

Schmidt, L. and P. Sevak (2006), "Gender, marriage and asset accumulation in the United States," *Feminist Economics*, Vol. 12(1–2), pp. 139–166.

Sen, A.K. (1980), *Equality of What? Tanner Lectures on Human Values*, Cambridge University Press, pp. 197–220.

Stewart, F. (2016), "Horizontal inequalities," in *World Social Science Report. Challenging Inequalities: Pathways to a Just World*, UNESCO, Paris, pp. 52–54.

Stewart, F. (2008), *Horizontal Inequalities and Conflict: Understanding Group Violence in Multiethnic Societies*, Palgrave, London.

Stewart, F. (2002), "Horizontal inequality: A neglected dimension of development," WIDER Annual Development Lecture 2001, Helsinki.

Stewart, F., G. Brown and A. Langer (2008), "Policies towards horizontal inequalities," in Stewart, F. (ed.), *Horizontal Inequalities and Conflict: Understanding Group Violence in Multiethnic Societies*, Palgrave, London, pp. 301–326.

Todd, J. and J. Ruane (2012), "Beyond inequality? Assessing the impact of fair employment, affirmative action and equality measures on conflict in Northern Ireland," in Brown, G., A. Langer and F. Stewart (eds.), *Affirmative Action in Developing Countries: International Experience*, Palgrave, London, pp. 182–208.

Weichselbaumer, D. and R. Winter-Ebmer (2005), "A meta analysis of the international gender wage gap," *Journal of Economic Surveys*, Vol. 19(3), pp. 479–451.

Wimmer, A., L.-E. Cederman, and B. Min (2009), "Why do ethnic groups rebel? New data and analysis," *World Politics*, Vol. 62(1), pp. 87–119.

World Bank (2012), *World Development Report: Gender Equality and Development*, World Bank, Washington, DC.

Yamokoski, A. and L.A. Keister (2006), "The wealth of single women: Marital status and parenthood in the asset accumulation of young baby boomers in the United States," *Feminist Economics*, Vol. 12(1–2), pp. 167–194.

5.

Inequality of Opportunity

François Bourguignon

This chapter discusses what is meant by inequality of opportunity (i.e., "ex ante inequality"), in the sense of how different circumstances involuntarily inherited or faced by individuals could affect their economic achievements later in life. This concept is also taken to include how fair the procedures are. The chapter presents the theoretical principles that can be used for measuring inequality of opportunity. Practical issues of measurement are illustrated through examples and stylized facts from the applied literature on inequality of opportunity and, in particular, on inter-generational economic mobility. The chapter summarizes the nature of the data needed to monitor the observable dimensions of inequality of opportunity and makes recommendations on the statistics that should be regularly produced for effectively monitoring them.

François Bourguignon is Emeritus Professor at the Paris School of Economics. The author wishes to thank Angus Deaton, Martine Durand, Marco Mira D'Ercole, Joseph Stiglitz, other members of the High-Level Expert Group, and participants in seminars in Mexico City and the World Bank for their most helpful comments. The author also thanks the participants in the HLEG workshop on "Inequality of Opportunity" held in Paris, France, on January 14, 2015, hosted by the Gulbenkian Foundation and organized in collaboration with the OECD. The author retains full responsibility for any remaining error or inaccuracy. The opinions expressed and arguments employed in the contributions below are those of the author and do not necessarily reflect the official views of the OECD or of the governments of its member countries.

Introduction

Conceptually, economic inequality can be considered from two different angles. The *ex post* view looks at differences in individual economic results or "outcomes," like economic well-being, living standards, earnings, income, etc. The *ex ante* view looks at the degree of difference between the circumstances involuntarily inherited or faced by individuals and affecting their economic achievements; this is also taken to include the procedural aspect of inequality—how fair the procedures are. The *ex post* view is referred to as "inequality of outcome," with income inequality probably the most common example. The *ex ante* view is referred to as "inequality of opportunity." Both types of inequality are clearly linked but in an asymmetric way. An increase in *ex ante* inequality will, all things being equal, increase *ex post* inequality. In the same way, inequality of outcome at a point of time or within a generation may affect inequality of opportunity in the future or in the next generation. However, a higher level of *ex post* inequality can also result from changes in people's economic behavior, independently of circumstances, and in how the economic system transforms given individual circumstances into economic results.

A marathon where runners don't start from the same line provides a useful analogy. *Ex post* inequality would essentially be the distribution of the finishing times. *Ex ante* inequality would refer to the distance competitors have to run to reach the finish line. *Ex post* and *ex ante* inequality are not the same because competitors may not have expended the same effort during the race. The winner might well be the one who had the least distance to cover. But it may also be the one who had the most to run but had the strongest will to win and suffered the fewest setbacks.

Focusing on one type of inequality or another may depend on the value judgment made on inequality. The most common value judgment behind concentrating on *ex post* inequality is "egalitarianism"; the one behind *ex ante* and procedural inequality is "fairness." In the marathon race, egalitarian observers would simply like to minimize the gap between the performance of the winner and that of the loser, irrespective of the starting position of the runners. More liberal observers would insist on fairness and try to make the runners run the same distance, irrespective of the distribution of performances. Of course, doing so would most likely also reduce the differences between finishing times, so that in practice the two approaches to inequality are not necessarily opposed to each other.

Another aspect of inequality of opportunity is that it may reduce the aggregate efficiency of an economy, or the average outcome, by weakening incentives. This effect, which has been emphasized and debated in the recent economic literature, is easily understood. In the inegalitarian race, the contestants who have the longest distance to run have little incentive to run fast, as they will likely be among the last over the finish line. But the same holds for people running the shortest distances, who know they will be among the first to finish even without making much effort. In other words, *ex ante* inequality has two important consequences: on the one hand, it generates more *ex post* inequality; on the other hand, it may reduce the aggregate performance of society. Thus, correcting inequality of opportunity may strengthen incentives—whereas correcting the inequality of outcomes is often held to do the opposite.

Another difference between the two concepts of inequality is their measurement. Considerable knowledge has accumulated over the last 40 years or so on how to measure the inequality of scalar outcomes like earnings, income, or standard of living, and the value judgments behind these measures. Things are much less advanced for inequality of opportunity. Whereas statements like "there is less inequality in country A than in country B," or "at time t than at time t-1" are easily understood and may be solidly grounded in data in the case of outcomes, they are difficult to substantiate in the case of inequality of opportunity.

Defining inequality of opportunity, in the tradition of Dworkin (1981), Arneson,

(1989) or Roemer (1998), as inequality in "the circumstances beyond the control of individuals," the view taken in this chapter is that it will never be possible to observe differences among individuals across *all* the circumstances that may shape their economic success independently of their will. (The fact that personal "will" may itself be a "circumstance," thus introducing a circularity into the definition of the inequality of opportunity, is discussed below.) Besides, what is not under the control of individuals, i.e., circumstances, and what is often referred to as "efforts," may be extremely ambiguous. It should also be mentioned that circumstances and efforts may interact in producing some outcomes, thus making the distinction between them still more ambiguous. It follows that it is not possible to measure inequality of opportunity in the most general sense as we measure inequality of outcomes like earnings or income and compare it across space or time. However, this does not mean that it is not possible to measure *some* observable dimensions of inequality of opportunity and, most importantly, their impact on inequality of outcomes. This is actually what the inequality of opportunity literature does without always saying so. It is in this restricted sense that the expression will most often be used throughout this chapter.

Analyzing how a person's income depends on the education or income of their parents when that person was a child, on where they grew up, on gender, race, migration status, and so on informs us as to the role of specific circumstances—family characteristics, region of birth, or how the labor market discriminates across gender or race—in shaping the distribution of income. It matters for policy to know whether this role has increased or not, or that more inequality in the income of the present generation is likely to generate more inequality in future generations. Yet such analysis is essentially partial. On the one hand, nonobserved circumstances may counteract the effect of observed ones, so that concluding that there is more inequality of opportunity based on inter-generational earnings mobility may be misleading. On the other hand, measuring the influence of a given circumstance on outcomes does not say much about the channels through which this effect takes place and on the policies to correct it. Deeper analysis is needed for some specific policy to be recommended.

The ambition of this chapter is essentially practical. It is not to contribute to the normative debate on the definition of inequality of opportunity in some absolute sense, or to the positive debate on its potential efficiency cost. It is rather concerned with the evaluation of the inequality specific to a given individual characteristic, duly considered as a circumstance; and, more importantly, to measure its contribution to the inequality of outcomes. The latter objective also applies to the case where several circumstances are considered simultaneously, as there are various ways of mapping the inequality of specific circumstances onto the inequality of given outcomes. In short, the chapter is rather brief on purely conceptual issues, on whether such and such a type of inequality is socially fair or unfair. The emphasis is on measurement issues and the practical use to be made of available measures.

The chapter is organized into three sections. The first section addresses a few conceptual issues, in particular what is meant by inequality of opportunity, and discusses the theoretical principles that can be used for measuring it. Practical issues of measurement are taken up in the second section and illustrated through several examples and stylized facts from the burgeoning applied literature on inequality of opportunity, in particular on inter-generational economic mobility. The final section summarizes the nature of the data needed to monitor the observable dimensions of inequality of opportunity and makes recommendations on the statistics that should be regularly produced for effectively monitoring them.

Conceptual Issues in Defining and Measuring Inequality of Opportunity

This section first addresses the definition of opportunity as distinct from other factors that may contribute to the inequality of outcomes. It then discusses a few theoretical principles that may guide the measurement of inequality of opportunity.

Opportunities and Economic Outcomes: Normative and Positive Issues

Figure 5.1 summarizes the debate about the definition of inequality of opportunity as opposed to inequality of outcomes. The box on the left-hand side of the figure refers to factors beyond the control of an individual, called "circumstances," and likely to affect how she or he will manage and perform in the economic sphere. Some of them are observable, like personal traits—gender, ethnicity, disabilities, place of birth—or parental background. Others, like genetic traits, parents' social capital, or cultural values, generally are not. Together they form the basis for inequality of opportunity.

The circle beneath the circumstance box stands for individual preferences, those presumed to be independent from circumstances, thus representing some genetic origin or resulting from all sorts of life experiences, with no relationship with parental background. This assumption of course is quite debatable and will be discussed further below.

Circumstances, preferences, and some key parameters from the economic sphere, like prices and wages, determine individual economic decisions in the box at the bottom of the figure—arrows (1), (2), and (6). To the extent that these decisions determine the contribution of the individual to the economic system, they are called "efforts." A good example of this is the supply of labor, which may depend on the wealth of an individual, i.e., circumstances if inherited, the wage rate, taxes on labor income and, of course, preferences.

Given the market mechanisms and the policies implemented in the economic sphere, and some randomness in those mechanisms, the individual contribution to the economic sphere results—arrows (3) and (4)—in some individual economic outcomes, be they earnings, income, consumption expenditures, etc. The key point, however, is that circumstances may also determine outcomes, together with individual decisions, through the economic sphere. This is the case, for instance, if some personal traits affect labor market rewards, as where there is discrimination according to gender, migrant status, ethnicity, or social origin. This direct influence of circumstances on outcomes through the economic sphere is represented by arrow (5), going from the circumstance box to the economic sphere. The corresponding inequality in outcomes has to do with what is often termed "procedural" inequality. Circumstances may also indirectly affect individual decisions by modifying the prices and wages faced by an individual—through arrow (6).

Within this representation of the determinants of economic outcomes, the latter thus result *directly* from individual economic decisions, which result themselves from personal preferences and economic conditions, and *indirectly* from the way personal traits and parental influence may affect the rewards for a given effort in the economic sphere.

Figure 5.1. The Relationship Between Individual Circumstances, Opportunities, and Outcomes

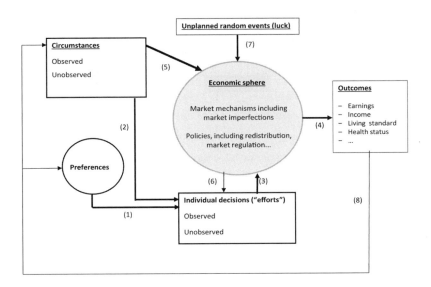

In this framework, inequality of opportunity corresponds to the diversity of individual circumstances and the way it maps onto unequal outcomes. However, in a dynamic setting, unequal outcomes may themselves map onto unequal individual circumstance. For instance, the thin dotted line (8) in Figure 5.1 may stand for the inter-generational transmission of inequality: successful people in the current generation provide better circumstances to their children in the next. Within a generation, that link may also stand for a random event at some point of life, which, given individual preferences (in particular with respect to risk), affects future earning potential, as in the case of poverty trap phenomena.

In the economic inequality literature, a key distinction is made between defining inequality in the space of circumstances and in the space of outcomes. This distinction clearly matters from the point of view of moral philosophy and normative economics.[1] For some authors, only inequality of individual circumstances should matter, as they are, to some extent, forced upon individuals, and people are not morally responsible for them. Social justice thus requires these sources of inequality to be compensated in the outcome space, for instance through cash transfers. In contrast, outcome inequality that arises from individual decisions or efforts should not be a matter of social concern as it essentially results from individuals' free will or preferences, so that individuals can be taken as morally responsible for them.[2] The opposite stream of the literature rejects this distinction between circumstances and efforts on the basis of preferences being themselves partly transmitted to individuals by their families or the social group they belong to. If so, most outcome determinants may be understood as circumstances, and the correction of inequality should entirely focus on the distribution of final outcomes.

At this stage, incentives must be taken into account. In the case where all determinants of outcome, including the taste for hard work, are considered as circumstances, compensating for all of them would lead to equalizing outcomes irrespective of individual actions and initiatives, thus eliminating work, entrepreneurship, or innovation incentives. In the case where only some income determinants are taken to be circumstances, compensating for differences in them and leaving uncorrected the inequality arising from individual decisions may not always be possible or efficient. In the case of labor market discrimination, for instance, we may know that women or children of immigrants are discriminated against on average, but it would be difficult, and certainly controversial, to establish this discrimination at the individual level. Even if it were possible, compensating through lump-sum payments those who are discriminated against would reinforce the market distortion created by discrimination, as people would get the same wage as before but would possibly expend less effort due to the lump-sum transfer. This is a clear case where inequality of opportunity is responsible for both inefficiency and inequality of outcomes, and where the only efficient corrective policy is to eliminate the market imperfection responsible for the inequality of opportunity in the first place.

Ambiguity and Observability Issues in Defining Opportunities

The framework shown in Figure 5.1, and the idea that inequality of opportunity could be compensated by transfers in the outcome space, has three fundamental weaknesses for practical application, in addition to the preceding inefficiency argument. First, there is a fundamental ambiguity about what can be defined as circumstances and individual decisions resulting from preferences supposedly independent of circumstances. Second, even if the distinction between circumstances and efforts were unambiguous, there is a problem with the fact that many circumstances and many efforts are not observable. Third, the relationship between opportunities and outcomes is actually two-way. If, at a point of time, inequality of opportunity is affecting inequality of outcomes when Figure 5.1 is read from left to right, the dotted array (8) in Figure 5.1 stands for the fact that inequality of outcome, possibly due to the free decisions of economic agents, may dynamically affect future inequality of opportunity. Taken together, these weaknesses justify focusing on the inequality of outcomes, while at the same time taking into account the sources of the inequality related to specific observable circumstances. These points are developed below.

The first critique of the distinction between circumstances outside individual control and individual decisions reflecting independent personal preferences is precisely that it is difficult to hold that preferences are under individual control, as if they were freely chosen by people. An in-depth critique of that assumption has been made by Arneson (1989). Somebody's taste for work, for thrift, or for entrepreneurship must come from somewhere, possibly from family background.[3] If so, the distinction between the inequality in outcomes due to circumstances and due to individual decisions becomes fuzzy and practically nonoperational.

The fact that many circumstances are not observed is another reason why the distinction between circumstances and efforts may have limited empirical relevance, at least as long as one is not ready to make several restrictive assumptions. Many circumstances that shape people's professional and family trajectory are not observable. Yet they may affect individual decisions as well as outcomes. For instance, parents may transmit to their children values or talents that will make them decide to go to graduate school and at the same time will help them in their career. If those values and talents are not observed, however, how could we disentangle in observed outcomes what is actually due to observed efforts—i.e., graduate school—and what is due to unobserved circumstances? It is only when it can be assumed that efforts do not depend on unobserved circumstances that also affect outcomes that such identification is possible. If this is not the case, the contribution of efforts to outcomes cannot be properly identified, which makes again the distinction between circumstances and efforts somewhat artificial.[4]

Another weakness of the distinction between inequality of opportunity and inequality of outcomes illustrated by Figure 5.1 is that, if outcomes are determined by circumstances and individual decisions, then outcomes at one point of time may determine future circumstances. As a matter of fact, the whole framework is set in static terms, when it should actually be dynamic. Outcomes of one generation or at one point of time are likely to affect circumstances in the next generation or at a future point of time, for instance, through accumulating or running down wealth or human capital, taken as a circumstance. Under these conditions, ignoring that part of the inequality of outcomes that comes from individual decisions implies ignoring a future source of inequality in the space of circumstances. It may also be noted that, in such a dynamic framework, the measurement of the inequality of outcomes raises some issues. If the unit of time is a generation, how should outcomes be defined? Certainly not by their value at a point of time. Within a dynamic intra-generational analysis, isn't it the case that many "individual decisions" quickly become circumstances, so that again the distinction between circumstances and efforts yields limited insights?

Summing up, the focus put by some moral philosophers and normative economists on inequality of opportunity rather than on inequality of outcomes may be perfectly justified in theory. Practically, however, the distinction that has to be made between factors that are under individual responsibility (efforts) and those that are not (circumstances) is most often blurred, in part because of observability issues. Even when relying only on observed circumstances and efforts, disentangling which part of inequality of outcome is due to one or the other is difficult upon admitting that observed and unobserved circumstances may affect both outcomes and efforts. Actually, the only solid empirical evidence that can be relied upon is the way outcomes depend on observed circumstances, i.e., essentially some personal traits and family-related characteristics.

Measuring Inequality of Observed Opportunities

Data on specific outcomes, some circumstances and, possibly, some types of efforts are available in household surveys or from administrative sources. On the basis of that data, it is possible to estimate the relationship between specific outcomes, circumstances, and efforts.

Before getting into the measurement of inequality of opportunity, or rather some dimensions of it, within these databases, it is worth formalizing that relationship and the arguments in the preceding section. Assume that a survey sample of the population is available with information on individual or household economic characteristics and background. Denote by y_i the outcome of interest for an individual i in the sample; denote his/her observed circumstances by C_i; and his/her efforts by E_i. We can represent the way in which circumstances and efforts determine outcome by the relationship:

$$y_i = f(C_i, E_i) + u_i$$

where $f(\ )$ is some function to be specified below and u_i stands for the role of unobserved circumstances and efforts as well as temporary shocks or measurement errors on the observed outcome. In empirical work, that relationship is often assumed to be log-linear:

$$Log\ y_i = a.C_i + b.E_i + u_i \qquad (1)$$

where a and b are vectors of parameters. Such a specification of the function $f(\ )$ is very restrictive, as one would expect some interaction between circumstances and efforts in determining outcome. Yet it is simple and quite sufficient for our purpose.

The argument in the preceding section and in the annex at the end of this chapter suggests that E_i is correlated to the observed circumstances, C_i, and the unobserved circumstances, U_i. Because of the latter, it is thus not possible to get unbiased estimates of a and b. Under these conditions, the only empirical relationship that can be reliably estimated is a reduced-form model where the outcome depends only on observed circumstances:

$$Log\ y_i = \alpha.C_i + v_i \qquad (2)^5$$

where α is a set of coefficients that describe the effect of observed circumstances on the outcome directly or indirectly through their correlation with efforts (observed or not observed), and v_i stands for all outcome determinants different from observed circumstances. It should be noted, however, that for α to be estimated without bias, it is necessary to assume that all these unobserved outcome determinants are independent of the observed circumstances, C_i. Otherwise, the estimated

α coefficients will also include the effects of all unobserved outcome determinants that are correlated in one way or another with C_i.

Estimating models of type (2) through Ordinary Least Squares (OLS) is a trivial exercise that has been performed under a variety of specifications for the outcome variable, y_i, and the explanatory variables, C_i. Perhaps the most familiar specification is the famous Mincer equation that includes the earnings rate of employed people as the outcome variable, and schooling[6] and personal traits as explanatory variables.

There is a burgeoning literature on the measurement of inequality of opportunity based on models of type (1) or (2). Using model (1), it essentially consists of comparing the actual inequality in outcomes to the inequality that would be observed if all individuals in the data sample were facing the same circumstances, or were all expending a given level of effort. This literature is exhaustively summarized in Ramos and Van de Gaer (2012) and Brunori (2016). We take here a simpler approach based on the fact that efforts are either not observed or endogenous—i.e., correlated with unobserved outcome determinants—so that model (2) is the only solid basis to measure the inequality of opportunities described by the variables in C_i.

It can be noted that, in some cases, it is possible to measure the inequality of single components of C irrespectively of outcomes and model (2). For instance, parental income or cognitive ability may be components of C, the inequality of which can be observed in some databases.[7] The higher the inequality of a component of C, the more unequal the distribution of outcomes, provided that the corresponding coefficient in α is strictly positive.

The inequality of the distribution of C may also be expressed in terms of the inequality of outcomes. When the latter is measured by the variance of logarithms and when there is a single component in C, model (2) implies that:

$$Var(Log\ y) = \alpha^2\ Var(C) + Var(v)$$

Thus, the inequality of that single component of C can also be expressed as what could be the inequality of outcomes if other determinants of outcomes were neutralized, i.e., in the case where they were the same for all individuals. If the inequality of outcomes is measured by the variance of logarithms *(VL)*, the inequality of *C*, $I_{VL}(C)$, could in that case be written as:

$$I_{VL}(C) = \alpha^2 \, Var(C) \qquad (3)$$

and

$$I_{VL}(C) = \alpha' \; Covar(C)\alpha$$

when there is more than one component in *C*.

This definition can be generalized to any measure of outcome inequality $M\{\ \}$ —i.e., Gini, Theil, mean logarithmic deviation—and to any number of components in *C* in two ways.

First, define the "virtual" outcome, $y^\circ(C_i,v^e)$, for every individual *i*, as what would be the outcome of that individual if all the outcome determinants other than the opportunities in *C* were equal to some exogenous value, v_e, common to all, i.e.:

$$Log \, y^\circ(C_i,v^e) = \alpha C_i + v^e \qquad (4)$$

Then compute the measure of inequality $M\{\ \}$ on the distribution of $y^\circ(C_i,v^e)$ in the whole sample. An absolute measure of the inequality of opportunities in *C* is then given by $M\{y^\circ(C,v^e)\}$, where $y^\circ(C,\ v^e)$ stands for the whole distribution of $y^\circ(C_i,v^e)$ in the sample. Fleurbaey and Schokkaert (2012) labeled this measure the "direct unfairness" *(du)* of the inequality of opportunity associated with *C*:

$$I_M^{\frac{du}{}}(C) = M\{y^\circ(C.,v^e)\} \qquad (5)$$

Thus, $I_M^{\frac{du}{}}(C)$ measures the inequality of opportunities in *C* by considering their impact on the inequality of outcome, irrespective of all other outcome determinants. Of course, a measure of inequality of opportunities in *C* can be defined for each measure $M\{\ \}$ of outcome inequality. As most outcome inequality measures $M\{\ \}$ are scale invariant, the arbitrary value of v_e does not actually matter.[8]

Second, one may use the "dual" of the preceding definition of inequality of opportunities in the following sense. Instead of equalizing the outcome determinants other than *C*, one may define a virtual income resulting from the equalization of the opportunities in *C* across all individuals in the sample. Let C^e be the common value of opportunities and $y^*(C^e,\ v_i)$ the corresponding virtual income:

$$Log\ y \cdot (C^{\epsilon},\ v_i) = \alpha C^{\epsilon} + v_i \qquad\qquad (6)$$

Then another absolute measure of inequality of opportunities in C may be defined for any outcome inequality measure $M\{\ \}$ as the difference between the actual inequality of outcome and that which would result from equalizing circumstances among all individuals in the sample. Fleurbaey and Schokkaert (2012) proposed to label this the "fairness gap" (fg) measure of inequality of opportunity associated with C:

$$I_M^{fg}\ (C.) = M\{y.\} - M\{y^{*}(C^{\epsilon},\ v.)\} \qquad\qquad (7)$$

As before, this measure is independent of the arbitrary value, C^{ϵ}, taken for opportunities when the outcome inequality measure is scale invariant.

Both measures of inequality of opportunities may also be defined in "relative" terms by expressing them as a proportion of the actual inequality of the outcome being studied, $M\{y.\}$. They will be denoted respectively $\widetilde{I}_M^{du}\ (C.)$ and $\widetilde{I}_M^{fg}\ (C.)$.

The preceding notations may seem complicated. Their interpretation is extremely simple and intuitive when applied to actual data, as illustrated by the following remarks.

1. Consider equation (2) as a standard regression equation of outcomes on a set of observed opportunities, with the unobserved outcome determinants, v, as the residuals of the regression. Then, if the inequality measure of outcome $M\{\ \}$ is the variance of logarithms, then both the direct unfairness (5) and the fairness gap measures (7) are equal to *the variance of the logarithm of outcome explained by the opportunities C*, and the corresponding relative measure is simply the familiar R^2 statistic associated with regression (2).

2. Consider now the individual "types" defined by combinations of the variables in C with a minimum number of observations. For instance, with only gender in C, there would be two types. With gender and two possible values for the education of the parents, there would be four types: men from low-education parents, women from high-education parents, etc. It turns out then that the direct unfairness inequality of opportunity (5) is very close to the familiar *between group* inequality of outcomes *when groups are defined by*

types, except that the inequality is defined on the mean of the logarithm of outcomes rather than on the outcome means.[9]

3. The preceding expressions to evaluate the inequality of observed opportunities refer to the linear case, where the opportunities being considered have independent effects on the outcome of interest. Of course, it is also possible to take into account interactions between opportunities as, for instance, between gender and education in explaining the inequality of earnings.

4. When considering types, the above formulas seem to leave little room for the inequality of outcomes within types. This is not completely true since the outcome inequality between types corresponding to (5) is not the same as the inequality between the types' mean outcomes, the difference depending on the distribution of outcomes within types. An approach that takes more explicitly into account outcome inequality within types is the inequality of opportunity measure that can be derived from the principles set in Roemer (1998):

$$I^R = \frac{1}{\bar{y}} \int_0^1 [\bar{q}(\pi) - Min_t\{q_t(\pi)\}]\, d\pi \qquad (8)$$

where $q_t(\pi)$ is the outcome of the quantile of order π in the outcome distribution for type t, $\bar{q}(\pi)$ is the (weighted) mean of those quantiles across types, and $y_{-1,i}$ is the overall mean outcome. In other words, inequality of the opportunities defined by types is the mean across quantiles of a Rawlsian type of inequality measure across types for each quantile.[10]

The preceding inequality measure corresponds to the case where the residual term, v, in (2) is heteroskedastic with a distribution, and hence a variance, that depends on the observed circumstance variables, C, or differs across types. This is perfectly consistent with the usual assumptions that the residual term v has zero expected value and is orthogonal to C. With heteroskedasticity, however, defining the inequality of opportunity through (5) or (7) is not possible anymore. The definition of the virtual income in (4) ignores the dependency of the residual term on C, and the equalizing of circumstances in (6) should require modifying the v_i term, so that its distribution does not depend on C anymore or, equivalently, is the same across types.

Practical Issues and Some Stylized Facts in Measuring Inequality of Opportunity

The discussion in the preceding section has focused on conceptual issues in the definition and measurement of inequality of opportunities. We now turn to the way these principles and approaches to measurement are handled in the empirical literature, and present stylized facts about some specific dimensions of inequality of opportunity.

The focus will first be on single dimensions of inequality of opportunities, without necessarily making reference to specific outcomes. More direct applications of the measurement tools discussed above will then be considered with various combinations of outcomes (income, earnings) and sets of opportunities. Special emphasis will be put on the measurement of inter-generational transmission of inequality, which has attracted much attention among social scientists, and which may be considered as a particular case of the measurement principles set out above. Emphasis will also be put on labor market discrimination, which raises some interesting questions when studied from the perspective of inequality of opportunity.

Direct Measures of Some Particular Dimensions of the Inequality of Opportunity

The measurement of specific dimensions of inequality of opportunities can be undertaken in an autonomous way, without explicit reference to economic outcomes. This direct approach simply consists of analyzing the distribution of particular circumstances, C. Many individual characteristics could be analyzed in this way, provided they are described by some quantitative index. Given its huge importance in the literature on inequality of opportunity, this section focuses on cognitive ability and then briefly considers the difficulty of handling directly other single dimensions of inequality of opportunity.

Cognitive Ability as an Opportunity and as an Outcome

The PISA initiative by the OECD provides firsthand data to measure inequality in one of the most important dimensions of individual circumstances: cognitive ability. It now gathers the scores of samples of 15-year-old students in more than 70 advanced and emerging economies in three tests: one on reading (i.e., answering questions about a short text); another on mathematics; and the third on science. This instrument has been fielded at 3-year time intervals since 2000. In addition to students' answers to these assessment tests, the database also reports information on their family background and on the characteristics of their schools.

Considering PISA scores as circumstances implicitly supposes that cognitive ability at age 15 is one of the important determinants of future individual economic outcomes, earnings in particular, and acknowledges that it essentially depends on genetic factors and the family context. People cannot be held responsible for that part of their life, so that inequality of PISA scores among 15-year-olds today will be responsible for some of the inequality of opportunity they will face later in their lifetime. But PISA scores may also be seen as the outcome of the educational process and, as such, as dependent on family circumstances, the efforts of the children, and the educational system itself.[11] Hence the debate on how schools may correct for the inequality of opportunity arising from family background. It is however the former perspective—i.e., cognitive scores as a circumstance—that is discussed in what follows.

Much publicity is given at each new edition of PISA to mean scores by country, to the ranking of countries and how rankings change over time. From the viewpoint of measuring inequality of opportunities, however, what matters most is the statistical distribution of these scores, or their disparities across students.

Figure 5.2 plots the inequality of PISA scores in mathematics, as measured by the coefficient of variation, against the mean score in the 2012 exercise for OECD countries. Interestingly, there is a clear negative relationship between the inequality and the mean of scores (putting aside the three emerging economies, Chile, Mexico, and Turkey, where the coverage of the PISA survey is much lower than in advanced countries, essentially because a nonnegligible proportion of 15-year-olds have already dropped out of school).[12] This is presumably because better mean scores are logically obtained by improving the lower tail of the distribution, more so than making improvements to the upper tail. Yet what may be more important is the substantial difference in the inequality of scores for countries in the same range of average scores. For instance, inequality is 30% higher in Belgium than in Finland or Estonia, in the upper part of the scale of mean scores; the same holds true for France compared with Denmark in the middle.

Figure 5.2. Mean and Coefficient of Variation of PISA Mathematics Scores in OECD Countries, 2012

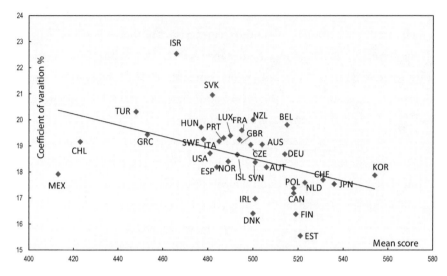

Source: OECD (2014), PISA 2012 Results: What Students Know and Can Do. StatLink 2 http://dx.doi.org /10.1787/888933839582.

Cognitive ability can be considered as a dimension of economic opportunity only insofar as it is a significant determinant of an outcome like earnings or the standard of living of an individual. In this respect, it is important to stress that test scores in surveys like PISA, the OECD's Survey of Adult Skills (PIAAC), or its predecessor (the International Adult Literacy Survey, IALS), only explain a limited part of earning differences across individuals. Murnane et al. (2000) and Levin (2012) make this point on the basis of US data. According to the former, a 1% increase in high school test scores entails a 2% increase in earnings when students are 31 years old, which is substantial.[13] However, the variance of adults' (log) earnings explained by high school test scores is small, slightly less than 5% for men (Murnane et al., 2000, p. 556). Family background is a more powerful determinant of earnings, all the more so when considering that test scores are very much dependent on the education and income of parents.

Instead of cross-country comparisons as in Figure 5.2, it would be interesting to see how inequality, or more exactly the whole distribution of scores, changes over time in a given country. Data reported by the OECD in 2012 include the 90/10 inter-decile and 75/25 inter-quartile ratios for the four exercises since 2003. These measures are remarkably constant except for emerging economies where inequality goes down at the same time as mean scores go up due to the lower tail moving up. France is one of the few advanced countries where the 90/10 inter-decile ratio increased significantly over time. As France's mean score did not change much, this would suggest that good performers do better and bad ones do worse, possibly a clear sign of an increase in inequality of that specific component of opportunities. A careful country-by-country study of the evolution of the whole distribution of test scores might reveal other interesting features. It is surprising that so much emphasis is being put on the evolution of the means without considering distributional features.

The same kind of analysis, based on different tests, is being performed for students at younger ages by a number of organizations, for instance, the Progress in International Reading Literacy Study, led by the International Association for the Evaluation of Educational Achievement. However, the results have not received as much publicity, even though they are equally, if not more, relevant in the analysis of inequality of opportunity, as numerous studies have shown that differences in individual cognitive abilities appear very early in life. Pre-school tests already show high variability among children depending on their family background, and several studies have shown that these differences might have long-lasting effects, as school systems would at best compensate for only part of them. Experiments with preschool programs aimed at leveling the playing field—like the Perry program or the Abecedarian program in the United States— have provided evidence of this (Kautz et al., 2014). As shown in recent work by Heckman,[14] these preschool inequalities are due in large part both to "parenting"—i.e., the care the parents devote to their young children—and to health factors.

Other Single Dimensions of the Inequality of Opportunity

Initial inequality in noncognitive skills is also important throughout people's lifetime, and may be considered as another dimension of inequality of opportunity, even though no synthetic measure is actually available, which makes comparing societies over space or over time difficult.

Health status is another dimension of childhood circumstances related to family background, and another component of human capital. In the same way that cognitive skills at age 15 influence future earnings and are heterogeneous across young people, health status at earlier ages is known to potentially influence the whole career of people and to be heterogeneous too.[15] The difficulty here is to monitor inequality in health status. There is an important literature, for instance, on birth weights as a predictor of health status, future education achievements, and adult earning levels (e.g., Currie, 2009). The same may be true of anthropometric indices at early ages, although most indices are strongly influenced by weight at birth. It is somewhat surprising that more attention is not given to the evolution of inequality in these indices and, as for educational test scores, their dependency on parental characteristics.

Another single dimension of the inequality of opportunity, different from human capital, is inherited financial capital. It is certainly possible to measure inequality of inheritance flows during a given period. Wolff (2015) does so for the United States using data from the University of Michigan's Panel Study of Income Dynamics (PSID) and provides Gini coefficients of inheritance flows both for the whole population and among recipients. However, this is not very informative because of the heterogeneity in the age of inheritors. The extent to which inheriting the wealth of one's parents at the age of 55, something frequent these days, may be considered as a component of inequality of opportunity is not totally clear, except if, somehow, one has been able to borrow, effectively or virtually, much earlier in life against this future wealth flow. As the credit market is highly imperfect, and the inheritance date or the amount to be inherited highly uncertain, it is not even certain it would make much sense to try to estimate something like the inequality in discounted expected inheritance flows of all 25-year-old individuals. Further, donations as well as inheritances would have to be taken into account.

Inheritance is a dimension of the inequality of opportunity whose inequality is difficult to evaluate as such, even though, when considering cohorts beyond a certain age, it is a key factor shaping inequality in economic outcomes, like income or standard of living, that are seldom reported in surveys.

Outcome-Based Measures of Inequality of Opportunities

Rather than considering the inequality of various dimensions of opportunities in an isolated way, it is possible to measure it indirectly through their overall effect on the inequality of the outcomes under study, using a relationship of type (2) above. It was seen that, in various ways, this relationship provides an indirect scalar metric of inequality of opportunity. Various illustrations of this approach are shown below, while also reporting stylized facts on some key components of inequality of opportunities.

Inter-generational Mobility of Earnings

Much work has been devoted to the estimation of models of type (2) where the outcome y_i is the (full-time) earnings of an observed individual, i, and C_i is the (log) (full-time) earnings of their parents, most often their father, observed roughly at the same age. Denoting the latter by $y_{-1,i}$, the basic specification of the model is thus:

$$Log\ y_i = \gamma\ Log\ y_{-1,i} + a + v_i \qquad\qquad (9)^{16}$$

where a is a constant and v_i is a zero mean random term, standing for all unobserved earnings determinants independent of fathers' earnings. The coefficient E_1 summarizes all the channels through which fathers' earnings, and their own determinants like education, may affect sons' earnings.

This model, reminiscent of the famous Galton (1886) analysis of the correlation of height across generations, is generally presented as belonging to the literature on inter-generational mobility, with the least square estimate $\hat{y}$ being interpreted as the inter-generational elasticity (IGE), or the degree of immobility across generations. Equivalently, in a Galtonian spirit, the coefficient $1 - \hat{y}$ is interpreted as the speed of "regression toward the mean."

This approach to inter-generational mobility is based on a parametric specification and the estimation of a specific parameter. Nonparametric specifications come under the form of mobility matrices showing the probabilities, p_{ij}, for the earnings of sons whose fathers' earnings are in income bracket i to be in bracket j. We consider these two approaches in turn.

Parametric Representation of Inter-generational Mobility

To see more clearly the relationship between IGE and inequality of opportunity, one may consider applying directly the alternative definition of inequality of opportunities provided in the preceding section of this chapter. Applying (4)–(7) to model (9) and assuming that the inequality measure $M\{\ \}$ is scale invariant, it can be shown that:

$$I_M^{du}\left(y_{-1.}\right) = M\{y_{-1.}^{\hat{y}}\} \text{ and } I_M^{fg}\left(y_{-1.}\right) = M\{y_.\} - M\{\exp(\hat{v}_.)\}$$

where the notation ^ refers to least square estimates. In the particular case where $M\{\ \}$ is the variance of logarithms, VL, it turns out that the two measures in absolute terms are identical because of the additivity property of the variance:

$$I_M^{du}\left(y_{-1.}\right) = I_M^{fg}\left(y_{-1.}\right) = \hat{y}^2 VL\{y_{-1.}\}$$

while in relative terms:

$$\tilde{I}_M^{du}\left(y_{-1.}\right) = \tilde{I}_M^{fg}\left(y_{-1.}\right) = \frac{\hat{y}^2 VL\{y_{-1.}\}}{VL\{y_.\}} = R^2 \qquad (10)$$

where R^2 is the measure of the explanatory power of the independent variables in regression (9) or, in the present case, the square of the correlation coefficient between the (log) earnings of parents and children.

It can be seen that there is a difference between the inter-generational mobility of earnings (IGE) and inequality of opportunity linked to fathers' earnings. The former is proportional to the latter with a coefficient equal to the ratio of the inequality of children's earnings to that of their fathers.[17] In other words, it is only in a world where the inequality of earnings does not change across generations that both the inequality of opportunity, based on the variance of logarithm, and the IGE coincide.

In their study of geographical differences in inter-generational mobility in the United States, Chetty et al. (2014a) use the ranks of parents and children in the earnings distribution as a relative measure of mobility. Based on the "copula" of the joint distribution of the (log) earnings of the two generations—i.e., the joint distribution of father/children ranks in their respective earnings distribution—this measure is independent of the marginal distributions of log earnings. It turns out that the rank-rank correlation is not very different from the log earnings correlation for reasonable small values of the latter. Through (10), it is thus possible to recover the IGE from the rank-rank correlation.

Nonparametric Representation: Mobility Matrices

Another way of representing the inter-generational mobility of earnings is through a transition matrix representing the way a two-generation dynasty transitions from a given earnings level for fathers to another (or the same earnings) level for sons. Let N earning brackets be denoted by Y_k, and denote $\hat{p}_{ij}$ the probability that the sons of fathers in bracket Y_i find themselves in bracket Y_j. The distribution of earnings is given by the total rows and columns of the matrix $P = \{p_{ij}\}$, but it is also possible to break free from these distributions by defining the income brackets as the quantiles (deciles, vintiles . . . of the distribution of the earnings for fathers on the one hand, and for sons on the other.[18]

Whether the transition or "mobility" matrix is defined in terms of income brackets or quantiles is not without implications for the interpretation that may be given to the comparison of two matrices. When referring to income brackets, the matrix shows "absolute" mobility, i.e., the probability that children's earnings could be higher, or lower, than their parents', a concern of many parents today. Conversely, defining the matrix in terms of quantiles permits to analyze "relative" mobility, irrespectively of earnings levels. The difference between the two approaches lies

Table 5.1. Inter-generational Transition Matrix for Earnings

Sons\Fathers	Y_1	Y_2	Y_3	...	Y_N	Total
Y_1	P_{11}	P_{12}	P_{13}	...	P_{1N}	$P_{1.}$
Y_2	P_{21}	P_{22}	P_{23}		P_{2N}	$P_{2.}$
Y_3	P_{31}	P_{32}	P_{33}		P_{3N}	$P_{3.}$
...	...	...	...	...	...	...
Y_N	P_{N1}	P_{N2}	P_{N3}		P_{NN}	$P_{N.}$
Total	$P_{.1}$	$P_{.2}$	$P_{.3}$	...	$P_{.N}$	1

StatLink 2 http://dx.doi.org/10.1787/888933839601.

essentially in the fact that the latter does not take into account the change in the distribution of earnings across generations.[19]

There is a huge literature on how to draw mobility indicators from such a representation of the influence of parents' earnings on children's earnings—see Fields and Ok (1999) or the survey by Jäntti and Jenkins (2015). For instance, mobility is often measured by one minus the trace of the mobility matrix. Shorrocks (1978) suggested a "Normalised Trace" measure given by $[N-trace(A)]/(N-1)$, where A is the matrix P with rows normalized to 1—i.e., the N probabilities p_{ij} are divided by the row sum p_i. Other measures are based on the expected number of jumps from one bracket, or decile, to another.

Rather than comparing transition matrices on the basis of mobility indices, some dominance criteria have also been developed, which may lead to incomplete ordering and, thus, to cases of noncomparability between two matrices. For instance, the diagonal criterion says there is less mobility in a transition matrix than in another if *all* diagonal elements, rather than their sum, are smaller in the former than in the latter. Shorrocks (1978) proposed a stronger criterion, the "strong diagonal view," according to which there is more mobility in matrix A than in B if $a_{ij} \geq b_{ij}$ for all $i \neq j$.

Although related, this kind of measure based on the transition probabilities has only an indirect link with measures of inequality of opportunity in the sense that it is not expressed in terms of the distribution of outcomes, which logically should be here the distribution of children's earnings. There are various ways in which such a link may be established:

- The Roemer inequality of opportunity formula (8) would be one way, although apparently seldom used, mostly because the transition matrix consistent with it would be conceptually different from P above. Indeed, the children's earnings brackets should be row-dependent so as to correspond to the deciles—or other quantiles—of the distribution of earnings among children from parents in a given earnings bracket or quantile.

- An alternative would consist of associating to each row of the matrix a scalar depending on the mean earnings and its distribution within the row. In a more general context, Van de Gaer (1993) suggested measuring the inequality of opportunity by the inequality of the mean earnings across "types," i.e., fathers' earnings here, which is actually a measure of type I^{du} as defined in (4). Lefranc, Pistolesi, and Trannoy (2009) argued in favor of combining the mean with some inequality measure within type. More generally, one could consider the observed distribution of children's earnings with the same father's earnings as being that of the *ex ante* random earnings of the typical child in that type. Then one would associate to each row of the transition matrix the certainty equivalent of the distribution of earnings in that row for a given level of risk aversion. This would be equivalent to associating to each row of the matrix the equivalently distributed earnings (EDE) for that row, in the sense of Atkinson (1970), and then defining inequality of opportunity as the inequality of these EDEs across rows.[20]

- A social welfare approach to the measurement of inter-generational mobility has been proposed by Atkinson (1981) and Atkinson and Bourguignon (1982), which differs somewhat from the inequality of opportunity analytical framework presented here. It consists of defining social welfare on father-son pairs, so that each cell of the transition matrix is given a utility $U(Y_i, Y_j)$ and the social welfare of society is defined by the mean value of this utility, weighted by the transition probabilities, P_{ij}. The simplest case is when $U(\ )$ is additive in the earnings of parents and children. Atkinson and Bourguignon (1982) derived dominance criteria to compare transition matrices on that basis, depending on the properties of the function $U(\ )$.

- A similar line of thought has been pursued by Kanbur and Stiglitz (2015), who extend the preceding approach by considering a steady state of an economy consisting of infinitely lived dynasties under the assumption of constant transition matrix and earnings distribution across generations. Within that framework, they identify a social welfare based dominance criterion of one matrix over another or, in other words, of one stationary state of an economy with some inter-generational mobility feature over another stationary state with a different mobility matrix.

In the perspective of inequality of opportunity, there are problems with the last two approaches. On the one hand, the assumption of a fully stationary economy and a social welfare dominance comparison based on dynasties with an infinite number of generations seems extreme, even though the stationarity assumption is often implicit in statements about inter-generational earnings mobility. On the other hand, it is a problem that the very nature of circumstances is used to make comparisons of outcomes across groups of individuals with identical circumstances. In other words, the mobility of children with rich parents may matter less than that of poor parents. What should matter from the point of view of inequality of opportunity is how different the distribution of earnings is across parents' earnings levels, with no particular importance being given to those levels.

In summary, there is some ambiguity about the way in which inequality of opportunity corresponding to nonparametric specifications of the inter-generational mobility of earnings can be measured. There are various ways mobility can be evaluated or transition matrices compared based on social welfare criteria. But the link with measures of inequality of opportunity of the kind that can be derived from simple parametric models of type (9)—at least under the assumption of homoscedasticity of the residual term, v—is unclear. For this reason, the rest of this section looks at the parametric case.

Data Requirements

A priori, the data requirement to estimate the IGE or the parents-children earnings transition matrix seems extremely demanding. One should observe the earnings of parents, generally the father, and that of the children, generally the sons, at more or less the same age or during the same period of their lifecycle. Long panel databases extending over 20 years and more would allow this to be done. For instance, the PSID in the United States has been collecting data on the same families and their descendants for almost 50 years. The British and the German household panels also extend over 25 years and more. In some countries, register data, most often tax data, allow researchers to follow people throughout their lifetime and from one generation to the next, but only a few countries have open and anonymized register data at this stage.

However, panel data are not really necessary to estimate model (9). The availability of repeated cross-sections over long periods is sufficient. Moreover, they permit the IGE to be estimated in a consistent—i.e., asymptotically unbiased—manner, something which is not certain with panel data.

To see this, it must be noted that the observation of $Log\, y_{-1}$ is most likely to include measurement errors or, at least, transitory components of fathers' earnings that are unlikely to have had any effect on their sons' earnings. Estimating y in (9) with OLS and without precaution for measurement error will thus lead to the so-called attenuation bias, a bias that has been shown to be quite substantial in intergenerational mobility studies.[21] The solution is to "instrument" $Log\, y_{-1}$ by regressing that variable on some fathers' or parents' characteristics at that time, Z, at the same date, say t_{-1}, and to use the predicted rather than the observed value when estimating (9) with OLS. Thus, if the parents' characteristics Z are observed at time t in the same database as their children's earnings, and if an earlier cross-section is available at time t_{-1}, this allows us to estimate the log earnings of adults with characteristics Z. Running OLS on (9) using the predicted earnings of the parents at time t_{-1} will yield an asymptotically unbiased estimator of the IGE. Through this so-called two-sample instrumental variable (TSIV) estimation strategy (Björklund and Jäntti, 1997), repeated cross-sections with information on respondents' parents and covering a long-enough period are sufficient to estimate the IGE.[22]

There are two important caveats to the preceding method. First, the instrumental variable approach just sketched is valid only to the extent that the instrument Z may be assumed to be orthogonal to the income of the children. It must be recognized, however, that this is unlikely to be the case, as most observable parents' characteristics, like education, occupation, wealth, etc., may be thought of as influencing the economic achievements of children. Second, even if the TSIV strategy did allow the IGE to be estimated consistently with repeated cross-sections rather than with panel data, it would not permit the corresponding inequality of opportunity to be estimated as defined by (10). This is because the variance of the instrumented earnings of parents is not the same as the variance of their true earnings.

Measurement errors are also likely to affect the estimation of mobility measures, social welfare dominance tests, and inequality of opportunity through the transition probability matrix methods mentioned above. In that case, both the error on fathers and sons matter. The former may be responsible for misclassifying fathers in the income scale, whereas the latter introduces noise in the transition probabilities.

Stylized Facts

The best illustration of this literature on the measurement of inter-generational mobility is the well-known "Great Gatsby" curve, building on the work of Miles Corak and popularized by Alan B. Krueger. It plots estimates of IGE against the level of inequality—in the contemporaneous generation—for a set of developed and developing countries. This curve is shown in Figure 5.3 below.

Along the vertical scale of the chart, one observes a rather wide dispersion of the estimated IGE, from 0.2 for Nordic countries—Sweden being a little above that level—to 0.5 in the United States and 0.6 in Latin American countries. If it is assumed that the inequality of earnings is similar among parents and children, then (10) suggests that a consistent measure of inequality of opportunity is the square of the IGE, or the R^2 of the regression of the log of sons' earnings over the log of fathers'. Then it can be seen that inequality of opportunity corresponding to the fathers' earnings alone is extremely low in Nordic countries, amounting to less than 4% of the variance of log earnings, while it is more substantial in the United States, amounting to 25% of sons' earnings inequality. Yet this would still leave considerable room for mobility if it were the case that no other circumstance, orthogonal to parents' earnings, constrained children's earnings, which seems unlikely.

The plot also shows a strong correlation between earnings immobility (i.e., IGE) or inequality of opportunity, and the degree of inequality, as measured by the Gini coefficient of household disposable income, at a point in time. Several explanations have been given for the negative correlation shown in Figure 5.3. The most frequent one relies on some convexity in the relationship between parents' income and their investment in the human capital of their children, or possibly some unequal access to quality schooling depending on parents' income. If rich parents invest a higher proportion of their own income in the education of their children, or if only the children of parents above some level of income have access to good quality schools, then more income inequality among parents should generate less intergenerational mobility.

The preceding argument is equivalent to assuming some nonlinearity in the

Figure 5.3. The Great Gatsby Curve

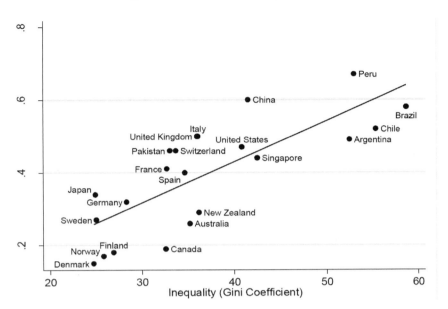

Source: Corak, M. (2012), "Here is the source for the Great Gatsby Curve," in the Alan B. Krueger speech at the Center for American Progress on January 12, https://milescorak.com/2012/01/12/here-is-the -source-for-the-great-gatsby-curve-in-the-alan-krueger-speech-at-the-center-for-american-progress/.

basic model (9) or, more exactly, that the IGE may depend on the level of income. If the IGE increases with income, as just suggested, then the linear approximation (9) would indeed yield an OLS estimate of the IGE that increases with the degree of income inequality.[23]

That the IGE may vary with the level of income is shown in the case of the United States by Landersø and Heckman (2016), p. 22, as can be seen in Figure 5.4 below.[24]

Another, more mechanical, explanation of the negative slope of the Great Gatsby curve is based on (10) above. If one compares two countries where income inequality was the same in the older generation, then it is the case that, with the same correlation coefficient (R^2) between the earnings of the two generations, the IGE will be higher in the country with the highest inequality today. For instance, Landersø and Heckman (2016, p. 17) show that the IGE in Denmark would be much bigger than what it is if the distribution of children's earnings was identical to the US distribution. This again illustrates the difference between the concept of immobility

Figure 5.4. Nonlinear Inter-generational Elasticity in the United States

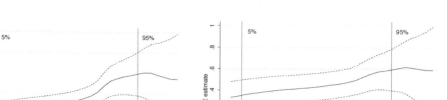

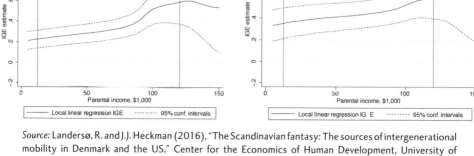

Source: Landersø, R. and J.J. Heckman (2016), "The Scandinavian fantasy: The sources of intergenerational mobility in Denmark and the US," Center for the Economics of Human Development, University of Chicago.

as described by IGE and that of inequality of opportunity related to parents' earnings. Yet it is unlikely that Figure 5.3 would be fundamentally different if the IGE were replaced by the inequality of opportunity as defined in (10).[25]

Other available explanations of the upward sloping Gatsby curve go from mobility to inequality rather than the opposite. For instance, Berman (2016) stresses that if the distribution of the residual term, v, is constant, model (9) leads to a steady-state distribution of earnings whose inequality is given by: $VL(y) = \frac{Var(v)}{1-\gamma^2}$. Thus, inequality of income increases with IGE. As a matter of fact, it should be noted that this property does not hold only at a steady state. Among two societies with the same distribution of earnings in one generation, inequality will be higher, all things being equal, in the society where parents transmit more of their earning capacity to their children. Formally, (9) implies that:

$$VL(y) = \gamma^2 \, VL\left(y_{-1}\right) + Var(v)$$

which is increasing in γ.

One might ask whether this positive relationship between inequality and inter-generational immobility may also hold inter-temporally. Interestingly enough, Aaronsson and Mazumder (2008) show that trends in wage inequality between 1940 and 2000 in the United States coincide with trends in IGE, with a compression in the first part of the period and increasing disparities in the later part.[26] However, not enough data are available to test that hypothesis on a cross-country basis.

The same type of analysis may be undertaken with other economic outcomes. However, to keep with the spirit of model (9) it is important to make sure that the same variable can be observed for both parents and children. For instance, having parents' earnings on the right-hand side of the equation and income per capita (or per adult equivalent) on the left-hand side is interesting, but the interpretation is not anymore in terms of inter-generational transmission of earning potential, as income per capita also depends on family size, marriage, and labor supply. There is also an issue with the period of observation of the right-hand variable. Presumably, one would expect parents' income to influence the life-time earnings of children. This may not be reflected when observing children during a short period at some stage of their life.

Chetty et al. (2014a) address this issue when analyzing the spatial heterogeneity of inter-generational income mobility in the United States, as they indeed use life-time pre-tax family income as income variables in both generations as drawn from administrative tax data. They find considerable spatial variation of income mobility across "commuting zones": "The probability that a child reaches the top quintile of the national income distribution starting from a family in the bottom quintile is 4.4% in Charlotte (North Carolina) but 12.9% in San Jose (California)."

Taking advantage of the length of register data, Chetty et al. (2014b) also study the time evolution of inter-generational mobility, in effect the rank correlation between fathers' and sons' earnings. They find no significant change across birth cohorts born between 1971 and 1982. This is in line with the results found earlier by Lee and Solon (2009) for the US using the PSID panel data set for cohorts born between 1952 and 1975. Both results diverge somewhat from Aaronsson and Mazumder (2008). Nonconsensual results are also found in other countries, as shown by the critiques by Goldthrope (2012) to the finding by Blanden et al. (2011) that mobility would have fallen in the United Kingdom.

Another interesting concept, closer to the sociological view on mobility, has recently been studied by Chetty et al. (2017). "Absolute mobility" is defined as the proportion of 30-year-old children whose real income is higher than their parents' when they were 30. Combining register data since 1970 with assumptions on rank correlation together with cross-sectional data for the period before, absolute mobility has declined continuously from the 1940 to the 1965 birth cohort—i.e., the baby boomers. It then stabilized but fell again soon because of the financial crisis—i.e., for cohorts born in the late 1970s.

Somewhat surprisingly, much less work has been done on the inter-generational transmission of wealth inequality and on the key role of inheritance in the inequality of opportunity. This is in part due to the availability of data. Typical household surveys generally do not include data on wealth. When they do, they do not necessarily include data on parents, or they are not repeated over a period long enough to apply the TSIV methodology. As for panel data, some waves of PSID do include wealth questionnaires. They have been used by Charles and Hurst (2003) to estimate an IGE for wealth. Unfortunately, no information is available that would allow to correct for measurement error bias. The British and German household panels do include data on wealth but the number of observations is too small to estimate IGE for wealth at mid-life, an age at which the wealth concept becomes relevant for both parents and children. One could also think of using estate statistics, but these actually lack relevance as their link to inequality of opportunity is through the heirs, whose wealth is not observed.

In Nordic countries, several recent studies of inter-generational wealth dynamics have relied on administrative data. Boserup, Kopczuk, and Kreiner (2014) provide estimates of the wealth IGE at mid-life in Denmark, and Adermon, Lindahl, and Waldenström (2015) do the same for Sweden. Both studies cover more than two generations. In both countries, the wealth IGE estimates are comparable and of limited size (around 0.3), a value comparable to the earnings IGE in Sweden but twice as large in Denmark.

Generalized Inter-generational Mobility Analysis and Inequality of Observed Opportunities

Parental income is only one of the circumstances affecting the economic outcome of an individual, even though it may be correlated with other circumstances. To provide a more complete picture, fathers' earnings, y_{-1} in equation (9), can be replaced or complemented by a vector of variables referring to the parental characteristics of an individual in the current generation. Labor force or household surveys often give information on the parents of respondents (education, occupation, residence, age when respondent was 10). Rather than using the TSIV approach to estimate parental earnings or income based on these characteristics, one may simply measure the related inequality of opportunity by the share of the inequality of income or earnings in the current generation that is accounted for by parents' characteristics, including the determinants of their own earnings.

Formally, model (9) is replaced by:

$$Log\ y_i\ =\ \beta\ Z_i\ +\ v_i \qquad\qquad (11)$$

where y_i is a particular economic outcome; Z_i a vector of variables that include all observed parental characteristics and some other characteristics beyond individual control, like gender; and v_i all the unobserved determinants of the economic outcome that are orthogonal to Z_i. In agreement with the definition (7), the R^2 statistics of that regression may be interpreted as the inequality of opportunities associated with individual characteristics in Z_i when measuring the inequality of outcomes with the variance of logarithms. Some authors prefer using other measures of inequality.[27]

In comparison with model (9), model (11) may be considered as a model of "generalized" mobility in the sense that more parental characteristics are taken into account that do not necessarily include the outcome being explained in the current generation. It can also be noted that this model is identical to the model used in the inter-generational mobility analysis of earnings when instrumenting the earnings of the parent by a set of characteristics available in the database—i.e., the TSIV approach. Model (11) would then correspond to the "reduced" form of the earnings mobility model, necessarily less restrictive than the structural form (9).

Figure 5.5 illustrates this approach to inequality of opportunity, drawing on a paper by Brunori, Ferreira, and Peragine (2013) that puts together estimates of some observed dimensions of inequality of opportunity in selected countries as reported in several papers, including Checchi, Peragine, and Serlenga (2010) and Ferreira and Gignoux (2011b). The inequality of opportunities measure used in these papers is the one defined in (5), with the mean logarithmic deviation as a measure of inequality.[28] The figure shows the relative inequality of

Figure 5.5. Inequality of Outcomes and Share Due to Observed Dimensions of Inequality of Opportunity, Selected Countries Around 2005

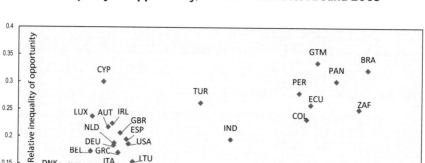

Source: Based on Brunori, P., F. Ferreira, and V. Peragine (2013), "Inequality of opportunity, income inequality and economic mobility: Some international comparisons," *IZA Discussion Paper*, No. 7155. StatLink 2 http://dx.doi.org/10.1787/888933839620.

observed opportunities (vertical axis) against the total inequality of outcomes (horizontal axis).

Figure 5.5 is in some sense the equivalent of the Great Gatsby curve, with the IGE being replaced by the inequality of observed opportunities.[29] This generalization of the Great Gatsby curve, which consists of replacing parental earnings by observed parents' characteristics and individual traits, leads to a relationship between inequality of observed opportunities and inequality of outcomes that is still positive. However, that relationship disappears when restricting the sample to advanced countries, unlike what is observed in Figure 5.3.

This difference must be taken with very much precaution, though. On the one hand, countries are not the same. On the other hand, both the outcome variables and the observed circumstances Z in Brunori, Ferreira, and Peragine (2013) may not be the same across countries. The economic outcome, y, refers to labor earnings for the EU countries and the United States,[30] household income per capita in Latin American countries, household earnings per capita in India, and household gross income per capita in South Africa. An important lesson to be drawn from these exercises is the need to use uniform definitions of variables. This is not always possible across countries, but is absolutely necessary for comparing the same country over time.

Another important caveat is that the inequality of observed opportunities reported in Figure 5.5 is estimated on the whole population rather than on specific age cohorts as in studies of inter-generational earnings mobility. In other words, the implicit assumption is that this inequality is uniform across age groups, or cohorts, in national populations. This is far from granted. The way an economic outcome depends on individual and parental circumstances may change over the life cycle, and may change across cohorts. Cohorts are definitely the most relevant statistical reference. What policy-makers and analysts are interested in is whether younger cohorts are less dependent on their family background than older cohorts, presumably at the same age.[31]

Improving and standardizing generalized mobility analyses of the type described above—to make them comparable across countries, over time, and across cohorts—might be easier to implement than standardizing inter-generational earnings mobility studies. It should permit key determinants of the inequality of outcomes to be monitored effectively—be it earnings, income, or subjective well-being—and to identify forces behind the evolution of the inequality, or possibly behind its stability. Done in a systematic way, such analyses should be most helpful for policy-making in the field of inequality.

It should also be noted that the same nonparametric matrix specification used for inter-generational mobility analysis can be used here. The matrix P in Table 5.1 would differ simply by the definition of the rows. Instead of referring to the earnings of parents, they would refer to types of individuals in the current generation, the types being defined by the most frequent combinations of individual characteristics, Z. This would not be a mobility matrix or a copula anymore but simply a matrix comparing the distribution of a given economic outcome across individuals with different social and family background or individual traits. The corresponding inequality of opportunity could be measured using the Roemer-like measure (8) above or some of the suggestions made when discussing the measure of inter-generational mobility.

Sibling Studies

Other approaches have been used in the literature to identifying what part of the inequality of outcomes has its roots in family background in the strict sense, rather than in the mixed bag of characteristics, Z, that can be found in household surveys. In this context, the idea of using differences or similarities among siblings or twins is particularly attractive.

If the economic outcome being studied is labor earnings, the square of the correlation coefficient of earnings between siblings is a direct measure of the share of the inequality of outcomes that comes from a common family context. This requires some assumptions on the underlying earnings model.[32] If these assumptions are found to be reasonable, then this correlation coefficient logically accounts for all observed and unobserved family background characteristics as well as presumably for other circumstances that were common to siblings in their childhood or adolescence. Because of this, it is expected that the share of outcome inequality explained in this way be higher than that of other estimations based on observed circumstances, even though siblings may not share all the family background factors susceptible to affect their earnings later in life. At first sight, however, orders of magnitude seem comparable to what is obtained in inter-generational earnings mobility studies—in the few countries where both estimates are available. For instance, the correlation coefficient between brothers' earnings is 0.23 in Denmark (Jäntti et al., 2002) and 0.49 in the United States (Mazumder, 2008). The former value is somewhat above what is shown in Figure 5.4, whereas the latter is roughly the same.

Sibling analysis of this type may well be able to capture a bigger part of the overall effect of family circumstances on outcome inequality but, contrary to the type of study described in the preceding sub-section, it does not say much about the channels behind this effect. Also, this type of analysis cannot be performed on the basis of standard household surveys, which are the most commonly used source for measuring outcome inequality.

Outcome Inequality Related to Gender or Other Personal Traits

The characteristics Z considered in the generalized inter-generational mobility approach may be of different kinds. They may be personal traits like gender, ethnicity, or migrant status, family background characteristics, or more generally the assets people may have received from their family, including schooling. The analysis of the inequality of observed opportunities discussed above did not make any distinction between these various components of Z. Yet the inequality associated with them may be subject to different value judgments and may have different policy implications in terms of the inequality of outcomes.

Gender is a case in point. If gender were the only component of the Z variables in the general model (11), then the associated decomposition of inequality would boil down to singling out the relative difference in the mean outcome across genders. This is the first step in the literature on gender earnings inequality, and more generally on "horizontal inequality," i.e., inequality in the mean outcomes of people with different personal traits (for example race, migrant status, or place of residence). Figure 5.6 on gender earnings inequality is typical of that literature. It shows how the male-female earnings differential fell substantially over the last decades in the OECD countries where it was the highest, but remains sizable, at around or above 15%, in a majority of countries.

At the same time, this figure raises questions that are directly related to the distinction between circumstance and effort in the inequality of opportunity literature. To what extent is the observed earnings differential due to different

Figure 5.6. Gender Wage Gap in Selected OECD Countries, 1975–2015

Percentage gap between median earnings of men and women, full-time workers

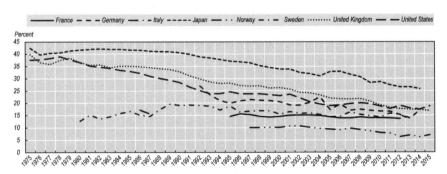

Source: OECD (2018), *OECD Earnings: Gross earnings: decile ratios* (database), https://doi .org/10.1787 /lfs-data-en. StatLink 2 http: //dx.doi.org/10.1787/888933839639.

occupational and career choices made by male and female workers, or to features completely outside their own control, like education or, most importantly,
employer discrimination in the labor market? Also, to what extent do the differentials shown in Figure 5.6 reflect differences in labor force participation rates,
themselves related to wage determinants like age or job experience? The answer
to these questions is of great importance for policy, in particular to identify the
role of labor market discrimination and the possible remedies to other sources of
earnings inequality. For instance, concluding from Figure 5.6 that gender earnings
discrimination has gone down by 15 to 20 percentage points in countries where
it was around 45% 40 years ago would not be correct if the composition of the
female (or male) labor force had changed over time or if the proportion of better
paid women increased.

Part of the answer to the questions mentioned above is obtained by adding other
personal traits and circumstances to gender as regressors in model (11). For instance,
if schooling is introduced as an additional circumstance variable, the coefficient of
the gender component would then reflect the male-female difference in earnings
once the effect of male-female differences in schooling on the earnings differential
had been accounted for. In a more general model, the gender coefficient would
measure the gender earnings gap that comes in addition to gender differences in
all observed earnings determinants. This coefficient is generally referred to as the
"adjusted" gender earnings gap.

It is possible to go further by making the model nonlinear through interactions
between gender and the other components of Z, namely:

$$Log\ y_i\ =\ \beta\,Z_i\ +\ \delta\,Z_i\ *\ G_i\ +\ v_i \qquad\qquad (12)$$

where G_i is a dummy variable that stands for the gender of person i and the δ coefficients measure the earnings differential associated with the individual characteristics in Z_i. Alternatively, model (12) can be estimated separately for male and
female workers:

$$Log\ y_i^g\ =\ \beta_g\,Z_i^g\ +\ v_i^g, g\ =\ M,F \qquad\qquad (13)$$

On the basis of the estimates of the two sets of coefficients β_g, the gender earnings gap may be decomposed into gender differences in the earnings determinants

and differences in the return to these determinants, i.e., between the estimated coefficients $\hat{\beta}_F$ and $\hat{\beta}_M$. For instance, women may be paid at a lower rate than men because they have less education, which was true for some time and still is for older cohorts, but they may also be paid less than men for any additional year of schooling, which might be considered as pure discrimination.

Formally, this so-called Blinder-Oaxaca decomposition is:

$$Log\ \bar{y}^{\,F} - Log\ \bar{y}^{\,M} = (n_F\hat{\beta}_F + n_M\hat{\beta}_M)(\bar{Z}^{\,F} - \bar{Z}^{\,M}) + (\hat{\beta}^{\,F} - \hat{\beta}^{\,M}).(n_F\bar{Z}^{\,F} + n_M\bar{Z}^{\,M}) \qquad (14)^{33}$$

where the notation $^-$ refers to means, and n_F and n_M are the weight of female and male workers respectively in the population sample. The first term corresponds to the contribution of differences in individual characteristics between men and women, i.e., the difference between the earnings gap and the adjusted earnings gap defined above. The second term stands for the true discrimination, i.e., the fact that the same characteristics are not rewarded in the same way among men and women. Actually, it is precisely the adjusted earnings gap defined earlier, the interest of (14) being that this adjusted gap can be decomposed into the contributions of the various components of Z. In the context of gender inequality, this adjusted gap may be considered as a measure of procedural inequality, i.e., the way the same characteristics are not rewarded in the same way for two groups of individuals.

Figure 5.7 illustrates this decomposition and at the same time exhibits quite a remarkable stylized fact. The figure is drawn from a meta-analysis of gender wage discrimination and shows the mean gender earnings gap and the adjusted earnings gap in a set of 263 papers covering a large number of countries at different points of time. The figure reports the means of all studies reporting estimates for a given year, year by year. A remarkable pattern emerges. Over time, the mean gender wage gap has declined substantially, as shown in Figure 5.6 for selected countries. At the same time the mean adjusted gap, or the second term in the Blinder-Oaxaca equation above, remains more or less constant on average. In other words, on average across countries, the main reason why the gender earnings gap declined is because the gender differences in wage determinants like education or job experience have declined, not because the returns to these determinants have become less unequal. Assuming the studies in this meta-analysis are fully comparable, this would mean

Figure 5.7. Gender Earnings Gap and Adjusted Earnings Gap in a Meta-analysis of the Literature

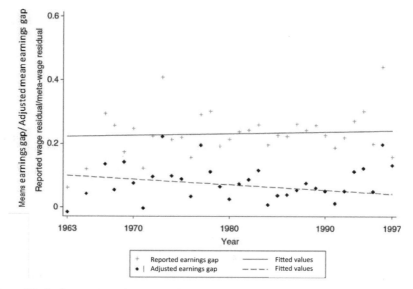

Source: Weichselbaumer, D. and R. Winter-Ebmer (2005), "A Meta-analysis of the international gender wage gap," *Journal of Economic Surveys*, Vol. 19(3), pp. 479–511.

that the inequality of opportunity related to labor market discrimination has not changed in the average country.

From a policy point of view, the Blinder-Oaxaca equation is of obvious interest since it shows the orientation to be chosen in order to reduce gender inequality, and therefore total earnings inequality. From a perspective of inequality of opportunity, however, it also raises an interesting issue, which is that focusing exclusively on circumstances as the source of inequality may not always be justified. The way efforts are rewarded by the economic system, depending on individual circumstances or personal traits, matters too.

As an example, consider the standard Mincer equation that explains the log of earnings or wages as a function of the number of years of schooling and job experience. A priori, it seems reasonable to consider years of schooling as a circumstance forced upon an individual by parents or family context, whereas job experience would more logically reflect decisions made by a person in adult life. But now, assume that the Blinder-Oaxaca decomposition shows that both education and job experience are rewarded differently for male and female workers. Then, the inequality of opportunity arising from labor market discrimination would actually depend on the inequality of circumstances—i.e., education—but also on efforts through the interaction between efforts and gender. In other words, the fact that a woman must make more effort to earn as much as a man with the same intrinsic productivity should be part of the inequality of observed opportunities.

Having said this, there remains the issue of the fundamental ambiguity of the distinction between efforts and circumstances. Are interruptions to job, labor force participation, and career caused by child rearing only the responsibility of women? Wasn't it society as a whole that constrained women's labor force participation and progressively relaxed that constraint under various economic and sociological pressures? These are difficult questions, which at the same time reveal the ambiguity of the very concept of gender-related inequality of opportunity and the measurement of it.[34] Under these conditions, it might be better to ignore the distinction between circumstances and effort and to make sure that we measure correctly the effect on the overall inequality of earnings of different personal characteristics, including job experience or part-time work, across gender, as well as the effect of differentiated rewards to these characteristics by the economic system.

To conclude these remarks on the measurement of the inequality of opportunity related to gender, the fact that the earnings gap or adjusted earnings gap refers exclusively to averaging operations within the two samples of male and female workers must be stressed. The fact that the spread of earnings rates around the mean may be quite different in the two groups should also be taken into account. In relation to model (11), this is equivalent to allowing for the variance of the residual term, v, to depend itself on gender, i.e., heteroscedasticity. This is a good case for using the Roemer measure defined in (8), or to follow the suggestion made above to replace the mean earnings by some function of the mean and the variance.

Overview of Practical Issues

Measuring inequality of opportunity, seen as the inequality of outcomes due to *all* factors completely outside individual control, seems unrealistic. The best that can be done is to measure the contribution to inequality of outcomes of *some* factors that seem beyond individual responsibility. In that sense, it is only possible to measure some dimensions of the inequality of opportunity. Yet even the distinction between circumstances outside individual control and voluntary individual decisions in the determination of economic outcomes is often ambiguous. Indeed, some dimensions of inequality of opportunity depend on these individual decisions, as is the case with discrimination within the labor market.

It is possible to measure directly some dimensions of inequality of opportunity, independently of their impact on economic outcomes. This is true, for instance, of cognitive ability, in adolescence or pre-school, potentially of noncognitive ability if some quantitative index is available,[35] or of health status. Note also that these individual characteristics may be considered as circumstances contributing to the inequality of individual outcomes like earnings or standard of living, but also as an outcome whose inequality may be explained by family-related characteristics. Most often, however, measuring the observable dimensions of the inequality of opportunity goes through the measurement of their impact on the inequality of economic outcomes.

The most obvious example of the measure of single dimensions of inequality of opportunity is the sizable literature on the inter-generational mobility of earnings, or other economic or socio-economic outcomes. The observed dimension of inequality of opportunity is the earnings of parents, and it is measured by its contribution to the inequality of children's earnings. This can be generalized to other observed family characteristics that may or may not include parental income or earnings, as well as personal traits like gender or ethnicity. Data requirements for this kind of analysis are much less demanding than what is needed for measuring the inter-generational mobility of earnings. Representative household surveys with recall information on the family background of respondents are the basic input. Of course, monitoring the corresponding dimensions of the inequality of opportunity over time or making comparisons across countries requires some uniformity of the information available in these surveys.

When applied to single personal traits, the preceding type of analysis is equivalent to measuring what is called "horizontal inequality" in the inequality literature, typically inequality of earnings or other income variable across gender, race, migrant status, or other individual characteristics. Combined with other individual circumstances that may depend themselves on individual traits, the measurement of these dimensions of inequality of opportunity allows for a detailed analysis of the observed discrimination that society exerts on individuals through the traits being studied.

The empirical literature on inequality of opportunity relies on various types of measures. When focusing on single scalar dimensions of the inequality of opportunity, it is not clear that the various measures available for economic outcomes—which are implicitly based on value judgments—are relevant. For instance, is the Gini coefficient adequate to represent the inequality of health status or cognitive ability? The variance, the coefficient of variation or quantile ratios may be sufficient to describe the spread of the distribution. Things are different when the observed dimensions of inequality of opportunity are measured in the outcome space, or by their contribution to the inequality of outcomes. In that case, a distinction must be made between parametric and nonparametric approaches.

A parametric specification of the relationship between outcomes and individual characteristics allows us to figure out what the inequality would be if only outcome differences due to individual characteristics were taken into account; or, alternatively, what difference ignoring them would make with respect to the overall inequality of outcomes. Then the resulting "virtual" outcome inequality can be evaluated by the usual measures of outcome inequality, including the Gini coefficient, the variance of logarithms, and the Atkinson measures. Based on the familiar log-linear relationship between economic outcomes and individual characteristics, this approach often leads to quite simple measures of the observed dimensions of the inequality of opportunity: the R^2 correlation coefficient when outcome inequality is measured with the variance of logarithms; the between-group component of decomposable inequality measures when the observed combinations of individual characteristics are used to define types of individuals; or the mean income gap in the case of a single individual trait like gender. Of course, as many measures of inequality of opportunity can be defined as there are measures of inequality of outcomes.

Things are different with nonparametric specifications that fully take into account the difference in the distribution of outcomes conditional on individual type. This includes the case where types correspond to the level of parental income as the dimension of the inequality of opportunity being studied, and where the inter-generational mobility of outcomes is described through a transition matrix; in these cases, comparing distributions requires comparing those matrices. Some interesting comparison criteria have been proposed that generally rely on strong assumptions about the way the social welfare of a society characterized by a given transition matrix is evaluated. At this stage, it cannot be said there is a consensus about these criteria.

The case where the overall inequality of outcomes is shown to result from different outcome distributions across various types of people, defined by a set of characteristics assumed to be outside their control, is the most general and realistic specification on which to ground the measurement of the observed dimensions of inequality of opportunity. It is equivalent to the parametric specification when the distribution of the effects of unobserved determinants of outcomes depends on the individual characteristics under study, i.e., heteroscedasticity in the core specification. Most measures used in the literature ignore this aspect of the measurement problem. For instance, the adjusted gender earnings gap ignores the fact that not only the mean but also the distribution of earnings expressed as a proportion of the mean differs across gender. The inequality measure drawn from Roemer (1998) would allow to remedy this.

Conclusions

Until now, concern about inequality focused mostly on inequality in key *outcomes* like earnings, gross or disposable income, standard of living, or wealth. Monitoring inequality of outcomes, or inequality *ex post*, is crucial to monitor social progress and redistribution instruments. Ideally, however, one would also want to monitor *ex ante* inequality, or inequality of opportunity, as it is a key determinant of *ex post* inequality. As argued throughout this chapter, however, there is something illusory in such an objective. The best that can be done is to monitor the observed dimensions of inequality of opportunity, or equivalently some determinants of inequality of outcomes that can be considered not to be the result of individual decisions or economic behaviors. Of course, such monitoring is of utmost importance for policy as it permits the sources of change in the distribution of the outcome considered to be identified and to adopt corrective policies if deemed necessary. These sources of change comprise the distribution in the population of individual characteristics like individual traits, family background including parental income or wealth, cognitive and noncognitive abilities, and all assets people can rely on to generate economic outcomes. They also include the way in which the economic sphere rewards the efforts of people with different traits or background, i.e., procedural inequality.

While some observed dimensions of the inequality of opportunity have received much attention in the recent economic literature, it is fair to say that their measurement still belongs to the realm of research. Unlike the inequality of disposable income or earnings regularly monitored through Gini coefficients or other inequality measures, few statistics related to inequality of opportunity are regularly produced by statistical institutes and publicly debated. For instance, we are ignorant in most countries about whether inter-generational mobility, one among many possible indicators of inequality of opportunity, has increased, remained the same, or decreased in the last decades. Progress has been made in monitoring mean educational achievements in many countries, most notably under the PISA initiative, but no systematic reporting or discussion takes place on the evolution of their dispersion. If the mean earnings gap across gender is reported regularly in most advanced economies, the same cannot always be said of the adjusted earnings gap or the gap across ethnic groups or between natives and first- and second-generation migrants. Yet, in most countries, data to evaluate these indicators on a regular basis either are available or could be made available at little cost.

Building off the analysis in this chapter, we list below the data required to improve the situation and monitor the observable dimensions of the inequality of opportunity in a systematic way rather than relying on the work done irregularly by researchers. We also list the statistics that should be published on a regular basis for a monitoring of inequality that would go beyond the Gini coefficient or other usual inequality measures of equivalized disposable income or earnings.

Data Requirements

Knowledge of the role that family background plays in determining inequality of earnings or income is essential for understanding the causes of inequality and possible changes in them. From that point of view, the ideal data by far are long-term panels such as the PSID in the United States, which has been running since 1968 and covers 5,000 families and all their descendants. With such long panels, one may observe many of the circumstances that surrounded the childhood and the adolescence of the younger cohorts of the panel, including parental income and wealth. Other long panels include the British Household Panel Study (BHPS) and the German Socio-Economic Panel. In Europe, the EU-SILC comprises longitudinal data but these are generally much shorter and do not follow descendants, so that family economic conditions during the youth of respondents are not observable.[36]

An alternative to long panels is the linkage of administrative data. Matching the tax returns of parents 30 years ago to that of their 40-year-old children today allows for the direct observation of income mobility. In some cases, it is even possible to link family characteristics other than income, thus allowing for more complete studies of the inter-generational sources of inequality. As established above, such data permitted detailed studies of the inter-generational transmission of wealth in Nordic countries and of the spatial heterogeneity of inter-generational mobility in the United States—as in Chetty et al. (2014a). Unfortunately, data such as these are still extremely scarce, even though steps could be taken by administrations to make them more systematically available in the future.

It is not because long panels are not always available that it is impossible to monitor the role of family background in generating inequality in economic outcomes. Repeated standard cross-sectional household or labor force surveys with recall information on the family characteristics of the respondents already allow for monitoring the impact of family background on the inequality of earnings, income, or standard of living. What is needed is to make sure that such information is available at regular time intervals and under the same, and possibly the most complete, format. It should not be too difficult to establish international norms in this area. Possible biases arising from the imperfect observation of top incomes in these data sources should not be ignored, and measures to prevent such biases should be seriously considered.

Some of the studies reviewed in this chapter show the use that could be made of such information (Figure 5.5). Note also that in a given cross-section, it is possible to conduct the analysis at the cohort level. The way the earnings of the 40- to 50-year-old depend at a given point of time on their family background is not the same as for the 30- to 40-year-old or the 50- to 60-year-old. With repeated cross-sections, it would then become possible to distinguish the cohort and the age effect. Finally, note that if the repeated cross-sections cover a long enough period, which is now the case in many advanced countries, then it is possible to use family background variables as instruments to estimate the earnings or income of parents, thus allowing for some monitoring of inter-generational income mobility, as in the study by Aaronsson and Mazumder (2008) mentioned earlier.

In the field of the inequality of wealth, cross-sectional data are scarcer, although several countries are now following the example of the Survey of Consumer Finances in the United States and its practice of oversampling the top of the distribution, where most wealth is concentrated. These surveys are extremely useful and one may only hope they will become more frequent. In particular, it would be interesting to investigate in more depth how it would be possible to monitor the role of bequests in generating wealth and income inequality, especially at a time where inheritance flows tend to grow faster than income, as suggested by Piketty (2014).

Horizontal inequality across gender and other personal traits can be followed through standard household or labor-force surveys. Here, the problem is not so much the availability of data as the use being made of them and the depth of the analysis conducted. As shown above, there is much to be learned from going beyond pure differences in earnings means. At a time where migration has become such an important issue in so many countries, data for monitoring the differences that natives and migrants face in the labor market should also be made available.

Students' skills surveys at various stages in childhood and adolescence, such as those assessed by PISA, are extremely helpful for detecting changes in a dimension of inequality of opportunity that is likely to entail changes in the inequality of outcomes later in life. PISA is a mine of information, although it was suggested above that more emphasis should be put on the inequality of test scores—on top of their differences across family backgrounds. Also, developing PISA-type instruments to measure inequality in cognitive abilities at younger age levels, including pre-school, is essential. For primary school, the data seem to exist, and it is perhaps only a matter of analyzing them in more detail, and certainly publicizing them better.

Priority Statistics

These data could and probably will generate many different types of statistics, related to various specific dimensions of the inequality of opportunity. It is important to define those that are likely to be the most useful in assessing social and economic progress, the most amenable to stimulating discussion among researchers, policy-makers, and civil society, and the most likely to be available in a timely manner in a reasonably large number of countries.

The lack of knowledge today in many countries of whether inter-generational mobility is increasing or decreasing is symptomatic of the data deficit and, until now, of the lack of interest by policy-makers and statisticians in monitoring key sources of outcome inequality beyond inequality itself as measured by the usual inequality indices. Yet the social demand for such information is mounting.

Three basic statistics should receive priority attention and should be harmonized as much as possible across countries and over time within countries:

- *Inequality of economic outcomes (earnings, income) arising from parental background* and its share in total inequality of outcome. Variance of logarithms of outcomes among various types of individuals and the R^2 statistics of family background variables (at least education, occupation, and age of the parents at respondent's birth) in explaining outcomes are the simplest examples of such statistics. Statistical institutes could seek to publish these statistics at 5-year intervals, possibly distinguishing across 5-year cohorts. Reflection should start about the key family background variables that could be systematically included in the analysis so as to develop international and inter-temporal comparability.
- *Variance analysis of scores in PISA and analogous surveys at earlier ages*, including pre-school, and the share of it explained by parental/social background, or the gaps in scores between students from different families. The 3-year periodicity of PISA seems adequate.
- *Gender inequality in earnings, unadjusted and adjusted for differences in education, age, job experience, occupation, etc.* Mentioning gender differences explicitly in basic coefficients like the return to education or to job experience, or simply showing both the unadjusted and the adjusted gaps as in Figure 5.7 would be helpful. This could be done easily for gender,

although this again requires defining standards to allow for comparability. Depending on the country, the same type of analysis should also be performed for race, religion, or migrant status.

Concerning the nature of the statistics to be released, the simplest option would be to rely on the parametric approach emphasized in this chapter and on the measures it leads to, as they are easily understood. But extending them to the nonparametric case, where the observed dimensions of the inequality of opportunity are represented in matrix form of individual types by outcome level, would also be desirable.

Annex: The Difficulty of Empirically Disentangling the Role of Opportunity and Effort in the Determination of Earnings

Consider a database with information on individual earnings, circumstances, and efforts and a linear model where (log) earnings of individual i, $Log\ y_i$, depends on the circumstances, C_i, and efforts, E_i, of the same person, both vectors being split into observed (C_{i1}, E_{i1}) and unobserved (C_{i2}, E_{i2}) components:

$$Log\ y_i = a + b_1 C_{i1} + b_2 C_{i2} + c_1 E_{i1} + c_2 E_{i2} + u_i \qquad (1)$$

where u_i summarizes all the other determinants of earnings, including luck and measurement error, and where a, b, and c are parameters, or vectors of parameters.

While a specification with interactions between circumstances and efforts would be more general, the points made below would be equally relevant with a more complete model—but a bit more intricate from a notational point of view.

Rearranging the terms in the preceding equation leads to:

$$Log\ y_i = a + b_1 C_{i1} + c_1 E_{i1} + \varepsilon_i \quad with \quad \varepsilon_i = b_2 C_{i2} + c_2 E_{i2} + u_i \qquad (2)$$

Where, without loss of generality, the residual terms, E_i, may be assumed to have zero expected value for each observation in the sample.

The objective is to estimate the two sets of coefficients b_1 and c_1 so as to disentangle the role of observed circumstances and efforts in observed earnings. To do so with standard Ordinary Least Squares would require the residual, ε, to be independent of the explanatory variables C_1 and E_1. This is problematic, however. Indeed, it is to be expected that the efforts expended by people to increase their earnings depend on the circumstances they face. This can be formalized as:

$$E_{i1} + \alpha_1 + \beta_{11} C_{i1} + \beta_{12} C_{i2} + \theta_{i1} \qquad (3)$$

$$E_{i2} + \alpha_2 + \beta_{21} C_{i1} + \beta_{22} C_{i2} + \theta_{i2} \qquad (4)$$

where θ_{i1} and θ_{i2} stand for other determinants of efforts, presumably independent of circumstances, but possibly mutually correlated. Substituting (3)-(4) into (2), it appears that ε_i is correlated to observed circumstances C_{i1} and observed efforts E_{i1} through unobserved circumstances and efforts, even when both are assumed to be orthogonal to their observed counterparts.

It follows that equation (2) cannot be estimated without a bias, and that disentangling the role of efforts and circumstances in the determination of earnings is generally impossible.[37]

This may not prevent estimating the *total effect* of observed circumstances on earnings. Substituting (3) and (4) in (2), gives:

$$Log\ y_i = \delta + \gamma . C_{i1} + \omega_i \qquad (5)$$

with:

$$\delta = a + c_1 . \alpha_1 + c_2 . \alpha_2; \gamma = (b_1 + c_1 . \beta_{11} + c_1 . \beta_{21}); \omega_i = (b_2 + c_1 \beta_{12}) . C_{i2} + c_2 E_{i2} + u_i + c_1 \theta_{i1}$$

For the residual term, ω_i, in (5), to be independent of the observed circumstance variables in C_1 it must be assumed that the unobserved circumstances and efforts E_2 and C_2 are orthogonal to observed circumstances. If this is not the case, this means that the coefficient γ in (5) accounts not only for the effects of observed circumstances, both directly and through efforts, but also for that part of unobserved circumstances and efforts correlated to observed circumstances.

Practically, parametric empirical analyses of inequality of opportunity are based on a model of type (5). This lessens the relevance of some of the theoretical measures of inequality of opportunity proposed in the literature, and justifies focusing on measures that can be derived from the reduced form (5) as shown in the main text.

Notes

1. This paragraph briefly summarizes an important literature in economics and in moral philosophy, which started with Rawls (1971) and whose major contributions are from Dworkin (1981), Arneson (1989), Cohen (1989), Roemer (1998), and Fleurbaey and Maniquet (2011).

2. This conclusion somewhat resembles Sen's emphasis on the "equality of capabilities" rather than "equality of functionings," at least when capabilities are defined as the set of functionings accessible to an individual (Sen, 1980, 1985). Interpreting functionings as a vector of outcomes, Sen's "capability equality" concept, similar to the concept of "equality of access to advantage" in Cohen (1989), would consist of equalizing the determinants of the set of accessible functionings, which are conceptually very similar to "circumstances" in the "equality of opportunity" framework. The only difference is that equalization in that case would be through equalizing those circumstances rather than compensation in the space of outcomes.

3. The debate in the sociological literature about the idea that people raised in a low socio-economic status environment may inherit low preferences for work effort illustrates that point. See a summary of that discussion in Piketty (1998).

4. A rigorous econometric analysis of this issue is provided in the annex at the end of this chapter.

5. The notation used for this equation is different from the one used in the annex at the end of this chapter.

6. Schooling being considered as a "circumstance," mostly determined by parental background.

7. Both sources of inequality are analyzed in detail below.

8. Thus, without loss of generality, v_e can be set to zero, its sample mean value, when (2) is estimated by Ordinary Least Squares.

9. With enough observations for each type, the two means differ by a factor that depends on the inequality of unobserved outcome determinants within the type.

10. Roemer justifies comparing outcomes across types for given quantiles by considering that individuals of different types (but in the same quantile of their own outcome distribution) expend the same efforts. The above formula does not appear in Roemer (1998) but it ensues logically from the specification of his objective function in the design of policies to minimize inequality of opportunities. Note also that $Min_t\{q_t(\pi)\}$ in (8) could be replaced by any standard outcome inequality measure across types.

11. This dependency of PISA scores on family background has been studied in detail by the OECD (2016) in an analysis where cognitive ability is precisely taken as an outcome rather than a circumstance.

12. Ferreira and Gignoux (2011a) analyze carefully this source of bias in a cross-country comparison.

13. The standard deviation in test scores being 7, this means that test scores at the end of high school may be responsible for earnings differentials of close to 30%.

14. See for instance the survey by Conti and Heckman (2012).

15. An interesting paper shows, for instance, the influence of in utero factors on adult earnings: see Almond, Mazumder, and Van Ewijk (2015).

16. Parameter notations differ from those used above or in the annex at the end of this chapter.

17. Note that this is true only for the variance of logarithm as an inequality measure.

18. When brackets are deciles (or other quantiles) of the distribution of earnings of parents for rows and of sons for columns, the transition matrix is bi-stochastic, with the sum of columns and rows being equal to 0.1 in the case of decile (and of 0.05 in the case of vintile, etc.). This mobility matrix is a representation of the copula of the joint distribution of father/children earnings defined above.

19. Sociologists, who are used to working with socio-economic classes rather than earnings or income, tend to emphasize "absolute" mobility, i.e., moving from one rung of the social ladder to another. Economists traditionally tend to work with "relative" mobility—although see the analysis of absolute earnings mobility in Chetty et al. (2017).

20. Note that this approach would also apply to the case where the parametric outcome model (2) is heteroskedastic, as discussed above.

21. See, for instance, Jäntti and Jenkins (2015, pp. 899–905) for examples drawn from the US literature.

22. Björklund and Jäntti (1997) apply this technique to compare mobility in Sweden and in the United States, whereas Aaronson and Mazumder (2008) do so to compare earnings mobility in the United States over time.

23. The argument is as follows: Let y in (9) depend linearly on [need eq.] for observation i, e.g., $y_i = y_0 + y_1 y_{-1,i}$, with $y_1 > 0$. Taking the means on both sides of (9), the average IGE for the whole population is then given by: $\bar{y} = y_0 + y_1 \frac{1}{n} \sum_i y_{-1,i}^2 / \bar{y}_{-1}$ where n is the size of the sample and $\bar{y}_{-1}$ the mean of parents' income. For a given mean parent income, the mean IGE in the sample thus increases with the variance, or more generally with the inequality of parents' income. Note however that the Gatsby curve refers to the inequality of household income at the time children's earnings are observed.

24. See also Chetty et al. (2014a), Figure 1b.

25. It is indeed unlikely that the change in inequality across generations could compensate for the differences in IGE.

26. Aaronsson and Mazumder (2008) use the TSIV method sketched above with US census data.

27. For instance, Bourguignon, Ferreira, and Menendez (2007) use the relative version of (7) with the Gini coefficient for the inequality measure $M\{\ \}$ and the mean of Z for the reference circumstance $C^{\ e}$ in (6). Brunori, Ferreira, and Peragine (2013) use the mean logarithmic deviation.

28. The mean logarithmic deviation (MLD) in a sample of individuals with economic outcome y_i is simply the difference between the log of the mean of the y's and the mean of the $\log y$'s. For some countries in Figure 5.5, a semi-parametric model is used, based on "types" of individuals, as defined by specific combinations of characteristics Z, rather than by these characteristics themselves.

29. It is the case that the relative inequality of observed opportunities based on the mean logarithmic deviation is close to the R^2 of the regression of outcomes on observed opportunities. From (9), this implies that the square root of that measure is comparable to the IGE.

30. This uniformity in the European case comes from being based on a common data source, the EU-SILC, which is roughly uniform across EU members. See Checchi, Peragine, and Serlenga (2010).

31. Such an analysis by cohorts is performed in Bourguignon, Ferreira, and Menendez (2007).

32. Essentially, homoscedasticity in a model of type (11).

33. Other expressions of the Blinder-Oaxaca decomposition use the β coefficients of one group in the first term and the mean characteristics of the other in the second rather than means over the two groups. The problem is that the decomposition then depends on what group is chosen for β. The formulation used here is path independent.

34. Additional difficulties would appear if, instead of focusing on wages, gender inequality focused on income, or more exactly household income (per capita or equivalized), as labor supply, marriage, assortative mating, and fertility would become important issues, on top of the fact that the distribution of income within the household is not directly observed (on these issues, see Meurs and Ponthieux, 2015).

35. For instance, through principal component analysis of answers to questions on non-cognitive ability in PISA.

36. In connection with EU-SILC, it should be noted that shorter panels may still be helpful in analyzing the inequality arising from involuntary shocks experienced by individuals in their recent past, which may be the main source of inequality of opportunity

appearing during adult life. In particular, such data should help to evaluate the hysteresis of such events and the role of social policies in neutralizing their long-run effects.

37. Bourguignon, Ferreira, and Menendez (2007, 2013) tried to find bounds on the b_1 and c_1 coefficients, but they proved to be too large to be of any use in identifying the inequality of opportunity conditional on efforts.

References

Aaronson, D. and B. Mazumder (2008), "Intergencrational mobility in the United States: 1940 to 2000," *Journal of Human Resources*, Vol. 43(1), pp. 139–172.

Adermon, A., M. Lindahl, and D. Waldenström (2015), "Intergenerational wealth mobility and the role of inheritance: Evidence from multiple generations," *IZA Discussion Paper*, No. 10126.

Almond, D., B. Mazumder, and R. van Ewijk (2015), "*In utero* Ramadan exposure and children's academic performance," with Almond, D. and R. van Ewijk, *Economic Journal*, Vol. 125, pp. 1501–1533.

Arneson, R. (1989), "Equality and equal opportunity for welfare," *Philosophical Studies*, Vol. 56(1), pp. 77–93.

Atkinson, A.B. (1981), "The measurement of economic mobility," in Eijgelshoven, P.J. and L.J. van Gemerden (eds.), *Inkomensverdeling en Openbare Financien*, Het Spectrum, Utrecht.

Atkinson, A.B. (1970), "On the measurement of economic inequality," *Journal of Economic Theory*, Vol. 2, pp. 244–263.

Atkinson , A.B. and F. Bourguignon (1982), "The comparison of multi-dimensioned distribution of economic status," *Review of Economic Studies*, Vol. 49, pp. 183–201.

Berman, Y. (2016), "The Great Gatsby curve revisited—Understanding the relationship between inequality and intergenerational mobility," Mimeo, School of Physics and Astronomy, Tel-Aviv University, Tel-Aviv, Israel.

Björklund, A. and M. Jäntti (1997), "Intergenerational income mobility in Sweden compared to the United States," *American Economic Review*, Vol. 87(5), pp. 1009–1018

Blanden, J. et al. (2011), "Changes in intergenerational mobility in Britain," in Corak, M. (ed.), *Generational Income Mobility in the United States and in Europe*, Cambridge University Press, Cambridge, pp. 122–146.

Boserup, S.H., W. Kopczuk, and C. Thustrup Kreiner (2014), "Intergenerational wealth mobility: Evidence from Danish wealth records of three generations," working paper, University of Copenhagen.

Bourguignon, F., F. Ferreira, and M. Menendez (2007), "Inequality of opportunity in Brazil," *Review of Income Wealth*, Vol. 53(4), pp. 585–618.

Bourguignon, F., F. Ferreira, and M. Menendez (2013), "Inequality of opportunity in Brazil: A corrigendum," *Review of Income Wealth*, Vol. 59(3), pp. 551–555.

Brunori, P. (2016), "How to measure inequality of opportunity: A hands-on guide," Working Paper No. 2016-04, Life Course Centre, University of Queensland, Australia.

Brunori, P., F. Ferreira, and V. Peragine (2013), "Inequality of opportunity, income inequality and economic mobility: Some international comparisons," *IZA Discussion Paper*, No. 7155.

Charles, K.K. and E. Hurst (2003), "The correlation of wealth across generations," *Journal of Political Economy*, Vol. 111(6), pp. 1155–1182.

Checchi, D., V. Peragine, and L. Serlenga (2010), "Fair and unfair income inequalities in Europe," *ECINEQ Working Paper*, No. 174-2010.

Chetty, R. et al. (2017), "The fading American dream: Trends in absolute income mobility since 1940," *NBER Working Paper*, No. 22910 (shortened version published in *Science*, Vol. 356(6336), pp. 398–406.

Chetty, R. et al. (2014a), "Where is the land of opportunity? The geography of intergenerational mobility in the United States," *Quarterly Journal of Economics*, Vol. 129(4), pp. 1553–1623.

Chetty, R. et al. (2014b), "Is the United States still a land of opportunity? Recent trends in intergenerational mobility," *American Economic Review*, Vol. 104(5), pp. 141–147.

Cohen, G.A. (1989), "On the currency of egalitarian justice," *Ethics*, Vol. 99(4), pp. 906–944.

Conti, G. and J. Heckman (2012), "The economics of child well-being," *IZA Discussion Paper*, No. 6930.

Corak, M. (2013), "Income inequality, equality of opportunity, and intergenerational mobility," *Journal of Economic Perspectives*, Vol. 27(3), pp. 79–102.

Corak, M. (2012), "Here is the source for the Great Gatsby Curve," in the Alan B. Krueger speech at the Center for American Progress on January 12, https://milescorak.com/2012/01/12/here-is-the-source-for-the-great-gatsby-curve-in-the-alan-krueger-speech-at-the-center-for-american-progress/.

Currie, J. (2009), "Healthy, wealthy, and wise: Socioeconomic status, poor health in childhood, and human capital development," *Journal of the Economic Literature*, Vol. 47(1), pp. 87–122.

Decancq, K., M. Fleurbaey, and E. Schokkaert (2015), "Inequality, income and well-being," in Atkinson, A.B. and F. Bourguignon (eds.), *Handbook of Income Distribution*, Vol. 2, pp. 67–140, Elsevier, North-Holland, Amsterdam.

Dworkin, R. (1981), "What is equality, Part 1," *Philosophy and Public Affairs*, Vol. 10(3), pp. 185–246.

Dworkin, R. (1981), "What is equality, Part 2," *Philosophy and Public Affairs*, Vol. 10(4), pp. 283–345.

Ferreira, F.H.G. and J. Gignoux (2011a), "The measurement of educational inequality: Achievement and opportunity," *IZA Discussion Paper*, No. 6161.

Ferreira, F.H.G. and J. Gignoux (2011b), "The measurement of inequality of opportunity: Theory and an application to Latin America," *Review of Income and Wealth*, Vol. 57(4), pp. 622–657.

Fields, G. and E. Ok (1999), "The measurement of income mobility: An introduction to the literature," in Silber J. (ed.), *Handbook of Income Inequality Measurement. Series on Recent Economic Thought*, Vol. 71, Kluwer Academic Publishers, Boston, pp. 557–598.

Fleurbaey, M. and E. Schokkaert (2012), "Equity in health and health care," in Barros, P., T. McGuire, and M. Pauly (eds.), *Handbook of Health Economics*, Vol. 2, Elsevier, North-Holland, Amsterdam, pp. 1003–1092.

Fleurbaey, M. and F. Maniquet (2011), "Compensation and responsibility," in Arrow, K.J., A.K. Sen, and K. Suzumura (eds.), *Handbook of Social Choice and Welfare*, Vol. 2, Elsevier, North-Holland, Amsterdam, pp. 507–604.

Galton, F. (1886), "Regression towards mediocrity in hereditary stature," *Journal of the Anthropological Institute of Great Britain and Ireland*, Vol. 15, pp. 246–263.

Goldthorpe, J. (2012), "Understanding—and misunderstanding—social mobility in Britain: The entry of the economists, the confusion of politicians and the limits of educational policy," *Barnett Papers in Social Research*, No. 2/2012, University of Oxford.

Jäntti, M. and S. Jenkins (2015), "Income mobility," in Atkinson, A. and F. Bourguignon (eds.), *Handbook of Income Distribution*, Vol. 2, Elsevier, North-Holland, Amsterdam, pp. 807–935.

Jäntti, M. et al. (2002), "Brother correlations in earnings in Denmark, Finland, Norway and Sweden compared to the United States," *Journal of Population Economics*, Vol. 15(4), pp. 757–772.

Kanbur, R. and J. Stiglitz (2015), "Dynastic inequality, mobility and equality of opportunity," *CEPR Discussion Paper*, No. 10542.

Kautz, T. et al. (2014), "Fostering and measuring skills: Improving cognitive and moncognitive skills to promote lifetime success," *OECD Education Working Papers*, No. 110, OECD Publishing, Paris, http://dx.doi.org/10.1787/jxsr7vr78f7-en.

Landersø R. and J.J. Heckman (2016), "The Scandinavian fantasy: The sources of intergenerational mobility in Denmark and the US," Center for the Economics of Human Development, University of Chicago.

Lee, C.-I. and G. Solon (2009), "Trends in intergenerational income mobility," *Review of Economics and Statistics*, Vol. 91, pp. 766–772.

Lefranc, A., N. Pistolesi, and A. Trannoy (2009), "Equality of opportunity and luck: Definitions and testable conditions, with an application to income in France," *Journal of Public Economics*, Vol. 93, pp. 1189–1207.

Levin, H. (2012), "More than just test scores," *Prospects*, Vol. 42(3), pp. 269–284, https://doi.org/10.1007/s11125-012-9240-z.

Mazumder, B. (2008), "Sibling similarities and economic inequality in the US," *Journal of Population Economics*, Vol. 21(3), pp. 685–701.

Meurs, D. and S. Ponthieux (2015), "Gender inequality," in Atkinson, A.B. and F. Bourguignon (eds.), *Handbook of Income Distribution*, Vol. 2, Elsevier, North-Holland, Amsterdam, pp. 981–1146.

Murnane, R. et al. (2000), "How important are the cognitive skills of teenagers in predicting subsequent earnings?," *Journal of Policy Analysis and Management*, Vol. 19(4), pp. 547–568.

OECD (2018), *OECD Earnings: Gross Earnings: Decile Ratios* (database), https://doi.org/10.1787/lfs-data-en.

OECD (2016), *PISA 2015 Results: Policies and Practices for Successful Schools (Vol. II)*, PISA, OECD Publishing, Paris, https://doi.org/10.1787/9789264267510-en.

OECD (2014), *PISA 2012 Results: What Students Know and Can Do (Vol. I, Revised Edition, February): Student Performance in Mathematics, Reading and Science*, PISA, OECD Publishing, Paris, http://dx.doi.org/10.1787/-en.

OECD (2013), *PISA 2012 Results: Excellence Through Equity (Vol. II): Giving Every Student the Chance to Succeed*, PISA, OECD Publishing, Paris, http://dx.doi.org/10.1787/-en.

Piketty, T. (2014), *Capital in the 21st Century*, Harvard University Press, Cambridge, MA.

Piketty, T. (1998), "Self-fulfilling beliefs about social status," *Journal of Public Economics*, Vol. 70, pp. 115–132.

Ramos, X. and D. van de Gaer (2012), "Empirical approaches to inequality of opportunity: Principles, measures, and evidence," *IZA Discussion Paper*, No. 6672.

Rawls, J. (1971), *A Theory of Justice*, Harvard University Press, Cambridge, MA.

Roemer, J. (1998), *Equality of Opportunity*, Harvard University Press, Cambridge, MA.

Roemer, J. and A. Trannoy (2015), "Equality of opportunity," in Atkinson, A.B. and F. Bourguignon (eds.), *Handbook of Income Distribution*, Vol. 2, Elsevier, North-Holland, Amsterdam, pp. 217–296.

Sen, A. (1985), *Commodities and Capabilities*, Elsevier, North-Holland, Amsterdam.

Sen, A. (1980), "Equality of what?," in McMurrin, S. (ed.), *Tanner Lectures on Human Values*, Vol. 1, Cambridge University Press, Cambridge.

Shorrocks, A. (1978), "The measurement of mobility," *Econometrica*, Vol. 46(5), pp. 1013–1024.

Van de Gaer, D. (1993), "Equality of opportunity and investment in human capital," PhD thesis, K.U. Leuven, Belgium.

Weichselbaumer, D. and R. Winter-Ebmer (2005), "A meta-analysis of the international gender wage gap," *Journal of Economic Surveys*, Vol. 19(3), pp. 479–511.

Wolff, E. (2015), *Inheriting Wealth in America: Future Boom or Bust*, Oxford University Press, New York.

6.

Distributional National Accounts

Facundo Alvaredo, Lucas Chancel, Thomas Piketty, Emmanuel Saez, and Gabriel Zucman

This chapter summarizes the concepts, methods, and goals of the WID.world project, the World Inequality Database, along with some first results from this source. WID.world builds on the experience of the World Top Incomes Database (WTID) to construct time series on the concentration of income at the very top of the distribution in more than 30 countries, to include wealth distribution and developing as well as developed countries. The ultimate goal of WID.world is to provide annual estimates of the distribution of income and wealth using concepts consistent with macro-economic accounts, i.e., to construct distributional national accounts (DINA). WID.world also aims to produce synthetic micro-files providing online information on income and wealth (i.e., individual-level data that do not result from direct observation but rather through estimates that reproduce the observed distribution of the underlying data). The long-run aim of the WID.world project is to release income and wealth synthetic DINA micro-files for all countries on an annual basis.

Facundo Alvaredo is Professor and Co-Director of WID.world at the Paris School of Economics and IIEP-UBA-Conicet, Lucas Chancel is Co-Director of WID.world at the Paris School of Economics and IDDRI, Thomas Piketty is Professor and Co-Director of WID.world at the Paris School of Economics, Emmanuel Saez is Professor and Co-Director of WID.world at University of California, Berkeley, and Gabriel Zucman is Professor and Co-Director of WID.world at the University of California, Berkeley. This chapter summarizes the recent work behind the WID.world project. In particular, we refer the reader to the following papers: Alvaredo et al., 2016; Piketty, Saez, and Zucman, 2016; Saez and Zucman, 2016; Garbinti, Goupille-Lebret, and Piketty, 2016, 2017; Piketty, Yang, and Zucman, 2017; Alvaredo, Atkinson, and Morelli, 2017, 2018; and Alvaredo et al., 2017. For the helpful discussions at the various meetings and seminars that took place since January 2014, we would also like to thank the members of the High-Level Expert Group on the Measurement of Economic Performance and Social Progress, as well as Marco Mira D'Ercole, Martine Durand, Jorrit Zwijnenburg, Peter Van de Ven (all from the OECD Statistics and Data Directorate), and participants at the HLEG Workshop on Measuring Inequalities of Income and Wealth (Berlin, September 2015). The opinions expressed and arguments employed in the contributions below are those of the authors and do not necessarily reflect the official views of the OECD or of the governments of its member countries.

Introduction

Renewed interest in the long-run evolution of the distribution of income and wealth has given rise to a flourishing literature over the past 15 years. In particular, by combining historical tax and national accounts data, a series of studies has constructed time series of the top income share for a large number of countries (see Piketty, 2001, 2003; Piketty and Saez, 2003; and the two multi-country volumes on top incomes edited by Atkinson and Piketty, 2007, 2010; see also Atkinson, Piketty, and Saez, 2011; and Alvaredo et al., 2013, for surveys of this literature). These projects generated a large volume of data, intended as a research resource for further analysis as well as a source to inform the public debate on income inequality. To a large extent, this literature has followed the pioneering work and methodology of Kuznets (1953) and Atkinson and Harrison (1978) on the long-run evolution of income and wealth distribution, extending it to many more countries and years.

The World Top Incomes Database, WTID (Alvaredo et al., 2011–2015), was created in January 2011 to provide convenient and free access to all the existing time series generated by this stream of work. Thanks to the contributions of over a hundred researchers, the WTID expanded to include time series on income concentration for more than 30 countries, spanning most of the 20th and the early 21st centuries, and, in some cases, going back to the 19th century. The key innovation of this research has been to exploit tax, survey, and national accounts data in a systematic manner. This has permitted the estimation of longer and more reliable time series on the top income shares than previous inequality databases (which generally rely on self-reported survey data, with usually large under-coverage and under-reporting problems at the top, and limited time span). These new series had a large impact on the discussion on global inequality. In particular, by making it possible to compare the shares captured by top income groups (e.g., the top 1%) over long periods of time and across countries, they contributed to reveal new facts and refocus the discussion on rising inequality.

In December 2015 the WTID was subsumed into WID.world (the World Wealth and Income Database, renamed in 2017 the World Inequality Database). In addition to the WTID top income shares series, the first version of WID.world included an updated historical database on the long-run evolution of aggregate wealth-to-income ratios and on the changing structure of national wealth and national income first developed in Piketty and Zucman (2014).[1] The name changed from WTID to WID.world in order to reflect the extension in scope and ambition of the database, and the new emphasis on both wealth and income.

In January 2017 a new website was also launched (www.wid.world), with better data visualization tools and more extensive data coverage. The database is currently being extended into three main directions. First, the project aims to go beyond only covering developed countries to focus more on developing countries; in recent years, tax information has been released in a number of emerging economies, including China, Brazil, India, Mexico, and South Africa. Second, WID.world plans to provide more and updated series on wealth-to-income ratios and the distribution of wealth, and not only on income. Third, it aims to cover the entire distribution of income and wealth, and not only of top groups. The overall long-run objective is to produce Distributional National Accounts (DINA).

The development of economic statistics is a historical lengthy process that involves economic theory, the limits of available data, the construction of a body of conventions, and the agreement of the community of scholars. Macro-economic aggregates (GDP, national income) from the System of National Accounts (SNA) are the most widely used measures of economic activity. In the beginning, national accountants were also experts in distributional issues, as the inter-linkages between the estimation of national income and its distribution were clearly recognized. However, the focus of the SNA has so far always been on the main sectors in the economy, only distinguishing results for the household sector as a whole, and not providing insights into disparities within the household sector. Partly as a result of these developments, the discrepancies between income levels and growth rates displayed in national accounts and the ones displayed in micro-statistics and underlying distributional data have been growing in all dimensions: income, consumption, and wealth (see, for example, Deaton, 2005; Bourguignon, 2015; and Nolan, Roser, and Thewissen, 2016). Scholars have been clearly aware of the discrepancies, and also have some ideas to explain the reasons behind them, but systematic and coordinated action to put them in a consistent framework has started only recently.[2] In 2011, the OECD and Eurostat launched a joint Expert Group to carry out a feasibility study on compiling distributional measures of household income, consumption, and saving within the framework of national accounts, on the basis of micro-data. This group, which was followed up by the creation of an OECD Expert Group on Disparities in National Accounts (EG DNA) in 2014, aimed to systematically combine micro- and macro-results to arrive at more granular breakdowns of the household sector available from the national accounts (see sidebar, "The Work of the OECD Expert Group on Disparities in a National Accounts Framework" for more information). One reason why this work has only started recently is quite clear: it is not a simple task.

A renovated approach to the measurement of economic inequality consistent with macro-aggregates should rebuild the bridges between distributional data available from micro sources and national accounts aggregates in a systematic way.

This is the main goal of the WID.world project pursued through DINA. The aim is to provide annual estimates of the distribution of income and wealth using concepts that are consistent with the macro-economic national accounts. In this way, the analysis of growth and inequality can be carried over in a coherent framework. In addition, the WID.world project aims to also include the production of synthetic micro-files (i.e., individual-level data that are not necessarily the result of direct observation but rather through estimations that reproduce the observed distribution of the underlying data, including the joint distribution of age, gender, numbers of dependent children, income, and wealth between adult individuals), providing information on income and wealth, which will also be made available online. The long-run aim is to release income and wealth synthetic DINA micro-files for all countries on an annual basis. Such data could play a critical role in the public debate, and be used as a resource for further analysis by various actors in civil society and in the academic, business, and political communities.

THE WORK OF THE OECD EXPERT GROUP ON DISPARITIES IN A NATIONAL ACCOUNTS FRAMEWORK

In response to the increased interest in household material well-being and its distribution, the OECD and Eurostat launched an expert group in 2011 to carry out a feasibility study of compiling distributional measures of household income, consumption, and saving across household groups within the framework of the national accounts. A methodology was developed according to a step-by-step approach that assists countries in building the best conceptual link between the micro- and macro-data; closing any gaps between the micro-data and the national accounts totals; imputing for any items that may be lacking in micro-data sources; and linking data across sources to arrive at consistent sets of accounts for various household groups. This work was continued in 2014 by EG DNA to improve the methodology and to look into possibilities to improve the timeliness of the distributional results. OECD Member countries have engaged in two exercises to compile experimental distributional results, and some countries have already started to publish their estimates (Australia, the Netherlands, and the United Kingdom).

The EG DNA project has a lot of similarities with the DINA project, as both aim to compile distributional results in line with national accounts totals, and overcome any discrepancies between the micro- and the macro-totals. Where DINA is focusing on income and wealth, the OECD project initially focuses on income, consumption, and saving, planning to include wealth in the second phase, probably in cooperation with the European Central Bank and Eurostat. While there are similarities, the projects also differ in some respects. First of all, the aim of the EG DNA project is to arrive at breakdowns of the household sector from the national accounts at an aggregated level, focusing on specific household groups, e.g., classified by income quintile, main source of income, or household composition, whereas DINA also aims to produce synthetic micro-data files for income and wealth. Second, the two projects apply different income definitions in deriving distributional results: whereas DINA aims to align the results to national income, i.e., for the economy as a whole (distinguishing five income concepts), the EG DNA project specifically targets the income of the household sector, with primary income, disposable income, and adjusted disposable income as main aggregates. A third difference relates to the unit of observation: while the DINA project focuses on individuals aged 20 years and older, the EG DNA considers the income of households (under the assumption that income is fully shared and that consumption decisions are made within the household), using equivalence scales to adjust for differences in household size and composition. These two methodological differences may lead to differences in distributional results derived from both projects.

Since the start of the OECD project, member countries have engaged in two exercises compiling first sets of experimental distributional results. Figure 6.1 presents an example of results derived from the exercise conducted in 2015: it presents estimates of the S80/S20 ratio, comparing the income of households in the highest income quintile with that of households in the lowest quintile. On the basis of these results, income inequality turns out to be

Figure 6.1. Ratio of Household-Adjusted Disposable Income of Households in the Top and Bottom Income Quintiles

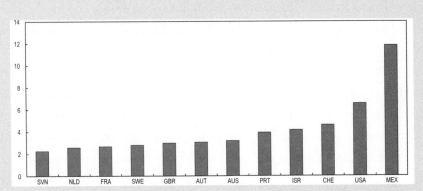

Note: Data refers to 2012 and 2011 for Australia, France, Netherlands, Portugal and Switzerland. *Source*: Zwijnenburg, J., S. Bournot, and F. Giovannelli (2017), "Expert group on disparities in a national accounts framework: Results from the 2015 exercise," *OECD Statistics Working Papers*, No. 2016/10, OECD Publishing, Paris, http://dx.doi.org/10.1787/daa921e-en. StatLink 2 http://dx.doi.org/10.1787/888933839696.

very high in Mexico, followed by the United States and Switzerland, whereas it is smallest in Slovenia, followed by the Netherlands, France, and Sweden. In addition to distributional results by income quintile, the experimental results also contain breakdowns into main source of income and household composition for a selection of countries, as well as information on the socio-demographic composition of the income quintiles.

While some countries have already started to publish distributional results according to EG DNA methodology, the OECD Expert Group is pursuing its work to improve the methodology to arrive at more robust and comparable results across a broader range of countries. In that perspective, the project faces similar challenges as the DINA, particularly in obtaining a better understanding of the reasons for gaps between micro-data and national accounts totals, gaps which for some items are very substantial; and in improving the methodology to impute for items for which micro-data are lacking. This should lead to a more robust methodology and to the publication of distributional results for a broader range of countries within the next couple of years.

Source: Text provided by Jorrit Zwijnenburg, OECD Statistics and Data Directorate.

It is worth stressing that the WID.world database has both a macro- and a micro-dimension. The objective is to release homogenous time series both on the macro-level structure of national income and national wealth, and on the micro-level distribution of income and wealth, using consistent concepts and methods. By doing so, we hope to contribute to reconciling inequality measurement and national accounting, i.e., the micro-level measurement of economic and social welfare and the macro-level measurement. In some cases, this may require revising central aspects of key national accounts concepts and estimates. By combining the macro- and micro-dimensions of economic measurement, we are following a very long tradition. In particular, it is worth recalling that Simon Kuznets was both one of the founders of US national accounts (and author of the first national income series), and the first scholar to combine national income series and income tax data in order to estimate the evolution of the share of total income going to top fractiles in the United States over 1913–48 (Kuznets, 1953).[3] This line of research continued with Atkinson and Harrison (1978), who made use of historical inheritance tax data and capital income data to study the long-run evolution of the distribution of personal wealth in Britain over 1922–72. We are simply pushing this effort further by trying to cover more countries and years, and by studying wealth and its distribution rather than only income.

Such an ambitious long-term objective—annual distributional national accounts for both income and wealth and for all countries in the world—will require a broad international and institutional partnership. The first set of methodological principles and recommendations are being set by ongoing work on the first version of the DINA Guidelines (Alvaredo et al., 2016). There are still many methodological decisions to be taken and agreed upon. It took from the 1910s to the 1950s before scholars (such as Kuznets, Kendrick, Dugé, Stone, Meade, and Frankel) could hand over the estimation of national income to official statistics bodies. It also took a long time (from the 1950s to the 2000s) before official national accounts were able to include standardized stock accounts. In fact, the first consistent guidelines for balance sheets—covering stocks of assets and liabilities—appear in the SNA manuals of 1995 and 2008 (in some key countries, such as Germany, the first official balance sheets were released only in 2010). Along the same lines, the development of a system of DINA is expected to take a long time before consensus among scholars and the statistical community is reached. In that regard, it is very encouraging that the OECD Expert Group on Disparities in National Accounts, which is working on compiling distributional results, has already engaged in two exercises, and that the first countries have already started to publish distributional results on the basis of the Expert Group's methodology (see sidebar).

We should stress at the outset that our methods and time series are imperfect, fragile, and subject to revision. The WID.world DINA project attempts to combine the different data sources that are available (in particular tax data, survey data, and national accounts) in a systematic way. We also try to provide a very detailed and explicit description of our methodology and sources, so that other users can contribute to improving them. But our time series and methods should be viewed in the perspective of a long, cumulative, collective process of data construction and diffusion, rather than as a finished product.

What Are the Concepts and Methods Being Discussed?

The concepts and methods used in the WTID series were initially exposed in the two collective volumes edited by Atkinson and Piketty (2007 and 2010), and in the corresponding country chapters and research articles. All country-level time series follow the same general principles: building on the pioneering work of Kuznets (1953), they combine income tax data, national accounts, and Pareto interpolation techniques in order to estimate the share of total income going to top income groups (typically the top decile and the top percentile). However, despite our best efforts, the units of observation, the income concepts, and the Pareto interpolation techniques were never made fully homogenous over time and across countries. Moreover, for the most part, attention was restricted to the top income decile rather than the entire distribution of income and wealth.

In contrast, the DINA time series and associated synthetic micro-files aim to be fully homogenous across all of these dimensions (or at least to make much more explicit the remaining heterogeneity in data construction) and, most importantly, to provide more detailed and comprehensive measures of inequality. In the DINA series, inequality is always measured using homogenous observation units, and taxable income reported on fiscal returns is systematically corrected and upgraded in order to match national accounts totals separately for each income category (wages, dividends, etc.) using various sources, imputation methods, and techniques to align the micro- and macro-data. Currently, WID.world aims to provide series on wealth (and not only on income) and on the entire distribution (and not only on top shares).

The two main data sources used in the DINA series continue to be income tax data and national accounts (just like in the WTID series), but we use these two core data sources in a more systematic and consistent manner, with fully harmonized definitions and methods, and together with other sources such as household income and wealth surveys, and inheritance, estate, and wealth tax data, as well as wealth rankings provided by "rich lists" compiled by the press. In most cases, the general trends in inequality depicted in the WTID series will not be very different in DINA series.[4] However, the latter will allow for more precise comparisons over time and across countries, more systematic world coverage, and more consistent analysis of the underlying mechanisms.[5]

In the DINA Guidelines (Alvaredo et al., 2016) the following key elements used in WID.world are discussed at length:

- The units of observation.
- The income concepts (pre-tax national income, pre-tax factor income, post-tax disposable income, post-tax national income, and fiscal income) and the wealth concepts (personal wealth, private wealth, public wealth, corporate wealth, and national wealth, as well as the corresponding notions of capital income flows and rates of return).
- The methods (e.g., imputation) employed to reconcile income tax returns and household survey micro-files with national accounts totals, as well as with wealth inequality sources.
- The methods employed to produce synthetic microfiles on income and wealth.
- The methods that can be used in the case of countries and time periods with more limited data sources.

In this section, we briefly refer to the units of observation and the income and wealth concepts used in WID.world, but the interested reader should consult the DINA Guidelines for the full documentation and a thorough investigation of details, problems, limitations, and challenges.

As was the case with the development of national accounts, the methodological discussion starts from the perspective of the developed countries, given the higher (though not perfect) quality and availability of data from all sources. A number of additional and important problems arise when we consider developing countries. In many cases—e.g., in China, India, or Mexico today—we only have income tax data for the top of the distribution, and the questions involve how to combine them with the household survey data that exist for the lower part of the distribution, and even the representativeness of tax data. Piketty, Yang, and Zucman (2017) provide an illustration for the case of China. In this respect, it should also be noted that in developing countries, the underground and informal economy may play a more significant role than in developed countries, possibly requiring different imputation techniques and different means of bridging gaps between micro-data and national accounts totals. Additionally, the discrepancies of both levels and trends from the existing data sources can be very large (Bourguignon, 2015) and deserve special and case-by-case attention.

The Units of Observation

One of the major limitations of the WTID series was the lack of homogeneity of the micro-level observation unit. Most WTID series were constructed by using the "tax unit" (as defined by the tax law of the country at any given point in time) as the observation unit. In joint-taxation countries like France and the United States, the tax unit has always been defined as the married couple (for married individuals) or the single adult (for unmarried individuals), and the top income shares series that were produced for these two countries did not include any correction for the changing structure of tax units (i.e., the combined income of married couples is not divided by two, so couples appear artificially richer than nonmarried individuals). This is problematic, since variations in the share of single individuals in the population, or in the extent of assortative mating in couples (being in a couple with a person similar to you socio-economically), could potentially bias the evolution of income inequality in various and contradictory ways. In some other countries, the tax system switched to individual taxation over the course of the history of the income tax (e.g., in 1990 in the United Kingdom), which creates other comparability problems in the WTID series (see Atkinson, 2005, 2007).

In order to correct for these biases, our DINA series try to use homogenous observation units. Generally speaking, our benchmark unit of observation is the adult individual. That is, our primary objective is to provide estimates of the distribution of income and wealth between all individuals aged 20 years and over (such as the shares of income and wealth going to the different percentiles of the distributions of income and wealth). Whenever possible, we also aim to construct estimates of individual income and wealth distribution that can be decomposed by age, gender, and number of dependent children. Ideally, we aim at producing synthetic micro-files providing the best possible estimates of the joint distribution—by age, gender, and number of dependent children—of income and wealth between adult individuals. But at the very least we want to be able to describe the distribution of income and wealth between all adult individuals.

One key question is how to split income and wealth between adults who belong to a couple (married or not) and/or to the same household (i.e., adults who live in the same housing unit). To the extent possible, we want to produce for each country two sets of inequality series: "equal-split-adults series" and "individualistic-adults series." In the equal-split series, we split income and wealth equally between adults who belong to the same couple. In the individualistic series, we attribute income and wealth to each individual income recipient and wealth owner (to the extent possible).

We should make clear that both series are equally valuable in our view. They offer two complementary perspectives on different dimensions of inequality. The equal-split perspective assumes that couples redistribute income and wealth equally between the partners. This is arguably a very optimistic perspective on what couples actually do: bargaining power is typically very unequal within couples, partly because the two members come with unequal income flows or wealth stocks. But the opposite perspective (zero sharing of resources) is not realistic either, and tends to underestimate the resources available to nonworking spouses (and therefore to overestimate inequality in societies with low female participation in the labor market). By offering the two sets of series, we give the possibility to compare the levels and evolutions of inequality over time and between countries under these two different perspectives. Ideally, the best solution would be to organize synthetic microfiles in such a manner that the data users can compute their own inequality series based upon some alternative sharing rules (e.g., assuming that a given fraction of the combined income of couples is equally split) and/or some alternative equivalence scales (e.g., dividing the income of couples by a factor less than two). This is our long-run objective.

Regarding the equal-split series, an important question is whether we should split income and wealth within the couple (narrow equal-split) or within the household (broad equal-split). In countries with significant multi-generational cohabitation (e.g., grandparents living with their adult children), this can make a significant difference (typically, broad equal-split series assume more private redistribution and display less inequality). In countries where nuclear families are prevalent, this makes relatively little difference. Ideally, both series should be offered. We tend to favor the narrow equal-split series as the benchmark series, both for data availability reasons (fiscal data are usually available at the tax unit level, which in a number of countries means the married couple or the nonmarried adult) and because there is possibly more splitting of resources at the narrow level (which is also arguably the reason why fiscal legislation usually offers the possibility of joint filling and taxation at the level of the married couple rather than at the level of the broader household, whose exact composition can vary and is not regulated by a legal relationship). However, in countries where fiscal sources are limited and where we mostly rely on household survey data (e.g., in China), it is sometime easier to compute the broad equal-split series. This should be kept in mind when making comparisons between countries (see the discussion in Piketty, Yang, and Zucman, 2017; and with the comparison between DINA series for China, France, and the United States).

Finally, when we look at inequality of post-tax disposable income, we introduce dependent children into the analysis, in order to be able to compute the relevant cash and in-kind transfers to parents (family benefits and tax credits, education allowances, etc.).

In the individualistic series, observed labor income and pension income is attributed to each individual recipient. This is easy to do in individual-taxation countries like the United Kingdom today, where by definition we observe incomes at the individual level. In general, labor income and pension income are also reported separately for each spouse in the tax returns and income declarations used in joint-taxation countries like France. In some cases, however (e.g., in US public-use tax files), we only observe the total labor or pension income reported by both spouses, in which case we need to use other sources and imputation techniques in order to split income appropriately between spouses (see Piketty, Saez, and Zucman, 2016).

The issues are more complicated for capital income flows. In individual-taxation countries, we usually observe capital income at the individual level. However, in joint-taxation countries, capital income is usually not reported separately for both spouses, and we generally do not have enough information about the marriage contract or property arrangements within married couples to be able to split capital income and assets into common assets and own assets. So in joint-taxation countries we simply assume in our benchmark series that each spouse owns 50% of the wealth of a married couple and receives 50% of the corresponding capital income flow. If and when adequate data sources become available, we might be able to offer a more sophisticated treatment of this important issue.

The Income and Wealth Concepts

One of the other major limitations of the WTID time series was the lack of homogeneity of the income concept and its dependence on the tax laws of each country. In contrast, the income concepts used in DINA series are defined in the same manner in all countries and time periods, and aim to be independent of the tax legislation of the given country/year. We use four basic pre-tax and post-tax income concepts to measure income inequality: (1) pre-tax national income; (2) pre-tax factor income; (3) post-tax disposable income; and (4) post-tax national income (see Alvaredo et al., 2016, for a detailed discussion of definitions and challenges).[6] All of them are anchored on the notion of national income (i.e., gross domestic product, minus consumption of fixed capital, plus net foreign income, for the economy as a whole) defined by using the same concepts as those proposed in the latest international guidelines on national accounts, as set forth by the 2008 UN System of National Accounts (SNA). However, in attributing income to the household sector, we apply a broader definition than is used in the 2008 SNA, as we also distribute the income of the other sectors in the economy (i.e., corporations, general government, and nonprofit institutions) rather than focusing on the household sector as defined in the national accounts. In the same way as for the income concepts, our wealth concepts refer to the latest international national accounts guidelines, based on which we define personal wealth, private wealth, public wealth, corporate wealth, and national wealth.[7]

We should make clear at the outset that our choice of using national accounts income and wealth concepts for distributional analysis certainly does not mean that we believe that these concepts are perfectly satisfactory or appropriate. Quite the contrary: our view is that official national accounts statistics are insufficient and need to be greatly improved. In particular, one of the central limitations of official GDP accounting is that it does not provide any information about the extent to which the different social groups benefit from GDP growth. By using national accounts concepts and producing distributional series based upon these concepts, we hope to contribute to addressing one important shortcoming of existing national accounts, to reduce the gap between inequality measurement and national accounts and also maybe between the popular individual-level perception of economic growth and its macro-economic measurement. The other reason for using national accounts concepts is simply that these concepts at this stage represent the only existing systematic attempt to define notions such as income and wealth in a common way, which (at least in principle) can be applied to all countries independently from country-specific and time-specific legislation and data sources.

One important limitation of existing official national accounts is the fact that consumption of fixed capital does not usually include the consumption of natural resources. In other words, official statistics tend to overestimate both the levels and the growth rates of national income, which in some cases could be much lower than those obtained for GDP. In the future, we plan to gradually introduce such adjustments to the aggregate national income series provided in the WID.world database. This is likely to introduce significant changes both at the aggregate and distributional level. We should also make clear that official national accounts are fairly rudimentary in a number of developing countries (and also sometimes in developed countries). Often they do not include the level of detail that we need to use the income and wealth definitions proposed below. In particular, proper series on consumption of fixed capital and net foreign income are missing in a number of countries, so that official series do not always allow national income to be computed.[8]

Countries/Years with Limited Income and Wealth Data

The construction of DINA series is very demanding in terms of data needs. Countries do not usually have all the data sources required, the limitations being very pronounced in many countries/years. This problem was also at the center of the development of national accounts: designing the SNA meant accepting that the standards could not be set at the level of the best, i.e., their implementation had to be feasible in less well-advanced countries. Methods need to be developed in the case of countries and periods with more limited data sources, typically on the basis of income tax tabulations rather than income tax micro-files, and/or with income tax data covering only a subset of the population rather than the entire population, and/or inadequacy of income tax data due to, for example, large or complete exemptions for capital incomes. The DINA Guidelines refer to each of these problems and illustrate the methods that can be applied with the cases of China (a country with limited access to income tax data; see Piketty, Yang, and Zucman, 2017) and France (a country with detailed tax data but where only income tax tabulations—rather than micro-files—are available prior to 1970; see Garbinti, Goupille-Lebret, and Piketty, 2017).[9]

What Can We Say Based on Available Evidence? First Results from WID.world and DINA

Income Inequality Dynamics: The United States, China, France

We first present some selected results on income inequality for the United States, China, and France (a country that is broadly representative of the West European pattern) in Figure 6.2. All series shown follow the same general DINA Guidelines (Alvaredo et al., 2016). National accounts, surveys, and fiscal data are combined in a systematic manner in order to estimate the full distribution of pre-tax national income (including tax-exempt capital income and undistributed profits). For more detailed results and discussions, we refer to the country-specific papers (Piketty, Saez, and Zucman [2016] for the United States; Piketty, Yang, and Zucman [2017] for China; and Garbinti, Goupille-Lebret, and Piketty [2017] for France).[10]

The combination of tax and survey data leads to a markedly upward revision of the official inequality estimates of China. The corrected top 1% income share is around 13% of total income in 2015, as compared to 6.5% in survey data. We stress that these estimates should be viewed as lower bounds, due to tax evasion and other limitations of tax and national accounts data, but we regard them as more realistic

Figure 6.2. Distribution of Income in China, the United States, and France, 1978–2015

Panel A. Top 1% income share   Panel B. Bottom 50% income share

Note: Distribution of pre-tax national income (before taxes and transfers, except for pensions and unemployment insurance benefits) among adults. Corrected estimates combine survey, fiscal, wealth, and national accounts data. Equal-split-adult series (the income of married couples is divided by two). *Sources:* US: Piketty, T., E. Saez, and G. Zucman (2016), "Distributional national accounts: Methods and estimates for the United States," *NBER Working Paper,* No. 22945; France: Garbinti, B., J. Goupille-Lebret, and T. Piketty (2017), "Income inequality in France, 1900–2014: Evidence from Distributional National Accounts (DINA)," *WID.world Working Paper,* No. 2017/4; China: Piketty, T., L. Yang, and G. Zucman (2017), "Capital accumulation, private property and rising inequality in China 1978–2015," *WID.world Working Paper,* No. 2017/6. StatLink 2 http://dx.doi.org/10.1787/888933839677.

and plausible than survey-based estimates. The estimates illustrate the need for more systematic use of administrative records, even for countries where the tax administration is far from perfect. China had very low-income inequality levels in the late 1970s, but it is now approaching the United States, where income concentration is the highest among the countries shown. In particular, we observe a complete collapse of the bottom 50% income share in the United States between 1978 and 2015, from 20% to 12% of total income, while the income share of the top 1% rose from 11% to 20%. In contrast, and in spite of a similar qualitative trend, the share of the bottom 50% remains higher than the top 1% share in 2015 in China and, even more so, in France.[11]

In light of the massive fall of the pre-tax incomes of the bottom 50% in the United States, our findings also suggest that policy discussions about rising global inequality should focus on how to equalize the distribution of primary assets—including human capital, financial capital, and bargaining power—rather than merely discussing ex-post redistribution through taxes and transfers. Policies that could raise the pre-tax incomes of the bottom 50% include improved education and access to skills, which may require major changes in the system of education finance and admission; reforms of labor market institutions, including minimum wage, corporate governance, and workers' bargaining power through unions and representation in the board of directors; and steeply progressive taxation, which can affect pay determination and pre-tax distribution, particularly at the top end (Piketty, Saez, and Stantcheva, 2014; Piketty, 2014).

The comparison between the United States, China, and France illustrates how DINA can be used to analyze the distribution of economic growth across income groups. As shown in Table 6.1, national income per adult increased in the three countries between 1978 and 2015: by 811% in China, by 59% in the United States, and by 39% in France. Nevertheless, performance has been very different across the distribution. There has been a clear pattern of rising inequality: top income groups enjoyed higher growth. In China, people at the top experienced very high growth rates of their income, but average growth was so large that the average income of the bottom 50% also grew markedly, by 401%. This is likely to make rising inequality more acceptable. In contrast, there was no growth at all for the bottom 50% in the United States (–1%). France illustrates another type of situation: people

Table 6.1. Real Income Growth Across the Distribution, 1978–2015

Percentages

Income group (distribution of per-adult pre-tax national income)	China	US	France
Full Population	811	59	39
Bottom 50%	401	–1	39
Middle 40%	779	42	35
Top 10%	1294	115	44
Top 1%	1898	198	67
Top 0.1%	2261	321	84
Top 0.01%	2685	453	93
Top 0.001%	3111	685	158

Note: Distribution of pre-tax national income (before taxes and transfers, except pensions and unemployment insurance benefits) among adults. Corrected estimates combining survey, tax, wealth, and national accounts data. Equal-split-adult series (income of married couples divided by two).
Sources: US: Piketty, T., E. Saez, and G. Zucman (2016), "Distributional national accounts: Methods and estimates for the United States," *NBER Working Paper*, No. 22945; France: Garbinti, B., J. Goupille-Lebret, and T. Piketty (2017), "Income inequality in France, 1900–2014: Evidence from Distributional National Accounts (DINA)," *WID.world Working Paper*, No. 2017/4; China: Piketty, T., L. Yang, and G. Zucman (2017), "Capital accumulation, private property and rising inequality in China 1978–2015," *WID.world Working Paper*, No. 2017/6. StatLink 2 http://dx.doi.org/10.1787/888933839658.

at the very top of the distribution experienced above-average income growth, but this pattern of rising inequality happened only for very high and numerically relatively negligible groups, so that it had limited consequences for the majority of the population. In effect, the bottom 50% income group enjoyed the same income growth as average growth (39%).

Private and Public Wealth-to-Income Ratios: The United States, China, France, the United Kingdom, Japan, Norway, and Germany

Next, we present findings on the evolution of aggregate wealth. We observe a general rise of the ratio between net private wealth and national income in nearly all countries in recent decades. It is striking to see that this phenomenon was largely unaffected by the 2008 financial crisis. The unusually large rise of the ratio for China is notable: net private wealth was a little above 100% of national income in 1978, while it was above 450% in 2015. The private wealth-to-income ratio in

China is now approaching the levels observed in the United States (500%), the United Kingdom, and France (550–600%).

The structural rise of private wealth-to-income ratios in recent decades is due to a combination of factors, which can decomposed into: (1) *volume factors* (high saving rates, which can themselves be due to aging and/or rising inequality, with differing relative importance across countries, combined with growth slowdown); (2) *relative asset prices*; and (3) *institutional factors*, including the increase of real estate prices (which can be due to housing portfolio bias, the gradual lift of rent controls, and lower technical progress in construction and transportation technologies as compared to other sectors) and of stock prices (which can reflect higher power of shareholders leading to the observed increase in Tobin's Q ratios—i.e., the ratio between market and book value of corporations).

Figure 6.3. The Decline of Public Property and the Rise of Sovereign Funds

(share of public wealth in national wealth)

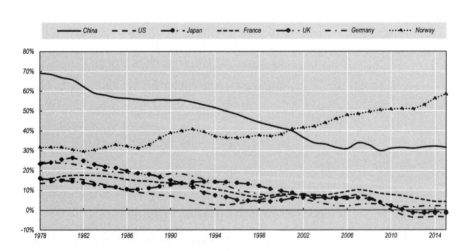

Note: Share of net public wealth (public assets minus public debt) in net national wealth (private plus public).
Source: China: Piketty, T., L. Yang, and G. Zucman (2017), "Capital accumulation, private property and rising inequality in China 1978–2015," *WID.world Working Paper*, No. 2017/6; other countries: Piketty, T. and G. Zucman (2014), "Capital is back: Wealth-income ratios in rich countries, 1700–2010," *Quarterly Journal of Economics*, Vol. 129(3), pp. 1255–1310, and WID.world updates. StatLink 2 http://dx.doi.org/10.1787/888933839715.

Another key institutional factor driving the rise of private wealth-to-income ratios is the gradual transfer from public wealth to private wealth. This is particularly spectacular in the case of China, where the share of public wealth in national wealth dropped from about 70% in 1978 to 35% by 2015, as shown in Figure 6.3. The corresponding rise of private property has important consequences for the levels and dynamics of inequality. Net public wealth has become negative in the United States, Japan, and the United Kingdom, and is only slightly positive in Germany and France. This arguably limits government's ability to redistribute income. The only exceptions to the general decline in public property are oil-rich countries with large public sovereign funds, such as Norway.

Wealth Inequality Dynamics: The United States, China, France, and the United Kingdom

Finally, we present findings on wealth inequality in Figure 6.4. We stress that currently available statistics on the distribution of wealth are highly imperfect. More transparency and better access to administrative and banking data sources are sorely needed if we want to gain knowledge of the underlying evolutions. In WID. world, we combine different sources and methods to reach robust conclusions: the income capitalization method (using income tax returns), the estate multiplier method (using inheritance and estate tax returns), wealth surveys, national accounts, and "rich lists." Nevertheless, our series should still be viewed as imperfect, provisional, and subject to revision. We provide full access to our data files and computer codes so that everybody can use them and contribute to improving the data collection.[12]

We observe a large rise of top wealth shares in the United States and China in recent decades, and a more moderate rise in France and the United Kingdom. A combination of factors explains these trends. First, higher-income inequality and severe bottom-income stagnation explain higher wealth inequality in the United States. Next, the very unequal process of privatization and access by Chinese households to quoted and unquoted equity probably played an important role in the very fast rise of wealth concentration in China. The potentially large mitigating impact of high real estate prices should also be taken into account; this effect, which benefited the middle class, is likely to have been particularly strong in France

Figure 6.4. Top 1% Wealth Share in China, the United States, France, and the United Kingdom, 1890–2015

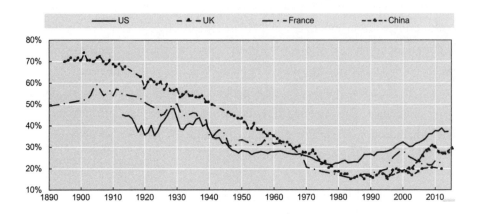

Note: Distribution of net personal wealth among adults. Corrected estimates (combining survey, fiscal, wealth, and national accounts data). For China, US, and France, equal-split-adult series (wealth of married couples divided by two); for UK, adult series.
Source: US: Saez, E. and G. Zucman (2016), "Wealth inequality in the United States since 1913: Evidence from capitalized income tax data," *Quarterly Journal of Economics*, Vol. 131(2), pp. 519–578; UK: Alvaredo, F., A.B. Atkinson, and S. Morelli (2018), "Top wealth shares in the UK over more than a century," forthcoming, *Journal of Public Economics*, and Alvaredo, F., A.B. Atkinson, and S. Morelli (2017), "Top wealth shares in the UK over more than a century," *CEPR Discussion Paper*, No. 11759; France: Garbinti, B., J. Goupille-Lebret, and T. Piketty (2016), "Accounting for wealth inequality dynamics: Methods, estimates and simulations for France (1800–2014)," *WID.world Working Paper*, No. 2016/5; China: Piketty, T., L. Yang, and G. Zucman (2017), "Capital accumulation, private property and rising inequality in China 1978–2015," *WID.world Working Paper*, No. 2017/6. StatLink 2 http://dx.doi.org/10.1787/888933839734.

and the United Kingdom, where housing prices have increased significantly relative to stock prices.

Given all these factors, it is not easy to predict whether the observed trend of rising concentration of wealth will continue. In the long run, steady-state wealth inequality depends on the inequality of saving rates across income and wealth groups, inequality of labor incomes and of rates of returns to wealth, and the progressivity of income and wealth taxes. Numerical simulations show that the response of steady-state wealth inequality to relatively small changes in these structural parameters can be large (Saez and Zucman, 2016; Garbinti, Goupille-Lebret, and Piketty, 2016). This instability reinforces the need for increased democratic transparency about the dynamics of income and wealth.

Conclusions

We have very briefly described the basic concepts, sources, and methods that we apply in the World Inequality Database (WID.world) and in the development of the DINA project. We should stress again that these methods are fragile, exploratory, and subject to revision. As more countries join the database, new lessons will be learned, and the methods will be refined and updated. Accordingly, new updated versions of the DINA Guidelines will be regularly released on WID.world.

We have also presented selected results on income and wealth inequality dynamics based on the DINA project. Global inequality dynamics involve strong and contradictory forces. We observe rising top income and wealth shares in nearly all countries in recent decades. But the magnitude of rising inequality varies substantially across countries, suggesting that different country-specific policies and institutions matter considerably. High GDP growth rates in emerging countries reduce between-country inequality, but this in itself does not guarantee acceptable within-country inequality levels and ensure the social sustainability of globalization. Access to more and better data (administrative records, surveys, more detailed national accounts, etc.) is critical to monitor global inequality dynamics, as this is a key building block to properly understand the present as well as the forces that will dominate in the future, and to design appropriate policy responses.

Notes

1. See also Piketty (2014) for an interpretative historical synthesis on the basis of this new material and of the top income shares time series.

2. Social Accounts Matrices are a related precedent.

3. Kuznets (1953) was preceded by ten years in this by Frankel and Herzfeld (1943), who made estimates of the European income distribution in South Africa based on income tax returns, making use of control totals from the census of population and from the national accounts.

4. Results of these comparisons are already available for France (Garbinti, Goupille-Lebret, and Piketty, 2017) and the United States (Piketty, Saez, and Zucman, 2016).

5. As new DINA series become available, we will systematically compare the inequality trends obtained in the old and the new series and analyze the sources of biases.

6. We also keep the *fiscal income* definition associated with the first top income share series (Atkinson and Piketty, 2007, 2010; Alvaredo et al., 2011–15).

7. Readers are referred to the DINA Guidelines Appendix, where we provide an Excel file with the formulas linking the income and wealth definitions to the SNA 2008 classification codes.

8. WID.world provides estimates of the consumption of fixed capital in countries where these series are not available in SNA series. WID.world also estimates missing income from tax havens to correct net foreign income flows (see Blanchet and Chancel [2016] for a discussion of methods). While these imputations are far from fully satisfactory, they increase the level of comparability of national income aggregates across countries.

9. The DINA Guidelines also discuss how the initial WTID time series, based on a fiscal income concept, can be corrected so as to be more directly comparable to new DINA series. In order to construct DINA/WID.world series for countries and time periods with limited data, we strongly recommend using the "Generalized Pareto interpolation" (gpinter) web interface available on-line (http://WID.world/gpinter). See Blanchet, Fournier, and Piketty (2017) for full technical details on Pareto curves and the corresponding interpolation techniques.

10. The series for China make use of the data recently released by the tax administration on high-income taxpayers and include a conservative adjustment for the undistributed profit of privately owned corporations.

11. These series refer to pre-tax, pre-transfer inequality. Post-tax, post-transfer series (in progress) are likely to reinforce these conclusions, at least regarding the US–France comparison.

12. We refer to the country-specific papers for detailed discussions: Saez and Zucman, 2016; Alvaredo, Atkinson, and Morelli, 2017, 2018; Garbinti, Goupille-Lebret, and Piketty, 2016; and Piketty, Yang, and Zucman, 2017.

References

Alvaredo, F., A.B. Atkinson, and S. Morelli (2018), "Top wealth shares in the UK over more than a century," forthcoming, *Journal of Public Economics*.

Alvaredo, F., A.B. Atkinson, and S. Morelli (2017), "Top wealth shares in the UK over more than a century," *CEPR Discussion Paper*, No. 11759.

Alvaredo, F. et al. (2017), "Global inequality dynamics: New findings from WID.world," *American Economic Review Papers & Proceedings*, Vol. 107(5), pp. 404–409.

Alvaredo, F. et al. (2016), "Distributional National Accounts (DINA) guidelines: Concepts and methods used in the World Wealth and Income Database," *WID.world Working Paper*, No. 2016/2.

Alvaredo, F. et al. (2011–2015), *The World Top Incomes Database*, online between January 2011 and December 2015.

Alvaredo, F. et al. (2013), "The top 1% in international and historical perspective," *Journal of Economic Perspectives*, Vol. 27(3), pp. 3–20.

Atkinson, A.B. (2007), "Measuring top incomes: Methodological issues," in Atkinson, A.B. and T. Piketty (eds.), *Top Incomes over the 20th Century: A Contrast Between Continental European and English-Speaking Countries*, Oxford University Press, Oxford, pp. 18–43.

Atkinson, A.B. (2005), "Top incomes in the U.K. over the 20th Century," *Journal of the Royal Statistical Society*, Vol. 168(2), pp. 325–343.

Atkinson, A.B. and A.J. Harrison (1978), *Distribution of Personal Wealth in Britain*, Cambridge University Press, Cambridge.

Atkinson, A.B. and T. Piketty (2010), *Top Incomes: A Global Perspective*, Oxford University Press, Oxford.

Atkinson, A.B. and T. Piketty (2007), *Top Incomes over the 20th Century: A Contrast Between Continental European and English-Speaking Countries*, Oxford University Press, Oxford.

Atkinson, A.B., T. Piketty, and E. Saez (2011), "Top incomes in the long run of history," *Journal of Economic Literature*, Vol. 49(1), pp. 3–71.

Blanchet, T. and L. Chancel (2016), "National Accounts series methodology," *WID.world Working Paper*, No. 2016/1.

Blanchet, T., J. Fournier, and T. Piketty (2017), "Generalized Pareto curves: Theory and applications to income and wealth tax data for France and the United States, 1800–2014," *WID.world Working Paper*, No. 2017/3.

Bourguignon, F. (2015), "Appraising income inequality databases in Latin America," *Journal of Economic Inequality*, Vol. 13(4), pp. 557–578.

Deaton, A. (2005), "Measuring poverty in a growing world (or Measuring growth in a poor world)," *Review of Economics and Statistics*, Vol. 87(1), pp. 1–19.

Fesseau, M. and M. Mattonetti (2013), "Distributional measures across household groups in a national accounts framework: Results from an experimental cross-country exercise on household income, consumption and saving," *OECD Statistics Working Papers*, No. 2013/04, OECD Publishing, Paris, http://dx.doi.org/10.1787/k3wdjqr775f-en.

Frankel, S.H. and H. Herzfeld (1943), "European income distribution in the Union of South Africa and the effect thereon of income taxation," *South African Journal of Economics*, Vol. 11(2), pp. 121–136.

Garbinti, B., J. Goupille-Lebret, and T. Piketty (2017), "Income inequality in France, 1900–2014: Evidence from Distributional National Accounts (DINA)," *WID.world Working Paper*, No. 2017/4.

Garbinti, B., J. Goupille-Lebret, and T. Piketty (2016), "Accounting for wealth inequality dynamics: Methods, estimates and simulations for France (1800–2014)," *WID.world Working Paper*, No. 2016/5.

Kuznets, S. (1953), *Shares of Upper Income Groups in Income and Savings*, National Bureau of Economic Research.

Nolan, B., M. Roser, and S. Thewissen (2016), "GDP per capita versus median household income: What gives rise to divergence over time?," *INET Oxford Working Paper*, No. 2016-03.

Piketty, T. (2014), *Capital in the 21st Century*, Harvard University Press, Cambridge, MA.

Piketty, T. (2003), "Income inequality in France, 1901–1998," *Journal of Political Economy*, Vol. 111, pp. 1004–1042.

Piketty, T. (2001), *Les hauts revenus en France au 20e siècle : Inégalités et redistributions, 1901–1998*, Grasset, Paris.

Piketty, T. and E. Saez (2003), "Income inequality in the United States, 1913–1998," *Quarterly Journal of Economics*, Vol. 118(1), pp. 1–39.

Piketty, T., E. Saez, and S. Stantcheva (2014), "Optimal taxation of top labor incomes," *American Economic Journal: Economic Policy*, Vol. 6(1), pp. 230–271.

Piketty, T., E. Saez, and G. Zucman (2016), "Distributional national accounts: Methods and estimates for the United States," *NBER Working Paper*, No. 22945.

Piketty, T., L. Yang, and G. Zucman (2017), "Capital accumulation, private property and rising inequality in China 1978–2015," *WID.world Working Paper*, No. 2017/6.

Piketty, T. and G. Zucman (2014), "Capital is back: Wealth-income ratios in rich countries, 1700–2010," *Quarterly Journal of Economics*, Vol. 129(3), pp. 1255–1310.

Saez, E. and G. Zucman (2016), "Wealth inequality in the United States since 1913: Evidence from capitalized income tax data," *Quarterly Journal of Economics*, Vol. 131(2), pp. 519–578.

UNECE (2011), *The Canberra Group Handbook on Household Income Statistics* (2nd ed.), Geneva, United Nations, www.unece.org/fileadmin/DAM/stats/groups/cgh/Canberra _Handbook_2011_WEB.pdf.

Zwijnenburg, J. (2016), "Further enhancing the work on household distributional data—

Techniques for bridging gaps between micro and macro results and nowcasting methodologies for compiling more timely results," paper prepared for the 34th IARIW General Conference, Dresden, Germany.

Zwijnenburg, J., S. Bournot, and F. Giovannelli (2017), "Expert Group on Disparities in a National Accounts Framework: Results from the 2015 exercise," *OECD Statistics Working Papers*, No. 2016/10, OECD Publishing, Paris, http://dx.doi.org/10.1787/daa921e -en.

7.

Understanding Subjective Well-Being

Arthur A. Stone and Alan B. Krueger

This chapter evaluates progress in measuring subjective well-being since the 2009 Stiglitz-Sen-Fitoussi Report. It summarizes approaches based on evaluative measures, experiential well-being, and eudaemonia (the extent to which a person believes that his or her life has meaning and purpose). It notes a tremendous uptake of subjective well-being measures by National Statistical Offices since 2009, and the growth in research on subjective well-being in the scientific literature. The chapter takes stock of what we have learned from global analyses of social and economic progress "beyond GDP" since 2009, including through the UN World Happiness Report, *the US National Academy of Science* Report on Measuring Subjective Well-Being, *the OECD* "How's Life?" *series and its Better Life Initiative. It also describes progress in acquiring new knowledge about subjective well-being and progress in applying this to policy. The chapter identifies some of the key issues that will need to be addressed to gain a more complete understanding of subjective well-being, including causality and data collection.*

Arthur A. Stone is Professor of Psychology, Economics, and Public Policy at the University of Southern California and Alan B. Krueger is Bendheim Professor of Economics and Public Affairs at Princeton University. The authors wish to thank all members of the HLEG, many of whom contributed sections to this chapter. They especially thank Professor Sir Angus Deaton for his contributions. At the OECD, Carrie Exton also provided sections for the chapter and did extensive editing. Finally, the authors thank the participants in the HLEG workshop on "Multi-dimensional Subjective Well-Being" held in Turin, Italy, on October 30–31, 2014, organized in collaboration with the OECD, the International Herbert A. Simon Society, and Collegio Carlo Alberto, and with the financial support of the Compagnia di San Paolo. The opinions expressed and arguments employed in the contributions below are those of the authors and do not necessarily reflect the official views of the OECD or of the governments of its member countries.

Introduction

Extensive progress has been made in collecting, analyzing, and improving subjective well-being data since the report of the Stiglitz, Sen, and Fitoussi Commission (SSF) was published in 2009. Many National Statistical Offices (NSOs) have already invested in ambitious measurement programs, and these are yielding important insights into the relationship between subjective well-being and a wide variety of characteristics and experiences.

Measures of subjective well-being (see sidebar, "What Are Subjective Well-Being Measures?") ask individuals to self-report ratings of aspects of their lives, including satisfaction with their life as a whole, their feelings at a particular moment, or the extent to which they feel that their lives have meaning or purpose. These measures focus on what people believe and report feeling, not their objective conditions, although they can be related to objective conditions. Thanks to large investments on the part of NSOs and governmental research agencies such as the US National Institute on Aging, there is today growing evidence to support the idea that these measures can be the basis of useful indicators of individual and societal welfare, and that they provide relevant information that is not reflected in more conventional economic statistics such as GDP. Of course, these more conventional statistics also capture information that subjective well-being measures do not.

On an individual level, subjective well-being data give insight into the way that people learn, work, and live, and what makes their lives satisfactory and happy, or what causes them pain and stress. There is now an increasing consensus that broader measures of societal progress should take into account how people feel about and experience their own lives, alongside information about their objective conditions. At a social level, subjective well-being measures are potentially powerful indicators that can signal wider problems in people's lives, capture prevailing sentiment, and predict behavior. For example, one recent study (Ward, 2015) shows that subjective well-being measures can predict voting behavior—even more effectively, in fact, than macro-economic variables. Subjective well-being measures can also be significant predictors of future health outcomes (Steptoe, Deaton, and Stone, 2015) and yield new insights that challenge our intuitive understanding of the world. For example, many studies have shown that in advanced, English-speaking Western countries, evaluative subjective well-being improves after middle age when we might have expected a decline due to higher rates of disease at older ages (Stone et al., 2010). Another surprising finding is that the impact of income differentially impacts evaluative and experiential well-being. At lower levels of income, there is a positive association between money income and subjective well-being, while at higher levels, only evaluative well-being is associated with income, whereas experiential well-being is not (Kahneman and Deaton, 2010).

Advances in research are facilitating the use of subjective well-being data in the public and private sectors. For example, businesses routinely access the satisfaction of their employees and customers; and "big data" on consumers' ratings and choices are used to recommend products to purchase, movies to watch, and music to listen to.

The rapid progress achieved in the use of subjective well-being data since SSF in 2009 suggests that there is much more to learn and that this work should continue. Larger databases of harmonized subjective well-being data, and panel data that connect subjective well-being indicators to observed outcomes are needed to reach conclusions about how these measures can most effectively be used—so collection of subjective well-being data requires continued support and commitment.

Such support will also depend on demonstrating the usefulness of these measures, which is already being done by several promising initiatives, policy applications, and societal indicators.

Progress in Measuring Subjective Well-Being Since the 2009 Stiglitz-Sen-Fitoussi Report

There has been dramatic progress in terms of both methodology and availability of subjective well-being data today relative to 5 years ago, and the Stiglitz-Sen-Fitoussi report was a catalyst for much of this progress.

WHAT ARE SUBJECTIVE WELL-BEING MEASURES?

"Subjective well-being" is subjective—that is, it is based on a person's self-reports of their beliefs and feelings. In this respect, it differs from objective well-being measures that may include observable health or material outcomes. A subjective well-being measure is one for which there is no obvious reference point that an external observer can use to evaluate a person's self-report.

Broadly speaking, there are three types of subjective well-being measures:

- *Evaluative measures* require a person to reflect upon and evaluate his or her life (or some aspect of it, such as health). This is often measured using questions such as: "The following question asks how satisfied you feel, on a scale from 0 to 10. Zero means you feel 'not at all satisfied' and 10 means you feel 'completely satisfied.' Overall, how satisfied are you with life as a whole these days?" (OECD, 2013). There are other evaluative measures including the Cantril ladder and Diener's multi-item scale (Diener, 1984).

- *Experiential well-being* is the measure of someone's feelings, states, and emotions, e.g., happiness, stress, pain, or sadness. These measures are optimally assessed at a given moment or over the course of a day, though longer recall periods are sometimes used (which may yield a more evaluative than experiential measure). This is often called "hedonic" well-being or "affect," though this chapter uses the broader term "experiential" well-being, which goes beyond purely affective states and includes pain and other miseries (Stone and Mackie, 2015). The rationale for this extension of hedonic well-being is that misery and pain are an important part of our momentary experience of life and concepts that fit into the broader experiential well-being construct. These concepts are often measured using questions (in daily assessment) such as: "On a scale from 0 to 10, where 0 means you did not experience the emotion at all, and 10 means that you experienced the emotion all the time, how much [enjoyment/stress/anger . . .] did you feel yesterday?" (Stone and Mackie, 2015). An advantage of collecting experiential data in real-time is that the reports can be linked to objective data on time-use as well as activities and resources. For example, feelings can be related to the type of activity individuals engaged in at the time (e.g., TV watching) and resources available (e.g., the size of the TV).

• *Eudaemonia* is the extent to which a person believes that his or her life has meaning and purpose (Ryff, 2014), but can also refer to other psychological states such as the idea of flourishing or thriving. Although scales of eudaemonia are available, recent national data collections have included questions such as: "Overall, to what extent do you feel that the things you do in your life are worthwhile?" (OECD, 2013), with responses given on a 0 to 10 scale where zero denotes "not at all worthwhile" and 10 denotes "completely worthwhile." There are also multi-item scales available.

Life evaluation (or life satisfaction) and experiential or hedonic well-being (both positive and negative) were described in Diener (1984). Eudaemonia is a term that has come into common use since the publication of the first

Stiglitz-Sen-Fitoussi report to describe aspects of people's psychological functioning not falling under Diener's definition. See OECD (2013) for further information.

We must be clear when speaking of "subjective well-being" to specify exactly which type of subjective well-being we mean, because the determinants and correlates differ among the measures. It is also apparent that confusion ensues when authors or policy-makers use the term "happiness" without saying which aspect of subjective well-being they have measured—sometimes they mean evaluative well-being, other times experiential well-being, and occasionally a mixture of the two.

There has been a tremendous uptick of subjective well-being measures by NSOs, but there has also been growth in research on subjective well-being in the scientific literature. The sidebar below provides a sampling of the breadth of scientific questions where subjective well-being was a major predictor or outcome in articles published in 2015 from the Web of Science platform. There has also been much progress in the theoretical understanding of the use of subjective well-being as a national indicator (e.g., Benjamin et al., 2014; Fleurbaey and Blanchet, 2013).

ARTICLES RELEASED IN 2015 UTILIZING SUBJECTIVE WELL-BEING AS EITHER A PREDICTOR OF OTHER OUTCOMES OR AS AN OUTCOME IN ITS OWN RIGHT

- Subjective well-being as a predictor of childbearing behavior and fertility decisions (Aassve, Arpino, and Balbo, 2016)
- How subjective well-being is linked to the "dark triad" of narcissism, psychopathy, and Machiavellianism (Aghababaei and Błachnio, 2015)

- Reasons for the decline of subjective well-being in China (Graham, Zhou, and Zhang, 2015)
- The link between subjective well-being and access to a cash margin among adult Swedes (Berlin and Kaunitz, 2015)
- Subjective well-being as a measure to assess suffering in cancer patients (Anglim et al., 2015)
- The subjective well-being of rural Anglican clergy (Brewster, 2015)
- Subjective well-being as a proxy for valuing health status (Brown, 2015)
- How subjective well-being is linked to trust and social cohesion (Cramm and Nieboer, 2015)
- The prediction of later life subjective well-being from early life experiential well-being (Coffey, Warren, and Gottfried, 2015)
- How different types of subjective well-being vary by age and their association with survival at older ages (Steptoe, Deaton, and Stone, 2015)
- How homeostatic processes may produce stable levels of subjective well-being (Cummins et al., 2015)
- Subjective well-being as a predictor of self-esteem in head and neck cancer patients (Devins et al., 2015)
- Subjective well-being as a moderator in the association of emotion and stress (Extremera and Rey, 2015)
- The impact of taking care of a family member on the subjective well-being of Japanese adults (Niimi, 2015)
- The impact of a comprehensive treatment on the subjective well-being of autistic young adults (Gal et al., 2015)
- Subjective well-being as a correlate of workplace air and noise pollution (García-Mainar, Montuenga, and Navarro-Paniagua, 2015)
- Teacher connectedness as a predictor for students' subjective well-being (García-Moya et al., 2015)

- Subjective well-being as a means for evaluating efforts to cope with unemployment (Hahn et al., 2015)
- Subjective well-being data as a tool for assessing workplace conditions in Spain (García-Mainar et al., 2015)
- Comparing the subjective well-being of Mexican immigrants with native-born Mexican Americans (Cuellar, Bastida, and Braccio, 2015)
- The impact of employment on the subjective well-being of older Korean immigrants living in the United States (Kim et al., 2015)
- The impact of daily energy management by employees on their subjective well-being (Kinnunen et al., 2015)
- Using subjective well-being data to explore social networks among older Japanese people (Saito et al., 2015)
- The association between health and subjective well-being among Europeans (Read, Grundy, and Foverskov, 2016)
- The relationship between locus of control and cell phone use to subjective well-being (Li, Lepp, and Barkley, 2015)
- Attitudes of older caregivers and their impact on their subjective well-being (Loi et al. 2015)
- Grand-parenting and its effects on subjective well-being (Muller and Litwin, 2011)
- Gender differences and subjective well-being (Meisenberg and Woodley, 2015)
- The correlation of immunological markers and subjective well-being in HIV patients in Uganda (Mwesigire et al., 2015)
- The correlation between academic performance and subjective well-being in adolescents (Steinmayr et al., 2015)
- How living with parents affects the subjective well-being of young adults (Nikolaev, 2015)
- The impact of smoking laws on subjective well-being (Odermatt and Stutzer, 2015)

- Self-control and emotion regulation as predictors of subjective well-being (Ouyang et al., 2015)
- Female infertility and self-compassion as predictors of subjective well-being (Raque-Bogdan and Hoffman, 2015)
- The association between body mass index and subjective well-being (Linna et al., 2013)
- The effects of labor market policies on the subjective well-being of the unemployed (Sage, 2015)
- The effects of indoor cleaning on subjective well-being in Japan (Shiue, 2015)
- Evaluating the impact of public parks on subjective well-being (Woodhouse et al., 2015)
- The impact of bright lights on subjective well-being (Stemer et al., 2015)
- The impact of plant closures on the subjective well-being of workers in Sweden (Stengård et al., 2015)
- The association between crime rates and subjective well-being in former Soviet countries (Stickley et al., 2015)
- The link between natural disasters and subjective well-being (Tiefenbach and Kohlbacker, 2015)
- The link between time spent exercising and subjective well-being (Wicker, Coates, and Breuer, 2015)
- The impact of technological improvements on subjective well-being (Zagonari, 2015)
- Subjective well-being as a moderator of cortisol secretion (Zilioli, Imami, and Slatcher, 2015)

National Statistical Office Data Collection

The availability of survey data on subjective well-being, including panel data, has increased at a rapid pace. NSOs are increasingly including subjective well-being questions in their surveys, and a majority of OECD countries now collect at least some subjective well-being data (Table 7.1). For example, NSOs in all but one OECD country have collected life evaluation data in recent years, and more than three-quarters of NSOs have collected some data on aspects of eudaemonia and experiential well-being.[1] This represents very significant progress since 2009. The *OECD Guidelines on Measuring Subjective Well-Being* (OECD, 2013), which provide clear directions and proposed modules for including subjective well-being questions in surveys, have galvanized this movement. Nevertheless, in some cases different measurement approaches continue to be adopted, particularly with regard to eudaemonia and experiential well-being, where broad consensus on best practice is still lacking. To ensure greater comparability and take-up of the data, further work is needed to coordinate and harmonize measurement efforts across countries, and to increase the frequency with which data are collected (see Exton, Siegerink, and Smith [2018], for a review of recent progress).

In 2013, the *EU Statistics on Income and Living Conditions*, or EU-SILC (Eurostat, 2013), included an ad hoc module on subjective well-being, which included a question for each of its three main elements. This has produced comparable subjective well-being data for all 28 European member states, as well as Iceland, Norway, Switzerland, and Turkey. In 2015, Eurostat (the statistical office of the European Union) also launched a publication on *Quality of Life – Facts and Views* (Eurostat, 2015), with explanatory pages and an interactive tool to make the data more easily accessible to a wide variety of users. This was complemented by a Eurostat analytical report on subjective well-being published in 2016. All quality-of-life indicators, including subjective well-being, have been evaluated by the Eurostat Expert Group.

On the basis of these experiences, Eurostat is now considering adding a question on life satisfaction in the core part of the EU-SILC questionnaire on a yearly basis in the near future, while every 6 years an ad hoc module with around 20 variables on the topic will supplement this information. This will provide a remarkable resource to the research and policy community: a harmonized cross-country data set with a sufficiently large sample size to estimate the relationship of subjective well-being to a host of individual and geographic characteristics over time. Eurostat's plan for annual measurement is an important step that will help to establish a time series for more than 30 countries.

There have also been advances in including subjective well-being in time-use surveys. This is particularly important to improve our understanding of experiential

Table 7.1. Data Collections on Subjective Well-Being Undertaken by National Statistical Offices in OECD Countries

	EU SILC (included life evaluation, eudaimonia and affect in 2013)	European Health Interview Survey (included affect in 2013-2015)	Other (additional) NSO data collections		
			Life evaluation	Affect/experiential well-being	Eudaimonia
Australia			From 2014, every 4 years	From 2001, every 3-4 years	
Austria	•	•	From 2004, now annually		
Belgium	•	•			
Canada			From 1985, annually	From 2015, annually	2016, frequency tbc
Chile			From 2011, biennially		
Czech Republic	•	•			
Denmark	•	•	From 2015, frequency tbc	From 2015, frequency tbc	From 2015, frequency tbc
Estonia	•	•			
Finland	•	•			
France	•	•	From 2011, annually	From 2011, annually	
Germany	•	•			
Greece	•	•			
Hungary	•	•	From 2013, biennially		From 2013, biennially
Iceland	•	•			
Ireland	•				
Israel			From 2006, annually	From 2002, annually	
Italy	•	•	From 2012, annually		

Country				2013-2015 (Social Integration Survey)	2013-2015 (Social Integration Survey)
Japan					
Korea			From 2013, annually		
Latvia	•	•			
Luxembourg	•	•			
Mexico			In 2012, frequency tbc	2012 and 2013, experimental	2013/14, frequency tbc
Netherlands	•		From 1974, now annually	2016, frequency tbc	2016, frequency tbc
New Zealand			From 2014, biennially	From 2008, biennially	From 2014, biennially
Norway	•		From 2011, now annually	From 2011, every 4 years	From 2015; every 4 years
Poland	•	•		From 2011, every 4 years	
Portugal	•	•			
Slovakia	•	•			
Slovenia	•	•	From 2012, annually		
Spain	•	•		2011	
Sweden	•	•			
Switzerland	•		From 2007, annually	From 2013, annually	From 2011, annually
Turkey	•	•			
United Kingdom	•	•	From 2011, annually	From 2011, annually	From 2011, annually
United States			2010, 2012, 2013 (ATUS); from 2005 (CDC), irregular frequency	From 2010, annually (National Health Interview Survey); 2010, 2013 (ATUS)	From 2005 (CDC), irregular frequency
Total	26	24	18 (34 including EU SILC)	14 (33 including EU SILC)	10 (31 including EU SILC)

Source: Exton, C., V. Siegerink, and C. Smith (2018), "Measuring subjective well-being in national statistics: Taking stock of recent OECD activities," forthcoming, OECD Publishing, Paris. StatLink 2 http://dx.doi.org/10.1787/888935839753.

well-being, since it enables the examination of the link between people's activities, daily circumstances, social contact, and feelings. Some countries (the United
States, France, Poland, Luxembourg, the United Kingdom, and Canada) have
incorporated some version of experiential well-being into their time-use surveys.
For example, in the United States a governmental agency, the Bureau of Labor Statistics, regularly conducts a time-use survey of over 12,000 individuals (the American Time Use Survey, ATUS). In 2010, 2012, and 2013, a well-being module was
included in ATUS that sampled three time-use episodes for each person and asked
a number of experiential well-being questions. Unfortunately, the module was limited to three rounds even though a strong recommendation to continue collection
of these experiential well-being data was issued by a National Academy of Sciences
panel (Stone and Mackie, 2015).

The investment of NSOs in measuring subjective well-being is extremely important and should continue (see sidebar, "The Experience of the UK Office for
National Statistics in Measuring Subjective Well-Being"). As with other indicators such as GDP, subjective well-being data is at its most valuable when one can
observe and compare trends, which requires tracking data over long periods. Continued methodological progress would be facilitated by the collection and dissemination of long time series in large, high-quality data sets. Collection of such data
will also facilitate the generation of policy-relevant insights. Researchers can help
support this process by ensuring that analyses of the data that do exist are carried
out and disseminated, demonstrating their usefulness; conversely, NSOs can help
by ensuring that micro-data are available in a timely manner. Nevertheless, the
methodological and conceptual issues raised later in this document must be taken
into account when interpreting the data collected. To take one example, Deaton
(2012) and Deaton and Stone (2016) suggest that tracking of subjective well-being
data can be disrupted by a change in the questionnaire design or by the provision
of inappropriate cues, and that such factors do not always average out.

THE EXPERIENCE OF THE UK OFFICE FOR NATIONAL STATISTICS IN MEASURING SUBJECTIVE WELL-BEING

In November 2010, supported by the then Prime Minister David Cameron, the UK Office for National Statistics (ONS) launched the Measuring National Wellbeing (MNW) program with the aim of establishing "an accepted and trusted set of National Statistics which help people to understand and monitor national well-being." Alongside a six-month national debate that asked people "what matters" to them, ONS began its program by developing and adding four questions on subjective well-being (called "personal" well-being, in the ONS initiative) to one of its largest household surveys (the Annual Population Survey). Some reflections on ONS experiences and lessons learned are the following:

• *A robust set of personal well-being questions was developed.* ONS undertook extensive work to develop a robust and credible set of four questions to capture personal well-being and introduced them into the UK's largest household survey. Challenges faced in the process included investigations into interview mode effects, different response scales, question placement, and cognitive interviewing. These questions were then added to the Annual Population Survey, whose large sample size provided the opportunity to analyze personal well-being alongside numerous other variables while also minimizing survey cost. The findings from ONS testing and development were used as best practice in informing the *OECD Guidelines on Measuring Subjective Well-Being.*

• *Experience from asking these questions has been positive.* The four ONS personal well-being questions take only 75 seconds to ask and complete. Since survey space is at a premium, they are an efficient use of both time and space. Feedback from interviewers has been positive, with many reporting that the questions provide an opportunity to build a rapport with respondents; by providing a focus on how people feel about their lives, the questions have also helped avoid refusals.

• *Demand for personal well-being data continues to grow.* Since their introduction into the Annual Population Survey in April 2011, ONS subjective well-being questions have been used in over 20 government surveys covering areas such as crime, household wealth, and visits to the natural environment. Researchers have used these data to improve understanding of the relationship between personal well-being and a range of other outcomes.

• *Personal well-being does not tell the whole story.* The national debate managed by ONS reinforced the wealth of factors that people consider as important to their well-being, and added legitimacy to the Measuring National Wellbeing program. ONS developed a suite of 41 measures of national well-being, including both subjective and objective measures across a range of domains, including for example "Our Relationships," "Health," "the Economy" and "the Natural Environment." ONS also recognized that presentation would be critical to acceptance of the measures and understanding of the wider program, and developed the National Wellbeing Wheel to respond to this challenge; the Wheel was recently replaced by a new interactive dashboard, accessible by the increasing number of users relying on mobile devices, which provides "live" updates as new estimates become available for each indicator.[1] While most media attention still falls on measures of personal well-being, a growing number of policy studies have used the domains of the National Wellbeing Wheel as a framework to structure approaches to policy evaluation and improvement.

• The *What Works Centre for Wellbeing* was established in late 2014. Since its introduction, the Centre, which is dedicated to bridging the gap between evidence and policy, has helped ensure that high-quality evidence is available to support policy-making, giving a focus to attempts to improve well-being across the United Kingdom. ONS seconded its head of personal well-being for a period of two years to help establish the Centre and cement links between evidence and policy.

- *Policy use of subjective well-being is increasing.* Estimates of personal well-being, within the framework of wider measures of national well-being, helped policy-makers understand how their decisions affect people's life. Examples of policy use of personal well-being data include: the Public Health Outcomes Framework, which monitors the four measures of personal well-being as part of its vision to improve and protect the nation's health and well-being; the presentation of personal well-being results by occupation, to support young people in making a more informed choice about their career; and the employment of a well-being valuation approach in attempts to monetize the human cost of crime.

- *There is no appetite for a single index of national well-being.* ONS is frequently asked to consider a single measure to summarize progress and place well-being on the same footing as GDP. While the advantages of a single indicator (particularly in aiding communication) are recognized, ONS has no intention of producing a single index of well-being: too many conceptual and methodological hurdles are, as yet, unresolved to allow progress in that direction.

1. www.ons.gov.uk/visualisations/dvc364/dashboard/index.html.

Source: Text provided by Jil Matheson.

Global Reports and Tools

Several global analyses of social and economic progress beyond (or in addition to) GDP have been published and widely disseminated since 2009, including the Legatum Institute's Prosperity Index (O'Donnell et al., 2014); the *World Happiness Report*,[2] released annually since 2012 by the UN Sustainable Development Solutions Network (Helliwell, Layard, and Sachs, 2018); the US National Academy of Science *Report on Measuring Subjective Well-Being* (Stone and Mackie, 2015); and the OECD's *How's Life?* series and Better Life Index (OECD, 2015a). While all these projects include sections on subjective well-being, each takes a different approach to the analysis and comparison of well-being across countries. This diversity of approaches and initiatives helps to advance our understanding of subjective well-being and how it can be used.

Two particularly important documents—the *OECD Guidelines on Measuring Subjective Well-Being* (OECD, 2013) and the US National Academy of Science *Report on Measuring Subjective Well-Being*—lay out the current experience in collecting data on subjective well-being and provide a focal point for a growing consensus around methodology. We view these documents as "required reading" for policy-makers and researchers working with subjective well-being measures because they carefully consider many of the various conceptual and methodological issues that are only briefly touched upon below.

Furthermore, a US National Institute on Aging–supported conference on time-use and experiential well-being was held in 2015 to take stock of progress since the publication of the day reconstruction method (DRM) and to identify remaining challenges. A report of the conference proceedings (Stone and Smith, 2015) outlines many issues and questions that remain about the DRM, despite its use in dozens of research studies. Two other documents—the Legatum Institute report and the *World Happiness Report*—speak more to the policy uses of subjective well-being measures and are discussed in a later section of this chapter.

Improvements in Methodology

The Stiglitz, Sen, and Fitoussi (2009) report identified some of the methodological and interpretive issues that caused concern about using subjective well-being measures. Since the publication of the report, solutions have been presented and explored for many of those issues. A short summary of the issues is provided in Table 7.2 alongside the most promising solutions. While a deep examination of these issues is important to improving the measurement of subjective well-being, it is equally important to avoid setting a uniquely high standard for subjective well-being in contrast to other indicators, such as income, consumption, or wealth inequality, which, as shown in the other chapters in this volume, can be quite difficult to calculate or are similarly derived from self-reported measures that are equally sensitive to the survey vehicle used (for example, the length of the recall period used for expenditure diaries can have dramatic effects on consumption estimates, Beegle et al., 2011) or may have other issues related to self-reports more generally.

Some of the methodological issues detailed in Table 7.2 can be partially addressed by careful standardization of questionnaires, which may reduce framing and potential context effects.[3] For this reason, the continued collection of standardized questions across countries is needed. Following the *OECD Guidelines* is a good way to ensure that questions are standardized, as they represent the state of the art for question formulation and survey administration. Eurostat's 2013 EU-SILC ad hoc module on subjective well-being followed the *OECD Guidelines*, and was based on its recommended questionnaire. The EU-SILC and its ad hoc modules have a legal basis, with a common list of variables, concepts, classifications, and survey requirements translated in all EU languages. The legislation is accompanied by EU-SILC methodological guidelines, including the recommended questionnaire, translated in all languages. Importantly, the legislation requires that all EU countries contribute data to this effort.

To illustrate the importance of the concerns over systematically different response styles and bias, we provide a more detailed discussion here. If different groups of people show *systematic differences* in how they interpret subjective well-being questions or use response scales (for example, due to some common characteristic such as language or culture), then simply comparing the *level* of subjective well-being between these groups can yield misleading conclusions. The extent to which this is a problem will depend, in part, on the question the data are being used to answer. In some cases, this will not matter if the main focus of interest is whether the *change* in a variable produced a *change* in subjective well-being within a specific population, rather than direct comparisons between groups of individuals.

However, in simple descriptive analyses where *levels* of subjective well-being are compared across groups, such as gender or occupations, or across countries, then systematic differences in question interpretation or response styles between groups has the potential to cause bias. For example, if the elderly understand or respond to a subjective well-being question in a way that is systematically different to younger people, or if richer people have a response style that is somehow different to that found among the poor, then we might over- or under-estimate differences in subjective well-being between these groups. In order to have more concrete ideas about the extent to which this may be a problem, we should have a better idea of why such differences may exist in the first place, and have some theoretical justification for a concern with systematic differences in how subjective well-being questions are interpreted and answered.

Concerns about systematic biases, in particular their potential interaction with context effects, are not solved through the use of panel or longitudinal data if the goal is to compare levels of well-being between groups at a single point in time. A salient example of this is provided by Deaton (2012) on context effects, with its implications further refined in Deaton and Stone (2016) using subjective well-being data collected by the Gallup Organization. In this work, Deaton found evidence of a large impact of a set of political questions placed prior to an evaluative well-being question (the Cantril ladder), an effect that was larger than that of the 2008 recession. This effect was driven by respondents who reported feeling that the country was going in the wrong direction, which exerted a strong downward bias on their answers to the subsequent life evaluation question. Importantly, these context effects varied by race or ethnicity. For example, the negative treatment effect of the political polling questions (compared with a control without such questions) was smaller for blacks than for whites. This meant that, while whites in the control group on average reported life evaluations almost 0.2 scale points higher than blacks (on a 0–10 scale), in the treatment group there was almost no difference between the two groups (less than 0.03 scale points). This contrasts with results for gender, age, and income, where the size of the context effects remained stable across different population groups.

The finding that context effects can work differently for different populations complicates the interpretation of group differences in subjective well-being and requires more extensive study. Since NSOs are very unlikely to ask political polling questions, it will be important to understand whether other lead-in questions can also produce a significant shift in responses. For example, Lee et al. (2016) found that asking a self-rated health question immediately before a subjective well-being question prompted a stronger correlation between the answers compared with a situation when the question ordering was reversed. This effect was driven by a subsample of respondents who reported one or more chronic health conditions: among those without chronic health conditions, question ordering did not produce a significant difference in the size of the correlation.

Taken together, these studies reinforce the importance of question ordering for both survey design and data comparability. Unless explicitly tested through split-sample methods, the effects of question ordering will tend to remain hidden from view.

While systematic group differences in response styles are insufficiently addressed in the literature, several advances have been made. These include the use of vignettes (Crane et al., 2016; although see Grol-Prokopcsyk et al., 2015, and OECD, 2013, for concerns about these methods) when analyzing data from migrants (Senik, 2014; Exton, Smith, and Vandendriessche, 2015), and using individual fixed effects models with panel data. However, in general we view these concerns as unresolved and recommend continuing research.

Another continuing area of methodological development pertinent for experiential subjective well-being research is the use of real-time and near-real-time data capture—for example, with momentary data recording such as ecological momentary assessment (EMA), which is based on the administration of brief questionnaires in real time in people's everyday lives (Stone and Shiffman, 1994; Shiffman, Stone, and Hufford, 2008), daily diaries, and day reconstruction methods (Kahneman et al., 2004). These are important techniques because of their potential to assess experiential subjective well-being with less retrospective bias than measures using (relatively) long recall periods that ask about fluctuating levels of emotions and pain. Long recall periods conflate actual memories of experiences with broad beliefs that do not necessarily accurately reflect experience. However, from a pragmatic perspective of data collection in national surveys, momentary methods can be unwieldy, burdensome, expensive, and impractical in some cases (e.g., while people are driving, or when they are engaged in activities that cannot be interrupted), yielding selection effects. As result, methods that ask about the prior day have become the standard; these include simple overall questions about the day before (as used in the UK ONS survey and the Gallup World Poll); so-called hybrid measures based on the DRM—which capture some details about the day, for example, the number of hours engaged in various activities (Christodoulou, Schneider, and Stone, 2014; Miret et al., 2012)—and DRM surveys (addressing the entire day or sections of the day, as done by the Survey on Health, Ageing and Retirement in Europe [SHARE]).

Table 7.2. Summary of Methodological Issues with Subjective Well-Being Measures

		Problem	Progress	Outstanding issues
Issue applying uniquely to subjective well-being variables	Adaptation	There are two parts to this issue. First, people may truly adapt to shifting conditions, although some evidence suggests this does not happen completely. Second, over time people may change their standards for evaluating their lives (i.e. scale recalibration), which may suggest that adaptation has occurred when in reality it has not.	Work continues on exploring scale recalibration and hedonic adaptation using both evaluative and experiential well-being measurements.	One promising area for future research is the analysis of factors that promote true adaptation to negative shocks (resilience). Another area is novel measurement approaches that reduce scale recalibration.
Issues generally applying to all self-reported variables	Shared method variance	Variables collected using the same method (for example, the same survey) may be influenced by similar individual characteristics or external factors (e.g. day of the week). This can bias the estimated relationship between the variables away from zero.	Recommendations: Avoid, or use caution, if using perception-based data from the same survey as both independent and dependent variables. Use panel data to adjust for individual fixed effects when possible. Use data less subject to potential biases (e.g. medical incidents rather than satisfaction with health) when possible; and self-reported demographic variables, which are usually relatively bias-free.	

		Problem	Progress	Outstanding issues
Issues generally applying to all self-reported variables	Sensitivity to survey methodology	Question order and other survey context effects: people who have answered questions on politics or other salient topics prior to a subjective well-being question may give answers that are shaped by those preceding questions and the feelings or reactions they generated (i.e. cueing or framing effects).	Recommendations: Place subjective well-being questions at the beginning of the survey/ module, or immediately after relatively neutral, factual reports, such as basic demographic information. Also, randomize question placement, to "average out" context effects. Standardize question order so that context effects are similar over surveys. Buffer text can be used to separate subjective well-being modules, although there is mixed evidence on the effectiveness of this. Context effects are not limited to question order: they may also be prompted by factors external to the survey, such as major news events, or public holidays. This means that national surveys should ideally be administered on a continuous basis throughout the year, as is the case for many routinely collected economic statistics (such as labor force statistics), which can themselves show pronounced seasonality.	Research is needed (and some is on-going) regarding the possible interaction of context effects with group variables (e.g. age group). Such interactions could distort group effects. Further develop effective buffer text to reduce context effects is a priority. If it can be demonstrated that seasonality is a problem for subjective well-being data, techniques for seasonal adjustment should be considered.

		Problem	Progress	Outstanding issues
Issues generally applying to all self-reported variables	Measurement error	Responses to eudaimonic and evaluative subjective well-being questions are influenced by occasion-specific factors that are unrelated to the underlying construct that one wishes to examine (e.g. weekends, holidays, news...). However, it is expected that daily events are associated with fluctuations in experiential well-being.	Large samples, frequent surveys, adjustment for day of week and holidays. Time-use surveys and experiential sampling, although the measurement error may be high with single-day assessments and multiple days are recommended when possible.	More work is needed to understand the reliability of subjective well-being measurements, especially with experiential assessments.
	Scaling	Response options for survey questions are typically presented on a bounded scale (e.g. with 4 or 10 at the maximum). While these scales are often treated as cardinal variables in statistical analysis, they are not.	Recommendation: Ensure that results are robust to different treatments of the bounded variable (e.g. using ordered logic, or using the percent of respondents above or below a threshold).	The U-index helps to address some concerns about interpersonal use of scales as long as individuals apply the same scales to positive and negative affect, but it has not been widely applied or studied.
	Systematic response styles and biases	Groups may interpret the question (or use the available response options) differently. If there are systematic differences in how groups of respondents behave, linked to particular characteristics (e.g. age or language), this may be problematic when making comparisons across such groups.	Recommendations: Use caution when interpreting level differences across groups if there are reasons for believing that those groups understand and use response scales in systematically different ways. Show robustness to adjustment.	This remains an important outstanding issue; additional work is needed to appraise and overcome this issue.

		Problem	Progress	Outstanding issues
Issues applying to most empirical evidence in general	Heterogeneity	Using the average can obscure important differences between population groups (e.g. by sex, age, or minority group status), and differences in trends within these groups. Relationships between variables can also be different for different sub-groups of the population (meaning that "what works on average might not work for you").	Recommendations: Report summary statistics not only in terms of the mean but also distributions (e.g. what percent of people are miserable) and differences between groups (sex, age, minority groups, employment status...). Examine moderation effects and identify subgroups for whom results may need to be assessed separately (where sample sizes permit).	Work on the development of reasonable thresholds for classification is needed (at what level or with which combination of subjective wellbeing measures is a person "not doing well"?)
	Identifying causality	Care must be taken to carefully consider factors relevant to affirming causal associations.	Development of testable theories should be a priority. Panel data and repeated cross sections can help identify effects from natural experiments. In addition, randomised evaluations provide evidence of causality in specific settings, and may provide support for relationships observed in more general setting, although the ecological validity of such manipulations may be questionable – i.e., whether or not the treatment bears any relationship to real-world events.	Establishing causality is important for informing policy decisions, as is consideration of potential unintended consequences. It is also important to identify heterogeneous treatment effects (see previous row), and individuals may sort in terms of their exposure to various stimuli based on their preferences.

StatLink 2 http://dx.doi.org/10.1787/888933839772.

Complementary approaches to survey questions have been, or are being, developed. Several approaches exist, or are being developed, that can complement survey questions. For example, big data is being used to "nowcast" subjective well-being (see sidebar, "Use of Big Data to 'Nowcast' Subjective Well-Being"), and new approaches are being developed to elicit people's preferences, including information on how they value trade-offs between competing goals. "Automatic data capture," which combines data such as GPS measurement or continuous health measures with survey questions on subjective well-being, is another example of these innovative approaches.

AGING AND SUBJECTIVE WELL-BEING

An intriguing line of research pursued by psychologists, sociologists, and economists is whether and how subjective well-being shifts with age. There are now dozens of articles examining this question. In short, the pattern is that evaluative well-being (as measured by instruments gauging life satisfaction, such as the Cantril ladder) is relatively high in an individual's 20s, falls to its lowest point in their late 40s and early 50s, and then improves to the highest levels in their 70s (although there may be declines in older age; see Figure 7.1). This pattern holds for English-speaking, wealthy countries, but not for poorer, non-Western countries (Steptoe, Deaton, and Stone, 2015). There is also evidence that the pattern is not attributable to cohort effects, which could have explained the pattern by different cohorts of individuals experiencing various historical events (Blanchflower and Oswald, 2008). Less is known about how experiential subjective well-being changes with people's age, but at least in the United States patterns of different affects are not U-shaped. For example, Stone et al. (2010) found that stress is high from age 20 through to about age 50, followed by a rapid decline through the 70s (the right side of this pattern is consistent with the evaluative well-being pattern of improving outcomes in older age). What is surprising about these patterns, at least for Western countries, is that the improvement in subjective well-being occurs at an age when the prevalence of chronic disease is on the increase, and that the presence of illness is associated with lower subjective well-being. Theoretical explanations, with some empirical support, focus on a shift in priorities and in social engagements and time use in older people, resulting in higher well-being.

Figure 7.1. Life Evaluations and People's Age Across the World

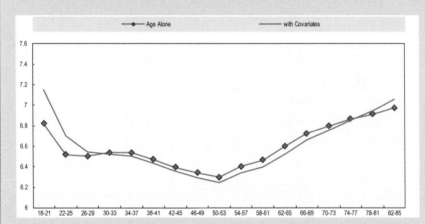

Note: Mean life evaluations, plotted by 4-year age groups. The continuous line represents unadjusted data, while the dotted line represents data adjusted for 4 covariates (the share of the population who are women living with a partner, with a child at home, and unemployed). *Source*: Stone, A.A. et al. (2010), "A snapshot of the age distribution of psychological well-being in the United States," *Proceedings of the National Academy of Sciences of the United States of America*, Vol. 107(22), pp. 9985–9990. StatLink 2 http://dx.doi.org/10.1787/888933839791.

USE OF BIG DATA TO "NOWCAST" SUBJECTIVE WELL-BEING

Big data offer opportunities to complement NSO-generated measures of subjective well-being, though there are significant cautions that must also be considered. Subjective well-being measures derived from Big Data can potentially provide more timely estimates, high-frequency information, local level data, and early warning signals. Big Data are also multi-dimensional—Google search queries (a form of revealed behavior), for example, can be used to cover a wide range of states, such as pain. The wealth of big data means that the impact of various shocks (e.g., the impact of the financial crisis across and within US cities) can be investigated in a timely fashion.

There are, however, challenges. Much big data suffers from selection bias and noise, and disaggregating results by different population groups can be problematic. A particularly important problem is that it is difficult to credibly infer the intent of people who contribute data points: researchers have no way of validating their assumptions about why and when people tweet or search for particular terms on Google (which may also be considered selection factors). For this reason, interpretive exercises carried out using big data sources should be approached with caution; research focusing on subjective well-being constructs measured with big data as compared with more traditional data collection methods could illuminate our understanding of these selection factors.

Substantive Progress:
New Knowledge About Subjective Well-Being

The Global Picture

Setting aside the measurement issues outlined above, which may impact the substance of what follows, Gallup World Poll data show that evaluative subjective well-being is highest, on average, in the Nordic countries, Switzerland, the Netherlands, Canada, New Zealand, and Australia; and lowest in the poorer countries of sub-Saharan Africa, and in countries experiencing war, such as Syria and Afghanistan (see sidebar, "Subjective Well-Being Across the World"). Changes in average reported life evaluation across countries since the SSF 2009 report also provide evidence that subjective well-being indicators are useful measures of social progress. The biggest drop in average life evaluations between 2005–07 and 2012–14 was in Greece, followed by Egypt and Italy (Helliwell, Layard, and Sachs, 2015)—although this analysis excludes 5 of the world's current 10 lowest-ranking countries, including Syria and Afghanistan, due to lack of data in earlier waves of the Gallup World Poll.

SUBJECTIVE WELL-BEING ACROSS THE WORLD

New evidence from the Gallup World Poll shows that the positive relationship between evaluative well-being and income runs throughout the range of GDP per capita, from the poorest to the richest countries. This pattern was not easily seen from the World Values Survey, which does not include the really poor countries in Africa, and had to wait until the Gallup World Poll came along to become firmly established. Prior to that, many researchers had observed that, when plotted against per capita GDP, countries' evaluative well-being flattened out at some point so that, at income levels above those of a country like Morocco, higher average income did not lead to higher evaluative well-being. This led many researchers in the field to conclude that income did not matter once countries were no longer poor. In his early papers, Easterlin used this as evidence that income did not improve the human lot, at least once we were not dealing with real poverty anymore (Easterlin, 1974).

Using the Gallup World Poll, Deaton (2008) showed that this conclusion was wrong. When life evaluation is plotted against the logarithm of income, the result is very close to a straight line. There is certainly diminishing marginal utility with respect to GDP per capita, but doubling income has the same effect at the bottom as at the top of the income scale, though the absolute changes in income are much smaller at the bottom than at the top (Figure 7.2). Of course, there is a lot of scatter, so that if you do not take the whole range, the relationship is much less obvious. For example, using plots limited to rich countries, an observer might conclude that there is not much of a relation there.

The variability in the association is also important, because it shows that countries are not trapped by their level of GDP per capita. Some countries do much worse than others, some much better. One interpretation is that these deviations indicate the policy space: governments can promote high subjective well-being even with limited resources, and countries like the United States can have relatively poor outcomes in terms of subjective well-being, even when they are very rich in terms of GDP per capita. Many factors besides GDP per capita determine people's subjective well-being levels, from employment status to health, and from environmental quality to social relationships. Nevertheless, some of the international variation may also be due to reporting styles. It is certainly plausible that people with different cultures use the scale differently. For example, countries of the former Soviet Union are way below the line, but first, there are good reasons for this, and second, income measures for these countries are likely to be affected by large measurement errors, so perhaps there is no need to invoke "Slavic dourness." In general, we should also remember that in these global comparisons involving per capita GDP

Figure 7.2. Log GDP per Capita Is Associated with Life Evaluations Worldwide

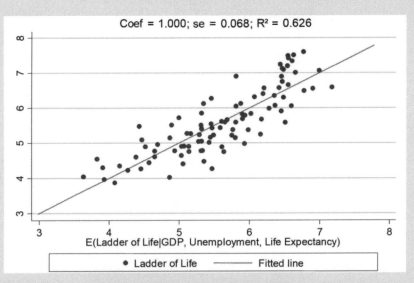

Note: N = 107 countries and territories. Pooled observations, 2009–13.
Source: Gallup World Poll and World Bank World Development data; Exton, C., C. Smith, and D. Vandendriessche (2015), "Comparing happiness across the world: Does culture matter?," OECD Statistics Working Papers, 2015/04, OECD Publishing, Paris. http://dx.doi.org/10.1787 /jrqppzd9bs2-en.

measured in purchasing power parity (PPP) terms, there is huge uncertainty about GDP measures; so not everything has to be attributed to oddities in life evaluation measures.

Another remarkable finding from the Gallup World Poll data is that experiential well-being measures are much less associated with per capita GDP than evaluative well-being, such as that measured using the Cantril ladder. At the country average level, there is only a small positive correlation between positive emotions (the sum of smiling/laughing, enjoyment, and feeling well rested a lot "yesterday") and log GDP per capita, while negative emotions (feeling anger, worry, and sadness a lot "yesterday") show essentially no relationship (Exton, Smith, and Vandendriessche, 2015). People in some African countries report as many instances of positive emotions yesterday as do people in much richer countries. If, as argued by Benthamite hedonistic utilitarians, the purpose of policy should be to maximize experiential happiness, then Gallup World Poll data would imply that Kuwait, Trinidad and Tobago, and Paraguay should be giving aid to Syria, Iraq, and Armenia, at least if aid improves happiness. Stress (for which Philippines is champion, and the United States is near the top), worry (Iraq), and anger (Algeria, Iran, Iraq, Turkey) are also not strongly related to income, while pain is highest in the Middle East. So higher national income tends to come with higher life evaluation, but does little to improve the emotional lives of citizens.

Despite these findings, the association between money income and subjective well-being is not yet settled. Stevenson and Wolfers (2012), for example, claim that the derivative of the Cantril ladder–based evaluative measure with respect to the log of income is around 0.30, pretty much no matter where you look over time.

Other findings from Gallup data show that the U-shape between life evaluation and age is not universal across countries, or at least across regions of the world (Figure 7.3). It is no puzzle that the ladder falls with age in the former Soviet Union countries, given that the elderly experienced the greatest losses from the transition away from a planned economy. But there are also areas of the world, like sub-Saharan Africa, where the relation between life evaluation and age is flat; others, like Latin America and southern Europe, where life evaluations fall with age; and some, like China, that share the English-speaking U-pattern. Of course, these are cross-sectional results, but it is not clear how to reconcile them with a universal U that is biological, based on evidence from primates, as has been argued (Weiss et al., 2012). The life-cycle patterns of experiential well-being are more uniform across the world, with a lot of what originally reported in Stone et al. (2010) showing up in many places. Negative emotions really do seem to become less prevalent with age around the world. This should perhaps replace the U-shape in evaluative well-being as the new stylized fact.

Figure 7.3. Life Evaluations and Age in Four World Regions

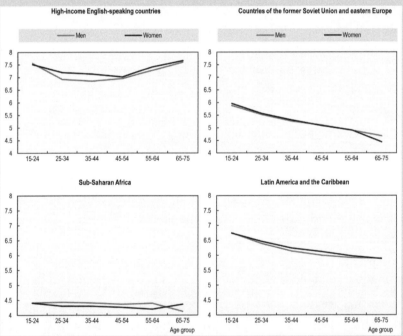

Source: Steptoe, A., A. Deaton, and A.A. Stone (2015), "Subjective wellbeing, health, and ageing," *The Lancet*, Vol. 385(9968), pp. 640–648. StatLink 2 http://dx.doi.org/10.1787 /888933839810.

Correlates and Determinants of Subjective Well-Being

At an individual level, there is a growing consensus around the factors that are correlated to higher life satisfaction: being employed and having higher income, better health, and stronger relationships are among the most important factors (see, for example, Eurostat's "Analytical Report on Subjective Well-Being," published in 2016). A large number of other correlates has been identified in some data sets, such as environmental conditions and pollution (Silva, de Keulenaer, and Johnstone, 2012). See the sidebar above for a partial list of the research findings on correlates of subjective well-being.

There is also new work on the importance of childhood as a critical period for later subjective well-being. Children's emotional health is the largest predictor of adult life satisfaction, above cognitive skills (Layard et al., 2014; OECD, 2015b). This indicates that while children's subjective well-being is important in and of itself, it matters also because it is likely to be a driver of adolescent and adult outcomes (such as adult life satisfaction, employment, or school achievement). Children's subjective well-being and emotional health are, in turn, correlated with a variety of family characteristics such as financial difficulties, family structure, moving to a different residence, and the quality of the parent relationship. One way that this research might help policy-makers would be to better understand why some children are resilient to detrimental circumstances or events, but others are not, and what the implications for public service investments are. Eurostat is currently developing a module for EU-SILC on children's health and material well-being that will likely be collected every 3 years in the future. When these data become available, they will provide many opportunities for deeper analysis on this topic.

Levels of subjective well-being are not only determined by the events that make people better or worse off, but also by the degree to which they "bounce back" after such events. Resilience is a concept closely related to that of (true) adaptation, and several papers in recent years have added to this literature. The picture that is painted by these studies is, however, mixed: there is evidence that life satisfaction adapts to some life events (such as marriage or childbirth), but less so to others (such as disability, entry into poverty, international migration, or unemployment; see, for example, Lucas, 2007; Clark et al., 2008; Oswald and Powdthavee, 2008; Frijters, Johnston, and Shields, 2011; Clark and Georgellis, 2013; Clark, D'Ambrosio, and

Ghislandi, 2016; and Helliwell, Bonikowska, and Shiplett, 2016). One potential explanation is that people adapt more to positive life events than to negative life events—which may point to a relationship between loss aversion and adaptation. Again, we point out the importance of specifying which type of subjective well-being is being assessed: this is because experiential and evaluative subjective well-being are likely to have different patterns of adaptation.

Progress has also been made in analyzing subjective well-being not only as an outcome, but also as a predictor or, in the framework of a production function, as an input to other life outcomes. Steptoe, Deaton, and Stone (2015) have shown that, for example, there is evidence that the three components of subjective well-being predict individual morbidity and mortality even when controlling for a wide variety of individual characteristics. Similarly, a growing body of research has supported the idea that meaning and purpose in life (i.e., eudaemonic well-being) is associated with health and mortality. For example, recent findings from the *Midlife in the United States* study demonstrate that subjective well-being is linked to the metabolic syndrome, a group of factors that raises the risk for heart disease and other health problems such as diabetes and stroke (Boylan and Ryff, 2015). However, recent data from the UK Million Women study show that ratings of "happiness" (admittedly an ambiguous construct from the multi-dimensional subjective well-being perspective advanced here—see "What Are Subjective Well-Being Measures?") are not linked to mortality when personal and health conditions at the first assessment point were considered in the regressions (Liu et al., 2016). Although the study omitted men, it could have been more refined in the subjective well-being measures employed, and it may have over-controlled co-varying health status, its conclusions challenge the prevailing sentiment about this issue.

What Do People Mean When They Say They Are "Satisfied with Their Life"?

To know what is behind these measures, and in particular to help understand how different measures relate to each other and might be combined, it is very important to understand what people mean when they say that they are satisfied with their lives, and how they weigh different well-being outcomes—that is, what matters for people's subjective well-being.

The correlates of the three types of subjective well-being present a generally coherent picture and provide predictive evidence that the measures are performing as expected. Nevertheless, a strong case can be made for more deeply understanding the origins of the ratings—that is, how people are generating them. In this regard, most work has been done on evaluative measures like life satisfaction, where there have been investigations into the aspects of life that bear the most on judgments of life satisfaction by simply regressing overall satisfaction measures on ratings of specific domains of life such as work satisfaction, partner satisfaction, social satisfaction, and so on (Helliwell, Layard, and Sachs, 2016, special section). However, simple, atheoretical analytic approaches may result in misleading conclusions and, importantly, lead to incorrect policy inferences. More recently, an econometric approach to decomposing global life satisfaction using stated preferences has been proposed and tested by Benjamin et al. (2014). This study has shown that people's decisions about the future are based on a complex weighting of ratings of anticipated well-being in several imagined outcomes. In another approach to the question, new work is ongoing employing traditional qualitative methods to understand the thought processes associated with making life satisfaction ratings—for example, via the use of "think aloud" techniques (Broderick et al., 2016).

Progress in Applications to Policy

Direct applications of subjective well-being to policy are at still an early stage. The years since 2009 have been immensely productive for the implementation of subjective well-being data collection in many countries, for understanding the issues in using subjective well-being data, and for the development of many techniques to cope with these issues. New research is now needed to better understand how subjective well-being measures can be transformed into a useful metric for policy-makers, and in what way they can provide meaningful information that contributes to better policy decisions. Yet another commission, from the Legatum Institute, focused on subjective well-being and governmental policy and provided a refreshingly pragmatic and thoughtful approach (O'Donnell et al., 2014). In many policy applications, some benefits and costs are recognized, but are not easily or accurately quantifiable in monetary terms, because explicit markets for these benefits and costs do not exist, and implicit valuations can only be imperfectly, if at all, placed on these factors. Thus, even if subjective well-being measures are imperfect, they have the potential to advance policy-making when compared with the imperfect measures of benefits and costs often available.

Cost-Benefit Analysis

Some work has used subjective well-being measures in cost-benefit analysis, as a method for valuing nonmarket outcomes (O'Donnell et al., 2014; Fujiwara and Campbell, 2011). The principle underlying this work is that many policies have costs and benefits that are difficult to monetize. As a result, standard cost-benefit analysis, which compares monetary costs and benefits, will lead to policy decisions that underweight those nonmonetary costs and benefits if these are not taken into account. In the case of valuing nonmarket factors for cost-benefit analysis, current methods have serious limitations, so complementing existing methods with subjective well-being-based valuations could provide additional information. The UK Treasury's *Green Book*, which provides formal guidance to government agencies on the appraisal and evaluation of policy proposals, was updated in 2011 to include a section on valuation for social cost-benefit analysis, including through subjective well-being-based methods. However, additional work needs to be done to make this approach more credible. In particular, there are many problems with monetizing differences in levels of subjective well-being (Kahneman and Krueger, 2006)—not least a lack of data sets containing high-quality measures of both personal income and subjective well-being, as well as conceptual problems in identifying a unit of measure with which to convert subjective well-being into dollars or euros. As with other measurement issues, the difficulties in using subjective well-being for cost-benefit analysis must be seen in light of the difficulties in other methods for cost-benefit analysis—and subjective well-being-based methods should be seen as a complement to, rather than a replacement for, more traditional techniques.

Program and Policy Evaluation

Several policy and program evaluations have included subjective well-being as an outcome indicator, and its inclusion can help both to assess the impact of a program and to understand its mechanisms with more confidence. These studies not only support the idea that subjective well-being can be used to meaningfully measure policy impact; they also support the underlying construct of subjective well-being and its responsiveness to life circumstances. Another advantage of using subjective well-being measures in policy evaluations is that they may show that interventions have benefits that are not measured by conventional outcomes; or, conversely, to show that while conventional methods may show benefits, these benefits could be offset by lower subjective well-being (and, in both cases, providing a richer understanding of program impact).

For example, an in-work support program in the United Kingdom was found to have unexpected negative impacts on the subjective well-being of people who participated in these programs (Dorsett and Oswald, 2014). Similarly, an unconditional cash transfer program in Kenya found positive impacts on the subjective well-being of participants, but negative spill-over effects on nonparticipants (Haushofer, Reisinger, and Shapiro, 2015). In Morocco, while household connections to the municipal water supply showed no impact on health or income, they resulted in increased happiness (Devoto et al., 2012). Other studies suggest a positive impact of access to insurance on mental health (Finkelstein et al., 2012), of family leave policies on the life satisfaction of parents (D'Addio et al., 2014), and of participation in the National Citizen Service in the United Kingdom on the subjective well-being of participants (United Kingdom Cabinet Office and Ipsus MORI, 2013). Finally, Ludwig et al. (2013) found that subjective measures of mental health improved among participants in the Moving to Opportunity experiment in the United States before such results showed up in physical health. Measures of subjective well-being also have the potential to improve our understanding of people's economic insecurity (see sidebar, "Subjective Well-Being and Economic Insecurity"), as also argued in Chapter 8 of this volume.

While work on refining the measurement and understanding of subjective well-being should continue, experimentation in policy applications should commence. As with many domains, experiments in policy applications and foundational work on measurement and understanding are likely to complement one another, in a mutually reinforcing process.

SUBJECTIVE WELL-BEING AND ECONOMIC INSECURITY

There are several possible threads through which one can link subjective well-being and economic insecurity. Research on both topics confronts several shared methodological issues, especially with respect to subjective economic insecurity. In addition, a primary concern about economic insecurity is that it reduces subjective well-being (even if the bad event does not actually happen). Eurostat's "Analytical Report on Subjective Well-Being" (2016) showed, for example, that people's inability to face unexpected expenses drastically reduces their subjective well-being, even when controlling for the impact of other variables such as their income or employment status.

A recent analysis of economic trends highlighted the differential effects of positive and negative GDP growth on people's subjective well-being (De Neve

Continuing Issues and New Questions

Issues to Be Addressed to Gain a More Complete Understanding of Subjective Well-Being

Causality

First, as with all other types of analysis, careful attention must be paid to establish credible causality. It is difficult to reach strong conclusions about causality on the basis of much of the subjective well-being research that is currently available, which relies mainly on observational and self-reported data. In order for the field to advance, it will be important to focus less on exploratory and hypothesis-generating studies, and more on developing and testing theories. These theories, and the research designed to test them, should ideally take into account the complex interrelationships among subjective well-being correlates, in order to identify which variables are acting as mediators or moderators, and which are causing actual shifts in subjective well-being. Panel data, especially panel data that can take advantage of a discontinuity such as a policy shift, are likely to be beneficial in this respect. As mentioned earlier, this endeavor is facilitated, and indeed perhaps only possible, when explicit models and theories are used to inform analyses and interpretations.

et al., 2015), using data from the Gallup World Poll, the US Behavioral Risk Factor Surveillance System, and Eurobarometer. Motivated by inferences from prospect theory (Kahneman and Tversky, 1979), the authors found that average evaluative well-being (life satisfaction) reacted more strongly to negative GDP growth than to positive growth in all three surveys (a pattern that is consistent with loss aversion). On the other hand, experiential well-being was only impacted by negative GDP growth: daily happiness and enjoyment decreased and stress and worry increased during periods of economic declines.

These findings have implications for both economic theory and macroeconomic policies, including the impact of unemployment, and nicely demonstrate the utility of taking a multi-faceted view of subjective well-being.

Understanding the nature of sorting with respect to preferences is also a priority for future research. For example, Krueger and Schkade (2008) provide some evidence that workers sort themselves across jobs based on their preferences, with workers who are more extroverted tending to be employed in jobs that require more social interactions.

Heterogeneity

Second, and related, analyses of subjective well-being need to go beyond the average and examine heterogeneity. Focusing on the average subjective well-being of a group or nation is misleading in the same way as focusing on the average income of a group or nation. There may be large inequalities in subjective well-being, including inequalities among people with different demographic characteristics. It is also important to consider the possibility of different levels and correlations among different groups in order to more fully understand the dynamics of subjective well-being. However, any sub-group analysis requires large sample sizes, which are not always available, although there are certainly some large-scale data sets in development, and data from NSOs will have a particularly important role to play here. In addition, data quality on the dimensions of interest for disaggregation is often poor among existing data sets, in particular income. This is a substantial problem for research on the relationship between income and subjective well-being. Again, large official data sets such as EU-SILC allow this disaggregation and analysis, with high-quality information on a range of covariates collected in a standardized way across countries. Most of these indicators and analyses are published—in the data sets and Eurostat publications—with a variety of different breakdowns such as those for sex, age, income, education level, employment status, country (for most countries also region) of residence, and degree of urbanization.

A theoretical model detailing the factors and processes underlying observed differences in subjective well-being would be invaluable for understanding and for designing possible interventions to remedy these inequalities. Building up a long time series of data across a wide range of countries will also be essential for testing these models, and to assess the dynamic relationships among drivers and outcomes.

Similarly, relatively little is known about the tails of the distribution of subjective well-being, particularly those who rate themselves as having extremely low levels of subjective well-being (including those who live with high levels of pain). These people are likely to represent a particular policy concern, and much may be learned from research focusing on them.

Finally, research efforts should continue to focus on adaptation and resilience, as these are among the most promising, if difficult, research avenues. Further investigation of the role of public goods and services in supporting people's resilience might lead to findings that could be directly acted upon by policy-makers; in other situations, such research might highlight the resources that are needed to restore subjective well-being after a life challenge.

Data Collection and Analytic Issues

Data Collection and Availability

As described above, data collection on subjective well-being has expanded enormously. There are, however, two important priority areas where there is still a lack of data on subjective well-being, and where the inclusion of subjective well-being questions is likely be relatively low cost. The first priority is the expansion of high-quality data collection on subjective well-being to poor countries, for example, by including a life satisfaction and experiential well-being module in household surveys conducted in these countries. As well as casting important light on the societal conditions and policy environments that can influence changes in subjective well-being over time, research into differences in well-being among countries has potential for addressing persistent methodological and conceptual questions concerning the meaning of subjective well-being responses from people in different cultural and economic settings. Have people in poor countries adapted to their circumstances, and are they using the subjective well-being scales in entirely different ways than those in wealthy countries? And if so, what do country comparisons mean?

The second priority is the inclusion of subjective well-being measures in official time-use surveys in order to increase our understanding of experiential well-being, as recommended in the National Academy of Science (NAS) report mentioned above. Such efforts could be supported by more guidance on which approach is best for this purpose, and by increasing the research output linked to existing efforts. The *Guidelines on Harmonising Time Use Surveys* (UNECE, 2013) have been useful in this area, but additional analysis of different approaches to collecting experiential well-being data are necessary in order to provide empirical guidance on best practice in this area. As mentioned above, the inclusion of subjective well-being items in ongoing time use surveys, such as the American Time Use Survey, is an efficient way to achieve this goal. Collecting time-use data and experiential well-being in poor countries would also be particularly useful, as little is known about the daily activities or experiential well-being of rural populations.

Finally, timely access to these data is critical, as is responsiveness by researchers to the new data. Measurement initiatives will push forward our knowledge and understanding of subjective well-being, but researchers must have access to these data in order to achieve this outcome. In turn, researchers must demonstrate the usefulness of these measures, or the measures risk being dropped. Increased cooperation among various actors would improve the quality and usage of data on subjective well-being, and networks can play an important role in this respect.

Data Analysis and Interpretation

As discussed above, one of the most important issues inadequately addressed by current research is that of systematic differences in question interpretation and response styles between population groups. Is there conclusive evidence that this is a problem? And, if so, are there ways to adjust for it? Information is needed about which types of group comparisons are affected, about the magnitude of the problem, and about the psychological mechanisms underlying these systematic differences.

While some of the methodological issues that have been associated with sub-jective well-being measures are, to varying degrees, minimized through the use of standardized questionnaires, this issue is not resolved through standardization alone. So far, only limited analysis has been performed for the assessment of the 2013 EU-SILC ad hoc module regarding the viability of cross-national compari-sons (Eurostat, 2016). The analysis that exists has been mostly undertaken through internal and external validation (correlations with certain variables of interest), and the results are encouraging.

Some progress has also been made on using vignettes to address this issue, but this approach has limitations. For example, people's responses to the circumstances described in vignettes are very likely to be shaped by the policy environment in which they live—because the implications of, for example, living with a chronic health condition depend on factors such as health care cost and availability, as well as disability benefits. This means that "correcting" subjective well-being self-reports of own conditions according to international differences in how people rate the same vignettes could ultimately remove the most policy-relevant part of the international variation in well-being, effectively throwing the baby out with the bathwater.

The U-index, which calculates the share of time that individuals spend in an unpleasant state—defined as a period when the strongest reported emotion is a negative one (Kahneman and Krueger, 2006)—is a promising method for neutral-izing differences in the extent to which response scales are used differentially across countries or groups of people. While some work is available supporting its utility, its application so far has been limited to measures of experiential well-being. More work is needed to see actually how large is the problem of inter-personal differences in the use of response scale, and to find new cost-effective solutions.

Subjective well-being questions are generic, but there are times when they should be tailored to the application at hand. For example, in the Moving to Opportunity project in the United States, feelings of security and anxiety were especially relevant for program participants and were specifically targeted. In many medical studies, pain may be a particularly relevant type of experiential well-being, whereas misery may be especially relevant in studies of refugees.

More population-level work is needed on subjective well-being beyond life satisfaction, i.e., extending measurements to eudaemonic and experiential well-being. At present, a variety of different approaches are being used across OECD statistical offices to collect this type of information (see Exton, Siegerink, and Smith, forthcoming, for further details). As described in the sidebar above, measures of subjective well-being belong to three different categories. Life satisfaction is generally the most widely used measure of subjective well-being, and the one for which there has been the most research, for example, on adaptation. A focus on a single indicator is, on the one hand, beneficial and pragmatic, as it ensures a wider evidence base for at least one indicator. On the other hand, there are surely missed opportunities, as there is likely much to be learned from data on the other dimensions of subjective well-being.

We concur with the conclusion of the NAS report (Stone and Mackie, 2015) that research on subjective well-being should be explicit about the types of measure used, and should ideally include more than one type of measure. More effort should be given to understanding eudaemonia and experiential well-being, to describing the relationship between the different measures, and to ensuring that these outcomes are not being neglected.

Work on the other aspects of subjective well-being needs to be balanced with the need for clarity in communication with those outside the research community. While a synthetic indicator that combines different dimensions of subjective well-being is probably not a strategy that is well grounded in current understanding of the different constructs, there is often some demand for combining information in summary form. Effort should be made to ensure that these measures, if they are to gain traction in a policy setting, are reasonably easy to understand and compare.

Related to this question is an issue that studies on subjective well-being share with other topics in this volume: how to think about, and communicate, what constitutes a *meaningful change* or difference in the measure considered. Especially in large samples, a very small difference may be statistically significant but not very important for policy-making. This can be particularly problematic when considering differences on a scale that has no inherent meaning. One option is to phrase differences in terms of some calibration (i.e., a difference of magnitude x corresponds to the increase in subjective well-being associated with an increase in personal income of y, although much more research is needed to establish a universal unit of measurement). It should also be noted that the original work on the day reconstruction method presented differences in experiential well-being across groups by aligning those differences with the affect associated with typical daily activities, providing an informative ruler for interpreting affective differences.

Applications to Policy

Experimentation and Innovation

The application of subjective well-being to policy is at an early stage, and there is still much to learn. At this point, there is sufficient understanding of methodological issues and consensus on the best way to address most of those issues to cautiously move forward. Experimental initiatives will, in turn, generate new questions and more progress on the methodological issues. However, many policy applications will have to wait until a sufficiently large and long cross-country data set has been built up, which will take time. In the meantime, there are a variety of ways that progress can be made.

Subjective well-being can complement existing policy analysis methods, and we recommend taking steps to consider all three dimensions of subjective well-being in order to obtain a complete picture. However, we realize that this recommendation is much less specific than we would like it to be, and the reason for this follows. Evaluative measures of subjective well-being (life satisfaction, Cantril ladder, Diener scale) seem to us to have a conceptual advantage over the eudaemonic and experiential subjective well-being measures in that they target people's summary evaluations of their current lives, which at face value appears more consistent with their choices and therefore with the economic concept of "utility."

Experiential measures may be less ideal because of concerns about true adaptation to changing environmental situations (see Sen's "happy peasant" arguments), though experiential measures do capture an essential aspect of well-being—how one feels. Eudaemonia addresses broader meaning and aspirations, which are undoubtedly an important aspect of life, yet it appears less directly applicable as a measure of utility. An example of this approach tracked evaluative and experiential well-being for people who migrated from Tonga to New Zealand, and showed how these measures illuminated their complex psychological transition (Stillman et al., 2015).

There are drawbacks, though, with exclusively adopting evaluative well-being as the primary measure for policy. First, as mentioned above, we believe that experience is an essential part of subjective well-being that should not be omitted. Second, as reviewed in the methodological sections of this chapter, evaluative measures are prone to being perturbed and, possibly, biased by a number of irrelevant factors, which raises questions about recommending their use for policy-making—particularly if the data are to be used as a proxy for utility, rather than as one of a variety of subjective well-being measures that might inform policy decisions.

Additional work should be done on cost-benefit analysis, to understand whether and how results from analyses based on subjective well-being valuation can complement existing methods. Early efforts have produced some extreme results, potentially due to income measurement issues (i.e., if the estimated partial effect of income on subjective well-being is small, and does not represent the "true" value of income, scaling other effects by this coefficient will lead to implausibly large monetary effects); and because models and theories were not sufficiently developed to allow sound interpretation. In addition, some other measures are particularly amenable to links with subjective well-being research—for example, the Quality-Adjusted Life Year (QALY) and the Well-Being-Adjusted Life Year (WELBY).

Some fairly low-cost initiatives would be to routinely collect, and report on, subjective well-being indicators in program evaluation questionnaires, and to routinely add subjective well-being questions to questionnaires such as labor force surveys or surveys carried out in schools. In the European context this will be done using the EU-SILC as a vehicle, as two to three indicators (including life satisfaction) will be collected on a yearly basis. As shown in the sidebar on page 213 listing articles released in 2015, data on subjective well-being is an important outcome not only in itself, but also as an input or driver of other outcomes of interest, and can help researchers provide a richer data analysis.

Researchers, in turn, need to spur applications to policy, in part to demonstrate to NSOs that investment in subjective well-being data is worthwhile. Much of the current research on subjective well-being is difficult to apply to policy, even experimentally. A greater focus on policy applications in the literature (e.g., on policy-amenable drivers of subjective well-being) would be helpful. Coordination among researchers, policy-makers, and NSOs may be very valuable, a role that the OECD may be well placed to play.

Cautions in Using Subjective Well-Being Data for Policy

Well-meaning but naive policy changes may make people worse off due to the complex inter-relationships between choices, prices, and heterogeneity in subjective well-being, as well as general equilibrium effects. Airport noise is one example: people live near airports for a reason, typically because of lower housing prices, or because they do not care too much about noise, and well-meaning policy (e.g., to reduce traffic at night) could actually make them worse off because of the effect of lower noise in raising house prices. (This example is taken from a personal communication with Angus Deaton.) We need to understand why people live where they do, and build models forecasting how location could change in response to policy changes. Hedonic models of sorting are well established in labor economics (e.g., Rosen, 1986) and urban economics (e.g., Roback, 1982), and this type of work can be extended to subjective well-being.

A less ambitious but still important goal for policy is simply to provide information on subjective well-being and let people and businesses use it as they see fit. To use a term from David Halpern, "de-shrouding" subjective well-being means giving the public information on the correlates of subjective well-being—informing them, for example, that priests, or people without children, or people who live in Denmark are happier than others (clearly, some of this has already occurred in the news media). To some extent, this is simply providing information, which might in principle be useful to someone considering a move to Copenhagen.

However, such information may also be misleading, partly because of the considerable challenges in identifying causality in these studies. The types of people who become priests are very special, and the standard battery of variables used to control for differences between groups (e.g., sex, age, educational background, income) is unlikely to fully control for the difference between people who become priests and those who select other occupations. In this regard, subjective well-being data are no different from data on average income: while it is informative to know that doctors earn more than the average worker, it is the case that many individuals do not have the training, aptitude, or temperament to work as doctors. Therefore, to continue with the subjective well-being example, entering the clergy may not yield the expected gains in subjective well-being that were anticipated on the basis of the de-shrouded well-being averages.

In addition, results from observational studies are averages, even if they are averages within groups, and as such may not apply to a given individual. So the application of subjective well-being data must be done in a considered way, given that the potential for unintended consequences are far from academic.

Conclusions

Up to this point, we have not made recommendations for how subjective well-being measures could be used in policy applications, i.e., recommendations beyond the generic suggestion echoed from the 2015 NAS report for the use of both evaluative and experiential subjective well-being measures. While we continue to agree that this is a reasonable approach, here we describe our concerns about this position and lay out recommendations taking those concerns into account.

The choice of the subjective well-being measure that will be used to inform policy should be directed by a theory or model of whatever phenomenon is under consideration, which should direct the subjective well-being construct that best serves the model and policy objectives. As discussed throughout this chapter, explicit depiction of the potential pathways by which subjective well-being influences or is influenced by other variables is paramount for properly specifying the measures selected, for study design, for structuring analyses, and for allowing appropriate interpretation of the results. Without such considerations, investigators are prone to arrive at incorrect, and possibly counterproductive, conclusions about how subjective well-being is impacted by a specific policy.

In the light of the considerations made in the preceding sections, we would like to conclude by providing a limited number of recommendations that could guide research, measurement efforts, and policy application of subjective well-being data in the future.

1. Continue regular, frequent, and standardized collection of subjective well-being data by NSOs. Use the *OECD Guidelines* to create a standardized evidence base, and aim for re-evaluation of guidelines in the future, once a sufficient evidence base is established.
2. Ensure that these data are collected in a way that allows estimation of the joint distribution of subjective well-being with other variables, and that the other variables (in particular, income) are well measured.
3. Focus on subjective well-being measures beyond life evaluation, and examine the relationship between different aspects of subjective well-being.
4. Continue to collect information on time use and experiential well-being, and intensify efforts to collect such data in low-income countries.
5. Focus efforts to resolve methodological issues on systematic inter-personal differences in response styles, which are not amenable to solution through standardized questionnaires.
6. Develop theories and build models of how different types of subjective well-being function as predictors and outcomes, and how they relate to the other variables one is considering; and develop models of people's sorting based on preferences and policy changes.
7. Add subjective well-being measures as outcomes in studies of randomized experiments and natural experiments to help identify causal mechanisms.

Notes

1. Albeit often looking at longer-term aspects of affective experience, such as feelings and emotions in the last two weeks, which can confound evaluative and experiential well-being.

2. http://worldhappiness.report/.

3. A remaining concern is that, even though context effects can be reduced or eliminated through good survey design, the notion that subjective well-being measures are particularly vulnerable to them would imply that the underlying construct is not stable. This is, however, difficult to test empirically and is controversial. That said, substantial evidence on the validity of life evaluation measures, and their consistent relationship to objective factors, suggests that people can and do provide meaningful responses to these evaluative questions.

References

Aassve, A., B. Arpino, and N. Balbo (2016), "It takes two to tango: Couples' happiness and childbearing," *European Journal of Population*, Vol. 32(3), pp. 339–354, https://pdfs.semanticscholar.org/5f7f/cf43dcfcbca04e4d8cc90ab078f3190c4661.pdf.

Aghababaei, N. and A. Błachnio (2015), "Well-being and the dark triad," *Personality and Individual Differences*, Vol. 86, pp. 365–368, https://doi.org/10.1016/j.paid.2015.06.043.

Beegle, K. et al. (2011), "Methods of household consumption measurement through surveys: Experimental results from Tanzania," *Journal of Development Economics*, Vol. 98(1), pp. 3–18.

Benjamin, D.J. et al. (2014), "Beyond happiness and satisfaction: Toward well-being indices based on stated preference," *American Economic Review*, Vol. 104, No. 9, pp. 2698–2735.

Berlin, M. and N. Kaunitz (2015), "Beyond income: The importance for life satisfaction of having access to a cash margin," *Journal of Happiness Studies*, Vol. 16(6), pp. 1557–1573, https://ideas.repec.org/a/spr/jhappi/v16y2015i6p1557-1573.html.

Blanchflower, D.G. and A.J. Oswald (2008), "Is well-being U-shaped over the life cycle?," *Social Science & Medicine*, Vol. 66, pp. 1733–1749.

Boylan, J.M. and C.D. Ryff (2015), "Psychological well-being and metabolic syndrome: Findings from the midlife in the United States national sample," *Psychosomatic Medicine*, Vol. 77(5), pp. 548–558.

Brewster, C.E. (2015), "Churchmanship and personal happiness: A study among rural Anglican clergy," *Rural Theology: International, Ecumenical and Interdisciplinary Perspectives*, Vol. 13(2), pp. 124–134, www.tandfonline.com/doi/abs/10.1179/Z.00000000050.

Broderick, J.E. et al. (2016), "A qualitative study of themes considered in life satisfaction ratings in the U.S.," unpublished manuscript, University of Southern California.

Brown, T.T. (2015), "The subjective well-being method of valuation: An application to general health status," *Health Services Research Journal*, Vol. 50(6), pp. 1996–2018, www.ncbi.nlm.nih.gov/pubmed/25762183.

Christodoulou, C., S. Schneider, and A.A. Stone (2014), "Validation of a brief yesterday measure of hedonic well-being and daily activities: Comparison with the day reconstruction method," *Social Indicators Research*, Vol. 115, pp. 907–917.

Clark, A.E., C. d'Ambrosio, and S. Ghislandi (2016), "Adaptation to poverty in long-run panel data," *Review of Economics and Statistics*, Vol. 98(3), pp. 591–600.

Clark, A.E., S. Flèche, and C. Senik (2015), "Economic growth evens out happiness: Evidence from six surveys," *Review of Income and Wealth*, Vol. 62(3), pp. 405–419.

Clark, A.E. and Y. Georgellis (2013), "Back to baseline in Britain: Adaptation in the BHPS," *Economica*, Vol. 80, pp. 496–512.

Clark, A.E. et al. (2008), "Lags and leads in life satisfaction: A test of the baseline hypothesis," *Economic Journal*, Vol. 118, pp. F222–F243.

Coffey, J.K., M.T. Warren, and A.W. Gottfried (2015), "Does infant happiness forecast adult life satisfaction? Examining subjective well-being in the first quarter century of life," *Journal of Happiness Studies*, Vol. 16(6), pp. 1401–1421, https://link.springer.com /article/10.1007%2Fs10902-014-9556-x.

Cramm, J.M. and A.P. Nieboer (2015), "Social cohesion and belonging predict the wellbeing of community-dwelling older people," *BMC Geriatrics*, Vol. 15(1), p. 30, www.researchgate.net/publication/275051964_Social_cohesion_and_belonging _predict_the_well-being_of_community-dwelling_older_people.

Crane, M. et al. (2016), "Correcting bias in self-rated quality of life: An application of anchoring vignettes and ordinal regression models to better understand QoL differences across commuting modes," *Quality of Life Research*, Vol. 25(2), pp. 257–266.

Cuellar, I., E. Bastida, and S.M. Braccio (2004), "Residency in the United States, subjective well-being, and depression in an older Mexican-origin sample," *Journal of Aging and Health*, Vol. 16(4), pp. 447–466, https://doi.org/10.1177/0898264304265764.

Cummins, R.A. (2001), "The subjective well-being of people caring for a family member with a severe disability at home: A review," *Journal of Intellectual and Developmental Disability*, Vol. 26(1), pp. 83–100.

Cummins, R.A. et al. (2015), "A demonstration of set-points for subjective wellbeing," *Journal of Happiness Studies*, Vol. 15(1), pp. 183–206, http://dx.doi.org/10.1007/-013 -9444-9.

D'Addio, A. et al. (2014), "Using a quasi-natural experiment to identify the effects of birth-related leave policies on subjective well-being in Europe," *OECD Journal: Economic Studies*, Vol. 2013/1, http://dx.doi.org/10.1787/_studies-2013-5k3tvtg6fvmq.

Deaton, A. (2012), "The financial crisis and the well-being of Americans," *Oxford Economic Papers*, Vol. 64(1), pp. 1–26.

Deaton, A. (2008), "Income, health and wellbeing around the world: Evidence from the Gallup World Poll," *Journal of Economic Perspectives*, Vol. 22(2), pp. 53–72, https://dx .doi.org/10.1257%2Fjep.22.2.53.

Deaton, A. and A.A. Stone (2016), "Understanding context effects for a measure of life evaluation: How responses matter," *Oxford Economic Papers*, Vol. 68(4), pp. 861–870, https://academic.oup.com/oep/article-lookup/doi/10.1093/oep/gpw022.

De Neve, J-E. et al. (2015), "The asymmetric experience of positive and negative economic growth: Global evidence using subjective well-being data," *Review of Economics and Statistics*, Vol. 100(2), pp. 362–375.

Devins, G.M. et al. (2015), "Distancing, self-esteem, and subjective well-being in head and neck cancer," *Psycho-Oncology*, Vol. 24(11), pp. 1506–1513, https://doi.org/10.1002/pon.3760.

Devoto, F. et al. (2012), "Happiness on tap: Piped water adoption in urban Morocco," *American Economic Journal: Economic Policy*, pp. 68–99.

Diener, E. (1984), "Subjective well-being," *Psychological Bulletin*, Vol. 95(3), https://ssrn.com/abstract=2162125.

Di Tella, R. et al. (2010), "Happiness adaptation to income and to status in an individual panel," *Journal of Economic Behavior & Organization*, Vol. 76(3), pp. 834–852.

Dorsett, R. and A.J. Oswald (2014), "Human well-being and in-work benefits: A randomized controlled trial," *IZA Discussion Paper*, No. 7943.

Easterlin, R.A. (1974), "Does economic growth improve the human lot? Some empirical evidence," in David, P.A. and M.W. Reder (eds.), *Nations and Households in Economic Growth: Essays in Honor of Moses Abramovitz*, Academic Press, New York.

Eurostat (2016), "Analytical report on subjective well-being," *Eurostat Statistical Working Papers*, http://ec.europa.eu/eurostat/web/products-statistical-working-papers/-/KS-TC-16-005.

Eurostat (2015), *Quality of Life: Facts and Views*, Eurostat Statistical Books, http://ec.europa.eu/eurostat/web/products-statistical-books/-/KS-05-14-073.

Eurostat (2013), *2013 EU-SILC Module on Wellbeing: Assessment of the Implementation*, http://ec.europa.eu/eurostat/documents/1012329/1012401/2013+Module+assessment.pdf.

Exton, C., V. Siegerink, and C. Smith (2018), "Measuring subjective well-being in national statistics: Taking stock of recent OECD activities," forthcoming, OECD Publishing, Paris.

Exton, C., C. Smith, and D. Vandendriessche (2015), "Comparing happiness across the world: Does culture matter?," *OECD Statistics Working Papers*, No. 2015/04, OECD Publishing, Paris, http://dx.doi.org/10.1787/jrqppzd9bs2-en.

Extremera, N. and L. Rey (2015), "The moderator role of emotion regulation ability in the link between stress and well-being," *Frontiers in Psychology*, Vol. 6, p. 1632, https://doi.org/10.3389/fpsyg.2015.01632.

Finkelstein, A. et al. (2012), "The Oregon health insurance experiment: Evidence from the first year," *Quarterly Journal of Economics*, Vol. 127(3), pp. 1057–1106.

Fleurbaey, M. and D. Blanchet (2013), *Beyond GDP: Measuring Welfare and Assessing Sustainability*, Oxford University Press, Oxford.

Frijters, P., D. Johnston, and M. Shields (2011), "Happiness dynamics with quarterly life event data," *Scandinavian Journal of Economics*, Vol. 113, pp. 190–211.

Fujiwara, D. and R. Campbell (2011), *Valuation Techniques for Social Cost-Benefit Analysis: Stated Preference, Revealed Preference and Subjective Well-Being Approaches*, Department for Work and Pensions, HM Treasury, London.

Gal, E. et al. (2015), "Integration in the vocational world: How does it affect quality of life and subjective well-being of young adults with ASD," *International Journal of Environmental Research and Public Health*, Vol. 12(9), pp. 10820–10832, https://doi.org/10.3390/ijerph120910820.

García-Mainar, I., V.M. Montuenga, and M. Navarro-Paniagua (2015), "Workplace environmental conditions and life satisfaction in Spain," *Ecological Economics*, Vol. 119, pp. 136–146, https://doi.org/10.1016/j.ecolecon.2015.08.017.

García-Moya, I. et al. (2015), "Subjective well-being in adolescence and teacher connectedness: A health asset analysis," *Health Education Journal*, Vol. 74(6), pp. 641–654, https://doi.org/10.1177/0017896914555039.

Graham, C., S. Zhou, and J. Zhang (2015), "Happiness and health in China: The paradox of progress," *Global Economy and Development Working Paper*, No. 89, Brookings, www.brookings.edu/wp-content/uploads/2016/07/happiness-health-progress-china.pdf.

Grol-Prokopczyk, H. et al. (2015), "Promises and pitfalls of anchoring vignettes in health survey research," *Demography*, Vol. 52(5), pp. 1703–1728.

Hahn, E. et al. (2015), "Coping with unemployment: The impact of unemployment duration and personality on trajectories of life satisfaction," *European Journal of Personality*, Vol. 29(6), pp. 635–646, https://doi.org/10.1002/per.2034.

Haushofer, J., J. Reisinger, and J. Shapiro (2015), "Your gain is my pain: Negative psychological externalities of cash transfers," working paper, www.princeton.edu/~joha/publications/Haushofer_Reisinger_Shapiro_Inequality_2015.pdf.

Helliwell, J.F., A. Bonikowska, and H. Shiplett (2016), "Migration as a test of the happiness set-point hypothesis: Evidence from immigration to Canada," *National Bureau of Economic Research Working Paper*, No. 22601, www.nber.org/papers/w22601.

Helliwell, J.F., R. Layard, and J.D. Sachs (eds.) (2018), *World Happiness Report 2018*, Sustainable Development Solutions Network, New York, http://worldhappiness.report/ed/2018/.

Helliwell, J.F., R. Layard, and J.D. Sachs (eds.) (2016), *World Happiness Report 2016*, Sustainable Development Solutions Network, New York, http://worldhappiness.report/ed/2016/.

Helliwell, J.F., R. Layard, and J.D. Sachs (eds.) (2015), *World Happiness Report 2015*, Sustainable Development Solutions Network, New York, http://worldhappiness.report/ed/2015/.

HM Treasury (2011), *The Green Book: Appraisal and Evaluation in Central Government*, HM Stationery Office, London.

Kahneman, D. and A. Deaton (2010), "High income improves evaluation of life but not emotional well-being," *Proceedings of the National Academy of Sciences*, Vol. 107(38), pp. 16489–16493.

Kahneman, D. and A.B. Krueger (2006), "Developments in the measurement of subjective well-being," *Journal of Economic Perspectives*, Vol. 20, pp. 3–24.

Kahneman, D. and A. Tversky (1979), "Prospect theory: An analysis of decisions under risk," *Econometrica*, Vol. 47, pp. 263–291.

Kahneman, D. et al. (2004), "A survey method for characterizing daily life experience: The day reconstruction method," *Science*, Vol. 306(5702), pp. 1776–1780.

Kim, B.J. et al. (2015), "The impact of employment and self-rated economic condition on the subjective well-being of older Korean immigrants," *International Journal of Aging and Human Development*, Vol. 81(3), pp. 189–203, https://doi.org/10.1177/0091415015607675.

Kinnunen, U. (2015), "Patterns of daily energy management at work: Relations to employee well-being and job characteristics," *International Archives of Occupational and Environmental Health*, Vol. 88(8), pp. 1077–1086, https://link.springer.com/article/10.1007%2Fs00420-015-1039-9.

Krueger, A.B. (2009), *Measuring the Subjective Well-Being of Nations: National Accounts of Time Use and Well-Being*, University of Chicago Press, Chicago.

Krueger, A.B. and D.A. Schkade (2008), "Sorting in the labor market: Do gregarious workers flock to interactive jobs?," *Journal of Human Resources*, Vol. 43(4), pp. 859–883.

Layard, R., A. Clark, and C. Senik (2012), "The causes of happiness and misery," in Helliwell, J.F., R. Layard, and J.D. Sachs (eds.), *World Happiness Report 2012*, Sustainable Development Solutions Network, New York.

Layard, R. et al. (2014), "What predicts a successful life? A life-course model of well-being," *Economic Journal*, Vol. 124(580), pp. F720–F738.

Lee, S. et al. (2016), "Question order sensitivity of subjective well-being measures: Focus on life satisfaction, self-rated health, and subjective life expectancy in survey instruments," *Quality of Life Research*, Vol. 25(10), pp. 2497–2510.

Li, J., A. Lepp, and J.E. Barkley (2015), "Locus of control and cell phone use: Implications for sleep quality, academic performance, and subjective well-being," *Computers in Human Behavior*, Vol. 52, pp. 450–457, https://doi.org/10.1016/j.chb.2015.06.021.

Linna, M.S. et al. (2013), "Body mass index and subjective well-being in young adults: A twin population study," *BMC Public Health*, Vol. 13, p. 231, https://doi.org/10.1186/1471-2458-13-231.

Liu, B. et al. (2016), "Happiness, health, and mortality reply," *The Lancet*, Vol. 388(10039), pp. 27–28.

Loi, S.M. et al. (2015), "Attitudes to aging in older carers—do they have a role in their well-being?," *International Psychogeriatrics*, Vol. 27(11), pp. 1893–1901, https://doi.org /10.1017/S1041610215000873.

Lucas, R.E. (2007), "Long-term disability is associated with lasting changes in subjective well-being: Evidence from two nationally representative longitudinal studies," *Journal of Personality and Social Psychology*, Vol. 92(4), pp. 717–730.

Ludwig, J. et al. (2013), "Long-term neighborhood effects on low-income families: Evidence from Moving to Opportunity," *American Economic Review*, Vol. 103(3), pp. 226–231.

Meisenberg, G. and M. Woodley (2015), "Gender differences in subjective well-being and their relationships with gender equality," *Journal of Happiness Studies*, Vol. 16(6), pp. 1539–1555, http://10.0.3.239/s10902-014-9577-5.

Miret, M. et al. (2012), "Validation of a measure of subjective well-being: An abbreviated version of the day reconstruction method," *PLoS One*, Vol. 7(8).

Muller, Z. and H. Litwin (2011), "Grandparenting and psychological well-being: How important is grandparent role centrality?," *European Journal of Ageing*, Vol. 8(2), pp. 109–118, https://dx.doi.org/10.1007%2Fs10433-011-0185-5.

Mwesigire, D.M. et al. (2015), "Relationship between CD4 count and quality of life over time among HIV patients in Uganda: A cohort study," *Health and Quality of Life Outcomes*, Vol. 13, p. 144, https://doi.org/10.1186/s12955-015-0332-3.

National Research Council (2012), "The subjective well-being module of the American Time Use Survey: Assessment for its continuation," Panel on Measuring Subjective Well-Being in a Policy-Relevant Framework, Washington, DC.

Niimi, Y. (2015), "The 'costs' of informal care: An analysis of the impact of elderly care on caregivers' subjective well-being in Japan," *MPRA Paper*, No. 67825, Munich Personal RePEc Archive, https://mpra.ub.uni-muenchen.de/67825/.

Nikolaev, B. (2015), "Living with mom and dad and loving it . . . or are you?," *Journal of Economic Psychology*, Vol. 51, pp. 199–209, https://doi.org/10.1016/j.joep.2015.08.009.

Odermatt, R. and A. Stutzer (2015), "Smoking bans, cigarette prices and life satisfaction," *Journal of Health Economics*, Vol. 44, pp. 176–194, https://doi.org/10.1016/j.jhealeco .2015.09.010.

O'Donnell, G. et al. (2014), *Wellbeing and Policy*, Legatum Institute, London.

OECD (2015a), *How's Life? 2015: Measuring Well-Being*, OECD Publishing, Paris, http:/ /dx.doi.org/10.1787/_life-2015-en.

OECD (2015b), *Skills for Social Progress: The Power of Social and Emotional Skills*, OECD Skills Studies, OECD Publishing, Paris, http://dx.doi.org/10.1787/-en.

OECD (2013), *OECD Guidelines on Measuring Subjective Well-being*, OECD Publishing, Paris, http://dx.doi.org/10.1787/-en.

Oswald, A.J. and N. Powdthavee (2008), "Does happiness adapt? A longitudinal study of disability with implications for economists and judges," *Journal of Public Economics*, Vol. 92, pp. 1061–1077.

Ouyang, Y. et al. (2015), "People higher in self-control do not necessarily experience more happiness: Regulatory focus also affects subjective well-being," *Personality and Individual Differences*, Vol. 86, pp. 406–411.

Raque-Bogdan, T.L. and M.A. Hoffman (2015), "The relationship among infertility, self-compassion, and well-being for women with primary or secondary infertility," *Psychology of Women Quarterly*, Vol. 39(4), pp. 484–496, https://doi.org/10.1177/0361684315576208.

Read, S., E. Grundy, and E. Foverskov (2015), "Socio-economic position and subjective health and well-being among older people in Europe: A systematic narrative review," *Aging and Mental Health*, Vol. 20(5), pp. 529–542, https://doi.org/10.1080/13607863.2015.1023766.

Roback, J. (1982), "Wages, rents and the quality of life," *Journal of Political Economy*, Vol. 90(6), pp. 1257–1278.

Rosen, S. (1986), "The theory of equalizing differences," in Ashenfelter, O.C. and R. Layard, *Handbook of Labor Economics*, Vol. 1, Elsevier, North-Holland, Amsterdam, pp. 641–692.

Ryff, C.D. (2014), "Self-realisation and meaning making in the face of adversity: A eudaimonic approach to human resilience," *Journal of Psychology in Africa*, Vol. 24(1), pp. 1–12.

Sage, D. (2015), "Do active labour market policies promote the subjective well-being of the unemployed? Evidence from the UK National Well-Being Programme," *Journal of Happiness Studies*, Vol. 16(5), pp. 1281–1298, https://doi.org/10.1007/s10902-014-9549-9.

Saito, M. et al. (2015), "Development of an instrument for community-level health related social capital among Japanese older people: The JAGES Project," *Journal of Epidemiology*, Vol. 27(5), pp. 221–227, https://doi.org/10.1016/j.je.2016.06.005.

Senik, C. (2014), "The French unhappiness puzzle: The cultural dimension of happiness," *Journal of Economic Behavior and Organization*, Vol. 106, pp. 379–401.

Shiffman, S., A.A. Stone, and M.R. Hufford (2008), "Ecological momentary assessment," *Annual Review of Clinical Psychology*, Vol. 4, pp. 1–32.

Shiue, I. (2015), "Less indoor cleaning is associated with poor health and unhappiness in adults: Japanese General Social Survey, 2010," *Environmental Science and Pollution Research*, Vol. 22(24), pp. 20312–20315, https://doi.org/10.1007/s11356-015-5643-8.

Silva, J., F. de Keulenaer, and N. Johnstone (2012), "Environmental quality and life satisfaction: Evidence based on micro-data," *OECD Environment Working Papers*, No. 44, OECD Publishing, Paris, http://dx.doi.org/10.1787/k9cw678dlr0-en.

Steinmayr, R. et al. (2015), "Subjective well-being, test anxiety, academic achievement: Testing for reciprocal effects," *Frontiers in Psychology*, Vol. 6, p. 1994, https://doi.org /10.3389/fpsyg.2015.01994.

Stemer, B. et al. (2015), "Bright versus dim ambient light affects subjective well-being but not serotonin-related biological factors," *Psychiatry Research*, Vol. 229(3), pp. 1011–1016, https://doi.org/10.1016/j.psychres.2015.05.068.

Stengård, J. et al. (2015), "Understanding the determinants of well-being and organizational attitudes during a plant closure: A Swedish case study," *Economic and Industrial Democracy*, Vol. 36(4), pp. 611–631, https://doi.org/10.1177/0143831X14527775.

Steptoe, A., A. Deaton, and A.A. Stone (2015), "Subjective wellbeing, health, and ageing," *The Lancet*, Vol. 385(9968), pp. 640–648.

Stevenson, B. and J. Wolfers (2012), "Subjective well-being and income: Is there any evidence of satiation?," *American Economic Review*, Vol. 103, pp. 598–604.

Stickley, A. et al. (2015), "Crime and subjective well-being in the countries of the former Soviet Union," *BMC Public Health*, Vol. 15, p. 1010, https://doi.org/10.1186/s12889 -015-2341-x.

Stiglitz, J.E., A. Sen, and J.-P. Fitoussi (2009), *Report by the Commission on the Measurement of Economic and Social Progress*, http://ec.europa.eu/eurostat/documents/118025 /118123/Fitoussi+Commission+report.

Stillman, S. et al. (2015), "Miserable migrants? Natural experiment evidence on international and objective and subjective well-being," *World Development*, Vol. 65, pp. 79–93.

Stone, A.A. and C. Mackie (2015), *Subjective Well-Being: Measuring Happiness, Suffering, and Other Dimensions of Experience*, National Academies Press, Washington, DC.

Stone, A.A. and S. Shiffman (1994), "Ecological momentary assessment (EMA) in behavioral medicine," *Annals of Behavioral Medicine*, Vol. 16, pp. 199–202.

Stone, A.A. and C. Smith (2015), "Developments in the day reconstruction method and related methods: Review and new directions," unpublished report, University of Southern California.

Stone, A.A. et al. (2010), "A snapshot of the age distribution of psychological well-being in the United States," *Proceedings of the National Academy of Sciences of the United States of America*, Vol. 107(22), pp. 9985–9990.

Tiefenbach, T. and F. Kohlbacher (2015), "Disasters, donations, and tax law changes: Disentangling effects on subjective well-being by exploiting a natural experiment," *Journal of Economic Psychology*, Vol. 50, pp. 94–112, https://doi.org/10.1016/j.joep.2015.07 .005.

UNECE (2013), *Guidelines for Harmonizing Time-Use Surveys*, United Nations Economic Commission for Europe, Geneva, www.unece.org/stats/publications/time_use_surveys .html.

United Kingdom Cabinet Office and Ipsos MORI (2013), *National Citizen Service 2013 Evaluation: Main Report*, www.ipsos-mori.com/researchpublications/publications /1692/National-Citizen-Service-2013-Evaluation.aspx.

Veenhoven, R. (2012), "Cross-national differences in happiness: Cultural measurement bias or effect of culture?," *International Journal of Wellbeing*, Vol. 2(4).

Ward, G. (2015), "Is happiness a predictor of election results?," *Centre for Economic Performance Discussion Paper*, No. 1343, http://cep.lse.ac.uk/pubs/download/dp1343.pdf.

Weiss, A. et al. (2012), "Evidence for a midlife crisis in great apes consistent with the U-shape in human well-being," *Proceedings of the National Academy of Sciences*, Vol. 109, pp. 19949–19952.

Wicker, P., D. Coates, and C. Breuer (2015), "Physical activity and subjective well-being: The role of time," *European Journal of Public Health*, Vol. 25(5), pp. 864–868, https:/ /doi.org/10.1093/eurpub/ckv053.

Woodhouse, E. et al. (2015), "Guiding principles for evaluating the impacts of conservation interventions on human well-being," *Philosophical Transactions of the Royal Society B: Biological Sciences*, http://dx.doi.org/10.1098/.2015.0103.

Zagonari, F. (2015), "Technology improvements and value changes for sustainable happiness: A cross-development analytical model," *Sustainability Science*, Vol. 10(4), pp. 687–698, https://link.springer.com/article/10.1007%2Fs11625-015-0311-y.

Zilioli, S., L. Imami, and R.B. Slatcher (2015), "Socioeconomic status, perceived control, diurnal cortisol, and physical symptoms: A moderated mediation model," *Psychoneuroendocrinology*, Vol. 75, pp. 36–43, https://doi.org/10.1016/j.psyneuen.2016.09.025.

8.

Economic Security

Jacob S. Hacker

This chapter examines what we know about economic security and what we still must learn. It defines economic security as vulnerability to economic loss, and treats "economic" as a description of the consequences (such as income loss) rather than the causes of insecurity. The chapter presents a series of recommendations for researchers and statistical agencies that would permit better measurement and analysis of economic security, both as a fundamental feature of economic life and as a major influence on subjective well-being and economic behavior. It synthesizes state-of-the-art theory and evidence regarding economic security and then lays out a small number of relatively well-developed measures. Drawing on the findings of this review and on the best available data, the chapter provides some preliminary evidence about the evolution of economic security in developed economies. The chapter then describes some of the continuing shortcomings of existing statistics in this field, and suggests ways to improve them.

Jacob S. Hacker is Director of the Institution for Social and Policy Studies and Stanley B. Resor Professor of Political Science at Yale University. The author wishes to thank Austin Nichols and especially Philipp Rehm—a true partner in conducting much of the research on which this chapter is based—as well as participants in the HLEG workshop on "Economic Insecurity: Forging an Agenda for Measurement and Analysis," held in New York on March 4, 2016, organized in collaboration with the OECD, the Washington Center for Equitable Growth, and the Yale Institution for Social and Policy Studies. Thanks to the Ford Foundation for funding and hosting the event. The author also thanks the HLEG members who commented on prior drafts. The opinions expressed and arguments employed in the contributions below are those of the author and do not necessarily reflect the official views of the OECD or of the governments of its member countries.

Introduction

In the wake of the financial crisis of the late 2000s, hundreds of millions of people in OECD countries faced significant economic dislocations, including unemployment, income volatility, and sharp drops in housing wealth and other assets. Opinion surveys showed a spike in people's worries about these and other economic risks, as well as a deterioration in their confidence that political leaders and public policies could effectively address them. In a phrase, citizens of crisis-affected countries grew more concerned about their "economic security," i.e., the degree to which they were vulnerable to hardship-causing economic losses. This heightened concern, in turn, influenced everything from their consumer and investment decisions, to their choices about family formation and geographic mobility, to their political behavior.

This chapter examines what we know about economic security and what we still must learn. The 2009 Stiglitz-Sen-Fitoussi report devoted relatively limited attention to economic security, whether as an influence on subjective well-being or as an objective feature of individuals' economic lives. It mentioned job security, health and medical spending security, and retirement security, but did not present measures of these phenomena. Its short section on economic security closed by arguing for a more comprehensive approach:

The many factors shaping economic security are reflected in the variety of approaches used to measure them. Some approaches try to quantify the frequency of specific risks, while others look at the consequences of a risk that materialises and at the means available to people to protect themselves from these risks (especially resources provided by social security programmes). A comprehensive measure of economic security would ideally account for both the frequency of each risk and its consequences, and some attempts in this direction have been made. A further problem is that of aggregating across the various risks that shape economic security, as the indicators that describe these risks lack a common metric to assess their severity. A final, even more intractable problem is that of accounting for the long-term consequences for quality of life of the various policies used to limit economic security (through their effects on unemployment and labour-force participation). (Stiglitz, Sen, and Fitoussi, 2009, pp. 201–202)

It is fair to say that the recommendations of the Stiglitz-Sen-Fitoussi report with regard to economic security—unlike its recommendations with regard to income inequality and subjective well-being—did not spark the investments in statistics, theory, and research necessary to achieve these ambitious goals. Given advances in concepts and data since 2009, however, the subject is ripe for a re-examination.

Key Features of Extant Measures

Before examining these measures, a few final points are in order. First, most measures focus on economic shocks that are unexpected and largely beyond the control of individuals. In practice, however, it is often difficult to know whether shocks are unexpected or involuntary. One approach is to focus on consumption, on the assumption that unexpected and involuntary shocks will have larger consumption effects. Yet consumption data are not widely available, nor are consumption drops the only possible measure of involuntary losses.

Second, while analysts frequently refer to the "risk" of economic loss, which implies a prospective outlook, most measures are in fact retrospective (the exception is measures of perceived security that ask respondents to offer their own assessment of various future events). In these cases, the risk faced by individuals or households is assumed to reflect past experience—their own, that of people like them, or a combination of the two.

Finally, and related, some measures are specific to people or households, while others can only be used to examine aggregate outcomes (for example, levels of security within regional or occupational groupings or among specific types of households). Perceived security is usually measured at the respondent level. By contrast, many measures of observed security are available only for aggregate groups, as they require observing the incidence of outcomes within defined populations.

This last point raises a final issue: the proper unit of analysis for measures of economic security. In general, security is an individual-level phenomenon. *People* experience insecurity, not groups. However, many of the most important forces that shape economic security, including the buffers people have against it, operate at the household level or even at higher levels of aggregation (communities, firms, regions, countries, and so on). Most measures are built up from either individual-level data or household-level data, with the choice depending on the specific measure used.[1]

What Is the State of Existing Statistics on Economic Security?

This section reviews the leading measures used to chart observed and perceived economic security, moving back and forth between concepts and data. Because data limitations are such a significant constraint, each measure is discussed in the context of the major data sources that are required to produce it. The section begins with measures of *perceived* security; it then turns to measures of *observed* security.

Measures of Perceived Economic Security

A wide range of surveys ask questions regarding people's perceived economic security. The main benefit of such surveys is that they directly capture individuals' perceptions of their personal and household economic experiences. To the extent that economic security is seen as synonymous with—or at least closely related to—individuals' psychological response to economic risks, surveys provide information about subjective perceptions that data on individuals' material circumstances cannot provide. And even if these perceptions are viewed "merely" as an effect or correlate of observed security, there is simply no way to understand the link between observed and perceived security without delving into these subjective responses.

Two key constraints, however, limit the utility of existing surveys for assessing perceived security. First, many survey questions are not asked repeatedly over any significant span of time, limiting the ability to examine *changes* in perceived security. Second, surprisingly few questions are replicated with similar wording in multiple national surveys, limiting the ability to examine *cross-national differences* in perceived security. The discussion that follows focuses on survey instruments that are available both over time and across at least a small subset of countries.

General Assessments of the Economy

Three broad categories of survey questions about perceived economic security appear regularly in major surveys. The first category comprises questions about how one feels about the economy or aspects of one's economic situation in the past or present. The most famous are the questions on one's own financial situation and the national financial situation, which are used to compile the University of Michigan Consumer Sentiment Index (Carroll, Fuhrer, and Wilcox, 1994).

The most common of these questions, however, seem weakly related to economic security—in particular, its forward-looking aspect. In addition, substantial research has shown that many of these general economic perceptions are heavily colored by assessments of incumbent parties, with partisans of the incumbent party offering more favorable assessments (Duch, Palmer and Anderson, 2000).

Perceptions of Buffers

A second category of questions, one that offers greater promise, concerns individuals' perceptions of their own ability to weather future economic shocks. Economic data often contain people's reports of specific levels of wealth or whether they have particular forms of insurance coverage. These questions, however, do not assess *perceived* security—they are simply designed to elicit information about households' material circumstances. Still, a number of surveys do include questions that involve a subjective component. The most common of such items concern the length of time the respondents believe they could remain economically comfortable if they were the victim of adverse economic shocks. Typically, these surveys find that the majority of individuals believe they could go only a limited amount of time before experiencing hardship—a reflection of the limited liquid wealth that many households have.

Similarly, some surveys ask people to assess whether they could rely on certain sources of support in the event of economic shocks, a line of questioning that also involves a subjective, forward-looking component. An example is the European Union's Survey of Income and Living Conditions (EU-SILC) 2015 ad hoc module's question on the possibility of the respondents relying on relatives, friends, or neighbors in case help (including financial help) is needed. Other examples of such questions are included in the EU-SILC—most notably, respondents are asked about their ability to make ends meet (current), their ability to face unexpected expenses (current, future), and their unmet needs (past) for medical and dental examination or treatment.

These questions contain a subjective component, and they provide an important indicator of individuals' preparation against major economic risks. Still, they are best thought of as measures of *buffers* rather than of *security* more generally. They are most useful, therefore, when they are accompanied by questions about the likelihood that individuals will experience economic shocks.

Expectations Regarding Future Shocks

This brings us to the third and final category of survey measures—namely, questions about one's likely economic situation in the future. These forward-looking measures seem closer to the concept of economic security than either of the survey items just discussed. More important, they provide something that measures of observed security cannot: individuals' own estimate of the risks they face.

Forward-looking questions fall into two broad subgroups.

- *Questions that ask about individuals' worry or anxiety with regard to specific risks.* Prior research shows that expressed worry is closely correlated with the expected probability of economic shocks; it also captures an emotional element of individuals' responses that other measures tend to miss. Unfortunately, surveys with these sorts of questions tend to be

country-specific—the most notable examples are US surveys, such as the
Survey of Economic Risk Perceptions and Insecurity (Rehm, Hacker,
and Schlesinger, 2012; Hacker, Rehm, and Schlesinger, 2013). Country-
specific surveys obviously cannot be used to examine differences across
nations, though, when repeated, they can be used to look at changes
over time.

- *Questions that ask individuals about the likelihood of economic loss.* Typically, these questions have asked people to rate the chance of an economic
event occurring on the basis of an ordinal scale (for example, 1 to 5, with
5 denoting the most insecure status). The most common of these types
of questions concern the risk of job loss. For example, the International
Social Survey Program has repeatedly asked respondents to express how
much they agree with the statement "my job is secure," with four answer options ranging from "strongly agree" to "strongly disagree." Several high-profile surveys, however, ask respondents to estimate the precise
numerical probability that they or someone like them will experience a
particular adverse economic shock (Manski, 2004; Hacker, Rehm, and
Schlesinger, 2013; Hendren, 2017).

Can We Believe Respondents' Estimates?

It might be wondered whether respondents can come up with meaningful estimates at the high level of precision that a 0–100 scale requires. To address this
concern, some surveys use categorical or more limited ordinal scales. However,
Hacker, Rehm, and Schlesinger (2013) show that with the appropriate survey
instruments—in their work, a sliding scale that shows visually the proportion
of the population that each percentage level represents—it is possible to get fine-
grained estimates that do not exhibit substantial clumping at 0% or 50%.

Moreover, their work and recent research by Rehm (2016) and by Hendren
(2017) shows that individuals do a reasonably good job forecasting the likelihood
of major economic shocks in the following year. A number of studies also show that
shocks affect the probabilities that individuals attach to future economic losses,
as well as their attitudes toward economic security more broadly. These findings
strongly suggest that measures of *perceived* and *observed* security may not be as

distinct as some analysts believe, at least when individual responses are averaged across larger groups.

Hendren's analysis also shows that measures of perceived and observed security can be used in conjunction with each other to assess the welfare loss associated with economic shocks. In brief, he looks at the drop in consumption that occurs not only when individuals lose their job, but also when individuals come to believe they have a high probability of losing it. The former measure is often used as a proxy for the welfare loss of unemployment, but as Hendren points out, if individuals cut back their consumption prior to unemployment because they expect to become unemployed, this approach will understate the negative welfare effects of unemployment—according to Hendren, by a substantial amount. Though Hendren's work does not consider the additional disutility associated with the fear or anxiety that such knowledge might produce, it does point to the promise of measures that utilize both perceived and observed security simultaneously.

Measures of Observed Economic Security

While measures of perceived security rely on individuals' own perceptions of their economic situation, measures of observed security draw on economic data that capture their material circumstances. Of course, much of this data comes from surveys of national populations (rather than, say, administrative sources). The difference is that these survey items are not designed to elicit information about respondents' perceptions but rather about their experiences and circumstances.

Four classes of measures of observed security are prevalent in the literature: (1) measures of household and individual buffers; (2) estimates of the probabilities of economic shocks; (3) indexes of observed security; and (4) various measures of over-time economic (in)stability.

Some measures are hybrids of these. For example, Bossert and D'Ambrosio present an indicator of insecurity that is a weighted combination of wealth levels (buffers) and past wealth dynamics (stability), while Hacker and his colleagues present a measure of the joint risk (probabilities) of income loss and medical spending shocks (stability) that includes a correction for household wealth (buffers). These hybrid measures are generally close to one of the major types (Bossert and D'Ambrosio, 2013; Hacker et al., 2014).[2]

Buffers

This class of measures looks at the adequacy of individuals' or households' savings, insurance, or other buffers against major economic shocks.

A major category of these measures defines and assesses asset sufficiency, i.e., whether households could maintain an adequate standard of living for a specified period merely by drawing down their wealth (usually, but not always, excluding housing because it is relatively illiquid and households need a place to live). In effect, these are measures of households' capacity for self-insurance. "Adequate" is defined differently in different studies, but a common metric in US analyses is the federal poverty line (a very low standard), with the specified period usually being 3 months (again, a low bar). Thus households are defined as "asset poor" when they have so little wealth they would not be able to support themselves at the US federal poverty line for at least three months if they lost their sources of income.

Cross-national analyses of asset poverty are rare, however, in part because of limited data. With regard to data, the Luxembourg Wealth Study has augmented the pool of cross-national wealth data, drawing on National Statistical Offices' micro-data regarding income and wealth. At the same time, the OECD and Eurostat have launched a project on household income consumption and wealth statistics, linking data on the distribution of each item based on micro-data. Yet these data are not always fully comparable cross-nationally, nor are high-quality wealth measures generally integrated into panel data, so wealth levels and vulnerability to shocks often cannot be examined inter-temporally side by side. Moreover, these wealth data generally do not do a good job measuring wealth at the top of the distribution—for that, specialized surveys that over-sample high-net-worth individuals like the US Survey of Consumer Finances are best. However, this is not a significant problem when looking at asset poverty, since the focus is on the lower part of the distribution.[3]

In addition to data challenges, conceptual issues bedevil cross-national analysis. These include how to set the minimum standard of living that assets are expected to provide, including whether it should be relative to the national income distribution or an absolute standard that is common across countries. No less vexing is whether to include housing wealth in asset measures, as housing valuation and prevalence differ substantially across countries, as does the ease of unlocking housing wealth when experiencing economic shocks (by, for example, borrowing against accumulated home equity).

Nonetheless, measures of asset sufficiency contain valuable information and are an important part of measuring economic security across countries, especially since they can be developed with existing data. To illustrate their value, Figure 8.1 compares income and asset poverty and "economic vulnerability" across OECD countries, using a relative poverty standard and adjusting income for household size ("equivalizing"). The "income poor" are those with equivalized income below 50% of the median income in each country. The "income and asset poor" are those with equivalized income below 50% of the median income and equivalized liquid financial wealth below 25% of the income poverty line (3-month buffer). The "economically vulnerable" are those who are not income poor but have equivalized liquid financial wealth below 25% of the income poverty line.

Three features of Figure 8.1 stand out. First, there is considerable overlap between income and asset poverty, though the degree of coincidence varies across countries. Most of the income poor are also asset poor. However, second, many of those who are not income poor lack adequate liquid financial wealth to weather economic shocks. Indeed, economic vulnerability is typically at least three times as high as income poverty. This suggests that vulnerability to economic shocks is a much broader phenomenon than economic deprivation. Third, levels of economic vulnerability vary greatly across countries. In Greece, for example, more than half the population lacks enough liquid financial wealth to maintain a poverty-level income for three months. By contrast, the share is roughly 1 in 5 in Austria and Norway.

Like other assessments of buffers, measures of asset sufficiency contain no information about the severity or character of the shocks that individuals or households face. Similar households with the same level of liquid wealth could experience very different levels of security based on their exposure to economic risks. Beyond this, asset measures do not typically take into account either borrowing capacity or informal sources of support, such as inter-household transfers. In principle, such measures could incorporate borrowing capacity through, for example, the use of credit ratings or (returning to perceived security) estimates of one's ability to borrow in the event of adverse shocks. But so far the focus has been squarely on household wealth.

Another weakness is that, in their emphasis on self-insurance, these measures leave out various types of *formal insurance* against major risks, such as health insurance and retirement pensions—both public and private. The OECD and the International Labour Organization (ILO) collect extensive data on the breadth of such protections, including the level of benefits, scope of coverage, duration of support, and stringency of qualifying conditions. Typically, these measures are based on statutory program rules or administrative data (or both). On the basis of these measures, analysts have produced indices of social program generosity that allow for comparison across countries.

Similarly, many countries collect data on the prevalence and characteristics of *private* insurance, such as commercial life and health insurance. These data are often collected at the household or individual level in surveys of income and

Figure 8.1. Income and Asset-Based Poverty

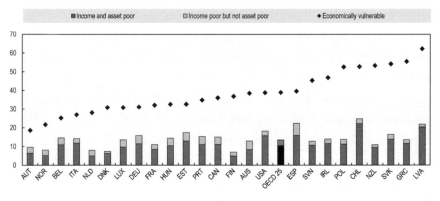

Note: Countries are ranked in ascending order of the share of individuals who are "economically vulnerable." The OECD average is the simple country average. The "income poor" are those with equivalized income below 50% of median income in each country. The "income and asset poor" are those with equivalized income below 50% of the median and equivalized liquid financial wealth below 25% of the income poverty line (3-month buffer). The "economically vulnerable" are those who are not "income poor" but have equivalized wealth below 25% of the income poverty line. Income poverty rates refer to household disposable income for Australia, Canada, Chile, Denmark, Finland, Italy, the Netherlands, New Zealand, Norway, and the United States, and to household gross income for the remaining countries. Liquid financial wealth includes cash, quoted shares, mutual funds, and bonds net of liabilities of own unincorporated enterprises.
Source: OECD (2017), *OECD Wealth Distribution Database*, https://stats.oecd.org/Index.aspx?DataSetCode=WEALTH. StatLink 2 http://dx.doi.org/10.1787/888933839848.

wealth, and at the aggregate level in surveys of national savings and production (or in commercial statistics on the breadth and characteristics of particular types of insurance).

For all their value, however, measures of formal insurance protection exhibit two salient weaknesses. First, with the exception of estimates based on household surveys, they are not usually available as individual- or household-level data that allow for comparison of levels of economic security across individuals or households, rather than across countries (or other geographic units).

Second, the tendency to focus on formal policy characteristics leaves these measures open to substantial slippage between assessed and actual risk protection. For example, not all benefits are "taken up" by those with formal coverage, nor do public and private implementers always carry out program instructions faithfully. With private benefits in particular, eligibility for specific benefits may be extremely complex to determine, as evidenced by US research on "surprise medical bills" (Cooper and Morton, 2016; Garmon and Chartock, 2016). Though actual protections are likely to be close to formal rules, important differences in economic security may still be missed, particularly when those most likely to experience economic dislocations—the poor, the young, the less educated—are most likely to fall through the gaps between promised and provided benefits.

Despite these caveats, measures of social program generosity provide crucial information about the extent to which public policies are designed to increase economic security. These indicators can be used to assess how broad and deep such protections are, as well as—alongside other measures of observed or perceived insecurity—how effective they are at achieving their purposes. Table 8.1 shows the most recent results (2010) for one broadly used collection of indicators of social program generosity, the Comparative Welfare Entitlements Dataset. The table shows the level (relative to the nation's average production wage), duration, and coverage for two important benefits: sickness pay and unemployment insurance. It orders the countries based on the data set's index of the comparative generosity of sickness pay, which normalizes these generosity indicators based on their historical (since 1980) and cross-country variation, equally weighting benefit levels, duration, and coverage.[4]

Shock Probabilities

Many students of political economy have examined discrete economic risks by looking at the cross-sectional prevalence of key economic shocks, most often unemployment. The goal is to calculate fine-grained measures of the risk of these shocks for particular groups, such as workers in different occupations. Rehm (2016), for example, develops "occupational unemployment rates," which are "calculated exactly as national unemployment rates are, except that the calculations are performed for detailed occupations," by dividing workers into up to 27 groups based on the International Standard Classification of Occupations (ISCO) developed by the ILO.

The logic—for which Rehm provides strong backing—is that "using a worker's occupation as a reference group and approximating the probability of job loss by the unemployment rate of his or her occupation provides a good measure of risk exposure" in the employment domain. Figure 8.2 shows, for instance, that these rates are strongly correlated with individuals' *perceived* job security. The figure pairs data from the US labor force survey and the US General Social Survey, showing the relationship between occupational unemployment rates (calculated for 27 occupation groups using labor force data) and whether a worker says it is "likely or very likely" they will lose their job in the coming year (calculated from the General Social Survey, with occupation groups assigned using the same ISCO standards). Given the imprecision of the survey question, the main point of interest is not the close numerical correspondence between the observed rate and perceived risk but the near-linear increase as occupational unemployment rates rise.

So far, unemployment has been the main focus of such inquiries, but similar group-specific measures of risk could in principle be constructed for other outcomes, such as reductions in pay or hours, entry into poverty, and reported sickness.[5]

These probability measures have the virtue of being readily understandable; moreover, in many cases they do not require panel data and thus can build on the large number of cross-sectional surveys already used by policy-makers. Indeed, labor force surveys are among the most widely available and reliable sources of data for inter-temporally and cross-nationally comparable indicators.

For all their virtues, however, these probability estimates can only be calculated for specific outcomes, and many important outcomes (such as large out-of-

Table 8.1. Welfare State Generosity, 2010

Country	Unemployment Generosity Index	Sickness Generosity Index
Norway	14.2	15.9
Sweden	8.2	14.9
Netherlands	11.9	13.8
Belgium	14.0	13.7
Germany	10.0	13.3
Switzerland	13.9	13.0
France	11.1	12.3
Denmark	9.5	12.2
Finland	9.2	12.1
Ireland	11.1	10.6
Austria	10.4	10.3
Chinese Taipei	5.4	10.3
Spain	11.7	10.0
Italy	5.7	9.6
Portugal	10.6	9.5
United Kingdom	8.3	8.0
Japan	5.3	7.6
Greece	7.3	7.3
New Zealand	7.1	6.3
Australia	7.1	6.3
Canada	8.1	5.2
United States	10.7	0.0
Korea	4.2	0.0

Note: Country characteristic scores are standardized using z-scores with mean and distribution based on a reference period. (Extreme values, including unlimited benefit duration, are dropped and assigned a maximum or minimum z-score.) These standardized characteristics for each program (unemployment, sick pay) are summed and the sum is multiplied by the coverage ratio. Thus, the sub-index is computed as: (Program generosity score) = [2*z(Benefit Replacement rate)+ z(ln(Benefit Duration weeks))+ z(ln(Benefit Qualification weeks)+ z(Waiting days)+12.5]*Insurance Coverage.
Source: Scruggs L. (2014), Comparative Welfare Entitlements Dataset (CWED2), University of Connecticut, and D. Jahn, University of Greifswald, http://cwed2.org/. StatLink 2 http://dx.doi.org/10.1787/888933839867.

pocket medical expenses) may be more difficult to see in standard economic data than is the case for unemployment. Furthermore, they can only be justified as estimates of the probability of these outcomes for a given individual or household with additional theory or evidence that supports the assumption that all members of an occupation or other group face risk more or less equal to the group's average probability.

Finally, because these measures are based on cross-sectional data—and, indeed, such fine-grained measures require samples of a size rarely achieved by panel studies—they cannot speak to the *cumulative* character of economic shocks. A group-specific unemployment rate, for example, only captures the share of a group that is out of work at any given time or during any given period. Yet the experience of unemployment is very different if particular individuals or households experience it again and again over time, as opposed to its incidence being spread broadly across the population.

Indices

Until now, the focus has been on discrete indicators, but a major class of measures used in time series and cross-national analysis attempts to bring together multiple

Figure 8.2. Occupational Unemployment Rates and Perceptions of Job Security, United States, 1972–2010

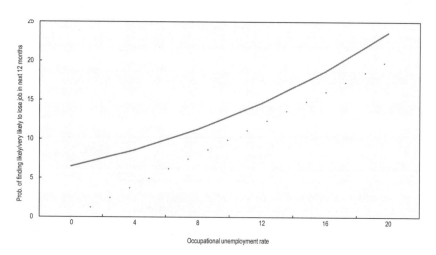

Note: The dashed line is the 45-degree line; the solid line shows the predicted probability of respondent saying he or she is likely or very likely to lose his or her job within the next 12 months, based on the US Current Population Survey (occupational unemployment rates) from 1972 to 2010 and the US General Social Survey (perceptions of job security within occupational groups) from 1972 to 2010, controlling for income, age, gender, work status, education, race, region (South versus outside South), and church attendance.

Source: Rehm, P. (2016), *Risk Inequality and Welfare States: Social Policy Preferences, Development, and Dynamics*, Cambridge University Press, Cambridge, MA. StatLink 2 http://dx.doi.org/10.1787 /888933839886.

indicators to "sum up" observed economic security. These indices range from the relatively simple measures of program generosity just discussed to relatively elaborate measures that try to capture both the probability of shocks and the strength of buffers within specific domains.

Among the latter, the work of Lars Osberg stands out as exemplary of domain-specific indices, which he calls the "named risks" approach. Though its implementation has evolved, the basic idea is that economic security is a product of (1) the probability of an adverse event and (2) the average consequence of that event, which is mediated by (3) the strength of the buffers available to protect people. Thus, Osberg's approach embodies the threefold distinction between shocks, losses, and buffers common to most definitions of economic security.

The four domain-specific indices developed by Osberg and his colleagues are meant to describe economic security for residents of a given country with regard to unemployment, family breakup, medical costs, and poverty in old age. In practice, the precise indices mix (1), (2), and (3) in different ways. With regard to unemployment, for example, the focus is on (1) and (3): "security from employment" is defined as a product of the unemployment rate (1) and the breadth of and fraction of prior wages provided by unemployment benefits (3).[6] With regard to family breakup, the focus is instead on (1) and (2): "security from single-parent poverty" is a product of the divorce rate (1) and the incidence and depth of poverty among single-female-parent families (2). In two cases—"security in the event of sickness" and "security from poverty in old age"—the index is based solely on (2): economic security with regard to medical costs is conceived of as (the inverse of) the average share of income spent on un-reimbursed medical expenses (2); and economic security in old age is conceived of as (the inverse of) the incidence and depth of poverty within a country among those older than 65.

The next section on key results that emerge from current evidence will consider these indices more fully, as well as nonindex *integrated* measures that attempt to capture economic security with a single indicator, such as the various measures of income volatility that have become so central to economic research over the last generation. For now, it suffices to lay out briefly the strengths and weaknesses of index measures in general and the index measures proposed by Osberg and his colleagues in particular (Osberg, 2015, 2010; Osberg and Sharpe, 2014, 2009).

A major strength of the domain-specific index approach is its ability to reflect the leading priorities embodied in public policy. That is, in this approach, deciding which domains to cover and how to conceptualize security within them can—and, indeed, *must*—be tailored to the goals of specific policies. Osberg bases his list of "named risks" on Article 25 of the United Nations' 1948 Universal Declaration of Human Rights, which reads, "Everyone has the right to . . . security in the event of unemployment, sickness, disability, widowhood, old age or other loss of livelihood in circumstances beyond his control." Consequently, Osberg's measures focus on economic security with regard to "unemployment," "sickness," "widowhood," and "old age."

This strength, however, is counterbalanced by a potential weakness. Basing measures on the priorities of public policy increases the chance that they will be relevant to policy-makers, but reduces the ability to assess whether those priorities are aligned with the realities of economic security. Implicitly, this is acknowledged in the substitution of "single parenthood" for "widowhood" in the index of family-related security: in an age in which most mothers work and family breakup is common, death of the (male) family breadwinner is no longer seen as the only or even most salient financial risk that parents face.

A concern common to all indices is the appropriateness of weighting. Domain-specific indices of economic security weight at two levels. The first is weighting done to construct the domain-specific index itself. In recent iterations of the index of "security in the event of unemployment," for example, Osberg and his colleagues have weighted the unemployment rate more heavily than unemployment benefits on the grounds that it has a larger effect on well-being. While this justification has merit, it moves the index away from a relatively simple measure—the joint product of the unemployment rate, the average replacement rate, and the share of workers covered—toward one that is more complex and potentially ad hoc.

Second, to the extent that these domain-specific measures are to be combined into a comprehensive index, there is the question of how to weight these different and possibly even incommensurable measures. At least four options present themselves: equal weighting (as in the Human Development Index); weighting on the basis of some measure of policy priority, such as spending on particular social benefits; weighting on the basis of the impact of each domain on household well-being; and weighting on the basis of measures of perceived security, such as the importance that individuals ascribe to security within a given domain, or the impact of shocks within that domain on perceived security. The last two approaches have considerable merit, but for the most part the evidence they require is lacking. If that evidence were stronger, moreover, it might well allow for more direct measures of observed security than the indices under consideration.

Another great strength of these domain-specific indices is that they rely on easily obtained and generally reliable data. The flipside is that these aggregate-level data may not correspond closely with individual experience or lend themselves to finer-grained comparisons across groups. The potential slippage between formal benefit rules and actual implementation has already been discussed. Also problematic is the inconsistent treatment of public and private buffers. Some of the measures proposed—un-reimbursed medical expenses, old-age poverty—are designed to measure outcomes in the context of all public and private protections. In the case of unemployment, however, only public benefits are considered, even though personal savings, spousal labor supply, and other private buffers may be an important source of additional support.

Finally, these indices were designed to measure economic security at the country level and are not always easy to apply to less highly aggregated groups. Certainly, it is not possible to use them to say that particular individuals or households are economically secure since, like estimates of the probability of specific shocks, they require a reference group. Thus, they are less useful for calculating the distribution of economic security *within* countries than they are for comparing levels of security *across* countries.

Volatility

Over the past generation, a large literature on income and consumption volatility has accumulated, driven by advances in both data and theory (e.g., Gottschalk et al., 1994; Moffitt and Gottschalk, 2002; Hacker, 2008; Hacker and Jacobs, 2008; Dynan, Elmendorf, and Sichel, 2008; Acs and Nichols, 2010; Nichols and Zimmerman, 2008; Nichols and Rehm, 2014; Kopczuk, Saez, and Song, 2010;

Gorbachev, 2011; Dogra and Gorbachev, 2016). With regard to data, the growth of high-quality panel studies has made it feasible to examine the over-time fluctuation of economic outcomes at the individual or household level in a way that was rarely possible in the past.

Using these data, scholars have proposed a range of innovative measures of such over-time fluctuations—most of them falling into the broad category of "volatility" estimates. Generally, volatility estimates are meant to describe the magnitude of inter-temporal fluctuation of some economic variable at the household or individual level. Typically, these measures focus on earnings or household income but sometimes they examine consumption. Moreover, they usually treat volatility as variance *relative to* longer-term trends, such as lifetime growth in earnings. Thus, volatility measures provide a rough estimate of income or consumption risk. The "Measures of Volatility" sidebar provides a more in-depth look at various volatility measures.

The primary implication of the burgeoning body of research on volatility is that income (and, to a lesser extent, consumption) varies enormously over time. Though most of the existing work has been done on the United States—which, it is becoming increasingly clear, has higher levels of volatility compared with other affluent countries—the conclusion holds across all countries for which panel data exist. People's economic circumstances change a great deal over time—so much so that, according to one recent calculation using the US Panel Study of Income Dynamics (PSID), more than half of adult Americans between the ages of 25 and 60 experienced at least one year below 150% of the federal poverty line (around $12,000 for an individual in 2015) in the period 1968–2009 (Rank, Hirschl, and Foster, 2014). This means, in turn, that many more people utilize social benefits aimed at cushioning major economic shocks during their lives than a static snapshot of the income distribution might suggest.

Whether income or consumption volatility has risen over time is a different question, which will be taken up in the next section. But the fact of volatility, hitherto hidden from view by the near-universal reliance on one-shot cross-sectional samples, is not in dispute.

Nonetheless, volatility is not the same as economic security for at least two reasons.

- Volatility measures treat gains and losses as symmetrical (except insofar as models assume diminishing marginal utility of income). Yet economic security is focused on losses, which, again, likely loom much larger in subjective well-being than do comparable gains.

- Volatility measures do not as a rule distinguish between different sources of losses (or gains). Yet not all losses threaten economic security. Losses that are freely incurred are different from less controllable shocks. For example, economic security is likely to be much more compromised by an involuntary job loss than by a planned hiatus from the workforce.

With regard to the source of economic shocks, some studies of volatility focus on outcomes that are unlikely to be voluntary, such as large shifts in consumption that are not explained by predictable changes in household needs. Most, however, treat all income or consumption changes similarly. Distinguishing voluntary changes from involuntary ones is difficult, since many life events involve elements of both. Early retirement, for example, is often associated with sickness or disability or with firms' efforts to shed older workers. Even divorce, almost by definition a choice for at least one partner, involves involuntary aspects, as the large literature on the negative consequences of divorce (particularly for women) suggests. Thus, determining voluntariness with regard to particular shocks can be difficult, especially with existing data. And since volatility analysts are usually interested in changes over time rather than absolute levels, putting to the side this thorny issue does not compromise their findings so long as the *relative* proportion of voluntary versus involuntary changes remains stable over time.

The issue of voluntariness should also be distinguished from the question of whether economic shocks are foreseeable. Foreseeability, too, is a matter of degree, and economic security is almost certainly not related to it in any unvarying manner. We know that people dislike uncertainty (Knight, 1921)—that is, situations in which they cannot even assign probabilities to future outcomes—and will pay to reduce that uncertainty (e.g., Ellsberg, 1961; Camerer and Weber, 1992; Di Mauro and Maffioletti, 2004). Thus, less foreseeable risks may well pose a greater threat to economic security, or at least to *perceived* security, all else equal.

MEASURES OF VOLATILITY

Many approaches to measuring volatility decompose variance in incomes into "persistent" components that are relatively stable over time (variance in long-run incomes across people, or inequality), and "transitory" components measuring inter-temporal variability or "volatility." These studies differ on many dimensions, including whether they focus on earnings or household income and whether they use administrative or panel data. A key difference is whether they use parametric or nonparametric models.

- *Nonparametric Models*: The seminal nonparametric computations of permanent and transitory variation from Gottschalk et al. (1994) have been followed by "error components models" (ECMs) or dynamic variance components models with persistent and transitory shocks. After the early work looking primarily at male earnings (often white male earnings in US data), numerous authors decomposed changes in household income inequality into persistent and transitory parts. Many of these ECMs identify a smaller role for transitory variation or volatility than for long-term or persistent differences across people; but even when transitory variation is small relative to persistent variation, the increase in transitory variation is often large.

- *Parametric Models*: A more recent body of work uses parametric decomposition, with most estimates informed by a series of papers by Gottschalk and Moffitt; the most prominent recent analysis using this approach is Kopczuk, Saez, and Song (2010). By contrast, Nichols and Zimmerman (2008), Acs and Nichols (2010) and Nichols and Rehm (2014) write income (not log income) as the sum of a permanent (time-invariant) component, a person-specific linear time trend, and transitory variability around trend. Persistent variance is the "inequality" (I) in longer-run incomes; variation in trends is called "mobility risk" (M); and variation around the trend is called "volatility" (V) or "inter-temporal variability around trend." Using a wide variety of data, Nichols and Rehm (2014) document large increases in volatility in the United States relative to Canada and other countries. They also conclude that tax and transfer programs have lesser volatility-mitigating effects in the United States than in other countries, and that the United States is diverging from its peers in the extent of volatility mitigation of its tax and transfer system.

Persistent variation across individuals in family or household resources tends to be much larger than inter-temporal variation in family or household income. In the United States, however, both persistent and transitory variations seem to have increased at comparable rates in recent decades. The increase in inter-temporal variation in household income stems from many sources, and more work is needed to ascertain its welfare consequences, but a substantial rise in the prevalence of large income drops (paired with a much smaller rise in the prevalence of large income gains) indicates that welfare-lowering risk has increased over past decades in the United States. This view is supported by recent work on consumption volatility by Dogra and Gorbachev (2016), who show that unexplained consumption variation has increased alongside higher income volatility—with the rise driven by increases among households with liquidity constraints (proxied by zero or negative wealth).

Source: Courtesy of Austin Nichols.

However, we also know from Rehm's research and related work (Rehm, 2016; Hendren, 2017) that people can more or less correctly anticipate many common economic shocks, at least to the extent that their perceptions of the likelihood correlate highly with observed measures of risk, and that they can update these perceptions on the basis of on new information or experiences. Indeed, one reason why commercial insurance against salient economic shocks is often inadequate or unavailable is such private information, which creates adverse selection (only high-risk individuals demand coverage), can destabilize or prevent the formation of viable private markets. This line of research suggests that economic security (or, at least, *perceived* security) depends not only on foreseeability but also on *what* is foreseen, with those who see the chance of a shock as high being less secure than those who are less certain or foresee a lower probability.

The third and final reason why volatility estimates are not direct measures of economic security is that they generally look only at household income, ignoring household wealth and major nondiscretionary expenditures such as out-of-pocket medical costs.[7] But liquid wealth is of course a major source of household protection against income volatility, and household well-being can be threatened by sharp spikes in nondiscretionary spending as well as by sharp drops in income. The small literature on consumption volatility is in part a response to these difficulties, but it suffers from its own weaknesses—most notably, the scarcity of high-quality consumption data.

Though economic security and economic volatility are not synonymous, the extensive and increasingly sophisticated literature on volatility provides crucial guidance for the measurement of economic security. One of the great virtues of this research has been its consistent focus on the refinement of individual-level measures that can be used for analysis at multiple levels, from the worker or household, to demographic or educational groups, to countries as a whole. This micro-level focus distinguishes volatility measures from some of the indices of economic security just considered, which are, by construction, limited to macro- or meso-level analysis.

In addition to offering crucial conceptual and methodological guidance, the literature on volatility also provides many valuable clues about the evolution of citizens' economic security. These central findings and their implications are discussed in the next section.

Hybrid Measures

Responding to some of the shortcomings of volatility measures as measures of economic security, Hacker and his colleagues have developed an alternative measure called the Economic Security Index or ESI (Hacker et al., 2014).[8] Despite the title, it is not truly an index; rather, it is a comprehensive measure of the incidence of large shocks to household economic standing that integrates multiple data sets covering income, wealth, and medical spending. This measure has been implemented using three major US panel data sources: the PSID, the Survey of Income and Program Participation (SIPP), and the Current Population Survey (CPS), which re-contacts households that remain in the same residence, allowing the formation of two-year mini-panels through an algorithm-based matching of households across adjacent years. All three of these sources show similar trends and demographic differences.

Unlike measures of volatility, the ESI focuses only on *drops*—in this case, a 25% or greater decline in "available household income" from one year to the next. The 25% threshold was chosen based on a separate opinion survey, which found that the median US household said they could go roughly three months without income before suffering "real hardship." (Other thresholds show similar trends, albeit at different levels.) The "one year to the next" criterion reflects the annual structure of most panel data, as well as the annual reporting and receipt of most public taxes and many public benefits.[9]

There are two other notable features of the ESI: first, it accounts for liquid financial wealth; second, it accounts for two of the most important nondiscretionary expenditures faced by many households, i.e., out-of-pocket medical costs (including insurance premiums) and debt service. Liquid (not total) household wealth enters in the calculation of the ESI as an exclusion criterion: households who have adequate liquid financial wealth to fully buffer their cumulative expected losses are not treated as "economically insecure" even when they experience a 25% or greater year-over-year income drop.[10] Medical costs and debt service enter in as constraints on income available for other consumption needs—i.e., these expenditures are subtracted from income when determining whether households experience a 25% or greater loss. Finally, household income is equivalized and then assigned equally to adult household members to provide an individual-level measure.

The ESI is thus a hybrid of the buffer and volatility approaches that produces a number similar to the estimates of the probability of adverse economic shocks discussed earlier. It is also a hybrid of an income-based and a consumption-based measure, since key nondiscretionary expenditures are subtracted from income. Like occupational unemployment rates, the individual-level measure is binary ("drop" or "no drop") and can only be turned into an estimate of economic security by looking at its incidence across a defined population. Though it would be possible to construct a truly individual-level measure with a long panel by looking solely at an individuals' past history (e.g., Stettner, Cassidy, and Wentworth, 2016), a probability estimate better captures the core aspect of economic security, namely that it involves the risk (but not certainty) of adverse outcomes. Like all observed measures, however, it is inherently backward-looking: future risk is assumed to be similar to (recent) past risk.

To bolster this approach, the research team that developed the ESI conducted a panel opinion survey that asked extensive questions about economic security, including whether individuals experienced large household income drops. These results allow not just for an independent verification of the estimates of the incidence of large drops made using the SIPP, PSID, and CPS. More important, given that none of these data sources contain questions about *perceived* economic security, they were used to verify that individuals experiencing large drops did in fact express lower levels of security. As already noted, they did: large income shocks were associated with much higher levels of worry, higher estimates of future shocks, and greater support for public policies designed to buffer these shocks. Wealth drops did not have such consistent effects, though the relatively small size of the sample—between 2,000 and 3,000 respondents—may have contributed to this (non)finding.

Nonetheless, the ESI has its own significant weaknesses. Like nearly every other measure discussed, it does not distinguish between voluntary and involuntary changes (although it does focus on sizable losses of 25% or greater that are least likely to be expected or voluntary). Nor does it capture all economic threats, including other salient nondiscretionary expenditures, most notably the unavoidable costs that come with participation in the labor force, such as child care and transportation costs (although there is much less agreement about the extent to which these expenses are nondiscretionary than there is with regard to medical costs.)

To date, no measure has been proposed that truly integrates over-time volatility with long-term risks such as retiring without adequate income. The ESI is no exception, though it does exclude earmarked retirement savings from the calculations of liquid financial wealth, on the grounds that spending down such savings jeopardizes household's economic security with regard to retirement. There is a large literature that looks at consumption drops at retirement (e.g., Banks, Blundell and Tanner, 1998; Aguiar and Hurst, 2005; Haider and Stephens Jr., 2007), and this focus might be integrated into the ESI approach. But such an integration would require accounting for the reduced income needs of retirees.[11]

Finally, in its focus on changes, the ESI does not treat people facing persistent but stable deprivation as economically insecure—a feature shared by all volatility measures. In practice, low-income individuals experience much greater instability of income and nondiscretionary spending than do higher-income individuals, and they have much more limited liquid financial wealth. Still, it remains true that volatility-based measures miss aspects of economic insecurity that do not involve economic instability.

In short, several measures have been proposed to assess economic security. Some of these measures are designed to capture only certain important aspects of economic security, such as the strength of household buffers, while others are closer to fully comprehensive measures. Even the latter, however, do not represent incontestable proxies, not least because the precise definition of economic security remains under discussion. Nonetheless, these measures of observed security clarify how analysts, policy-makers, and statistical agencies could better assess a critical feature of citizens' lives and a fundamental influence on their well-being. The next section turns to what these measures tell us about the character and evolution of economic security in recent decades.

What Can We Say About Economic Security Based on the Available Evidence?

This section presents a small number of indicators that can be used to compare economic security across individuals, households, socio-demographic groups, and countries. It focuses on observed economic security, and more specifically on two measures of observed security that are available or can be developed for multiple countries and time periods: Lars Osberg's "named risk" approach, a hybrid of the probability-of-shock and prevalence-of-buffers approach; and new estimates based on the approach embodied in the ESI, i.e., a volatility-based measure that focuses on large year-to-year income drops.

In presenting these results, this chapter draws on both published and unpublished research. In particular, the ESI-style estimates for countries other than the United States have been developed only recently and thus should be considered preliminary. Moreover, both these data and the evidence developed by Osberg and his colleagues are currently available only for affluent countries. As more and more countries develop high-quality economic data—and in particular panel data—it should become possible to develop similar measures for a broader range of countries.

The "Named Risk" Approach

Osberg's "named risk" measure of economic security is designed to capture the overall prevalence of and degree of protection against major economic shocks listed in the UN Universal Declaration of Human Rights, specifically unemployment, sickness, single-parent poverty, and poverty in old age. Results are available from 1980 through 2009 for 14 affluent democracies: Australia, Belgium, Canada, Denmark, Finland, France, Germany, Italy, the Netherlands, Norway, Spain, Sweden, the United Kingdom, and the United States.

In addition to the shock-specific measures, Osberg and his colleagues calculate an aggregate index of economic security, weighting each component based on the

Figure 8.3. Osberg's Index of Economic Security, Selected OECD Countries, 1980 and 2014

Source: Centre for the Study of Living Standards (2016), *Database of the Index of Economic Well-Being for Selected OECD Countries and Alberta, 1980–2014*, www.csls.ca/iwb/FinalIEWBAlbertaandOECD2014 .xlsx. StatLink 2 http://dx.doi.org/10.1787/888933839905.

share of the population in each year presumed to face the relevant risk (i.e., everyone aged 15 to 64 years in the case of unemployment; the entire population in the case of sickness; married women with children under 18 in the case of single-parent poverty; and adults aged 45 to 64 in the case of old-age poverty).

For ease of exposition, this aggregate measure is used in Figure 8.3 to compare all 14 countries, with the dark bar indicating the beginning of the series (1980) and the lighter bar the end (2014).

Figure 8.3 points to several notable features.[12] First, countries differ substantially in their overall level of economic security. In 2014, economic security was greatest in Norway, with a value of 0.83 (the indices are constrained to be between 0 and 1), followed by Denmark with a value of 0.81. By contrast, the United States had the lowest score at 0.48, followed by Spain (at 0.59).

Second, in most nations, the index does not change much between 1980 and 2014. Only three nations experienced a change in the index greater than 10%: Canada (12% increase), Spain (18% decline), and the United States (a 62% increase in economic security).

The relative stability of the aggregate index reflects relatively little change in most of the shock-specific indices.[13] The most notable trend in the shock-specific indices is an overall increase in "security from single-parent poverty" and "security in old-age poverty." These indices improve because of reductions in the prevalence and severity of poverty among single-parent households and the elderly, respectively.

Whether poverty is a good measure of economic security is an important question, and one that will be taken up in the conclusions. For now, it is simply worth noting that levels of poverty are not necessarily the same as the *risk* of poverty. Assessing risk requires looking at the probability that any individual or group will enter poverty over some defined interval, which in turn requires considering income dynamics. It is to the topic of income dynamics—and specifically the prevalence of large income drops—that we now turn.

The Prevalence of Major Income Drops

The second set of findings reviewed here is based on the Economic Security Index. Recall that the ESI is a hybrid measure constructed using panel data that captures the share of individuals experiencing a 25% or greater year-over-year decline in family-size-adjusted real household income net of out-of-pocket medical spending. The ESI excludes from this share both the very small portion of the population entering retirement between one year and the next and the larger (but still relatively small) proportion possessing liquid financial wealth sufficient to self-finance the loss.[14]

Unfortunately, neither out-of-pocket medical spending nor liquid financial wealth is reliably reported in many panel studies. Thus, what is presented here is a limited version of the ESI without the medical spending or wealth adjustments. This measure captures the share of the adult population experiencing a 25% or greater loss in (household-size-adjusted) individual income from one year to the next.[15] It can be thought of as a measure of income risk, whether for the population as a whole (when looking at the prevalence of 25% or greater losses nationwide) or for specific sub-groups (when looking at the prevalence among regional, occupational, or demographic groupings).

This measure is simple, feasible given existing data, and scalable, with a larger absolute loss required as income rises. Given this last characteristic, it is also comparable across countries with different average per-capita income levels. As noted previously, the 25% threshold was based on US survey questions that asked how long respondents could go without their income before experiencing hardship. Whether responses to this sort of question would be similar in other countries is unclear. It is worth reporting, however, that within a plausible range neither over-time trends nor the rankings of countries are particularly sensitive to the exact threshold chosen.

This measure can be constructed for almost forty countries, reflecting the growth of reliable panel studies in the past two decades. Since panel data are a crucial precondition for any approach that tracks individuals or households over time, it makes sense to begin with a brief summary of the data. The next section discusses the changing scope and character of panel data in greater depth.

Producing these estimates required assembling various panel studies that cover more than a few years and have been more or less continuous since their creation. For many of these studies, the period that can be analyzed is relatively brief. With the exception of a few pioneering panel studies—notably, the German Socio-Economic Panel (GSOEP), which starts in 1984, and the US PSID, which starts in

1968—country-specific panel studies mostly date from the 1990s. These encompass Australia, Canada, Korea, Sweden, Switzerland, and the United Kingdom. Another wave of studies began in the early 2000s with the launch of the European Union's Survey of Income and Living Conditions (EU-SILC), eventually encompassing more than 20 countries.

For the United States, in addition to the PSID, panel data can be obtained from the SIPP and from the matched CPS files. Though the SIPP, PSID, and CPS were all used to construct the Economic Security Index, the estimates presented here use matched CPS files, which produce the largest sample. The main drawback of matched CPS results is their short (two-year) panels, but they are sufficient to measure year-over-year income drops.[16]

Figure 8.4 provides a simple picture of the prevalence of large income losses in all the countries for which data are available, as well as changes over the most recent period encompassing the financial crisis (roughly from the early 2000s until the end of the data series). The length of the bars shows the range of prevalence estimates across the years (indicated next to the country abbreviation). The point marker shows that average for these estimates within each country across these years. Finally, if there is a trend in the data over the most recent period, this is indicated by an arrow showing the direction of the change.

Thus, the figure shows the average, range, and recent evolution of income risk in these countries.

As Figure 8.4 shows, the prevalence of large income losses varies substantially both across countries and within countries over time. Within the group considered by Figure 8.4, the countries with the greatest range and highest average prevalence of large income losses are generally those that were hit hardest by the financial crisis, including Spain, Greece, and Iceland. The countries with the lowest average prevalence of large income losses include the Netherlands, Sweden, Switzerland, Denmark, Norway, and Finland. The United States—the country that has been the focus of most analyses of income volatility—has a relatively high prevalence of large income losses.

Moreover, the ranking of countries is fairly consistent with the "named risk" approach, especially its measure of security in the event of unemployment. Figure 8.5 shows the correlation between this measure, averaged for 2006–08, and the average prevalence of large income losses over the same period in the 14 countries for which both estimates are available.

Finally, while the prevalence of large income losses generally rose between the early and late 2000s, this trend was largely cancelled out as countries recovered from the crisis. Indeed, only a handful of countries—most notably the United States—have experienced a secular rise in the prevalence of large income losses. Most countries have seen little or no increase in the incidence of large income losses, and a few (e.g., Switzerland, Norway, and Austria) witnessed a decline. Since these data encompass the period of the financial crisis and the slow recovery that followed, this is a notable finding, suggesting that some countries were able to reduce the fallout of the crisis and its aftermath, at least when it comes to income risk.

This hypothesis can be put to a more direct test by parsing the components of household income. In the literature on income inequality, researchers commonly

Figure 8.4. Average, Range, and Evolution of the Incidence of Large Income Losses

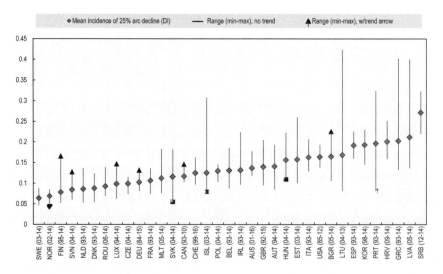

Notes: Based on the following panel data collections: ECHP, EU-SILC, CPS, CNEF (BHPS, SOEP, HILDA, KLIPS, SHP, SLID). For each country, the period covered is indicated on the horizontal axis. Arc-changes, unlike percentage changes, treat gains and losses symmetrically (e.g., an income gain from $50 to $100 implies a 100% change but a 67% arc-change; while an income loss from $100 to $50 implies a 50% change but a 67% arc-change); they are bound between +2 and −2. StatLink 2 http://dx.doi.org/10.1787/888933839924.

distinguish between inequality before and after taxes and transfers, and use the difference between the two as a rough measure of how much taxes and transfers reduce
inequality. More specifically, the standard approach is to calculate the difference
between the Gini coefficient of the distribution of market income [Gini(MI)] and
the Gini coefficient of the distribution of disposable income [Gini(DI)].[17] Because
Gini coefficients are summary indicators, this measure is necessarily calculated at
the aggregate level.

When looking at the prevalence of large income losses, an equivalent approach
would distinguish between losses in income before and after taxes and transfers,
and assess how many fewer citizens experience large income losses when taxes and
transfers are taken into account.[18] In other words, the reduction of risk would be calculated as the difference between the aggregate prevalence of market income losses

Figure 8.5. The Incidence of Large Income Losses versus Osberg's Scaled Index of Economic Security

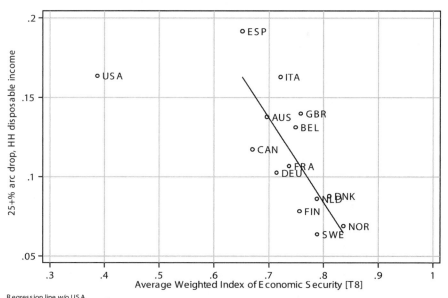

Regression line w/o USA
Coef: -.531, SE: .14, T: -3.8, R2: .53, N: 13

Note: Refer to Figure 8.3. Osberg's Index of Economic Security, Selected OECD Countries. Sample: AUS
2001–14, BEL 1993–2014, CAN 1993–2010, DEU 1984–2014, DNK 1993–2014, ESP 1993–2014,
FIN 1995–2014, FRA 1993–2014, GBR 1992–2014, ITA 1993–2014, NLD 1993–2014, NOR
2002–14, SWE 2003–14, USA 1985–2012.

[Risk(MI)] and the aggregate prevalence of disposable income losses [Risk(DI)], as follows: [Risk(MI) - Risk(DI)]/Risk(MI).

This approach, however, is less precise than necessary. When comparing summary measures such as Gini coefficients, there is no way to determine who changes rank as the income measure switches from market income to disposable income. By contrast, with the current measure of income risk, it is possible to know who is prevented from experiencing a large income loss by taxes and transfers. In particular, individuals can be classified into four categories based on whether they experience a qualifying drop in market income, in disposable income, or in both, as illustrated by the two-by-two matrix in Table 8.2.

The matrix shows the four possible combinations of market and disposable income dynamics. Those in the top-left cell [1] do not experience large income losses in either market income or disposable income. Pooling the data for all countries and years, about 81% of adults belong to that category. At the other extreme, those in the bottom-right cell [4] experience large income losses in both disposable income and market income. On average, about 10% of adults are in this unfortunate situation.

The top-right cell [3] refers to individuals who experience a large drop in market income, but not in disposable income. For these individuals, about 7% of adults,

Table 8.2. Incidence of Risk (Market Income versus Disposable Income)

		Large loss in market income	
		No	Yes
Large loss in disposable income	No	[1] Secure (no income loss) 81%	[3] Income loss mitigated 6%
	Yes	[2] Income loss aggravated 2%	[4] Risk (income loss) 10%

Note: Based on the following panel data collections: ECHP, EU-SILC, CPS, CNEF (BHPS, SOEP, HILDA, KLIPS, SHP, SLID). Sample: AUS 2002–16, AUT 1995–2014, BEL 1994–2014, BGR 2006–14, CAN 1994–2010, CHE 2001–16, CZE 2005–14, DEU 1985–2015, DNK 1994–2014, ESP 1994–2014, EST 2004–14, FIN 1996–2014, FRA 1994–2014, GBR 1993–2015, GRC 1994–2014, HRV 2010–14, HUN 2005–14, IRL 1994–2014, ISL 2004–14, ITA 1994–2014, KOR 2004–14, LTU 2005–13, LUX 2004–14, LVA 2007–14, MLT 2006–14, NLD 1994–2014, NOR 2003–14, POL 2005–14, PRT 1994–2014, ROU 2007–14, SRB 2013–14, SVK 2005–14, SVN 2005–14, SWE 2004–14, USA 1986–2011. StatLink 2 http://dx.doi.org/10.1787/888933839943.

the tax and transfer system serves as a safety net that keeps them from crossing the 25% threshold. Finally, the bottom-left cell [2] indicates the peculiar situation in which the tax and transfer system actually exacerbates income losses. Fortunately, these cases are rare, roughly 2% of observations.

These cells suggest a more precise measure of the buffering role of the tax and transfer system: the share of adults who experience a large loss in market income but not in disposable income. The proportion is substantial: on average, the tax and transfer system mitigates large income drops for about 41% of individuals experiencing large income drops $(7/(7+10) = 0.41)$. However, this number varies dramatically across countries and over time.

Figure 8.6 provides a summary picture of the role of taxes and transfers in reducing the prevalence of large income losses in our set of countries during the most recent period (again, roughly the early 2000s until the end of the relevant data series). The length of the bars shows the average share of adults who see their market income decline by 25% or more, but are prevented from experiencing a large disposable income loss by taxes and transfers. The arrows show whether this buffering role has increased or decreased over time.

The conclusion suggested by this figure is that countries with high levels of income risk (as shown in Figure 8.4) do relatively little to cushion large market income losses through the tax and transfer system. Moreover, the recent evolution of this buffering role indicates that countries have, if anything, increased the degree to which they reduce large income losses during the recent crisis. That is to say, a growing share of those who experience large market income losses are prevented from experiencing large disposable income losses thanks to the tax and transfer system. Whether this reflects a conscious change in policy or, more likely, the resilience of countries' safety nets during the economic crisis, it provides some reassurance to those who worry that national systems of social protection are becoming progressively less capable of covering contemporary risks to income. It remains to be seen whether this conclusion will continue to hold true once the deep employment effects of the crisis recede.

Finally, while all these estimates have looked at the adult population as a whole, they can be used to examine socio-demographic differences within countries. Figure 8.7 contains one such comparison looking at the average prevalence of large disposable income losses for adults with different levels of formal education. Not surprisingly, in most nations, income losses are much more likely among adults with limited formal education as compared with those with extensive formal education. Though not reported in Figure 8.7, income losses are also more prevalent among lower-income adults (when income is averaged across all available observations for each individual), workers who are not members of trade unions, heads of single-parent households, and younger adults.

Indeed, it is possible to look at more than just the differences across broadly defined groups. When panels are sufficiently long, it is also possible to construct individual-level or household-level measures for extended periods of time, as is done in the volatility literature.

Table 8.3, for example, shows the share of the working-age population experiencing one, two, three, or four or more large income losses over a decade.[19] Over 10 years, as the table shows, only a minority of working-age adults in Australia,

Figure 8.6. Effect of Taxes and Transfers on the Incidence of Large Income Losses

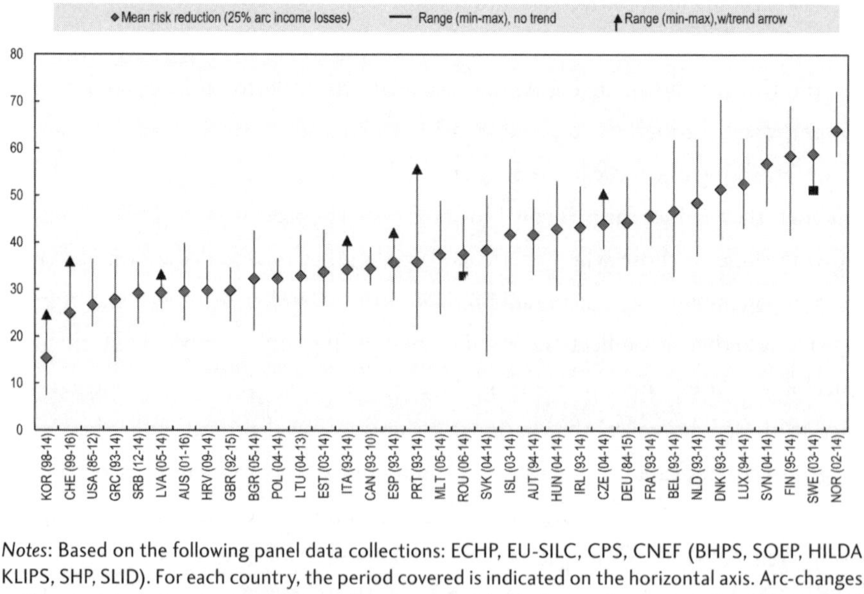

Notes: Based on the following panel data collections: ECHP, EU-SILC, CPS, CNEF (BHPS, SOEP, HILDA, KLIPS, SHP, SLID). For each country, the period covered is indicated on the horizontal axis. Arc-changes, unlike percentage changes, treat gains and losses symmetrically (e.g., an income gain from $50 to $100 implies a 100% change but a 67% arc-change; while an income loss from $100 to $50 implies a 50% change but a 67% arc-change); they are bound between +2 and −2. StatLink 2 https://doi.org/10.1787/888933839962.

Figure 8.7. Incidence of Income Losses by Education, Pre- to Post-secondary

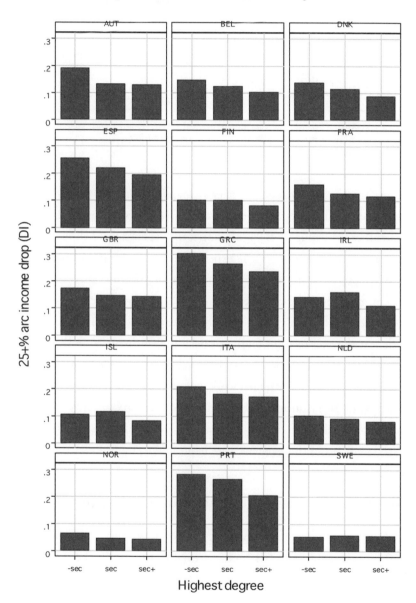

Note: Based on the EU-SILC for 2012/2013.

**Table 8.3. Number of Large Year-to-Year Income Drops Experienced
by Individuals over a Decade**

Drops	United States	United Kingdom	Switzerland	Germany	Australia
0	26.4%	39.5%	40.4%	41.1%	33.0%
1	31.1%	32.9%	33.9%	30.8%	32.1%
2	22.9%	16.1%	17.2%	17.4%	21.4%
3	12.3%	8.3%	6.1%	7.3%	9.6%
4+	7.4%	3.3%	2.4%	3.4%	4.0%

Note: Based on the CNEF panel data collection (PSID, BHPS, SHP, SOEP, HILDA). Sample: AUS 2002–16, CHE 2001–16, DEU 1985–2015, GBR 1993–2006, USA 1971–97. StatLink 2 http://dx.doi.org/10 .1787/888933839981.

Germany, the United Kingdom, Switzerland, and the United States were fortunate enough to escape the experience of a year-over-year income loss of 25% or more. On the other side, roughly 23% of Americans experienced 2 drops, about 12% experienced 3 drops, and over 7% experienced 4 or more drops, indicating that close to half of Americans experienced 2 or more large income losses in that decade.

In sum, the prevalence of large income losses appears to be a sensible measure of economic security that varies across countries and individuals in ways generally consistent with other relevant findings (including, as discussed in the last section, measures of *perceived* economic security). Still, it remains incomplete in some key respects, and significant additional work will need to be done to develop a broader evidence base for measuring other elements of economic security (such as large consumption shocks) and extending these measures to a larger set of countries. The next section discusses this evidence base in greater depth.

Are Available Statistics Adequate to Inform Policy?

As is clear from the discussion thus far, the low availability of reliable and cross-nationally comparable data has been a crucial constraint on the development of improved measures of economic security. Three shortcomings of existing statistics stand out: the limited pool of long-term and cross-nationally comparable panel data; the weaknesses of most administrative data for tracing individuals over time; and the lack of regular questions about economic security in conventional random-sample opinion surveys and, to even greater extent, in panel data. Nonetheless, these data have been rapidly improving, as shown when reviewing each of these major sources.

Panel Data

Measures that look at fluctuations in individuals' economic standing over time generally require panel data. Historically, this has been a key constraint on the development of better metrics on insecurity.

To be sure, panel data are not always necessary. Cross-sectional data can be used to develop a number of the measures discussed in this chapter, including assessments of the buffers that individuals and households have and estimates of the cross-sectional incidence of key economic shocks, such as unemployment. The challenge, however, is that such data can only provide insight into the point-in-time incidence of shocks, rather than their over-time prevalence. Moreover, it is generally not possible to use cross-sectional data to estimate how buffers *change* for particular households or individuals, or whether shocks are concentrated among specific groups rather than broadly distributed across the population.

Fortunately, a wide range of panel data sets have been inaugurated in the last two decades (see sidebar, "Major Panel Data Sources"). One weakness of many of these sources, however, is their lack of simultaneous data on income, consumption, and wealth. In addition, most do not contain questions that allow researchers to assess *perceived* economic security alongside *observed* economic security. Finally, differences in question wording and survey design can make it difficult to compare results across different panels. The recommendations presented at the end of this chapter aim to remedy these problems, and to increase the number of countries for which panel data are available.

MAJOR PANEL DATA SOURCES

For measuring economic insecurity, we would like multiple observations on income over a long period of time at a relatively high frequency. Typically, we have instead a short panel with high-frequency data collection, or a long panel with lower frequency.

In the United States, the PSID has measured incomes on an annual basis back to 1968, but has not been refreshed to stay representative in every year, and it switched to biennial reporting of incomes in 1997. The SIPP has measured monthly incomes every four months since 1984, but starts new panels every few years and switched to annual reporting in 2016. The CPS has annual income in March (matchable to the prior or subsequent March for a fraction of the sample) but does not follow movers. The Health and Retirement Survey and National Longitudinal Surveys are lower frequency and do not represent the full population.

Long panel surveys are available for many developed countries, including the Household, Income and Labour Dynamics (HILDA) in Australia, the Canadian Survey of Labour and Income Dynamics (SLID), the German Socio-Economic Panel (GSOEP), the Korea Labour and Income Panel Study (KLIPS), the Swiss Household Panel (SHP), and the British Household Panel Study (BHPS), plus harmonized country panel data sets in the Cross-National Equivalent File (CNEF) and the EU-SILC. China and many less developed countries have or are soon to have panel household surveys as well.

Source: Courtesy of Austin Nichols.

Administrative Data

New data sets linking tax and program data are becoming available in a handful of countries. These can be superior to panel data because of the well-known problems of recall bias and attrition in panel data. However, most administrative data sets remain limited, and they suffer from their own problems, including significant restrictions on their use by researchers (see sidebar, "Major Administrative Data Sources"). A promising new source of data is the large data sets being created by financial institutions. These data allow very fine-grained analysis of economic dynamics, but suffer from some serious problems, including limited availability, limited scope (often encompassing only transactions conducted through a single financial institution), and lack of representativeness of the individuals/households included.

MAJOR ADMINISTRATIVE DATA SOURCES

Administrative data from tax records are sometimes hard to access, but offer the possibility of longer panels with annual measures of income. In the United States, for example, the Longitudinal Employment and Household Dynamics (LEHD) data set, available in secure Census data facilities, links multiple administrative records on people and firms. Similarly, the Social Security Administration (SSA) hosts the Master Earnings File (MEF) containing all earnings reported to the SSA.

These sources offer long series of annual income thought to be of high quality because they are subject to auditing. Recently, efforts have been made to merge multiple administrative records with government survey data, as in the "Gold Standard File" created by the US Census and the SSA. An important point to bear in mind with matched data sources is that merge rates are never 100%, and matched samples may be less representative of the population of interest.

Federal government sources offer large sample sizes, but so too does a new generation of corporate data sources, both from regular clients and special surveys such as those conducted by AC Nielsen. Credit reporting agencies and major banks have in some cases better coverage of annual totals for both household income and expenditures, thanks to aggregating transaction-level data for account holders. Many of these sources can also track income across country boundaries and may include transactions not subject to third-party reporting and therefore missing from government files. Nevertheless, many low-income or unbanked individuals will never be observed in these files.

Source: Courtesy of Austin Nichols.

Questions About Economic Security in Conventional Opinion Surveys

As noted in the discussion of perceived security measures, opinion surveys sometimes include questions about economic security, particularly job security. These questions typically ask respondents to assess how likely it is that they will experience specific adverse economic events, or how well protected they would be if they experienced such events. Cross-nationally comparable survey questions are relatively rare, however, and overwhelmingly concern economic security in the domain of employment. Moreover, even within countries, panel surveys are relatively rare, making it difficult to assess the causes of changing perceptions of economic security at the individual level.

Nonetheless, a number of cross-sectional surveys do include questions regarding perceived job security. These include:

- International Social Survey Program (ISSP) Work Orientations I–III: "For each of these statements about your (main) job, please tick one box to show how much you agree or disagree that it applies to your job. My job is secure" (1989, 1997, 2005).

Figure 8.8. How Insecure Is My Job?

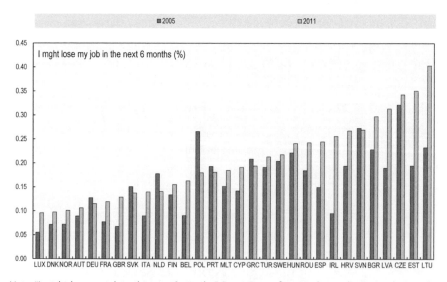

Note: "I might lose my job in the next 6 months." Percentage of respondents who "strongly agree" or "agree" (versus "neither agree nor disagree"/"disagree"/ "strongly disagree").
Source: Eurofound (2010), European Working Conditions Surveys (EWCS), 2005/2010, www.eurofound .europa.eu/surveys/european-working-conditions-surveys. StatLink 2 http://dx.doi.org/10.1787 /888933840000.

- European Social Survey (ESS): "Using this card, please tell me how true each of the following statements is about your current job. My job is secure" (2004, 2010).
- European Quality of Life Survey (EQLS): "Using this card, how likely or unlikely do you think it is that you might lose your job in the next 6 months?" (2003, 2007, 2011/12).
- Eurobarometer (EB): "Here is a list of statements about your current job. For each of them, please tell me if it is very true, quite true, a little true, or not at all true? My job is secure" (1996, 2009).

Figure 8.8 shows the country-year averages for one such question in the European Working Conditions Surveys (EWCS): "How much do you agree or disagree with the following statements describing some aspects of your job? I might lose my job in the next 6 months" (2005 and 2010):

Conclusions

This chapter has reviewed and extended the growing literature on economic security, outlining a range of measures and data that are improving analysts' and policy-makers' understanding of this critical aspect of economic life. This final section provides a series of suggestions for promoting more and better research on economic security and improving the base of data on which this work rests.

The core point is that researchers, national statistical agencies, and key international organizations should work together to improve and augment existing measures. No one doubts the fundamental importance of economic security. Yet few measures of this vital phenomenon are widely used and accepted. The goal of this chapter has been to lay out a small number of such measures that are consistent with available theory and evidence, can be relatively easily produced for multiple countries using extant data, and can guide policy-makers seeking to safeguard and increase economic security.

The task going forward will be to refine these measures to produce a small number of reliable indicators of economic security that can help experts and policy-makers evaluate economic well-being and social progress. These measures will necessarily be imperfect, and no single one will suffice on its own. Together, however, a small set of measures could provide a baseline for assessing and comparing economic security while creating the foundation for improved measures in the future.

Improving and Encouraging Research on Economic Security

The starting point for these efforts is a stronger conceptual foundation. Research on economic security requires a major collaborative program spanning policy-makers, researchers, and theorists to refine both theory and measurement. With regard to theory, the concept of economic security remains in its infancy. Substantial progress in the study of economic security will require its further refinement, with particular attention to the role of individual psychology. With regard to measurement, the development of stronger indicators will require grappling with the intertwined role of income, consumption, and wealth; the causes of losses (including the difficult question of how to establish causality given the ubiquity of confounders in this realm); and the improvement of measures of perceived security. It will also require better integration of measures of perceived and observed security within major data sources, the next focus.

Improving and Augmenting Data Related to Economic Security

Refinements in theory and measurement will only bear fruit if they rest on an adequate base of high-quality data. In particular, there is a pressing need for cross-national data efforts that bring together researchers and National Statistical Offices to develop panel data that are comparable across countries. These data should include perceived security measures alongside traditional panel economic variables, as is now done in a handful of panel studies. In addition, efforts should be made to link panel data with administrative data that incorporates public tax and program data sets.

At the same time, researchers and National Statistical Offices, as well as interested private survey firms, should work together to create a small subset of "security monitors" that could be incorporated into opinion surveys. On the whole, data on the subjective experience of economic security that could allow for monitoring of over-time or cross-country trends remain sparse. Fielding better cross-nationally comparable surveys is therefore imperative. Prior to that, however, extant measures should be compared with measures of *observed* security to see how closely they correspond. (For that purpose, including more questions about perceived security in panel data sets would again be invaluable.)

Any security monitors based on opinion surveys must be closely tied to the best available research on how to gauge security through a limited number of survey instruments. Here, survey designers should draw on the experience gained by the large community of researchers working on subjective well-being. Moreover, questions should be designed to cover a broad range of risks, not just those related to employment—including risks related to retirement and family dissolution, as well as access to and affordability of food, housing, and health care.

Finally, efforts should be directed at developing innovative new data sources that can be scaled up, including lab experiments that probe subjective risk perceptions and individuals' willingness to pay to insure themselves against key economic risks. A central question here will be how to distinguish "economic security" from general risk aversion, since the former is broader than the latter. Collaboration with private businesses and other institutions that provide financial services should also be encouraged to obtain new data on individual economic dynamics that address the major current limits of proprietary sources. In all these efforts, data should be designed to capture the joint distribution of income, consumption, and wealth, as argued elsewhere in this volume.

Identifying a Small Number of Core Measures of Economic Security

In the meantime, researchers, policy-makers, and national statistical agencies should work to develop a handful of core measures of economic security that can be incorporated into a "dashboard" of indicators of well-being. In addition to refined ESI-style measures of income risk, these indicators should include one or a few perceived measures of economic security; one or a few measures of buffers (such as asset poverty); and one or a few "named-risk measures" (probability multiplied by severity) for a few major risks such as unemployment, uninsured medical expenses, and inadequate retirement income.

There is a strong case, however, for *not* aggregating these various measures into a single index, since the logic of current weighting schemes is relatively weak. When employing Osberg's named-risk approach, moreover, it would be ideal to have all such measures focus on the same basic outcome: the uninsured income loss in the event of a particular adverse shock. Ideally, these estimates would also be based on panel data, reducing the gap between measures of income loss and the "named-risk" approach.

With regard to the ESI-style measure of income risk and the estimates developed, this chapter indicates that it should be possible to develop reliable measures that can be used to compare multiple countries. Nonetheless, several questions remain. For starters, is it possible to incorporate out-of-pocket medical spending into such estimates, as is done for the United States in the ESI? Out-of-pocket medical costs represent a substantial financial burden for many households, so ignoring their effect on economic security leaves an incomplete picture. However, rising out-of-pocket costs may reflect improvements in the quality or volume of care, so their welfare effects are ambiguous. How to treat medical costs is a question that research on economic security needs to better address.

Additional questions must be addressed as well. Perhaps the most pressing is whether wealth and consumption data can be integrated into measures of income loss. Should, for example, such measures subtract debt service or treat wealthy individuals differently from those without wealth, as is done in the ESI? Can consumption effects be used as a test of whether income losses are involuntary? Can measures better account for the differing consumption needs of different households?

A large set of questions also concern the *causes* of income losses. With present data, it is not always possible to link large losses to discrete changes in the standing of workers or their families. Improved data and measurement techniques should make it possible to pinpoint the causes of large losses more precisely. It is worth keeping in mind, however, that large losses are often the result of multiple simultaneous shocks, which presents difficulties for those interested in parsing their causes. Moreover, even with the best available data, it is always difficult to distinguish correlation from causation in observational studies.

Over the past few decades, economic security has gained heightened salience due to major changes in the workplace and the family, as well as mounting pressures on public programs and the erosion of key private protections. These changes—and the popular concerns they have generated—make it imperative that researchers and policy-makers better understand how economic security is changing, who is most affected by these changes, and what policies are best poised to address the resulting dislocations.

The findings and recommendations of this chapter point to major areas where our knowledge of economic security has improved. The chapter has also highlighted areas where work can and should be further advanced. Better concepts and measures would not only benefit economic research. They could also help policy-makers evaluate how well existing policies protect economic security and guide them as they sought to improve those policies. Few tasks are more vital today.

Notes

1. One reason for looking at household data is that earnings—the main focus of individual-level analyses—is only one source of income for most people. With increased labor force participation of women, and reforms to social programs that increase the incentive to work, there is good reason to think that the covariance of earnings and transfers has increased over time, and that the inter-temporal covariance of spouses' incomes has increased as well. Such increased covariances can result in higher family or household income variability even in the absence of increasing earnings volatility. It is important to note, however, that assigning household resources to individuals, as is common in insecurity research, requires assumptions about how household resources are shared within the family. An important agenda for this research—one essential to understanding the gendered character of insecurity—is to examine more closely how resources are actually pooled within the family.

2. Indices, by design, encompass multiple indicators that can, and often do, involve elements of measures (1), (2), and (4).

3. The *OECD Wealth Distribution Database* compiles data on wealth distribution sourced from surveys and administrative registers based on common definitions and classifications. OECD (2017) presents data on the distribution of wealth for 28 OECD countries and 3 emerging economies.

4. Unemployment insurance covers national insurance provisions earned without income-testing. Sick pay covers benefits paid in the event of short-term nonoccupational illness or injury. This includes provisions for mandatory private (employer-paid) benefits in addition to public insurance. Public pensions include only mandatory public programs (except for the nominally private Finnish earnings-related fund). Data are also provided for replacement rates of minimum pensions for those without work history. Replacement rates, eligibility criteria, and duration of benefits are calculated for a notional average production

worker in manufacturing who is 40 years old and has been working for the 20 years preceding the loss of income or the benefit period. Two different household types are accounted for: single (living alone, no children, or other dependents) and family (cohabiting with a spouse with no earnings, two children aged 7 and 12). Replacement rates are calculated by annualizing the first half year of benefits (i.e., calculating the benefit for the first 26 weeks and multiplying by 2). The reference wage for replacement rates is the "average production worker wage." General government cash transfers are accounted for when calculating the net wage; the replacement rate for families refers to income that includes child/family benefits (Scruggs, 2014a and 2014b).

5. A more elaborate example of a probability-estimate measure is the "Retirement Risk Index" developed by Munnell and colleagues to study changes in US economic security (Munnell, Webb, and Delorme, 2006). This measure is designed to capture the probability that working-age Americans who have yet to claim public and private retirement benefits will retire without adequate income. In essence, this risk measure marries the buffer approach discussed previously with the group-specific probability estimates currently under consideration. It does so by calculating available wealth for retirement (based on present wealth and its forecasted growth, plus expected public and private benefits) and then comparing this household-specific total with the amount needed to purchase an actuarially fair annuity that offers an income-replacement rate judged sufficient by established models of retirement planning. What makes it a group-specific risk measure is that these numbers are then used to calculate the future probability of inadequate retirement income as just defined for various educational and income groups and age cohorts. (The main finding is that retirement preparedness has declined sharply overall, particularly so for younger and poorer Americans.) Thus, this measure is conceptually equivalent to Rehm's—though it uses forecasted income rather than observed unemployment to assign probabilities.

6. Another example of such measure is the index of labor market security used by the OECD in the context of its OECD Job Quality Framework. This index is measured as the product of unemployment risk (the monthly probability of becoming unemployed times the average expected duration of completed unemployment spells in months) and (one minus) unemployment insurance (the coverage of the unemployment insurance/assistance times the replacement rates of public transfers received by the unemployed). See Cazes, Hijzen, and Saint-Martin (2015).

7. Just how discretionary medical spending truly is remains a major topic of analysis, which is not discussed here; suffice it to say that the largest out-of-pocket expenditures are likely to be the least within the immediate control of individual patients.

8. Another volatility-related hybrid measure is the approach of Bossert and D'Ambrosio (2013), who measure economic security as a weighted sum of household wealth and its past volatility. Like other volatility measures, this approach provides a household-level estimate of economic insecurity (which can be translated into an individual-level estimate by assuming equal distribution of household-size-equivalized resources—the common approach in the

volatility literature). Bossert and D'Ambrosio apply their approach to the US PSID and to the Italian Survey of Household Income and Wealth (SHIW). Without going into the precise characteristics of this measure—and, indeed, Bossert and D'Ambrosio say that researchers presently do not know exactly how to weight current wealth and past wealth volatility—its main strength is its integration of wealth levels and changes into a single measure. Its main weaknesses are, first, panel studies with high-quality wealth data are rare, certainly when compared with income data; and, second, there is limited evidence that changes in net worth are, by themselves, a major source of economic insecurity. In part, this is because wealth can change without any direct material hardship if asset prices fluctuate but individuals are not required to liquidate their wealth; in part, it reflects the aforementioned issue of how losses should be treated relative to gains (Bossert and D'Ambrosio are agnostic on this question, though they say that losses should be weighted *at least* as heavily as gains). By contrast, there is considerable evidence that large income losses make people feel less secure.

9. The SIPP has a shorter panel structure that allows assessment of whether the specific annual accounting period—i.e., what dates are considered as start and end points of a year—makes a significant difference to the results; it does not.

10. How much is required to buffer a loss is determined by using the PSID to determine how long it takes for the median household with similar characteristics experiencing a similar-sized drop to return to their pre-drop income level, and then summing the cumulative income shortfall over this period.

11. This could be done either by adjusting household income at retirement or by accounting for the full range of work-related nondiscretionary expenditures that retirees need not incur. At present, those retiring in the previous year are excluded from calculation of the ESI, so as not to confuse entrance into retirement with an adverse shock.

12. The next three paragraphs draw heavily on Osberg and Sharpe, 2014.

13. These trends in poverty, in turn, raise two questions: First, should poverty be assessed using country-specific poverty levels; and second, should these levels be absolute (i.e., the same across time or space) or relative (e.g., less than 50% percent of median income, the standard used by Osberg and his colleagues)? For comparing across countries, there is a strong argument for using country-specific thresholds. Poverty is commonly understood as deprivation relative to other members of a given society. It would be difficult, for example, to use the same standard for old-age poverty in Bangladesh as in Belgium; there would either be no poverty in the latter or near-universal poverty in the former. For over-time comparison, however, there is a stronger argument for using absolute poverty levels—for example, by fixing poverty levels for each nation at the beginning of a series—so as to separate out trends in economic security from trends in median income. This is particularly true when looking at short time intervals during which it is plausible to argue that the income levels that define poverty remain relatively constant.

14. Technically, the cumulative loss that occurs before income returns to its pre-drop level for a typical household with similar characteristics and a similarly sized loss.

15. Technically, the threshold is a 25 percent or greater arc-percent change. Arc-percent changes are calculated as 2*(Income[t]-Income [t-1])/[(Income[t]+Income[t-1])]. Unlike percent changes, arc-percent changes are bound by minus and plus 2, and they treat gains and losses symmetrically. For example, a respondent doubling her income from $50 to $100 experiences a 100 percent change (but a 67 arc-percent change). A respondent with a change in income from $100 to $50 experiences a 50 percent change (but a 67 arc-percent change). The arc-percent approach treats the change of $50 in a symmetric fashion.

16. All data were cleaned and standardized following established conventions. To deal with outliers as well as different top-coding and bottom-coding rules, income values were bottom-coded at 1 national currency unit (NCU) and top-coded at the 98th percentile. The main income variable used is total household income after taxes (including all cash benefits), adjusted by family size.

17. Usually, researchers calculate the percentage difference between the two [Gini(MI)-Gini(DI)]/Gini(MI)], though sometimes they use the absolute difference.

18. This approach raises issues that can only be touched upon here. The biggest one is the common assumption—embodied in the convention of calling pre-tax, pre-transfer income "market" income—that income before taxes and transfers is a pristine reflection of market forces, while disposable income after taxes and transfers captures the effects of government policy. In fact, taxes and transfers can greatly affect labor and capital markets, hence "market" income as well as disposable income. In addition, governments can and do attempt to shape market income through a range of tools besides taxes and transfers, including regulatory and macro-economic policies. For these reasons, it is best to think of the difference between market and disposable income as suggestive of the role of taxes and transfers but not, by itself, as offering a complete or definitive assessment.

19. The sample consists of respondents aged 25–60 with 10 consecutive years of nonmissing information on income drops (most recent spell). Weights from the final year of the spell are applied.

References

Acs, G. and A. Nichols (2010), *America Insecure—Changes in the Economic Security of American Families*, The Urban Institute, Washington, DC, www.urban.org/sites /default/files/publication/32906/412055-america-insecure.pdf.

Aguiar, M. and E. Hurst (2005), "Consumption versus expenditure," *Journal of Political Economy*, Vol. 113(5), pp. 919–948.

Banks, J., R. Blundell, and S. Tanner (1998), "Is there a retirement-savings puzzle?," *American Economic Review*, Vol. 88(4), pp. 769–788.

Bossert, W. and C. D'Ambrosio (2013), "Measuring economic insecurity," *International Economic Review*, Vol. 54(3), pp. 1017–1030.

Camerer, C. and M. Weber (1992), "Recent developments in modeling preferences: Uncertainty and ambiguity," *Journal of Risk and Uncertainty*, Vol. 5(4), pp. 325–370.

Carroll, C.D., J.C. Fuhrer, and D.W. Wilcox (1994), "Does consumer sentiment forecast household spending? If so, why?," *American Economic Review*, Vol. 84(5), pp. 1397–1408.

Cazes, S., A. Hijzen, and A. Saint-Martin (2015), "Measuring and assessing job quality: The OECD Job Quality Framework," *OECD Social, Employment and Migration Working Papers*, No. 174, OECD Publishing, Paris, http://dx.doi.org/10.1787/jrp02kjw1mr-en.

Cooper, Z. and F.S. Morton (2016), "Out-of-network emergency-physician bills—an unwelcome surprise," *New England Journal of Medicine*, Vol. 375(20), pp. 1915–1918.

Centre for the Study of Living Standards (2016), *Database of the Index of Economic Well-Being for Selected OECD Countries and Alberta, 1980–2014*, www.csls.ca/iwb /FinalIEWBAlbertaandOECD2014.xlsx.

Deaton, A. (1992), *Understanding Consumption*, Oxford University Press, Oxford.

Di Mauro, C. and A. Maffioletti (2004), "Attitudes to risk and attitudes to uncertainty: Experimental evidence," *Applied Economics*, Vol. 36(4), pp. 357–372.

Dogra, K. and O. Gorbachev (2016), "Consumption volatility, liquidity constraints and household welfare," *Economic Journal*, Vol. 126(597), pp. 2012–2037.

Doiron, D. and S. Mendolia (2012), "The impact of job loss on family dissolution," *Journal of Population Economics*, Vol. 25(1), pp. 367–398.

Duch, R.M., H.D. Palmer, and C.J. Anderson (2000), "Heterogeneity in perceptions of national economic conditions," *American Journal of Political Science*, Vol. 44(4), pp. 635–652.

Dynan, K.E., D.W. Elmendorf, and D.E. Sichel (2008), "The evolution of household income volatility," Federal Reserve Board and Brookings Institution, draft.

Ellsberg, D. (1961), "Risk, ambiguity, and the savage axioms," *Quarterly Journal of Economics*, Vol. 75(4), pp. 643–669.

Eurofound (2010), *European Working Conditions Surveys (EWCS), 2005/2010*, www .eurofound.europa.eu/surveys/european-working-conditions-surveys.

Friedman, M. (1957), "The permanent income hypothesis," in *A Theory of the Consumption Function*, pp. 20–37, Princeton University Press, Princeton.

Garmon, C. and B. Chartock (2016), "One in five inpatient emergency department cases may lead to surprise bills," *Health Affairs*, Vol. 36(1), pp. 177–181.

Gorbachev, O. (2011), "Did household consumption become more volatile?," *American Economic Review*, Vol. 101(5), pp. 2248–2270, https://doi.org/10.1257/aer.101.5.2248.

Gottschalk, P. et al. (1994), "The growth of earnings instability in the US labor market," *Brookings Papers on Economic Activity*, Vol. 1994, No. 2, pp. 217–272, www.jstor.org /stable/2554657.

Hacker, J.S. (2008), *The Great Risk Shift: The New Economic Insecurity and the Decline of the American Dream* (2nd ed.), Oxford University Press, New York.

Hacker, J.S. and E. Jacobs (2008), *The Rising Instability of American Family Incomes, 1969–2004: Evidence from the Panel Study of Income Dynamics*, Economic Policy Institute.

Hacker, J.S., P. Rehm, and M. Schlesinger (2013), "The insecure American: Economic experiences, financial worries, and policy attitudes," *Perspectives on Politics*, Vol. 11(1), pp. 23–49, https://doi.org/10.1017/S1537592712003647.

Hacker, J.S. et al. (2014), "The Economic Security Index: A new measure for research and policy analysis," *Review of Income and Wealth*, Vol. 60, pp. S5–S32).

Haider, S.J. and M. Stephens Jr. (2007), "Is there a retirement-consumption puzzle? Evidence using subjective retirement expectations," *Review of Economics and Statistics*, Vol. 89(2), pp. 247–264.

Hendren, N. (2017), "Knowledge of future job loss and implications for unemployment insurance," *American Economic Review*, Vol. 107(7), pp. 1778–1823.

Kahneman, D. and A. Tversky (2013), "Prospect theory: An analysis of decision under risk," in Maclean, L.C. and W.T. Ziemba (eds.), *Handbook of the Fundamentals of Financial Decision Making: Part I*, pp. 99–127, World Scientific.

Knight, F.H. (1921), *Risk, Uncertainty and Profit*, Houghton Mifflin, Boston and New York.

Kopczuk, W., E. Saez, and J. Song (2010), "Earnings inequality and mobility in the United States: Evidence from social security data since 1937," *Quarterly Journal of Economics*, Vol. 125(1), pp. 91–128.

Manski, C.F. (2004), "Measuring expectations," *Econometrica*, Vol. 72(5), pp. 1329–1376.

Moffitt, R. and P. Gottschalk (2002), "Trends in the transitory variance of earnings in the United States," *Economic Journal*, Vol. 112 (478), Conference Papers (March), pp. C68–C73.

Munnell, A., H.A. Webb, and L. Delorme (2006), *Retirements at Risk: A New National Retirement Risk Index*, Center for Retirement Research, Trustees of Boston College, http://crr.bc.edu/wp-content/uploads/2011/09/NRRI.pdf.

Nichols, A. and P. Rehm (2014), "Income risk in 30 countries," *Review of Income and Wealth*, Vol. 60, pp. S98–116, https://doi.org/10.1111/roiw.12111.

Nichols, A. and S. Zimmerman (2008), *Measuring Trends in Income Variability*, The Urban Institute, Washington, DC.

OECD (2017), *How's Life? 2017: Measuring Well-Being*, OECD Publishing, Paris, http://dx.doi.org/10.1787/_life-2017-en.

OECD (2017), *OECD Wealth Distribution Database*, https://stats.oecd.org/Index.aspx?DataSetCode=WEALTH.

Osberg, L. (2015), "How should one measure economic insecurity?," *OECD Statistics Working Papers*, No. 2015/01, OECD Publishing, Paris, http://dx.doi.org/10.1787/js4t78q9lq7-en.

Osberg, L. (2010), "Measuring economic insecurity and vulnerability as part of economic well-being: Concepts and context," in IARIW 31st General Conference, St. Gallen, Switzerland.

Osberg, L. and A. Sharpe (2014), "Measuring economic insecurity in rich and poor nations," *Review of Income and Wealth*, Vol. 60(S1), https://doi.org/10.1111/roiw.12114.

Osberg, L. and A. Sharpe (2009), *Measuring Economic Security in Insecure Times: New Perspectives, New Events, and the Index of Economic Well-Being*, Centre for the Study of Living Standards, Ottawa.

Rank, M.R., T.A. Hirschl, and K.A. Foster (2014), *Chasing the American Dream: Understanding What Shapes Our Fortunes*, Oxford University Press, Oxford.

Rehm, P. (2016), *Risk Inequality and Welfare States: Social Policy Preferences, Development, and Dynamics*, Cambridge University Press, Cambridge, MA.

Rehm, P., J.S. Hacker, and M. Schlesinger (2012), "Insecure alliances: Risk, inequality, and support for the welfare state," *American Political Science Review*, Vol. 106(2), pp. 386–406, https://doi.org/10.1017/S0003055412000147.

Scruggs, L. (2014), "Social welfare generosity scores in CWED 2: A methodological genealogy," *CWED Working Paper Series*.

Scruggs L. (2014), Comparative Welfare Entitlements Dataset (CWED2), University of Connecticut and D. Jahn, University of Greifswald, http://cwed2.org/.

Stettner, A., M. Cassidy, and G. Wentworth (2016), "A new safety net for an era of unstable earnings," The Century Foundation, New York, https://tcf.org/content/report/new-safety-net-for-an-era-of-unstable-earnings/.

Stiglitz, J.E., A. Sen, and J.-P. Fitoussi (2009), *Report by the Commission on the Measurement of Economic and Social Progress*, http://ec.europa.eu/eurostat/documents/118025/118123/Fitoussi+Commission+report.

Sullivan, D. and T. von Wachter (2009), "Job displacement and mortality: An analysis using administrative data," *Quarterly Journal of Economics*, Vol. 124(3), pp. 1265–1306.

Tversky, A. and D. Kahneman (1992), "Advances in prospect theory: Cumulative representation of uncertainty," *Journal of Risk and Uncertainty*, Vol. 5(4), pp. 297–323.

Western, B. et al. (2012), "Economic insecurity and social stratification," *Annual Review of Sociology*, Vol. 38, pp. 341–359.

9.

Measuring Sustainability

Marleen De Smedt, Enrico Giovannini,
and Walter J. Radermacher

This chapter outlines the principles of the capital approach and of the systems approach to measuring sustainable development. In the capital approach, human, social, natural, and economic capital are considered separately, with indicators presented on their stocks and how they change over time. While significant progress has been achieved in operationalizing this approach to sustainability, this approach, argue the authors, implicitly assumes the independence of these stocks, and does not easily lend itself to considering interactions between different parts of the systems that underpin human well-being and functioning ecosystems. The chapter considers how the systems approach should be taken forward to move from theoretical considerations to empirical applications. It explains the key notions underpinning the systems approach, including risk, vulnerability, and resilience, arguing that sustainability remains the ultimate objective. The chapter proposes a measurement agenda, suggesting steps to improve consideration of economic, human, and natural capital in the capital approach; and to improve the measurement of resilience and other aspects of the systems approach.

Marleen De Smedt is former Adviser to the Director-General of Eurostat, Enrico Giovannini is Full Professor of Economic Statistics at the Department of Economics and Finance of the University of Rome "Tor Vergata," and Walter J. Radermacher is Professor at the University of Rome "La Sapienza" and former Director-General of Eurostat. The authors wish to thank Paul Schreyer as well as other members of the HLEG for their comments on previous drafts of this chapter. They also thank the participants of the two HLEG workshops held in Rome, Italy, organized in collaboration with the OECD, on "Intra-generational and Inter-generational Sustainability" on September 22–23, 2014, hosted by the Einaudi Institute for Economics and Finance and the Bank of Italy and sponsored by SAS; and on "Measuring Economic, Social and Environmental Resilience" on November 25–26, 2015, hosted by the Einaudi Institute for Economics and Finance, supported by the Bank of Italy and ISTAT and sponsored by SAS. The section titled "Toward a Systems Approach to Inform Policy" largely relies on Manca, Benczur, and Giovannini (2017); therefore, the authors of this chapter are deeply grateful to Anna Manca and Peter Benczur for their contribution. The opinions expressed and arguments employed in the contributions below are those of the authors and do not necessarily reflect the official views of the OECD or of the governments of its member countries.

Introduction

Ensuring that individual and societal well-being can last over time requires preserving the resources needed by future generations. This approach (which underpins the definition of "sustainable development" provided by the 1987 Brundtland Report) implies that measures of economic and social progress must take into account changes in those resources that last over time (i.e., capital). These changes consist of depreciation, depletion, and erosion (all of which diminish capital) as well as investment, innovations, and discoveries (all of which increase capital). Without them, any account of sustainability is incomplete.

The very nature of "capital"—as a cornerstone of economic production, as an entrepreneurial code of conduct, and as a fundamental of bookkeeping and accounting—implies a close relationship between capital and sustainable development. Conceptually, capital can be broken down into economic, human, and natural capital (social capital is typically added too, but it is not discussed here, as it is addressed in Chapter 10).[1] At the same time, an exclusive focus on the measurement of different types of capital—and the deeply rooted belief that, with enough effort, signals about the future can be internalized via the right valuation of capital—may divert attention from investigating the measurement of sustainability from different but complementary perspectives.

One example of these complementary perspectives is provided by the notion of "footprints," which recognizes that the environment crosses country borders. This is why the UNECE insists that "[Sustainable Development Indicator] sets should reflect the transboundary impacts of sustainable development, by highlighting how a country in the pursuit of the well-being of its citizens may affect the well-being of citizens of other countries" (UNECE, 2014, p. 14). So pursuing sustainable development increasingly means considering not just individual countries but the entire globe. A capital approach allows for an integration of time, the "future," but it is less useful for the accounting of place, the "elsewhere" dimension, which is equally important when it comes to monitoring the sustainability of national activities.

Another complementary perspective is to look into "systems," their behavior over time and their inter-relationships. In this perspective, monitoring capital stocks is only part of the story: ultimately, the challenge is to manage—nationally and internationally, and over a long-time perspective—those complex and inter-dependent systems (economy, society, and nature) that shape the well-being of future generations. Such systems are complex, meaning they behave differently at different scales; they behave in nonlinear ways; they are often self-organizing; and they are characterized by uncertainties, resilience, tipping points, and irreversibility.

In a systems approach, the focus moves from measuring the stocks of assets to coming to grips with the resilience of economic, societal, and natural systems. Tackling these issues requires inter-disciplinary work, with a focus on the ability of the system to cope with risks and uncertainties in a broad and long-run perspective, and on the different ways to manage this coping ability (resilience) of systems. "Resilience" is indeed referred to in the UN's Sustainable Development Goals (SDGs) and by the targets of its 2030 Agenda.

As this chapter will show, despite a range of national and international initiatives (see sidebar, "Monitoring Sustainable Development in Practice: Some Examples"), measuring sustainable development still faces difficulties and limitations. Good and effective communication to all stakeholders about available as well as missing information is critical, especially for making decision-making processes more effective and participatory.

This chapter is organized as follows. The first section lays out the principles of the capital and of the systems approach. The next section describes progress achieved in measuring economic, human, and natural capital since the Stiglitz, Sen, and Fitoussi (2009) report. The third section dives deeper into the systems approach, which should be taken forward to move from theoretical considerations to empirical information. The concluding section draws up a measurement agenda for the years to come.

MONITORING SUSTAINABLE DEVELOPMENT IN PRACTICE: SOME EXAMPLES

Various initiatives aimed at improving the measurement of progress and sustainable development have resulted in international agreements and standardization, such as the adoption of the 2008 System of National Accounts (SNA), the G20 Data initiative, and the adoption of the System of Economic Environmental Accounting (SEEA) in 2012. With the adoption in 2015 of the 17 Sustainable Development Goals (SDGs, United Nations, 2015a) and 169 targets, and the later agreement on a set of 232 global indicators, much headway has been made toward a common set of sustainable development indicators at the global level.

Some countries, however, have tracked sustainable development for several years, even before the adoption of the UN SDGs, either through a national set of indicators or in a supra/international context, or both. Examples of such international developments include:

• The Recommendations of the Conference of European Statisticians (CES), providing guidance on how sustainable development indicators (physical and monetary) may be harmonized and made consistent across countries and institutions (UNECE, 2014).

- In the EU context, the European Statistics Sponsorship Group on Measuring Progress, Well-Being and Sustainable Development (European Statistical System, 2011), the Sustainable Development Indicators set, the biennial monitoring reports on the EU Sustainable Development Strategy (Eurostat, 2016a), the EU Commission Communication on the next steps for a sustainable European future (European Commission, 2016a), a proposal for a new European Consensus on Development (European Commission, 2016b), and the 2016 Eurostat report on sustainability (Eurostat, 2016b).
- Various OECD analyses, tools, and approaches, including the recent assessment of OECD countries on "Measuring Distance to the SDG Targets" (OECD, 2016b).
- The World Bank's Genuine Savings Indicator, which is directly based on the capital approach (World Bank 2006, 2011), and the UNEP reports on "Inclusive Wealth" (UNEP and UN-IHDP, 2012 and 2014);
- The Sustainable Development Solutions Network (SDSN).[1]

At the national level, since the publication of the 1987 Brundtland Report and the recommendations of the Stiglitz, Sen, and Fitoussi (2009) report, a number of countries have started to collect data and to establish indicators on sustainable development. Among others:

- In *Italy*, the National Statistical Office (ISTAT) and representatives of civil society developed a multi-dimensional approach to measure "equitable and sustainable well-being" (*Benessere equo e sostenibile*, BES), integrating measures of economic activity (GDP) and of the social and environmental dimensions of well-being, inequality, and economic, social, and environmental sustainability.

The indicators are published on the BES website, with a detailed analysis of indicators available in the BES Reports.[2] The BES system has now been incorporated in the annual cycle that drives economic and financial planning by the Government and Parliament.

- *Finland* has a long tradition in using indicators on sustainable development: the first set of sustainable development indicators was published in 2000 and this list—available on the Findicators website[3]—has been growing ever since.

- *Switzerland* uses a measurement framework based on a system structure to monitor sustainable development. The system (MONET)[4] comprises 73 indicators. Each indicator is published on the internet and evaluated (through "traffic light" symbols) according to the observed trend. The website also includes 9 indicators related to the global dimension of sustainable development.

- The 2016–19 Federal Sustainable Development Strategy (FSDS)[5] is *Canada*'s primary vehicle for sustainable development planning and reporting. It sets out priorities, goals, and targets, identifies actions to achieve them, and links these to 12 global SDGs, with sustainable development indicators published on different webpages.[6]

- In 2002, the *German* Federal Government adopted its "National Sustainability Strategy." The Strategy was revised in 2016, setting out the challenges that have arisen for Germany from the 2030 Agenda. At the core of the strategy is a "sustainability management system" that defines objectives with a timeframe for fulfillment and indicators for monitoring, as well as regulations for the management and definition of institutional design. Since 2006, the Federal Statistical Office has reported on the indicators of the National Sustainability Strategy in six reports.[7] The Federal Statistical Office has now been commissioned to continue its statistical monitoring based on the revised strategy.

1. http://unsdsn.org/resources/publication/type/data-monitoring-accountability.

2. www.istat.it/it/benessere-e-sostenibilità.

3. www.findikaattori.fi/en/kestavakehitys.

4. www.bfs.admin.ch/bfs/en/home/statistics/sustainable-development.html.

5. www.ec.gc.ca/dd-sd/default.asp?Lang=En&n=CD30F295-1.

6. www.ec.gc.ca/default.asp?lang=en&n=FD9B0E51-1.

7. The 2016 report by the Federal Statistical Office on the development of the indicators of the German sustainability strategy is available at: www.destatis.de/DE/Publikationen/Thematisch/UmweltoekonomischeGesamtrechnungen/Umweltindikatoren/IndikatorenPDF_0230001.pdf?blob=publicationFile.

Key Concepts and Approaches
The Capital Approach

Ensuring the well-being of present and future generations essentially depends on how societies choose to use their resources, i.e., their various forms of capital. These resources include physical elements, such as shelter and sub-soil assets or the quality of the natural environment, but also intangibles such as knowledge or the quality of social and institutional structures. Therefore, more than just including produced (economic) capital, the definition of capital should encompass social, human, and natural capital.

Measuring capital requires constructing and examining balance sheets for different types of capital, for each country and for the whole planet, and assessing their changes over time. This type of "capital approach" may be characterized as reflecting what, in the field of financial markets, has been described as a "microprudential perspective": all forms and appearances of capital are inventoried one by one. Measuring sustainability from a capital approach focuses on the net change in the volumes of the stocks of various assets, weighted by their "shadow prices" (i.e., a monetary value reflecting the true opportunity costs of all activities, taking into account all externalities and public goods generated by them); these shadow prices will in general differ from market prices, and depend on all other types of capital, technology, and societal preferences. Shadow prices should also reflect future actions and their discounted consequences, to make net changes in overall capital a true indicator of sustainability (for a full discussion of the theoretical issues associated with the capital approach, see Fleurbaey and Blanchet, 2013).

One important implication here is that adopting such a comprehensive capital approach would require reconsidering conventional distinctions between consumption and investment activities. For example, expenditures that contribute to a society's human and/or social capital (e.g., training of teachers) will enhance that society's long-term sustainability, rather than simply representing final or intermediate consumption as assumed in the current System of National Accounts (SNA). Thus, measures of investment, consumption, and national wealth in a sustainability perspective would generally differ from the one used in conventional economic statistics, as, in general, we lack a good understanding of the relevant flows of investment and depreciation. These difficulties were recognized in the Stiglitz, Sen, and Fitoussi (2009) report, which recommended establishing a sub-dashboard to provide information about changes of those "stocks" that underpin human well-being. For economic, human, and natural capital, the progress made in developing metrics in recent years and the current challenges, as well as recommendations for the future, are described in the next two sections.

The Systems Approach

One of the lessons learned from the financial crisis was that a micro-prudential approach of supervision and regulation is, in itself, insufficient to avoid financial crisis. A macro-prudential layer is also needed, as the interactions among individual financial institutions are, from a financial sustainability perspective, as important as the conditions of a single institution. To ensure overall sustainability therefore, a "systems approach" was needed.

The same dichotomy can be applied to complex systems in general, differentiating between the behavior of single components considered in isolation, and that of the full system with all interactions. Such a systems perspective (Costanza et al., 2014) allows the identification of relevant actors who play a particular role in the system, their behavior and their interactions with the other actors; and helps to address key questions of system dynamics applied to the society, economy, and environment we live in.

While these systems are complex by themselves, their interactions with each other add to complexity. As mentioned above, besides dynamics, complex systems are often characterized by nonlinearities (which can be negative or positive), emergent properties, self-organization, tipping points, and transformation. These characteristics make the system subject to self-generated (endogenous) shocks in addition to shocks coming from outside the system (exogenous). The interactions of these characteristics help to define the degree of vulnerability of a system to risks as well as its resilience.

The key notions underpinning the systems approach could be described as follows:

• *Risk* is here used with a double connotation: first, to describe threats for systems (i.e., systemic risks); second, when it is possible, to quantify the probability of an unknown event. Contrary to this situation, *uncertainty* is used if the "unknown" cannot be quantified. For decision making and citizens' participation in democratic societies, this distinction is critical. Individual well-being and social welfare are affected by these risks, but also depend on the *availability of information* about them. The availability of information—or the treatment of uncertainties—is particularly important concerning social inequalities linked to risk arising from economic activities.

• *Vulnerability* manifests itself in damage from a disturbance that might arise from external or internal factors. It ranges from "low" to "high," depending on the severity of the impact of the disturbance on the system. There are different definitions for vulnerability, ranging from vulnerability within a specific context, such as in an environmental context (climate change) or in a personal context (poverty, risky behavior, sickness), to more integrated approaches relating to both physical and social systems' susceptibility to multiple stresses generated by socio-economic and environmental changes. Complex systems may be vulnerable to all kinds of risks inherent in everyday life that are the result of decisions, naturally occurring events, or a combination of both. In this wider context, vulnerability is of a *multi-scale nature*; it is not evenly distributed among social groups, spatial units, or time. Vulnerability of a system is shown by its response to disturbances, and depends on the intrinsic characteristics of the system and on the severity and time of exposure of the disturbance.

- *Resilience*, rooted in the Latin word *resilire* (which means "jump back," "rebound"), is the capacity to recover from adversity (from temporary shocks—such as sudden flows of migration—or from continuous threats or slow-burn processes—such as the aging of societies), either returning to the original state or moving to a new steady state (from positive adaptation to transformation), often strengthened and more resourceful. Resilience, which is the centerpiece of the systems approach, can be a *characteristic of a system or sub-system, or of individuals*. This distinction is important because system-wide resilience is typically the result of a series of interactions among individuals and sub-systems. It thus provides us with a concept and a structure that allows us to identify components, the monitoring of which could underpin a policy framework. At the same time, resilience also makes *the role of dynamics* more explicit, by looking at disturbances and their short- and long-run impact.

Focusing on resilience should not be misunderstood as an attempt to abandon sustainability, but instead as an approach to retain or restore it when responding to shocks and threats. *Sustainability is and remains the ultimate objective.* The fact that we begin to examine how systems respond to shocks and threats does not lead us to give up on preventing shocks or negative events. Similarly, if a resilient system rebounds from a shock to re-establish its initial path, this is not good enough if the initial path was unsustainable. While resilience and sustainability are not inter-changeable concepts, addressing the resilience of systems is a way to build a system-level "macro-prudential" approach about how we can prevent and adapt to shocks and threats, and transform our society. The "pressure-state-response" used in environmental economics provides an early example of the systems approach (see sidebar below). A more in-depth discussion is included in the conclusion.

THE PRESSURE-STATE-RESPONSE APPROACH
AS AN EXAMPLE OF THE SYSTEMS APPROACH

The original pressure-state-response (PSR) approach, developed by Statistics Canada and popularized by the OECD with reference to natural capital, was later extended to Driver-Pressure-State-Impact-Response (DPSIR), adopted by UNDP in 1997 and used in the context of Environmental Economic Accounting (EEA). The DPSIR framework (Figure 9.1) contains the different elements describing the resilience of the State of the Environment and allows the classification of data and indicators for the different elements (drivers, pressures, states, and impact). On the basis of such data, and using estimation and extrapolation techniques, the Intergovernmental Panel on Climate Change (IPCC, 2015) has estimated the planetary boundaries for climate change. The limits of a resilient ecosystem and these boundaries were again stated in COP21 (UN 21st Conference of the Parties, Paris, 2015): we should keep global temperature well below 2°C above pre-industrial levels, and at least below 1.5°C.

Figure 9.1. The Pressure-State-Response Approach

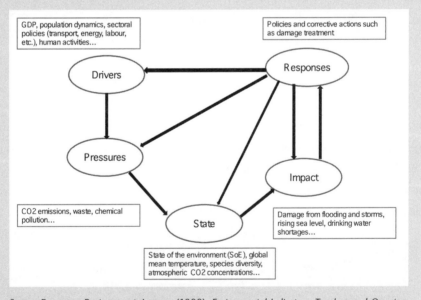

Source: European Environment Agency (1999), *Environmental Indicators: Typology and Overview*, Technical Report No. 25/1999, TNO Centre for Strategy, Technology and Policy, The Netherlands.

This example demonstrates that using the best available data and estimates, a scientific consensus could be reached on the planetary boundaries. Once these are set, it is possible to look at the scientific work and political actions needed to keep the system within these boundaries (see the discussion on carbon pricing in the next section).

What Is the State of Existing Capital Measures?

The capital approach builds on the notion of preserving or increasing the different stocks (capital) that drive our welfare and well-being. This "stock" approach to sustainability can either look at variations in each stock in physical terms or convert all these assets into a monetary equivalent. So the capital approach could evolve in two directions: either as a "mainstream economic approach," determining all types of capital and monetizing them; or as an "organizing framework," with physical indicators covering all the main assets. In the following, both interpretations are used, depending on the maturity of the data. Each type of capital is discussed separately.

Economic Capital

Progress Since 2009

During and after the global economic crisis, many of the issues raised in the Stiglitz, Sen, and Fitoussi (2009) report gained traction, while at the same time the failure to appropriately measure economic sustainability by conventional statistics became apparent. Risks and vulnerabilities built up over time in the economic system through increased debt levels, higher financial leverage (supported by more liberal finance laws and regulations), deteriorating quality of debt through higher credit default risks, price bubbles, and increased inter-connectedness across sectors and countries. This fragility went unnoticed due, partly, to the way that economic health was measured: it did not sufficiently measure risk.

During and immediately after the crisis, it was clear that many actors lacked appropriate and timely data to help them respond effectively. The G20 Data Gaps Initiative (DGI) has been an important source of progress in providing broader and more comprehensive measures of economic sustainability.[2] This initiative supports government efforts to provide comparable statistics on the build-up of risks in the financial sector, cross-border financial links, vulnerability to shocks, and communication of these statistics. It emphasizes the importance of having more and better information on how the assets and liabilities of one sector match those of others, as well as on currency and maturity mismatches. The G20 DGI provides templates for collecting balance sheet data that can be compared across countries. Many countries, especially within the EU, now make quarterly data available in a timely manner. Some even provide the institutional sector accounts discussed below.

One of the lessons on economic sustainability learned since the 2007 financial crisis is that there is no firm threshold for public debt beyond which we should expect GDP growth to fall significantly, even though high levels of public debt may raise concerns about the resilience of the economic system to shocks. Even studies showing correlations between public debt and GDP growth tell us little or nothing about causality. The only real test of the sustainability of public debt is provided by the market (i.e., the ability to sell government bonds), which is itself a function of the institutional setup of different countries (such as the existence of a central bank and the ability of monetary policy to maintain low interest rates) and of the assessment of future prospects for public finances given the evolution of demographic and other factors. There is also evidence that the relation between public debt and GDP growth may run from (low) growth to (high) public debt rather than the other way around in some circumstances.

The recovery from the crisis has been lackluster in much of the world and, in the United States and some other OECD countries, has further concentrated income gains at the top. Part of the reason for the unsatisfactory recovery across the world was the implementation of austerity measures, enacted under the misguided belief that there is a critical threshold above which debt lowers growth. Erosion of human capital due to unemployment and underemployment, discussed elsewhere in the report, is likely to have lowered growth for years to come. Investments in crumbling public infrastructure could have helped millions of people, maintained human capital stocks, and gone further toward helping the economy to recover.

Outstanding Issues and New Questions

While the 2008 SNA includes full balance sheets for economic assets and liabilities, many countries are still guided by a very limited (and possibly misleading) approach to sustainability. As described above, comparisons of (gross) public debt to GDP are incomplete measures of economic sustainability. It may be that part of the appeal of using the debt to GDP ratio as an indicator of sustainability is that it is relatively simple to calculate and understand.

However, sustainability has two additional aspects to be considered:

- A full balance sheet approach (i.e., taking stock of a broader range of associated risks and both assets and liabilities), by looking at:
  - the balance sheets of all sectors (banks, households, etc.) rather than the government alone;
  - both liabilities and assets (e.g., recognizing that fire sales of assets in depressed financial markets may worsen net worth);
  - the distinction between types of economic capital that add to productive capacity and those that do not (e.g., land), and between changes in volumes and changes in prices (see sidebar, "W versus K").
- A long-term sustainability analysis that takes account of the impact of demographic and other factors on the evolution of public finances.

With regard to the latter aspect, models and scenarios provide valuable guidance to societies on the choices they have to make to achieve sustainability. Models will become increasingly important to assess interactions between different types of capital and their determinants (see sidebar, "Modeling Public Finances").

W VERSUS K

Stiglitz (2015a), in his discussion of Piketty's (2015) finding of a long-term increase of the capital-output ratio, notes that such an increase should normally be accompanied by a decline in the returns to capital relative to labor and by a declining capital share in income. Neither is the case empirically, though, as data on declining labor shares and real wages indicate. Stiglitz's resolution of the puzzle lies in distinguishing between wealth (W) and capital services in production (K):

The distinction between W and K reflects the dual nature of capital, i.e., as a factor of production and a means of storing wealth. This distinction is a well-established feature in the literature on capital measurement (Jorgenson, 1963; Jorgenson and Griliches, 1967; Diewert and Schreyer, 2008; OECD, 2009) but is sometimes overlooked in the debate. Each aspect of capital is associated with a particular measure.

- The wealth aspect of capital requires a measure that reflects the market value of capital goods. W is the conceptually correct entry into balance sheets. Balance sheets relate to particular points in time, and valuation of wealth is at the prices prevailing at these points in time. The change in wealth between these points in time is made up of investment or other additions to the stock, minus depreciation or depletion, and revaluations.
- To capture the production aspect of capital, a volume measure K is required to reflect the flow of capital services into production. Unlike the wealth stock, the price of capital service is identified with user costs, designed to capture the marginal productivity of the different types of capital.

Stiglitz (2015a) explains: "The wealth income ratio could be increasing even as the capital income ratio is stagnating or decreasing. Much of wealth is not produced assets ('machines') but land or other ownership claims giving rise to rents. Some of the increase in wealth is the increase in the capitalised value of what might be called exploitation rents—associated with monopoly rents and rents arising from other deviations from the standard competitive paradigm. Some is an increase in the value of rents associated with intellectual property" (Stiglitz, 2015, p. 8).

This distinction implies that the evolution of the wealth-output ratio in nominal terms can be very different from the capital-output ratio in volume terms. The distinction also raises a question of scope of the two concepts— the inclusion or exclusion of some assets can modify the entire profile of the wealth-output and capital-output ratio. One such asset is land, and in several countries the rise in the overall wealth-output ratio has been driven by the steep revaluation of land, confirming Stiglitz's point. Despite the two distinct perspectives, the wealth and the production sphere are linked and so are its measures. Indeed, W and K should be constructed consistently and as part of an integrated framework, as laid out for instance by the 2008 SNA or in more detail by OECD (2009) and Jorgenson and Landefeld (2007).

MODELING PUBLIC FINANCES

Policy-makers in some countries are becoming more interested in modeling the path of public finances, acknowledging that demographic evolution (particularly aging) is a major factor in analyzing fiscal sustainability, alongside structural reforms and productivity developments. Notable examples of the approach include the United States,[1] Australia,[2] and European Union countries.[3]

This approach typically analyzes the situation of countries over the short, medium, and long term against their government debt level, their initial budgetary position, and the projected evolution of aging costs (notably old-age pensions, health care, and long-term care). It uses a range of assumptions, including on demographic evolution, real GDP growth, inflation, real interest rates, and labor market participation. An important aspect of the approach is to consider different scenarios, communicating clearly the sensitivity of the results with respect to the assumptions.

One advantage of this approach is that it is possible to analyze the projected

path of sustainability over time, thereby identifying particular future periods
of stress.

1. www.gao.gov/fiscal_outlook/federal_fiscal_outlook/overview.

2. https://treasury.gov.au/intergenerational-report/.

3. http://ec.europa.eu/economy_finance/publications/eeip/pdf/ip018_en.pd.

Arguably, macro-economic models should go further to reflect the joint determination of the paths of economic output and public debt levels by interest rates and
the government primary balance (i.e., government net borrowing or net lending,
excluding interest payments on consolidated government liabilities). This implies
recognizing that monetary policy and budget rules cannot be set independently
of each other, and that fiscal consolidation in a recession may have large effects
in terms of reducing GDP growth and limited effects in terms of reducing public
debt (possibly further increasing it). Macro-economic models should also highlight
the path that private demand is expected to follow under a given configuration
of policy instruments, and the need to adjust such instruments when the path of
private demand is inconsistent with macro-economic goals of full employment and
price stability.

A full balance sheet approach to economic sustainability would also imply a
more nuanced approach to sustainability, one that is not likely to rely on a "single
number." This makes it more difficult to decide, to take a pertinent example, when
it is appropriate to engage in fiscal stimulus.

In this context, a complete balance sheet would have several important
characteristics:

- Private wealth should be considered alongside the assets and liabilities
  of the public sector, as private liabilities may be converted into public
  liabilities if particular agents fail (due to bank bailouts, for example). In
  addition, the tax base upon which the government can draw for meeting
  its liabilities depends on the net wealth of the private sector. In both of

these respects, some sort of distributional information is important since aggregation may mask the fact that for many agents debt is not covered by assets. The share of households (or firms or banks) with negative net worth may be a useful indicator. There is also value in considering the transmission of wealth between generations through examining data on inheritance of assets more closely.

- A better balance sheet would also take into account the fact that, even though the value of an asset (e.g., land) has increased, and overall measures of wealth have gone up, this is not the same as an increase in the volume of productive assets.

- More detailed balance sheets of financial corporations and other institutional sectors are critical to understand risks and vulnerabilities. The G20 DGI recommends producing quarterly institutional sector accounts. We should also recognize that, when risk is not properly measured, we may underestimate the fragility of firms, households, and other institutions in the face of financial stress. Balance sheets should be more detailed, both in terms of showing more granular sub-sectors (to illuminate differences in vulnerabilities as measured, for example, by debt-to-income ratios) and more detailed data for each of those sub-sectors, while taking into account the costs and benefits of collecting and analyzing more detailed data. More detailed balance sheets within a sub-sector would allow for a better analysis of risk through examining inter-connectedness by having breakdowns by counterparty sector, or breakdowns of debt by maturity and currency.

- All relevant types of pension liabilities need to be included.

Even such improved and more detailed accounts, however, may not be sufficient to capture macro-economic risk. One reason for this is that no clear conceptual framework exists for capturing risks at a macro-level, and that a full understanding of the links between macro- and micro-level risks (such as the building up of sectoral risk) is still missing. Therefore, better indicators should be compiled to measure different types of risk (liquidity, solvency, maturity, currency, overexposure, contingencies, and guarantees) and their concentration in specific segments of the

economy. Aggregate data will not suffice. One also needs more granular information to assess what fraction of firms (or households) will face financial stress in the
event of changes in asset prices, and the importance of these firms for the whole
economy.

There are also other aspects to risk. For example, existing SNA conventions may
lead to considering higher risks as adding to the value of financial services. This
issue is reflected in an ongoing discussion about the measurement of "financial
intermediation services indirectly measured" (FISIM). Financial intermediar-
ies assume risks when they provide loans; hence, the core question is whether the
higher-risk premiums that banks may incur increase their output, or whether risk
is borne by other sectors or society at large and should not be reflected in the output of the financial sector. Doing so, one should make a clear distinction between
developments in current and in constant prices.

These issues form part of the "systems" and "resilience" issues discussed in the
conclusion.

Human Capital

Countries with higher human capital have stronger economic growth, and individuals with higher human capital and better capabilities achieve better individual outcomes. At the country level, OECD (2010) estimates that increasing PISA
scores (see sidebar on page 338, "PIAAC and PISA Surveys") by one standard deviation would increase GDP growth by 1.8 percentage points. At the individual level,
people with higher education live longer, have higher earnings and accumulated
wealth, better health, denser networks of connections, and are more active citizens.

Human capital has been defined as the "knowledge, skills, competencies and
other attributes embodied in individuals that facilitate the creation of individual, social and economic well-being" (OECD, 2001).[3] This OECD definition is
all-embracing: it incorporates various skills and competencies that are acquired by
people through learning and experience but may also include innate abilities. Some
aspects of motivation and behavior, as well as the physical, emotional, and mental
health of individuals, are also regarded as human capital in this broader definition.

In practice, however, the measurement concentrates on a narrower definition.

Knowledge, skills, and competencies certified by formal education have been the object of earlier research in the measurement of human capital. More recent developments have looked at other approaches to complement educational attainment indicators.

Measurement of human capital has implications for understanding the fundamental processes of societal development and economic growth. It also matters for estimating and understanding inequalities within societies. Measurements of human capital are important for the accountability of the education and health sectors. They help in accurately accounting for the costs and benefits of societal phenomena such as unemployment, and of the proposed policies to address those problems.

Human capital significantly determines a country's consumption and production possibilities, today and in the future. People's knowledge, skills, and competencies are "capital" in that they can be built up, but they can also decay, particularly during long periods of unemployment or sickness, or following shocks such as wars or migration. Failing to account for human capital could lead policy-makers to underweight investments in education, youth employment, and public health, with detrimental consequences for the future.

This is why in this chapter human capital is examined through the lens of sustainability. One of the motivations for focusing on human capital is a concern that, during and in the aftermath of the financial crisis of the late 2000s, estimates of the cost of the crisis did not reflect the decrease in human capital from high rates of youth unemployment, workers' layoff, loss of firm-specific human capital, and lower spending on training by firms. If these costs were underestimated, the response to the crisis in terms of fiscal stimulus or investment in education and skills may have been too weak.

While there is widespread agreement about the importance of maintaining and increasing human capital to ensure sustainability, there continue to be discussions on the best way to measure it, on the advantages and disadvantages of different definitions of human capital (what should be included and what can be measured given data limitations), and on different methods to value it (see sidebar, "Approaches to Measuring Human Capital").

APPROACHES TO MEASURING HUMAN CAPITAL

Traditionally, the most common approach to measuring aspects of human capital has been to use nonmonetary indicators of educational output, such as literacy or secondary school graduation rates. This type of indicator has the advantage of being widely available, both across countries and over time, even if data may not be fully comparable across countries. More recently, the indicators approach has been developed to take into account other aspects of human capital formation and stock characteristics. The use of standard classifications—for example, by type of education program—has improved the quality of these indicators.

Other approaches have aimed at producing a single summary measure of the stock of human capital in a country, expressed in monetary terms. These approaches include:

- *The cost-based approach* (Kendrick, 1976), where the stock of human capital is estimated as the depreciated value of the stream of past investments in human capital, such as teacher salaries and all other expenditures on education.
- *The lifetime income approach* (Jorgenson and Fraumeni, 1989, 1992a, 1992b), where the discounted value of the future labor income of individuals in the population for different education levels is calculated.
- *The indirect or residual approach*, which estimates the human capital stock as the difference between the discounted value of future consumption flows and the monetary value of other measured capital stocks. Because of its limitations, this approach is not recommended by the *Guide on Measuring Human Capital* (UNECE, 2016).

Summary measures of the stock of human capital may also be based on some combination of indicators and monetary measures. For example, the

stock of human capital in a country may be measured as a weighted average of the mean years of schooling of different segments of the population
(including those that are currently inactive), with weights based on estimates
of the "rates of return to schooling" for various educational categories used
to capture "quality."

Progress Since the 2009 Stiglitz-Sen-Fitoussi Report

Some progress has been made in measuring human capital, as reflected in the *Guide
on Measuring Human Capital* (UNECE, 2016). The guide provides reference and
support for different strategies and approaches to measuring human capital, with
an emphasis on preparing satellite accounts on human capital in line with SNA
guidelines.

There is today general agreement in the statistical community on basic methodologies toward measuring human capital as related to education and labor market
returns, though significant concerns remain. In general, in a national accounts
context, the most appropriate measures are either cost approaches or the discounted
lifetime income approach (in the tradition of Jorgenson and Fraumeni).[4]

While the lifetime income approach is appealing from a theoretical point of
view, it requires detailed data and a number of assumptions; in particular, the value
of human capital today depends on the assumptions you make about GDP growth
in the future. This complicates the estimation, for example, of the impact of the
economic crisis on future growth through the channel of reduced human capital.
Other assumptions about the future must also be made, for example on life expectancy, and these assumptions can have large impacts on the overall estimate of the
value of human capital.

The cost approach is based on past expenditure, but is also requires assumptions,
in particular about depreciation of, and future returns to, human capital. However,
for data availability reasons, the cost approach is most often preferred.

Several National Statistical Offices have recently undertaken initiatives to
develop monetary measures of human capital, to be used alongside indicators
of education quality and achievement. One common finding of these studies is
that, whatever approach is used, the value of human capital is high compared to

economic capital, even if the size of the discrepancies between estimates based on lifetime incomes and the cost approaches remains a puzzle (Liu, 2011). However, beyond the numerical estimates produced by these studies, considering educational expenditures as investment rather than consumption would have large impacts on how capital formation is defined and understood.

In addition, more recently, there has been substantial progress in the direct measurement of cognitive skills—in particular by the OECD through the PISA and, since 2011, the PIAAC survey (see sidebar below). The PISA survey, in particular, has played an important role by bringing human capital to the attention of policymakers in the educational community and beyond.

PIAAC AND PISA SURVEYS

Two OECD-sponsored instruments are increasingly used as a basis for computing human capital indicators:

The Programme for International Student Assessment (PISA) was run in 2006, 2009, 2012, and 2015. While all waves of PISA included tests in mathematics, science, and reading, the 2006 wave focused on science, the 2009 one on reading, and the 2012 one on mathematics. PISA testing also occurred in 2000 and 2003. In 2003 and 2012, tests were also offered in creative problem solving, while the 2012 wave included an optional test of financial literacy.

The Survey of Adult Skills, a product of the OECD Programme for the International Assessment of Adult Competencies (PIAAC), was designed to provide insights into the availability of some key skills in society and how they are used at work and at home. The first survey of its kind, it measures proficiency in several information-processing skills—namely literacy, numeracy, and problem solving in technology-rich environments.

Outstanding Issues and New Questions

Progress still needs to be made to improve the lifetime income approach for estimating the value of human capital and, more generally, to expand our understanding and measurement of human capital. Most of the analyses have thus far considered human capital as formal education or cognitive skills, and its returns as increased labor earnings. Future work needs to expand the measurement of human capital to match the understanding that it is broader than education and cognitive skills, and that its returns are larger than individual earnings. The initial focus on education and labor returns was in part a function of data availability, and of the fact that this concept was more straightforward to operationalize when limited to these aspects. Even so, measuring human capital in these narrow terms suggests that human capital investments are undervalued.

It is now important to build on this foundation to go beyond cognitive skills, education, and remunerated activities. This broader perspective requires addressing difficult measurement questions such as how to measure noncognitive skills and nonmarket benefits, both individual and social, and understanding and measuring specific human capital and networks.

It also implies taking life expectancy and the demographic structure of the population into account, as those who live longer and healthier lives are more productive both in the market and in society. Migration also has to be included in the measurement of human capital: there is a cost for the sending countries when the better-educated population migrates.

Improving the Lifetime Income Approach

Quantifying the relationship of future productive potential to both levels of human capital and human capital investment is critical to establishing support for a more comprehensive treatment of human capital accounts, even though such a task faces clear methodological challenges. Better and more consistent estimates of the returns to education require, for example, longitudinal studies that can account for cohort effects (Boarini, Mira d'Ercole, and Liu, 2012).

In addition, measuring *specific* human capital is more complicated than measuring *general* human capital. Specific human capital includes, for example, firm-specific human capital, or networks, while general human capital includes schooling or nonspecific work experience. Failing to take on-the-job training into account may bias the estimate of the returns to formal schooling.

Understanding the gap between cost-based estimates and income-based estimates requires simultaneous estimation of the two. Implementing satellite accounts for human capital would help in better matching the two types of estimates.

However, many of the data needed for implementing the lifetime income approach are not available for some countries, and not necessarily harmonized. A better understanding of human capital, and improvements in its measurement, will come from more cross-country research. For example, countries vary in the structure of the earnings reported (e.g., time period considered, which particular criteria are included in the earnings definition) and in the reporting of educational attainment. Harmonized data, where available, would allow researchers to improve their understanding of the role played by education.

Finally, there is a need to better understand what the lifetime income approach can be used for, given the sensitivity of estimates to changes in assumptions about the future. While these estimates serve a very important role in demonstrating that human capital forms a very large component of wealth, and that spending on human capital should be considered as investment rather than consumption, it is less clear what practical use can be made of the approach in terms of planning and measuring sustainability.

HUMAN CAPITAL CONSEQUENCES OF RECESSIONS

A substantial concern with recessions is that unemployment, particularly youth unemployment, erodes human capital, or limits human capital acquisition through on-the-job training. If the full cost of recessions (the long-term lower GDP growth due to lower human capital) were recognized, policy responses might be stronger. While it is difficult to measure the loss of human capital due to recessions, these effects are likely to be important, as graduates who enter the labor market during a recession can be expected to have permanently lower incomes; these efforts are ignored by most applications of the lifetime income approach.

Expanding the Measurement of Human Capital and Its Returns

A strategy that values human capital by estimating the impact of education on life-time income is also insufficient as it omits many important features on both sides of the equation: first, the human capital acquired outside of formal education, as well as noncognitive skills; and, second, the nonmarket benefits of human capital. A more comprehensive approach to human capital measurement would be important to lead policy-makers to recognize that education expenditure is a form of investment rather than consumption.

While the focus on formal education and market returns has been a function of pragmatically starting from where data availability and conceptual clarity were higher, it is important to increase data availability and conceptual clarity on human capital at all stages of capital formation, including its benefits and how it is embodied in individuals. For example, human capital investment takes place not only through education, but also through on-the-job training, parenting, and household production of nonmarket services (see sidebar, "Measuring and Valuing Unpaid Household Service Work"), as well as through participation in cultural activities. Destruction of human capital occurs, for example, in the presence of high youth unemployment, whose effects are not only lower consumption today but a lower long-run growth trajectory of the country tomorrow. Similarly, it is important to recognize that human capital is embodied in individuals not only through knowledge and cognitive skills, but also through noncognitive skills and traits. Its benefits encompass not only labor market returns, but higher subjective well-being, citizenship, caring, social trust, cooperation, and health. In this broader perspective, health care expenditures should be recognized as a kind of maintenance and repair flow for human capital, and better health conditions as nonmarket benefits from human capital. Human capital may also stimulate the accumulation of social capital: the norms and values that children develop at school will enable them to participate better in society as adults (OECD, 2010). In this broader perspective, developments in human capital can be seen in the context of the systems approach (outlined above in the section of that name), thanks to its links with developments in economic, social, and natural capital.

MEASURING AND VALUING UNPAID HOUSEHOLD SERVICE WORK

Even if unpaid household work contributes to preserve and improve human capital, most of it is excluded from the production boundary of the SNA. Various efforts have been undertaken in recent years to measure the amount and type of work carried out in the household and to estimate the monetary value of this work. Some countries have started to value these activities in a Household Satellite Account, which provides important information on the economy and society. Time-use surveys are an important tool to capture the amount of time spent by individuals to provide nonmarket services that benefit other household members or society more generally. Putting a value to household work is, however, not straightforward since the work is unpaid and because it often results in intangible services. A UNECE Task Force (UNECE, 2017) recently released a set of guidelines for valuing unpaid household services.

Beyond the Average

As with income or wealth, it is important to go beyond the average when examining human capital: there are important inequalities in human capital, which can vary by country and among population groups. In addition to understanding whether overall human capital is increasing or not, it is important to look at inequalities in human capital as these play an important role in shaping lifetime inequalities. For this reason, measures need to differentiate between adults and children, different groups in particular countries, and different household arrangements to understand how patterns are shifting over time.

Better measurement of these inequalities (in education and health care, for example) will contribute to a better understanding of inequality of opportunity. While gender inequalities in human capital are very important from a variety of perspectives (see sidebar), so are inequalities by income, race, caste, or religion.

GENDER INEQUALITIES IN HUMAN CAPITAL

While reducing inequalities in education would help reduce inequalities in life chances, gender-specific inequalities have an even broader impact as they affect fertility decisions, the health of children, gender relations in the family with regard to power, and gender division of labor and authority within households.

The goal of achieving gender parity in education by 2005 has not yet been fulfilled, despite significant improvements. By 2011 only 60% of countries achieved this goal at the primary level, and 38% at the secondary level. In the world, more girls than boys are out of school: girls make up 54% of the total number of children out of school. In the Arab States, the share is 60%, unchanged since 2000 (UNESCO, 2015; UN Women, 2015). The gender parity index has increased dramatically in Southern Asia, where inequality was highest in 1990 and is now the lowest. However, while sub-Saharan Africa, Oceania, Western Asia, and North Africa have made progress, girls are still disadvantaged relative to boys regarding enrollment in primary education. Social inequality also widened, and this inequality often interacts with larger social and economic cleavages.

Attending school does not necessarily mean achieving basic literacy skills. It is a particular concern for poorer countries with insufficient teacher resources, but also in rich countries. The partial closing of the gender gap in primary education has contributed to reducing the incidence of illiteracy among women, but women still account for more than 60% of all illiterate persons in the world.

In secondary education, progress has been even more uneven across countries. On average, across the OECD, 43% of 25- to 64-year-olds have achieved an upper secondary or post-secondary, nontertiary degree. The improvement from the older to the younger cohorts is particularly large for women. Across the OECD in 2015, 37% of 55- to 64-year-old women, but only 15% of 25- to 34-year-old women, had no upper secondary degree (OECD, 2015).

For developing regions as a whole, the gender parity index for secondary education increased from 0.77 in 1990 to 0.96 in 2012. However, there are large differences between regions, with girls enjoying an advantage in Latin America and the Caribbean, but lagging significantly behind boys in sub-Saharan Africa, Southern Asia, Western Asia, and Oceania. Southern Asia stands out as the region where the greatest progress has been made, with the region's index increasing from 0.59 to 0.93 between 1990 and 2012.

Sub-Saharan Africa, on the contrary, stands out as the region where girls have the worst chances, particularly in the poorest sections of the population and in rural areas. Only 9% were completing lower secondary education by the end of the 2000s, a share that has been declining over time. Based on recent trends, girls from the poorest families in sub-Saharan Africa are only expected to achieve lower secondary completion in 2111.

Overall, at past rates, low-income countries would not achieve universal primary and secondary education before the end of this century. Around half of 15- to 19-year-old girls and boys are expected to complete lower secondary education in low-income countries by 2030, while only 33% of boys and 25% of girls would complete upper secondary.

While gender-specific disadvantages still remain in primary and secondary education, in tertiary education the gender gap was closed by 2015 and in some countries even started to reverse, with women outnumbering men. In two out of five OECD countries, as well as in Lithuania and the Russian Federation, one out of every two young (25–34) women has a tertiary diploma. Only in Canada, Korea, Luxembourg, the Russian Federation, and the United Kingdom do men have such high rates of tertiary education. Gender differences, however, still remain in fields of specialization, with women concentrating in the humanities and men in the scientific and technical sectors. Furthermore, the gender balance again reverses at the upper tertiary level, with more men than women obtaining a PhD. Finally, although most tertiary graduates are women, men still have better labor market outcomes in terms of both participation and earnings (United Nations, 2015b).

Natural Capital

At a social and political level, concern about climate change and environmental sustainability has continued to grow since the Stiglitz, Sen, and Fitoussi (2009) report, though real progress in addressing these issues on a meaningful scale has been slow. At the same time, there has been a shift in the thinking about capital, from no longer thinking just about quantity and volume but about quality, biodiversity, and ecosystems.

The development of the capital approach as applied to natural capital has followed four historical episodes (and corresponding measurement tools), each of them driven by environmental crises:

1. Measuring volume and price changes, driven by energy crises and depletion of natural resources.
2. Measuring local changes of environmental quality, linked to growing degradation of air, land, and water quality, and poorer waste treatment.
3. Focus on measuring global phenomena, linked to awareness of ozone layer depletion and climate change.
4. Measurement of ecosystems and planetary boundaries.

We are now in this fourth episode, moving beyond the measurement of individual stocks of natural capital and toward ecosystems. This considers the "interplay of different assets (for example, within a forest, there is an interplay between water, timber, soil, and wildlife)." This definition, provided by the System of Environmental-Economic Accounting (SEEA) discussed below, makes clear that, in order to measure environmental sustainability, more than the measurement of stock is required. Ecosystems are not a collection of different stocks but, more fundamentally, *systems* and, as such, they can have greater or lesser degrees of resilience. They provide a multitude of services to society (for example, a forest not only supplies timber but may also provide water retention and flood or landslide protection, air filtration, carbon sequestration, habitat for rare species, and recreation).

A capital approach, applied to nature, could, in principle, allow values in the environment to be compared to values in the economy, providing a bridge between environment and economics. However, a common measurement framework is not easily adapted to the measure of ecosystems. This section summarizes progress in measuring environmental assets since the Stiglitz, Sen, and Fitoussi report (2009); identifies areas that require work most urgently; and sets out a path toward measurement of ecosystems as a key part of natural capital.

Progress Since the 2009 Stiglitz, Sen, and Fitoussi Report

Several advances in the measurement of natural capital have taken place since 2009, some of them codified in international frameworks and recommendations. In particular, the System of Environmental-Economic Accounting—Central Framework (SEEA CF) was adopted as a statistical standard by the United Nations Statistical Commission in 2012 (United Nations et al., 2014a). It covers the first three episodes described above: measuring volume and price changes, local environmental quality, and global phenomena.

The SEEA extends national accounting to include a broader set of environmental assets, for example fish stocks. It is designed to produce comprehensive and systematic information on environmental conditions linked to the economy to help guide policy-making, to understand the drivers of environmental change, and to assist with modeling and scenario building. The SEEA CF also covers initiatives taken to measure carbon emissions embedded in a country's imports and exports ("carbon footprints"), according to multi-country input-output tables. "Adoption of the System of Environmental-Economic Accounting" describes the progress that National Statistical Offices have made in implementing the SEEA CF.

The SEEA CF defines environmental assets as the "naturally occurring living and nonliving components of the Earth," together constituting the biophysical environment, which provide benefits to humanity. In the SEEA CF, environmental assets are viewed as individual components (including land, mineral, and energy resources, timber and aquatic resources, and water resources) that make up the environment. For these assets, physical as well as monetary asset accounts can, in principle, be compiled to describe the opening and closing stocks as well as the changes in these assets. In practice, many conceptual and data problems limit our ability to both quantify several of these assets in physical terms and to value them in monetary terms.

A significant further development in the field of measuring environmental sustainability that has occurred since 2009 is the development of the SEEA-Experimental Ecosystem Accounting (SEEA-EEA), published in 2014 (United Nations et al., 2014b), and which corresponds to ecosystems and planetary boundaries, the fourth episode described above. The SEEA-EEA represents initial efforts to define a measurement framework for tracking changes in ecosystems and linking those changes to economic and other human activity. In this framework, an ecosystem is a dynamic complex of plant, animal, and micro-organism communities and their nonliving environment interacting as a functional unit.

Human activity influences ecosystems across the world and significantly modifies many ecosystems. Several countries have begun to set up experimental accounts that describe ecosystem assets and the flows of services from these ecosystems. Ecosystem services include provisioning (e.g., food, water), regulating (e.g., flood protection, air filtration), and cultural (e.g., recreation) services.

ADOPTION OF THE SYSTEM OF ENVIRONMENTAL-ECONOMIC ACCOUNTING

A global assessment of SEEA implementation undertaken by the UN Statistics Division in 2014 indicated that 54 countries have established a program on environmental-economic accounting as part of their national statistical program, with 15 more planning do so in the short term. Topics covered by these current and prospective accounting programs differ between countries. In a nutshell, the UN assessment shows that developed countries' accounts tended to focus on air emissions, environmental taxes, material flows, the environmental goods and services sector, and physical energy flow accounts, while developing countries focused on water and energy. In the EU, the focus has been on physical and monetary flow accounts, while outside the EU the focus has been on natural resources accounting.

These differences in compilation practices may reflect differences in national priorities. The policy demand in developing countries may be understood as stemming from the need for better managing their endowments of natural resources and from specific security issues related to water and energy.

Natural capital accounting (NCA) considers natural capital as an important element in decision making for national development and economic growth, complementing GDP data with stock measures, particularly those of natural resources and ecosystems. The Wealth Accounting and Valuation of Ecosystem Services (WAVES) Partnership led by the World Bank and involving many UN agencies, national governments, academia, and NGOs aims to ensure that natural resources are mainstreamed into development planning and national accounts. WAVES has adopted the SEEA as the underlying statistical framework to inform policies.

As mentioned above, developing methodologies that allow valuing different systems (economic, social, and environmental), and that allow these values to be compared with one another, is important, and monetary valuations are often called upon to serve this role. However, pricing natural capital is difficult, not only conceptually but also technically. There are still no agreed methods to estimate the monetary value for many environmental assets, because the market prices of environmental assets are inadequate or nonexistent for several reasons. In a market context, economists use market prices to evaluate trade-offs, implicitly assuming that the price for a good or commodity obtained from the market reflects its marginal value for society as a whole. However, this relationship breaks down in the presence of externalities, which are large in the environmental sector, or when prices are not observed (as there are no transactions).

While accounting for nonfinancial, nonproduced assets remains a hurdle that has not yet been overcome, progress has been made on measuring land and subsoil assets (a set of issues belonging to the first historical episode in the development of the capital approach). A number of countries already produce monetary estimates for these assets. Other forms of natural capital remain, however, uncharted territory, in particular when it comes to ecosystems. A number of countries have started experiments to systematically describe ecosystem capital, and the first experimental estimates of their monetary value have been made.

Outstanding Issues and New Questions

The need to measure environmental assets and, in particular, ecosystems and planetary boundaries (episode 4 above) is now being recognized. Lots of research over the last 50 years has gone into measuring these assets and into developing valuation techniques that would allow monetary values to be estimated for them. However, the most critical measurement issues have still not been resolved.

Uncertainty remains over both how to measure quantities and conditions (of sub-soil assets, public goods, ecosystems, and their services) and how to price them. In the case of global phenomena, and in particular for ecosystems and planetary boundaries, these assets are nontraded, and so the market system will generally not provide the metrics for measuring and pricing. Reliable, widely accepted alternatives have yet to be established.

While all OECD countries establish measures of produced assets, only a handful of countries produce complete SNA balance sheets that also include the value of land and sub-soil assets: Australia, France, Korea, and the Netherlands. The value of other environmental assets is generally excluded.

More countries should apply the SEEA, and produce more timely and reliable environmental-economic indicators based on it. These could include measures of "resource productivity" (the amount of material consumed per unit of GDP) and measures of the "circular economy" (e.g., recycling rates or cyclical use rate, measuring the amount of materials that is reused in relation to total material use). These indicators do not need to be expressed in monetary units, but they should meet the same quality criteria as GDP.

It should be clear from the above discussion that the measurement of sustainability, in the narrow sense of keeping the total monetary value of the stock of natural capital constant, is plagued with uncertainties that result from a combination of challenges: difficulties to find price estimates in the absence of markets; difficulties to predict future demand; uncertainties about system behavior including lack of knowledge about the inter-dependence of different systems; and so on. A more comprehensive approach should aim to develop an information system that enhances our knowledge about all components of natural capital, including subsoil assets, land and the way it is used, and ecosystems. This is the ambition of the systems approach presented in the section of that name.

CARBON PRICING

The conceptual and data issues related to carbon pricing are relatively simple, and the underlying phenomena well understood compared to many other types of natural capital. However, even for such a relatively simple methodological approach, the following would have to be addressed.

- Carbon prices should fully reflect the social cost of emissions. This social cost is hard to predict and should not only include the costs of providing the global public good in question, but also take into account tipping points and nonlinearities in the damage from each additional unit of emissions.
- Carbon prices should incorporate time discounting appropriately. The discount rates applied should reflect both an element of "pure time discounting" (i.e., how much consumption tomorrow is valued by a person relative to consumption today) and an assessment of how much better off future generations will be relative to the current one. Deciding on this second element of the discount rate is not straightforward, but has a large impact on carbon pricing.
- Distributional effects complicate pricing carbon emissions. The effects of climate change will fall disproportionately on certain social groups and places, so the most appropriate carbon prices should reflect the degree of "aversion to inequality" of the community.
- Finally, the price of carbon emissions should take into account cross-border externalities, i.e., the effects of emissions in one country on other countries, as well as risks and resilience.

Toward a Systems Approach to Inform Policy

In the capital approach, the different forms of capital (human, social, natural, economic) are considered separately. This implicitly assumes their independence and, therefore, substitutability. Since we know, however, that they are not truly independent, a more adequate measurement approach would call for a further step, going beyond independently measured balance sheet items. To properly describe phenomena that are shaped by the interaction between complex systems (be they social, economic, or ecological), a more macroscopic approach is needed. In practice, the ambition to build balance sheets cannot be achieved for some assets, in particular when assets are difficult to value in monetary terms, either because of noneconomic benefits that flow from the asset or because the valuation of an asset is complicated or involves uncertainty (as in the case of sub-soil assets that have not yet been discovered). Further, certain government activities provide benefits to society as a whole (they may be public goods or the provision of commodities generating large externalities), whose value may bear little relation to the cost of the assets providing these services (unlike private sector activities, where in equilibrium, marginal benefits should equal marginal costs).

Another limitation of this approach is that deciding whether a particular situation is sustainable is difficult in the presence of risk and uncertainty. Whether a given situation is sustainable depends on the risk posed by that situation, implying that some evaluation is needed of whether that level of risk is acceptable. Apart from the fact that people are more loss averse than risk averse (i.e., they will take considerable risks if they don't expect to lose much), estimating the level of risk itself is difficult, and in the case of uncertainties it is impossible. People may have different preferences regarding risk and the best way of dealing with uncertainties, and those preferences may differ across generations, making it difficult to ascertain whether a particular development (as described by successive balance sheets) is sustainable or not. The global nature of sustainability adds a further layer of difficulty (with issues related to causalities, property rights, etc.) and complexity regarding attempts to measure the different stocks of capitals.

Most likely, the "holy grail" of a society-wide balance sheet, incorporating all types of capital and permitting the different sectors to "talk" to each other by assigning monetary values (under the assumption of "weak" sustainability) will never be fully achieved. Or it will be achieved only at the price of heroic assumptions. Setting shadow prices entails evaluating the future, which is a daunting task falling outside the remit of official statistics (Fleurbaey and Blanchet, 2013). Further, these estimations and assumptions would have such a large influence on the conclusions of the exercise that the exercise itself would likely be neither successful nor helpful as a contribution to a democratic debate on the societal choices related to sustainable development.

To better understand the complexity of our world, we should look at it from a systems perspective (Walshe, 2014; Borio, 2009; Fiksel, 2006; and Costanza et al., 1997) and examine how these systems—the ecological-social-economic-political systems—cope with changes and shocks. This broadens the notion of sustainability with the dimension of a given system's ability to cope with future, known and unknown, disturbances. This should ensure that the system remains sustainable, or at least that it has the ability to restore its sustainability after a temporarily unsustainable period.

The two main dimensions of shocks and of slow-burn processes (such as demographic changes) that determine how the system could respond to them (hence their resilience) are intensity and persistence. The interaction of these two dimensions determines the system's ability to sustain a resilient behavior; in turn, such

Figure 9.2. Shocks and Capacities

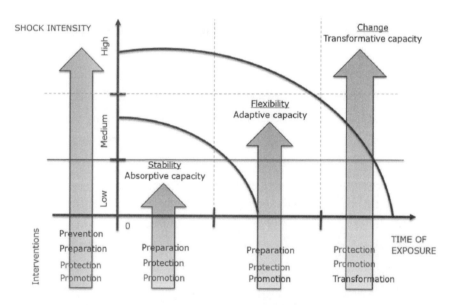

Source: Manca, A.R., P. Benczur, and E. Giovannini (2017), "Building a scientific narrative towards a more resilient EU society—Part 1: A conceptual framework," *JRC Science for Policy Report*, No. 106265, Publications Office of the European Union, Luxembourg, http://publications.jrc.ec.europa .eu/repository/bitstream/JRC106265/jrc106265_100417_resili ence_scienceforpolicyreport.pdf.

ability can be classified as "absorptive capacity," "adaptive capacity," and "transformative capacity." Each of the three can then be linked to different types of interventions aimed at enhancing the system's resilient behavior,[5] as described in Figure 9.2.

When the time of exposure is not too long and the intensity is not too large, the main characteristic of this ability is the *absorptive capacity*, which relates to stability and resistance, i.e., a situation where agents absorb the impact of shocks without changing their behavior. As the time of exposure or its intensity increases, and absorptive capacity is exceeded, *adaptive capacity* will start playing a role: agents adjust their expectations and aspirations when coping with deteriorating conditions. This requires flexibility, and involves incremental changes that are necessary to allow agents to continue functioning without major qualitative distress in response to disturbances. Agents try to mitigate potential damages and at best turn the adverse situation into an opportunity. Adaptation often takes place on multiple levels, as it is rarely related to a single specific stressor, but rather reflects a broad combination of many.

Ultimately, as the disturbance becomes unbearable (both in terms of its intensity and persistence) and adaptation would lead to too large a change, *transformative capacity* is the way forward. This transformation can be both the outcome of a deliberate decision and action of agents, like a regime change through a democratic election process, or a change forced by environmental or socio-economic conditions. The main feature of transformative capacity is that it does not only include technical and technological changes, but also cultural changes, behavioral shifts, and institutional reforms. Transformative resilience can be defined as the means of learning from past events and engineering changes, ideally toward a better condition given current constraints. Such a shift of the status quo may nevertheless be difficult to achieve.[6]

In real situations, different agents might experience the two dimensions differently. Moreover, disturbances seldom have a single channel of transmission; instead, they tend to originate from a chain of events and consequences and trigger multiplicative effects. This means that the three types of capacity often act simultaneously, at multiple levels (individuals, community, region, country, institutions) and with potentially different intensity at different levels. In other words, they are different perspectives of the same reality rather than opposing or competing components.

In this context,[7] a society is resilient if, when facing shocks or persistent structural changes, it keeps its ability to deliver individual and societal well-being in an inter-generationally fair way, i.e., ensuring current well-being without seriously compromising that of future generations. Absorptive and adaptive capacity means that, despite some initial inevitable losses after a shock, a resilient society tends to return to its original level of well-being and functionality, and potentially move to a better one. When the situation becomes unbearable and a transformation is necessary, the original level of well-being and functionality can no longer be sustained; however, these transformations should lead to a new, sustainable path, with acceptable levels of well-being.

This approach establishes a close link between resilience and sustainability, the former being the means to achieve the latter in a dynamic sense. While sustainability in the capital approach is about the quantity and value of the stock of the capital available (which acts as a buffer), a resilience approach focuses on the qualitative side, which in turn depends on many aspects of a "system" (diversity, the flow of assets, inter-connectedness). One way to think of this complementarity is that sustainability is the long-term design phase, while resilience is about reactive capacity, i.e., about managing imbalances and acting to keep or restore sustainability.

In the real world, where reaching a tipping point may determine "breaks" in some parts of the system, sustainability can become impossible because of nonlinearities: for example, political institutions can become unsustainable because of a prolonged recession and decline in people's standards of living. In this case a "revolution" may happen, leading to the collapse (a deep transformation) of the socio-economic system or to deep conflicts (foreign war, civil war, etc.).

Layers and Inter-dependences

One of the main implications of this approach is that resilience needs to be analyzed in the context of sustainability by looking at the entire ecological-social-economic-political system. Such a general approach may have several "sectoral" applications: for example, focusing on resilience of the ecosystems for the benefit of our generation and of the generations to come should be at the center of any long-term policy, such as the 2030 Agenda, no matter which specific economic or social policies are concerned.

In this perspective, the global system can be visualized as a "doughnut" with different layers: the economic, social, and environmental layers, with an indication of the planetary boundaries (and showing where these boundaries have already been crossed), as well as an area of safe and just space for humanity (Figure 9.3). Not only are systems embedded in one another, but there are layers within each of them.

In this perspective, society consists of individuals, communities, regions, nation-states, supranational and international entities, and humankind at large. The resilience of individuals should be considered in the context of resilience of communities, which in turn are embedded in regions and nation-states, and so on.

Figure 9.3. A Safe and Just Space for Humanity

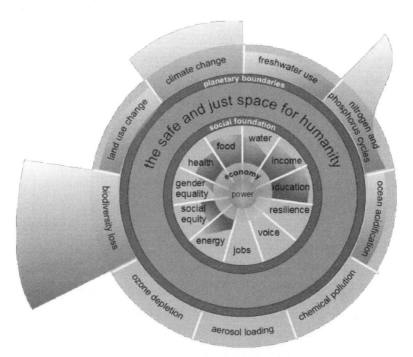

Source: Raworth, K. (2012), "A safe and just space for humanity. Can we live within the doughnut?," *Oxfam Discussion Paper*, February, www.oxfam.org/sites/www.oxfam.org/f/dp-a-safe-and-just-space-for-humanity-130212-en.pdf; and Rockström, J. et al. (2009), "Planetary boundaries: Exploring the safe operating space for humanity," *Ecology and Society*, Vol. 14(2), p. 32, www.ecologyandsociety.org/vol14/iss2/art32/.

The concept of resilience goes hand in hand with the situation of a system being hit by disturbances. If the risk materializes, a system can be vulnerable or not, depending on the intensity of the shock and the properties of the system. A vulnerable system can recover with a contained social welfare loss or not.

Resilience of systems should also be seen as inter-dependent with the people within those systems, as one might think of micro-, meso-, and macro-economies. While at a macro-level, a country's economy might be resilient to economic shocks, not all groups of people within the country might be resilient. So the analysis of macro-measures, such as GDP, might be misleading in the analysis of resilience if not accompanied with other socio-economic indicators and by in-depth analysis of vulnerable groups.

Improved measurement should be produced at each layer in order to understand their vulnerability and risks, but the links and interactions between all levels also need to be examined. The systems approach allows us to create different scenarios and estimate and demonstrate the related effects (similarly to stress tests). The challenge consists in increasing our capacities to distinguish between dangerous situations and sustainable pathways in an uncertain context. This approach could also help to generate a baseline against which to estimate the cost of different types of shocks and the risks associated with them, as well as estimates of investments to be made to make the systems more resilient.

While recognizing the limits of scenarios and forecasting, model results are important inputs in the design and implementation of policies and programs for reducing risk and increasing resilience. These results could provide a framework for a public discourse about choices that have to be made as society moves toward sustainability, choices which might include trade-offs between the "now" and "tomorrow" as well as between the "here" and "elsewhere" dimensions of sustainability.

A practical example of a systems approach is given in Figure 9.4, which describes the impact of changes in water quantity and quality on different system layers.

From an overall perspective, a starting point to understand how shocks spread among the different segments of the whole system, and where to intervene, is provided by the materially closed Earth system (Figure 9.5). Its three main ingredients are the inputs (the four types of capital stocks), the outputs (well-being and its determinants), and the engine (the overall "assembly" system) that translates inputs into outcomes and outputs. The final results of a system are ultimately determined

Figure 9.4. The Vulnerability to Variations in Water Availability and Quality

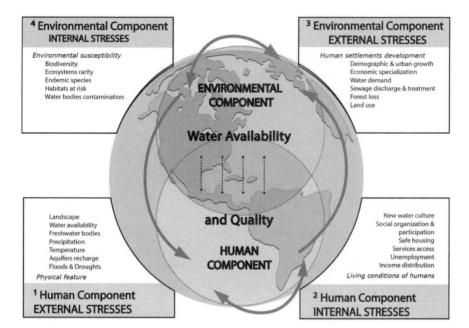

Source: Sosa-Rodríguez, F.S. (2016), "An alternative framework for analyzing the vulnerability of socio-ecological systems," *Realidad, Datos y Espacio. Revista Internacional de Estadística y Geografía*, Vol. 7(1), INEGI.

by the outcomes—i.e., societal and individual well-being—while shocks typically affect the inputs (capital stocks), and then the effects interact in the assembly system. In some cases, the engine might be in distress, and is the place where most of the policy interventions should occur.

With respect to measurement, this approach implies that we should concentrate on three aspects:

1. Resilience of assets, to be measured in the context of the capital approach.
2. Resilience of the engine, referring to eco- and social system services and to institutions, production processes, and their complex interactions. Measurement here is highly problematic, since it refers to the power of institutions to shape the production process, in a broad sense.
3. Resilience of outcomes/output, in terms of investment, consumption of goods and services, well-being, and negative externalities such as pollution, social marginalization, or poverty.

Figure 9.5. Ingredients of Resilience in the Materially Closed Earth System

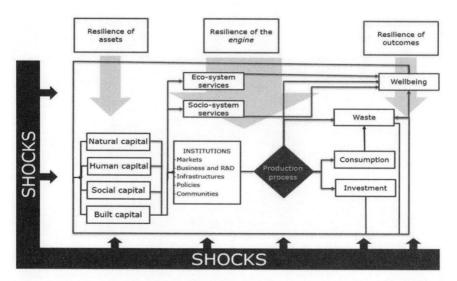

Source: Manca, A.R., P. Benczur, and E. Giovannini (2017), "Building a scientific narrative towards a more resilient EU society—Part 1: A conceptual framework," *JRC Science for Policy Report*, No. 106265, Publications Office of the European Union, Luxembourg, http://publications.jrc.ec.europa.eu/repository/bitstream/JRC106265/jrc106265_100417_resilience_scienceforpolicyreport.pdf, based on Costanza, R. et al. (1997), "The value of the world's ecosystem services and natural capital," *Nature*, Vol. 387, pp. 253–260.

Metrics for Resilience, Risks, and Uncertainties

A macro-prudential, system-wide approach in the sense described above does not yet exist either in policy or in statistical terms. Even in the SNA, and its extensions by the SEEA, a classical aggregation concept is used, rooted in the inventory and valuation of single capital goods. Nevertheless, it is possible to broadly outline the main conceptual components and procedural steps that would be necessary to explore and develop in detail a complementary way of accounting for a system's dynamics and resilience:

- *Scope and dimensions*: Available knowledge in various scientific disciplines should be used to evaluate and quantify risks, i.e., threats for the resilience and the sustainability of economic, social, and environmental systems. Priority should be given to the risks that are most relevant for sustainability, e.g., those that are pushing systems close to planetary boundaries, as defined by the scientific community. While micro-level accounting tends to undervalue natural and social capital, macro-level accounting can capture systemic interactions between environment, society, and economy.

- *Quantification*: Geographical Information Systems (GIS), accounting methods, and indicator systems (e.g., dashboards) should be combined to achieve the best possible and most far-reaching condensed presentation of the major risks (current, emerging).

- *Aggregation, valuation*: The actual price system does not work well with complex and/or systemic risks. Actuarial expertise (scientists or practitioners) that is used to estimate "premiums" necessary to ensure the major risks could provide valuable inputs for this exercise.

- *Scenarios*: These might be used to show the dynamic evolution of sustainability over time. A good example is old-age pensions. A society may confront a large stock of pension entitlements for only one cohort, obligations that will be costly to meet for some years but then the system stabilizes. A policy action might be needed to deal with short-term problems, but possibly a different one from that implied by a large stock of pension obligations toward all future cohorts. Inter-generational accounting models, which typically focus only on government finances, could be used to show that large fiscal deficits in the future could be met by higher taxes or though other ways of shifting the burden to households, in particular when households have low debt and high assets; private debt is already co-analyzed with government debt in the context of the EU Micro-Imbalances Procedure (MIP).

- *Communication*: It is important to integrate all societal stakeholders (science, civil society, business, policy) from the very early stages in generating knowledge of this kind. New metrics generated using this procedure should in particular facilitate a democratic dialogue. As a consequence, the processes of measurement and political discourse should be seen as mutually dependent and influencing each other. In this sense, new metrics, generated through new measurement processes, should be tailored and fit for specific purposes in the policy cycles.

VULNERABILITY, POVERTY, AND RESILIENCE

This chapter has argued that it is important to assess the risk properties of the economic system—i.e., its exposure to risk, its vulnerability, and its resilience. Changes in economic policy can have significant effects on "risk performance": increasing exposure to risk; making the economic system more vulnerable; reducing the capacity of individuals or other entities in the system to cope with risks; or making the system as a whole (or the units within it) less resilient. Some reforms may simultaneously improve average economic performance but reduce risk-performance. It is important not only to know when this is happening, but also to quantitatively assess the effects. If GDP growth increases but resilience decreases, we would want to know this. In some circumstances, a country might want some measure of resilience in its dashboard of key indicators.

While this is an area in which so far there has been limited progress—and it is an important arena for future research—some promising approaches include the following:

Vulnerability and poverty. When individuals move out of poverty, we would hope that that move is permanent. In reality, many of those who escape poverty often fall back into it again. Even those who have never been poor have a chance of falling into poverty. The threat of falling into poverty can loom large in the life of a person and other family members—it can be a source of anxiety that our national income statistics never pick up. One simple measure of vulnerability is the share of people who are not poor at any one date but may experience at least one year of poverty in the next five years (UNDP, 2014).

Resilience to economic phenomena. Vulnerability is a measure of the possibility of downward mobility. Resilience, by contrast, is a measure of "recovery," i.e., how quickly (if ever) a family or an economy that experiences a negative shock recovers. There can, of course, be many measures of resilience: how fast it takes for a family that winds up in poverty to move out of poverty; or how fast on average it takes for an economy that experiences a negative shock to return to its pre-crisis level, or to the level that it could have attained in the absence of a crisis. At each level, it is important to know the determinants of resilience, i.e., what makes some families or economies more resilient than others. In the light of the systems approach, it is also important to look at resilience from a broad societal perspective, beyond simple income or output measures.

A striking aspect of the 2008/2009 crisis was that different countries experienced shocks of different magnitudes; by and large, the recovery has also been slower than for previous economic downturns, which is understandable given the magnitude of the shock. In the beginning, some commentators had expected a "V-shaped recovery," with the economy quickly bouncing back; others thought, however, that the economy was less resilient, and that the recovery would be "U shaped." The latter perspective proved right, and in the following years the debate was about how long the flat bottom of the U would last. These experiences highlight that an economy can be resilient with respect to small shocks, and not with respect to big shocks.

Money-equivalent measures. This chapter has described the economy as a dynamic sub-system, connected to social and environmental sub-systems. In assessing changes in the economic system, we can measure its overall risk performance in a way similar to the Atkinson and Stiglitz measures for inequality and to the Arrow and Pratt measures for risk: how much society would be willing to pay to avoid the systemic risk that it confronts. Such a measure would compound the risk properties of the system as a whole and the aversion to risk of society.[1]

The chapter has described the properties of systems that affect the size of systemic risks. For instance, better automatic stabilizers could make the economic system more resilient—it would more quickly recover from an adverse shock. Thus, for a given degree of risk aversion, a more resilient economic system—one that recovers more quickly from an adverse shock—would presumably lower the systemic money-equivalence of the risk. This measure could provide guidance on the value that should be assigned to the risk aspects of various economic reforms.[2] For example, a move from a defined benefit to a defined contribution pension scheme could weaken automatic stabilizers since individuals are more exposed to business-cycle risks; in this situation, such a measure might provide some guidance as to how much "better" in some other way the defined contribution system has to be compared with the defined benefit to offset the loss in systemic stability.

1. The discussions of inequality and of risk highlighted the importance of money-equivalent measures. These measures ask how much a person would be willing to pay to avoid some risk, or society to avoid inequality. But in economics, we typically think of matters at the margin—how much we are willing to pay to get rid of a small amount of risk or inequality. In evaluating a new policy, we may ask what is the incremental value of the reduction in risk or inequality compared with the status quo baseline. Stiglitz has described such a marginal measure for income inequality (Stiglitz, 2015b).

2. There have been many attempts to measure individual risk aversion by looking at individuals' behavior with regard to risk—how much they are seemingly willing to pay to reduce the risks that they confront.

Conclusions

Since the Stiglitz, Sen, and Fitoussi (2009) report, a substantial amount of work has been carried out on measuring progress toward sustainable development, based on different models and approaches and in different geographical settings. However, further work is needed. Directions for future work include the following.

On the Capital Approach

Economic Capital

1. Distinguish between nominal wealth and the quantity of productive capital—data should be collected and displayed in such a way that the volume of productive capital is not obscured by revaluation effects. Also, the scope of nominal wealth and productive capital may be different and should be distinguished (for instance, nominal wealth includes net foreign financial assets, productive capital does not).

2. Use a balance sheet approach to help assess economic sustainability for all institutional sectors (e.g., banks, nonfinancial corporations, households) rather than for the government alone; and focus on both liabilities and as-

sets, recognizing that fire sales of assets in depressed financial markets will worsen net worth.

3. Improve fiscal modeling to incorporate demographic evolution and more generally engage in research on how much further to take simultaneity into account.

Human Capital

1. Increase efforts to understand and measure human capital stock and its formation process. In particular, skills (cognitive and noncognitive) and other components of human capital, and approaches to their measurement, need further discussion and analysis.

2. Develop satellite accounts for human capital using the cost approach together with more detailed nonmonetary indicators. In practice, satellite accounts for education and training should be a main building block. Coverage of nonformal education processes (e.g., on-the-job training) is important.

3. Pursue research on the income-based approach to provide more complete information, in particular on labor earnings from both market and nonmarket activity.

4. Increase efforts to understand and measure the noneconomic returns to human capital.

5. Rethink how the SNA treats public and private expenditures in human capital in view of capitalizing them.

6. Further explore the links between human capital and social capital.

Natural Capital

1. Improve measurement of environmental assets, including land and ecosystems (e.g., the extent and condition of different types, the services they provide).

2. Calculate and communicate at least annually how much carbon space is left before reaching potential "tipping points."

3. National Statistical Offices should apply the SEEA, and produce timely estimates of "resource productivity" and the "circular economy."

4. Improve the timeliness of indicators and accounts for natural capital applying the same now-casting techniques already used for economic variables like GDP.

On the Systems Approach

Stretching the Boundaries of Research

Interest in this complementary way of accounting for systems' resilience is growing, as shown by initiatives taken in the context of the European Commission's 7th Environmental Action Programme, or EAP (European Parliament and Council, 2013); the 2014 United Nations Development Programme (UNDP) framework; *European Environment—State and Outlook 2015*, also known as the SOER report (European Environment Agency, 2015); and the Joint Communication on "A Strategic Approach to Resilience in the EU's External Action" (European Commission, 2017).

While the maturity of research in this field is not yet comparable with other fields of research included in this book, multi-disciplinary cooperation should be enhanced. A macro-prudential approach to sustainability policies needs to be underpinned with high-quality information, best fit for this purpose. In this regard, the two workshops on resilience organized by the HLEG can only be seen as starting points. While necessary and fruitful for the first collection of ideas and questions, they exemplified the difficulties to overcome "silo" mentalities and cultures of scientific disciplines and to merge expertise from all "camps" in one broader program.

The Stiglitz, Sen, and Fitoussi (2009) report has shown that it is possible to breach the boundaries and traditional ways of thinking and thereby achieve essential progress. Similar progress should be made in the field of resilience by inviting researchers to contribute to this major set of questions.

Recommendations

1. Improve measurement of resilience so as to better understand vulnerability and risk at each level and across all dimensions, while also examining the links and interactions between all levels, and the dynamic properties of the

system. The international statistical community should establish a taskforce on the measurement of sustainability using the systems approach.

2. Further explore and document the complementarity of both the capital and the systems approaches, liaising theoretical considerations with empirical information.

3. Improve estimates and communication of risk and resilience to all stakeholders.

4. Involve various disciplines and assure horizontal cooperation to lay the basis of a special education path for sustainable development.

5. Introduce standardized terms and variables, which can serve as "ideal types" (in the sense of Max Weber), so that they fulfill expectations from both theoretical and empirical sides, thus helping to produce statistical metrics with high quality.

A New Impetus

The establishment of the 17 SDGs and 169 targets has given a new impetus to the development of common sustainable development indicators, and to the scientific work needed to underpin these indicators, so that progress toward sustainable development can be traced at global level, across countries and regions, in a reliable and timely manner. New measurement initiatives should take into account developments in statistical methodologies such as making use of big data or other approaches as proposed by the Global Conference on a Transformative Agenda for Official Statistics[8] and in the report by the Independent Advisory Group to the UN Secretary-General (United Nations, 2014).

However, in a world of complex systems, sustainability cannot be measured in full: there are limits to the measurement, and only part of the knowledge is available. According to good democratic principles, both the knowledge available—monetary and physical indicators as well as models such as those for considering resilience of systems—and the areas where knowledge is missing should be communicated in a correct way to all stakeholders to show possibilities as well as limits for governance.

More investment is also needed to develop analytical models at global scale to evaluate future scenarios and the impact of alternative policies for sustainable development employing a systems approach. Transboundary effects of policies and the global interactions of economic, social, and environmental phenomena can only be addressed by analytical models. Development of these models will require better and more-timely data from the international statistical system. A more continuous and fruitful dialogue, at global scale, between scientists and statisticians has to be established as soon as possible.

Notes

1. As is the case in the recommendations of the Conference of European Statisticians (UNECE, 2014).

2. www.imf.org/en/News/Seminars/Conferences/DGI/global-conferences-on-dgi.

3. Previous definitions of human capital by the OECD differed in that they referred to economic well-being only. Social capital is considered in Chapter 10 of this book.

4. However, some of the strong assumptions of the lifetime income approach to calculating human capital are not very appealing. For example, "rates of return to schooling" typically capture only labor market returns, while they should ideally be extended to capture nonmonetary returns (such as the longer life expectancies of better-educated people, though there is debate over causality in this relationship). However, capturing nonmonetary returns requires valuing them, which is frequently done using income. This is problematic, because such an approach might lead to the conclusion, with respect to life expectancy, that lives in poor countries are worth less than lives in rich countries, and by implication that the returns to human capital are lower. This approach is also less useful to explain future growth of GDP and productivity because the (real) service flows from that stock are themselves a function of the income streams expected in the future.

5. Adjusting the 3P + T framework of social protection (Devereux and Sabates-Wheeler (2004) to a broader resilience framework.

6. For example, the European Union faced a massive flow of migrants and refugees from 2015–16 onwards. This is likely to have a significant impact on the composition of European society in the coming decades. The ability of the EU to adapt to the new situation, and to transform itself through the integration of nonnative European citizens, will be key to avoiding a massive socio-economic crisis and instead build a strong cohesive society.

7. This interpretation of resilience draws on Manca, Benczur, and Giovannini (2017).

8. http://unstats.un.org/unsd/nationalaccount/workshops/2015/NewYork/lod.asp.

References

Adams, W.M. (2006), *The Future of Sustainability—Rethinking Environment and Development in the Twenty-First Century*, report of the IUCN Renowned Thinkers Meeting, January 29–31, 2006, IUCN, https://portals.iucn.org/library/sites/library/files/documents/Rep-2006-002.pdf.

Algan, Y., P. Cahuc, and A. Shleifer (2013), "Teaching practices and social capital," *American Economic Journal: Applied Economics*, Vol. 5(3), pp. 189–210.

Beck, U. (1992), *Risk Society: Towards a New Modernity*, SAGE Publications, New Delhi.

Berkes, F. and D. Jolly (2001), "Adapting to climate change: Social-ecological resilience in a Canadian western Arctic community," *Conservation Ecology*, Vol. 5(2), p. 18, www.ecologyandsociety.org/vol5/iss2/art18/.

Berman, R., C. Quinn, and J. Paavola (2012), "The role of institutions in the transformation of coping capacity to sustainable adaptive capacity," *Environmental Development*, Vol. 2, pp. 86–100.

Boarini, R., M. Mira d'Ercole, and G. Liu (2012), "Approaches to measuring the stock of human capital: A review of country practices," *OECD Statistics Working Papers*, No. 2012/04, OECD Publishing, Paris, http://dx.doi.org/10.1787/k8zlm5bc3ns-en.

Borio, C. (2009), "Implementing the macroprudential approach to financial regulation and supervision," *Financial Stability Review*, Bank of France, Vol. 13, pp. 31–41.

Brundtland, G.H. (1987), *Our Common Future*, Oxford University Press, Oxford.

Chambers, R. (1989), "Editorial introduction: Vulnerability, coping and policy," *IDS Bulletin*, Vol. 20(2), pp. 1–7.

Costanza, R. et al. (2014), *An Introduction to Ecological Economics* (2nd ed.), CRC Press, Boca Raton, FL.

Costanza, R. et al. (1997), "The value of the world's ecosystem services and natural capital," *Nature*, Vol. 387, pp. 253–260.

Cumming, G. and J. Norberg (2008), "Scale and complex systems," in Norberg, J. and G. Cumming (eds.), *Complexity Theory for a Sustainable Future*, Columbia University Press, New York.

Devereux, S. and R. Sabates-Wheeler (2004), "Transformative social protection," *IDS Working Paper*, No. 232, Institute of Development Studies, Brighton, United Kingdom, www.unicef.org/socialpolicy/files/Transformative_Social_Protection.pdf.

Diewert, W.E. and P. Schreyer (2008), "Capital measurement," in Durlauf, S.N. and L.E. Blume (eds.), *The New Palgrave Dictionary of Economics*, Palgrave Macmillan, London.

El Serafy, S. (2013), "Herman Daly Festschrift: Hicksian income, welfare, and the steady state," *The Encyclopedia of Earth*, www.eoearth.org/view/article/153484 (accessed on May 31, 2018).

European Commission (2017), "A strategic approach to resilience in the EU's external action," Joint Communication to the European Parliament and the Council, https://eeas.europa .eu/sites/eeas/files/join_2017_21_f1_communication_from_commission_to_inst_e n_v7_p1_916039.pdf.

European Commission (2016a), "Next steps for a sustainable European future—European action for sustainability," Communication from the Commission to the European Parliament, the Council, the European Economic and Social Committee and the Committee of the Regions, COM (2016), No. 739, https://ec.europa.eu/europeaid/sites /devco/files/communication-next-steps-sustainable-europe-20161122_en.pdf.

European Commission (2016b), "Proposal for a new European consensus on development: Our world, our dignity, our future," Communication from the Commission to the European Parliament, the Council, the European Economic and Social Committee and the Committee of the Regions, COM (2016), No. 740, https://ec.europa .eu/europeaid/sites/devco/files/communication-proposal-new-consensus-development -20161122_en.pdf.

European Environment Agency (2015), *The European Environment—State and Outlook 2015*, SOER synthesis report, Copenhagen, www.eea.europa.eu/soer.

European Environment Agency (1999), *Environmental Indicators: Typology and Overview*, Technical Report No. 25/1999, prepared by Smeets E. and R. Weterings, TNO Centre for Strategy, Technology and Policy, The Netherlands.

European Parliament and Council (2013), "Living well, within the limits of our planet," 7th EAP—The New General Union Environment Action Programme to 2020, http:// ec.europa.eu/environment/pubs/pdf/factsheets/7eap/en.pdf.

European Statistical System (2011), *Final Report on the Sponsorship Group on Measuring Progress, Well-Being and Sustainable Development*, http://ec.europa.eu/eurostat/web /ess/about-us/measuring-progress.

Eurostat (2016a), "Sustainable Development Indicators," http://ec.europa.eu/eurostat/web /sdi/overview.

Eurostat (2016b), *Sustainable Development in the European Union—A Statistical Glance from the Viewpoint of the UN Sustainable Development Goals*, Eurostat Statistical Books, Luxembourg, http://ec.europa.eu/eurostat/documents/3217494/7745644/KS -02-16-996-EN-N.pdf.

Eurostat (2003), "Household production and consumption: Proposal for a methodology of household satellite accounts," *European Commission Working Papers and Studies*, http: //ec.europa.eu/eurostat/documents/3888793/5823569/KS-CC-03-003-EN.PDF /e284578-a435-4bd8-b42d-b86d4a911637.

Fiksel, J. (2006), "Sustainability and resilience: Toward a systems approach," *Sustainability: Science, Practice and Policy*, Vol. 2(2), pp. 14–21, https://doi.org/10.1080/15487733 .2006.11907980.

Fleurbaey, M. and D. Blanchet (2013), *Beyond GDP: Measuring Welfare and Assessing Sustainability*, Oxford University Press, Oxford.

Folke, C. et al. (2002), "Resilience and sustainable development: Building adaptive capacity in a world of transformations," *AMBIO: A Journal of the Human Environment*, Vol. 31(5), pp. 437–440.

Galaz, V. et al. (2016), "Planetary boundaries: Governing emerging risks and opportunities," *Solutions*, Vol. 7(3), pp. 46–54.

Gallopin, G. (2003), "A systems approach to sustainability and sustainable development," Publications of the Economic Commission for Latin America and the Caribbean (ECLAC), Santiago de Chile.

Garavito-Bermúdez, D., C. Lundholm, and B. Crona (2016), "Linking a conceptual framework on systems thinking with experiential knowledge," *Environmental Education Research*, Vol. 22, pp. 89–110.

Hanson S.G., A.K. Kashyap, and J.C. Stein (2011), "A macroprudential approach to financial regulation," *Journal of Economic Perspectives*, Vol. 25(1).

Heal, G.M. (ed.) (1974), *The Review of Economic Studies: Symposium on the Economics of Exhaustible Resources*, The Society for Economic Analysis Limited, Longman, Edinburgh.

Hicks, J.R. (1939), *Value and Capital: An Inquiry into Some Fundamental Principles of Economic Theory*, Clarendon Press, Oxford.

Hjorth P. and A. Bagheri (2006), "Navigating towards sustainable development: A system dynamics approach," *Futures*, Vol. 38, pp. 74–92.

Holling, C.S. (2001), "Understanding the complexity of economic, ecological and social systems," *Ecosystems*, Vol. 4, pp. 390–405.

IPCC (2015), IPCC Assessment reports, www.ipcc.ch/publications_and_data /publications_and_data_reports.shtml.

Jorgenson, D.W. (1963), "Capital theory and investment behaviour," *American Economic Review*, Vol. 53, pp. 247–259.

Jorgenson, D.W. and B.M. Fraumeni (1992a), "Investment in education and U.S. economic growth," in *Scandinavian Journal of Economics*, Vol. 94, supplement, pp. 51–70.

Jorgenson, D.W. and B.M. Fraumeni (1992b), "The output of the education sector," in Griliches, Z. (ed.), *Output Measurement in the Service Sectors*, University of Chicago Press, Chicago.

Jorgenson, D.W. and B.M. Fraumeni (1989), "The accumulation of human and nonhuman capital, 1948–1984," in Lipsey, R.E. and H.S. Tice (eds.), *The Measurement of Savings, Investment and Wealth Studies*, University of Chicago Press, Chicago.

Jorgenson, D.W. and Z. Griliches (1967), "The explanation of productivity change," *Review of Economic Studies*, Vol. 34(3), pp. 249–283.

Jorgenson, D.W. and J.S. Landefeld (2007), "Blueprint for expanded and integrated U.S. accounts: Review, assessment, and next steps," in Jorgenson, D., J.S. Landefeld, and W. Nordhaus (eds.), *A New Architecture for the U.S. National Account*, University of Chicago Press, Chicago.

Kendrick J.W. (1976), *The Formation and Stock of Total Capital*, Columbia University Press, New York.

Klenow, P.J. and A. Rodríguez-Clare (1997), "The neoclassical revival in growth economics: Has it gone too far?," in Bernanke, B.S. and J. Rotemberg (eds.), *NBER Macroeconomics Annual 1997*, MIT Press, Boston, MA, www.nber.org/chapters/c11037.pdf.

Liu, G. (2011), "Measuring the stock of human capital for comparative analysis: An application of the lifetime income approach to selected countries," *OECD Statistics Working Papers*, No. 2011/06, OECD Publishing, Paris, https://doi.org/10.1787/5kg3h0jnn9r5 -en.

Lupton, D. (2013), *Risk*, Routledge, New York.

Manca, A.R., P. Benczur, and E. Giovannini (2017), "Building a scientific narrative towards a more resilient EU society—Part 1: A conceptual framework," *JRC Science for Policy Report*, No. 106265, Publications Office of the European Union, Luxembourg, http://publications.jrc.ec.europa.eu/repository/bitstream/JRC106265 /jrc106265_100417_resilience_sc ienceforpolicyreport.pdf.

Nyamu-Musembi C. and A. Cornwall (2004), "What is the 'rights-based approach' all about? Perspectives from international development agencies," *IDS Working Paper*, No. 234, Institute of Development Studies, Brighton, United Kingdom, www.ids.ac.uk /files/dmfile/Wp234.pdf.

OECD (2016a), *Education at a Glance 2016: OECD Indicators*, OECD Publishing, Paris, http://dx.doi.org/10.1787/-en.

OECD (2016b), "OECD and the Sustainable Development Goals: Delivering on universal goals and targets," www.oecd.org/development/sustainable-development-goals.htm.

OECD (2015), *Education at a Glance 2015: OECD Indicators*, OECD Publishing, Paris, https://doi.org/10.1787/eag-2015-en.

OECD (2010), *The High Cost of Low Educational Performance: The Long-Run Economic Impact of Improving PISA Outcomes*, OECD Publishing, Paris, http://dx.doi.org/10 .1787/-en.

OECD (2009), *Measuring Capital—OECD Manual 2009* (2nd ed.), OECD Publishing, Paris, http://dx.doi.org/10.1787/-en.

OECD (2001), *The Well-Being of Nations: The Role of Human and Social Capital*, OECD Publishing, Paris, http://dx.doi.org/10.1787/-en.

Perrings, C. (2006), "Resilience and sustainable development," *Environment and Development Economics*, Vol. 11(4), pp. 417–427.

Piketty, T. and G. Zucman (2013), "Capital is back: Wealth-income ratios in rich countries, 1700–2010," *Quarterly Journal of Economics*, Vol. 129(3), pp. 1255–1310.

Putnam, R. (2000), *Bowling Alone: The Collapse and Revival of American Community*, Simon and Schuster, New York.

Radermacher, W.J. and A. Steurer (2015), "Do we need natural capital accounts for measuring the performance of societies towards sustainable development, and if so, which ones?," *Eurostat Review on National Accounts and Macroeconomic Indicators*, Vol. 2015/1, pp. 7–18.

Rapport, D.J. and A. Friend (1979), *Towards a Comprehensive Framework for Environmental Statistics: A Stress-Response Approach*, Statistics Canada, Ottawa.

Raworth, K. (2012), "A safe and just space for humanity. Can we live within the doughnut?," *Oxfam Discussion Paper*, February, https://www-cdn.oxfam.org/s3fs-public /file_attachments/dp-a-safe-and-just-space-for-humanity-130212-en_5.pdf.

Rockström, J. et al. (2009), "Planetary boundaries: Exploring the safe operating space for humanity," *Ecology and Society*, Vol. 14(2), p. 32, www.ecologyandsociety.org/vol14 /iss2/art32/.

Rudinow Saetnan, A., H. Mork Lomell, and S. Hammer (2012), "By the very act of counting—the mutual construction of statistics and society," in Saetnan, R., H.M. Lomell, and S. Hammer (eds.), *The Mutual Construction of Statistics and Society*, Routledge, London.

Sachs R. (2014), "Emerging risk discussion paper: Risk transfer and uncertainty," discussion paper for the EEA Scientific Committee Seminar on Emerging Systemic Risks, Copenhagen, February 24, www.researchgate.net/publication/267369640 _Emerging_Risk_Diskussion_Paper_Risk_transfer_and_uncertainty.

Seccombe, K. (2002), "'Beating the odds' versus 'changing the odds': Poverty, resilience, and family policy," *Journal of Marriage and Family*, Vol. 64(2), pp. 384–394.

Shaw, R. et al. (1991), "Sustainable development: A systems approach," International Institute for Applied Systems Analysis, Laxenburg, Austria.

Solow, R.M. (1986), "On the intertemporal allocation of natural resources," *Scandinavian Journal of Economics*, Vol. 88, pp. 141–149.

Sosa-Rodríguez, F.S. (2016), "An alternative framework for analyzing the vulnerability of socio-ecological systems," *Realidad, Datos y Espacio. Revista Internacional de Estadística y Geografía*, Vol. 7(1), INEGI.

Stiglitz, J.E. (2015a), "New theoretical perspectives on the distribution of income and wealth among individuals: Part I. The wealth residual," *NBER Working Paper*, No. 21189, www.nber.org/papers/w21189.

Stiglitz, J.E. (2015b), "Inequality and Economic Growth," *Political Quarterly*, Vol. 86, pp. 134–155.

Stiglitz, J.E. (1979), "The use of prudential measures in the international banking markets," *BISA*, Vol. 7.18(15), *Papers Lamfalussy*, LAM25/F67, pp. 1–2.

Stiglitz, J.E., A. Sen, and J.-P. Fitoussi (2009), *Report by the Commission on the Measurement of Economic and Social Progress*, http://ec.europa.eu/eurostat/documents/118025/118123/Fitoussi+Commission+report.

UNDP (2014), *Human Development Report 2014—Sustaining Human Progress: Reducing Vulnerabilities and Building Resilience*, United Nations Development Programme, New York, http://hdr.undp.org/sites/default/files/hdr14-report-en-1.pdf.

UNECE (2017), *Guide on Valuing Unpaid Household Service Work*, United Nations, Geneva, www.unece.org/stats/publications/guideuhw.html.

UNECE (2016), *Guide on Measuring Human Capital*, United Nations, Geneva, www.unece.org/index.php?=44704&L=0.

UNECE (2014), "Conference of European Statisticians recommendations on measuring sustainable development," Geneva, www.unece.org/fileadmin/DAM/stats/publications/2013/CES_SD_web.pdf.

UNEP and UN-IHDP (2014), *Inclusive Wealth Report 2014: Measuring Progress Towards Sustainability*, UN University—International Human Dimensions Programme on Global Environmental Change and UN Environment Programme, Delhi.

UNEP and UN-IHDP (2012), *Inclusive Wealth Report 2012: Measuring Progress Towards Sustainability*, UN University—International Human Dimensions Programme on Global Environmental Change and UN Environment Programme, Delhi.

UNESCO (2016), "Gender review—creating sustainable futures for all," *EFA Global Monitoring Report 2016*, http://unesdoc.unesco.org/images/0024/002460/246045e.pdf.

UNESCO (2015), "Teaching and learning—achieving quality for all," *EFA Global Monitoring Report 2013/4*, http://unesdoc.unesco.org/images/0022/002266/226662e.pdf.

United Nations (2015a), "Transforming our world: The 2030 agenda for sustainable development," Resolution 70/1 of the UN General Assembly, www.un.org/ga/search/view_doc.asp?symbol=A/RES/70/1&Lang=E.

United Nations (2015b), "The world's women 2015—trends and Statistics," https://unstats.un.org/unsd/gender/worldswomen.html.

United Nations (2014), *A World That Counts: Mobilising the Data Revolution for Sustainable Development*, report prepared by the Independent Expert Advisory Group on a Data Revolution for Sustainable Development, New York, www.undatarevolution.org/wp-content/uploads/2014/11/A-World-That-Counts.pdf.

United Nations (2000), "Household accounting: Experience in concepts and compilation, Vol. 2, household satellite extensions," in *Handbook of National Accounting*, Studies in Methods, Series F, No. 75/Vol. 2, https://unstats.un.org/unsd/publication/SeriesF/SeriesF_75v2E.pdf.

United Nations et al. (2014a), *System of Environmental-Economic Accounting 2012—Central Framework*, https://unstats.un.org/unsd/envaccounting/seearev/seea_cf_final_en.pdf.

United Nations et al. (2014b), *System of Environmental-Economic Accounting 2012—Experimental Ecosystem Accounting*, https://unstats.un.org/unsd/envaccounting /seeaRev/eea_final_en.pdf.

UN Women (2015), *Summary Report: The Beijing Declaration and Platform for Action Turns 20*, New York, www.unwomen.org/-/media/headquarters/attachments/sections /library/publications/2015/sg%20report_synthesis-en_web.pdf?vs=5547.

Walshe, R. (2014), "Concept paper: A new systems approach to resilience," *Climate Exchange*, https://climate-exchange.org/2014/02/07/concept-paper-a-new-systems -approach-to-resilience (accessed June 4, 2018).

World Bank (2011), *The Changing Wealth of Nations: Measuring Sustainable Development in the New Millennium*, World Bank, Washington, DC., https://siteresources.worldbank .org/ENVIRONMENT/Resources/ChangingWealthNations.pdf.

World Bank (2006), *Where Is the Wealth of Nations? Measuring Capital for the 21st Century*, World Bank, Washington, DC, http://siteresources.worldbank.org/INTEEI/214578 -1110886258964/20748034/All.pdf.

10.

Trust and Social Capital

Yann Algan

This chapter discusses the role of trust for social progress and people's well-being. It reviews the different definitions and types of trust, including rational trust, moral trust, and social preferences, as well as the state of existing statistics on trust. The chapter argues in favor of the definition of trust provided by the OECD Guidelines on Measuring Trust *as "a person's belief that another person or institution will act consistently with their expectations of positive behaviour." It looks at why trust matters for the well-being of people and the country where they live, and assesses the available evidence on its role in supporting social and economic relations. It analyzes trust between individuals (inter-personal trust) and trust in institutions (institutional trust) as determinants of economic growth, social cohesion, and well-being, as a crucial component for policy reform and for the legitimacy and sustainability of any political system. Finally, the chapter stresses the importance of integrating survey measures of trust into the routine data collection activities of National Statistical Offices, and of implementing quasi-experimental measures of trust and other social norms based on representative samples of the population as a complement to traditional survey questions.*

Yann Algan is Professor of Economics at Sciences-Po Paris. The author wishes to thank Elizabeth Beasley, Axelle Charpentier, Angus Deaton, Martine Durand, Lara Fleischer, Sergei Guriev, Alan B. Krueger, Marco Mira D'Ercole, Fabrice Murtin, Joseph E. Stiglitz, and Yang Yao as well as participants in the HLEG workshop on "Measuring Trust and Social Capital," held on June 10, 2016, in Paris and organized in collaboration with Sciences-Po, the European Research Council, and the OECD. Yann Algan also thanks the European Community's Horizon H2020 Programme (H2020-ERC-2014-CoG Grant Agreement n° 647870) for its financial support of the SOWELL project. The opinions expressed and arguments employed in the contributions below are those of the author and do not necessarily reflect the official views of the OECD or of the governments of its member countries.

Introduction

Social capital, broadly understood as the set of shared norms and values that contribute to well-being (OECD, 2013a), has received a huge amount of academic and policy interest in the last quarter century as a key driver of social progress and well-being. The term "social capital" conveys the idea that cooperative human relations are crucial for improving various aspects of people's life, and that it consists of a stock that should be preserved and developed for the sustainability of well-being. This is why the influential report of the Commission on the Measurement of Economic Performance and Social Progress made specific recommendations to develop better measures of social connections and social capital (Stiglitz, Sen, and Fitoussi, 2009). Several initiatives since 2009 have advanced our understanding of social capital and of the data resources available for this effort. For example, the OECD has included aspects of social capital in the framework underpinning its bi-annual report *How's Life?* (OECD, 2011), while other international task forces have underscored the need to develop better measures of social capital for evaluating the sustainability of well-being over time (UNECE, 2013).

Given the very broad and heterogeneous nature of social capital, it is important to narrow and deepen the analysis of its various aspects one at a time, in order to make progress on its measurement and to document its policy relevance. This chapter focuses on the role of "trust" for social progress and well-being. While trust is only one component of social capital (see the "Social Capital and Trust" sidebar on the different definitions and dimensions of social capital), research shows that this dimension is indispensable for social and economic relations. Trust between individuals (inter-personal trust) and trust in institutions (institutional trust) have been shown to be a decisive determinant of economic growth, social cohesion, and well-being. They have also been shown to be a crucial component for policy reform and for the legitimacy and sustainability of any political system. These are also the two types of trust addressed by the *OECD Guidelines on Measuring Trust* (see the "OECD Guidelines on Measuring Trust" sidebar).

SOCIAL CAPITAL AND TRUST

Despite the high level of interest in social capital, there is little agreement about the best way to define and measure it. This has slowed down its incorporation in official statistics and hampered the development of internationally comparable data collection since the 2009 Stiglitz, Sen, and Fitoussi report. OECD (2001) defined social capital as the "networks together with shared norms, values and understandings that facilitate cooperation within or among groups," while Scrivens and Smith (2013) distinguish four main aspects of social capital:

- *Personal relationships* refer to people's networks (i.e., the people they know) and the social behaviors that contribute to establishing and maintaining those networks, such as spending time with others or exchanging news. This category concerns the extent, structure, density, and components of individuals' social networks.
- *Social network support* is a direct outcome of the nature of people's personal relationships and refers to the resources—emotional, material, practical, financial, intellectual, or professional—that are available to each individual through their personal social networks.

- *Civic engagement* measures activities through which people contribute to civic and community life, such as volunteering, political participation, group membership, and different forms of community action. High levels of volunteering and civic action can contribute to institutional performance as well as being a driver of trust and cooperation.

- *Trust and cooperation.* Following Coleman (1990), "an individual trusts if he or she voluntarily places resources at the disposal of another party without any legal commitment from the latter, but with the expectation that the act of trust will pay off." The different types of trust are discussed in this chapter.

OECD GUIDELINES ON MEASURING TRUST

The *Guidelines on Measuring Trust* address both producers and users of trust data (OECD, 2017) and are modeled after the successful *OECD Guidelines on Measuring Subjective Well-Being* (OECD, 2013b). They cover trust in both other people (also known as inter-personal trust) and in public institutions (institutional trust).

These *Guidelines* represent the first attempt to provide international recommendations on collecting, publishing, and analyzing trust data to encourage their use by National Statistical Offices. They describe why measures of trust are relevant for monitoring and policy-making, and why national statistical agencies have a critical role to play in enhancing the usefulness of existing measures. Besides establishing what is known about the reliability and validity of measures of trust, the *OECD Guidelines* describe best approaches for measuring it in a reliable and consistent way, and provide guidance for reporting, interpretation and analysis.

The *OECD Guidelines* also include a number of prototype survey modules

on trust that national and international agencies can readily use in their
household surveys. Five core measures were selected on the basis of their
statistical quality and ability to capture the underlying concepts of trust,
building on previous use in household surveys. While this core module is
recommended to be used in its entirety, its first question on generalized inter-
personal trust is considered as a "primary measure" that should be implemented at the very minimum, on account of the solid evidence available on
its validity. The five questions are as follows:

1. And now a general question about trust. On a scale from zero to ten,
   where zero is not at all and ten is completely, in general how much do
   you trust most people?
2. On a scale from zero to ten, where zero is not at all and ten is completely, in general how much do you trust most people you know
   personally?

*Using this card, please tell me on a score of 0–10 how much you personally trust
each of the institutions I read out. 0 means you do not trust an institution at all,
and 10 means you have complete trust.*

3. [COUNTRY'S] Parliament?
4. The police?
5. The civil service?

Why Does Trust Matter?

The academic research on trust has highlighted a number of relations between trust
and a range of outcomes that matter for the well-being of people and of the country
in which they live.

Trust matters for economic activity and GDP growth. Countries with higher levels
of trust tend to have higher income. Figure 10.1 illustrates this relationship by plot-
ting income per capita over 1980–2009 against average generalized inter-personal
trust (i.e., trust in people in general) over 1981–2008 for a sample of 106 countries.
The correlation is steady: one-fifth of the cross-country variation in income per

Figure 10.1. Cross-Country Correlation Between Average Income per Capita and Generalized Inter-personal Trust

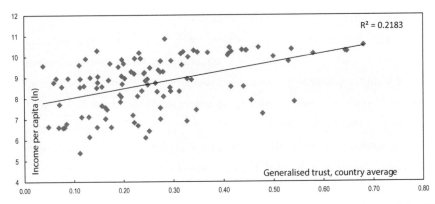

Note: Average income per capita (1980–2009) has been obtained from the Penn World Tables 7.0. Trust is computed as the country average from responses to the trust question in the five waves of the World Values Survey (1981–2008), the four waves of the European Values Survey (1981–2008), and the third wave of the Afrobarometer (2005). The question asks, "Generally speaking, would you say that most people can be trusted or that you need to be very careful in dealing with people?" Trust is equal to 1 if the respondent answers "Most people can be trusted" and 0 otherwise.
Source: Algan, Y. and P. Cahuc (2014), "Trust, growth and well-being: New evidence and policy implications," in Aghion, P. and S. Durlauf (eds.), *Handbook of Economic Growth*, Vol. 2, Elsevier, North-Holland, Amsterdam, pp. 49–120. StatLink 2 http://dx.doi.org/10.1787/888933840019.

capita is related to differences in generalized trust. As discussed later in the chapter, research carried out since 2009 has shown that this relationship is likely to be causal (Algan and Cahuc, 2010).

Early research on the roots of economic development stressed the role of technological progress and the accumulation of human and physical capital. But since those factors were unable to explain a large share of the cross-country differences in income per capita, the focus has progressively shifted to the role of formal institutions (North, 1990), considered as factors that support or weaken market institutions (Stiglitz and Arnott, 1991) and that shape the incentives to accumulate wealth and innovate (Acemoglu, Robinson, and Johnson, 2001; World Bank, 2002); and the focus has shifted to determining what extent those institutions could be distinguished from factors like human capital (Glaeser et al., 2004). More recently, attention has been directed toward deeper factors, in particular social capital and trust. Since the ground-breaking work of Banfield (1958), Coleman (1974), and Putnam (2000), generalized inter-personal trust—broadly defined as cooperative attitude outside the family circle—has been considered by many social scientists as a key driver of many economic and social outcomes (Knack and Keefer, 1997; Dasgupta and Serageldin, 2000; Dasgupta, 2005).

Arrow (1972) gives one likely explanation for the role of trust in economic development: "Virtually every commercial transaction has within itself an element of trust, certainly any transaction conducted over a period of time. It can be plausibly argued that much of the economic backwardness in the world can be explained by the lack of mutual confidence."

Arrow's intuition is straightforward. In a complex society, it is impossible to write down and enforce detailed contracts that encompass every possible state of the world for economic exchanges. Ultimately, in the absence of informal rules established by trust and trustworthiness, markets are missing, gains from economic exchanges are lost, and resources are misallocated. In that respect, trust and the informal rules shaping cooperation could explain differences in economic development. Arrow (1972) considers trust as being at the core of economic exchange in the presence of transaction costs that impede information and contracts. Fundamentally, the economic efficiency of trust flows from the fact that it favors cooperative behavior and thus facilitates mutually advantageous exchanges in the presence of incomplete contracts and imperfect information. In Arrow's term, trust in others acts as a lubricant to economic exchange.

Trust is critical to the well-being of citizens. Inter-personal trust does not only matter for economic outcomes. People seem to have more satisfying lives when they live in an environment of trust and trustworthiness, and when they are more trusting and trustworthy themselves, even controlling for income. For example, it seems that the nonmonetary dimension of having cooperative social relationships with others affects health and happiness above and beyond the monetary gains derived from cooperation.

Panel A of Figure 10.2 illustrates this relationship by using measures of life satisfaction from the World Values Survey question: "All things considered together, how satisfied are you with your life as a whole these days?" Life satisfaction ranges from 1 to 10, a higher score indicating a higher life satisfaction. The correlation between life satisfaction and generalized trust is positive: 17% of the variance in life satisfaction is associated with cross-country differences in generalized trust, with

Figure 10.2. Generalized Inter-personal Trust, Life Satisfaction, and Life Expectancy, 2002–14

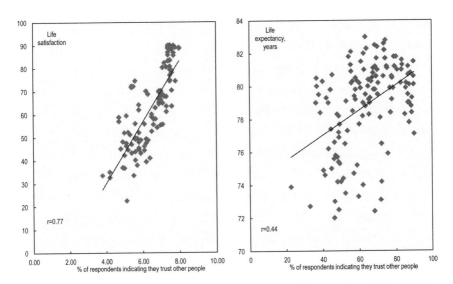

Note: Data on generalized trust is sourced from the European Social Survey, data on life satisfaction is sourced from the Gallup World Poll.
Source: OECD (2017), *OECD Guidelines on Measuring Trust*, OECD Publishing, Paris. StatLink 2 http://dx .doi.org/10.1787/888933840038.

few outliers, like Portugal. Panel B of the same figure also shows a steady positive relationship between generalized trust and life expectancy (OECD, 2016). Similar relationships have been found between generalized trust and different dimensions of health status and health-related behavior (Lochner et al., 2003; Lindström, 2005; Poortinga, 2006; Petrou and Kupek, 2008), and trust and suicide rates (Helliwell, 2007).

Trust improves community life and governance. Trust in institutions, or institutional trust, is also a key element of a resilient society and is critical for implementing effective policies, since public programs, regulations, and reforms depend on the cooperation and compliance of citizens (Blind, 2007; OECD, 2013a). Trust in institutions is a key driver of well-being and economic outcomes (OECD, 2015, 2016).

While inter-personal trust is of primary importance for measuring social capital, institutional trust is most relevant to evaluating the effectiveness of government policies and programs (e.g., Klijn, Edelenbos, and Steijn, 2010). When people have a high level of trust in institutions, they are more likely to comply with laws and regulations, and it is easier to implement policies that may involve trade-offs between the short and long term, or between different parts of society, e.g., through taxation or distributive policies (Marien and Hooghe, 2011; OECD, 2013a). Institutional trust is especially important to government activities that address market failures (e.g., health care, education, the environment) or where long-term gains require short-term sacrifices (e.g., education, pensions).

Figure 10.3, from the *OECD Guidelines on Measuring Trust* (OECD, 2017), shows the relationship between trust in two institutions—the national government and the judiciary—and GDP per capita. In both cases there is a strong positive correlation, in particular in the case of the judiciary. This makes intuitive sense, since the key channels through which institutions affect economic outcomes, such as contract enforcement or regulation of the market place, have a more direct link to the judicial system than to the government more generally. It should be stressed

Figure 10.3. Trust in Institutions and GDP per Capita, 2006–15

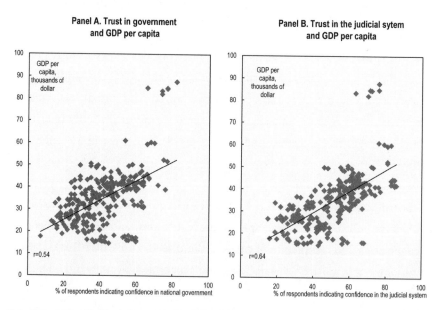

Panel A. Trust in government and GDP per capita

Panel B. Trust in the judicial sytem and GDP per capita

Note: Data on trust in government and on trust in the judicial system are sourced from the Gallup World Poll.

Source: OECD (2017), *OECD Guidelines on Measuring Trust*, OECD Publishing, Paris. StatLink 2 http://dx.doi.org/10.1787/888933840057.

that this correlation could also reflect an impact of GDP per capita on institutional trust, as discussed in the next sections.

What Does Trust Mean?

There is an extensive literature on the concept and theories of trust from a wide range of different disciplines within social sciences, including political science, sociology, economics, and psychology. A central feature of this literature is to consider trust as a "cognitive category with knowledge and belief" (Hardin, 2004), stressing that expectations are central, either expectations about the action of others or about the fact that others share the same values (Uslaner, 2008). But beyond this common element, the concept of trust has received many different interpretations, leading to different measures reviewed by OECD (2017) and different policy recommendations (see below). Following the *OECD Guidelines*, we will define trust as "a person's belief that another person or institution will act consistently with their expectations of positive behaviour." The different theories of trust are reviewed below.

Rational Trust

Trust can be thought of as a belief about other people's trustworthiness, that is, how others are likely to behave toward you. Cooperation is then a strategy to maximize one's own benefit and can only be sustained through reputation. This strategic nature of rational trust is made clear in the trust game of Berg, Dickhaut, and McCabe (1995). In this framework, two individuals are free to invest—or not—some amount that will enable them to produce jointly. Once they make this investment, the fact that the contracts are incomplete and unenforceable (as there is no way for a third party to verify that everything promised is performed) gives each player the chance to profit from the association at the expense of the other. The only possible outcome of this game is an absence of cooperation such that the players have no interest in participating ("Nash equilibrium"—a game theory concept where no player can gain anything by changing their chosen strategy if other players do not change theirs). This shows that the absence of cooperation may prevent mutually advantageous exchanges from coming about.

If trust is purely rational (i.e., self-interested), cooperation can only emerge as a reputation device and in presence of punishment. The spontaneous emergence of cooperative behavior in populations of large size is improbable if each individual is a pure *homo economicus* and they all interact anonymously. If they are not interacting anonymously, that is if people develop reputations over time, cooperation based on reputational trust can emerge, as supported by historical and experimental evidence. Greif (1993, 1994) in his analysis of the Maghribi and Genoese traders, and Dixit (2004) have shown that such cooperation can be supported when there is sufficient transmission of information (that is, a potential partner in a transaction can find out if someone has cheated before because they have a bad reputation), and there is coordinated implementation of strategies intended to punish those caught defecting. This is to say that cooperation may exist in the absence of any formal institution defining legal rules if the size of the population and the preference for the present benefit are sufficiently small. If these conditions are unmet, however, formal institutions explicitly laying down legal rules and sanctions are needed in order to sustain cooperation.

In this way, whether people trust or not depends on their perception of how well societal institutions function. If people believe that strong enforcement mechanisms are in place to discourage cheating or other forms of noncooperative or socially harmful behaviors, they will be more likely to trust others in general (Knack and Keefer, 1997; Rothstein, 2000; Beugelsdijk, 2006). In this case, efficient institutions in which individuals trust are a key driver of trust in others in a cross-section of countries (Rothstein, 2011).

The value of an understanding of trust as strategic and rational is that it highlights the role played by formal institutions in encouraging trust and coordination. However, this view of trust does not account for the cooperative behavior often experimentally observed to arise in anonymous, nonrepetitive, one-off human interactions (Bowles and Gintis, 2007; Fehr, 2009), which has been associated with moral trust and social preferences, as discussed below.

Moral Trust and Social Preferences

The main alternative to a rational notion of trust is the concept of moral trust, whereby trust is a value or preference inherited through socialization rather than a strategy chosen by an individual (OECD, 2017). In this interpretation, trust is still an expectation about how others will behave, but it is not a strategic expectation. In Uslaner's formulation, trust is a "moral commandment to treat people as if they were trustworthy." Trust is a belief that others share our fundamental values (Uslaner, 2002), and people extrapolate from their experiences with specific individuals or from their educational and cultural background to extend trust to groups of people with similar characteristics (Farrell, 2009).

In this line, Fukuyama (1995) considers trust as "the expectation that arises within a community of regular, honest, and cooperative behaviour, based on commonly shared norms, on the part of the other members of that community." A similar definition is also used in the economic literature, where trust and cooperative behaviors are the set of "shared beliefs and values that help a group overcome the free rider problem in the pursuit of socially valuable activities" (Guiso, Sapienza, and Zingales, 2011).

The concept of moral trust emphasizes the existence of an intrinsic motivation and social preferences linked to cooperation and to the psychological or nonmonetary cost of noncooperating (Bowles and Polania-Reyes, 2012). In this perspective, individuals are motivated by more than material payoffs, and value the act of cooperating in itself. In all these settings, individuals are assumed to have social preferences, or other-regarding preferences, and not just self-regarding preferences, which allow cooperation to emerge in anonymous groups of substantial size (see Bowles and Gintis, 2007, for a synthesis).

In this perspective, the literature distinguishes two main social preferences:

- *Altruism*, where people cooperate with others without expecting any payoff or reciprocity, deriving utility solely from "warm glow preferences" (Andreoni, 1989; Anderson, Goeree, and Holt, 1998).
- *Reciprocity*, or *conditional cooperation*, where people cooperate if others cooperate and are reciprocal, but may sanction those who do not respect cooperative norms (Fehr and Schmidt, 1999; Fehr and Gachter, 2000; Gintis et al., 2005; Falk and Fischbacher, 2006; Hoff, Kshetramade, and Fehr, 2011). Individuals display strong betrayal aversion and sanction noncooperative behaviors even if it entails a monetary cost that conflicts with their self-interest (Fehr, 2009).

Types of Trust

Regarding trust between individuals, since the seminal work of Banfield (1958) and Coleman (1990), social scientists have made a distinction between limited morality (directed to people one knows personally) and generalized morality (directed to all people, including strangers). Societies with limited morality promote codes of good conduct within small circles of related persons (family or kin), whereas selfish behavior is regarded as morally acceptable outside the small network. This behavior was described as "amoral familism" by Banfield (1958). Societies with generalized morality promote good conduct outside the small family/kin network, which allows the possibility of identifying oneself with a society of abstract individuals or abstract institutions.[1]

There is evidence that the two types of morality, generalized and limited morality, are really of two different natures, and may affect outcomes in opposite directions, as suggested initially by Banfield (1958). Ermisch and Gambetta (2010), drawing on a representative sample of the British population, find that people with strong family ties have a lower level of trust in strangers than people with weak family ties, and argue that this association is causal. They show that this owes to the level of outward exposure: factors that limit exposure to outsiders limit subjects' experience as well as motivation to deal with strangers.

The concept of trust in institutions is at an earlier stage of both theoretical and empirical development than that of inter-personal trust. The idea of institutional trust encompasses the degree to which people trust specific institutions of a political nature (such as the parliament, the police, or the justice system) or nonpolitical nature (such as banks or private business). The theoretical literature generally distinguishes between two main channels of institutional trust: "trust in competence," i.e., about the competence and knowledge of the persons working in an administration in charge of a public policy; and "trust in intentions," i.e., about their honesty and integrity (Nooteboom, 2007).

What Is the State of Existing Statistics on Trust?

The growing awareness of the importance of trust in social and economic progress has led to several initiatives to improve and expand measures of trust from the research community, governments, and international organizations. These include the OECD's Trust Strategy and *How Is Life?* reports, the UN Sustainable Development Goals, and the Praia City Group on Governance Statistics. Particular attention has been paid by the OECD to better understanding whether the trust measures commonly in use are of sufficient quality and accuracy in order to decide whether they can be considered "fit for purpose" and ready to be collected within official statistics.

Measures of Trust

Survey-Based Measures of Trust

So far, most of the research on the role of trust and cooperation draws on answers to survey questions. A large number of countries are covered by household surveys that have included questions on trust since the beginning of the 1980s. For the most part, these surveys are conducted by nonofficial data producers outside the official statistical system, such as private companies and academic initiatives. Overall, geographic coverage, collection frequency, and sample size vary considerably between surveys. For example, the annual Gallup World Poll has been collecting data on institutional trust since 2006. The World Values Survey (WVS) has been collecting data every 5 years since 1981, albeit for a smaller set of countries. The European Social Survey (ESS) has been collecting data every two years since 2002 for European countries and regions. The Latinobarometer has been collecting data for 19 Latin American countries yearly since 1995, and the Afrobarometer has covered 37 countries with a 2-year frequency since 2002. In addition, there have been occasional large-sample collections of data on trust by official data producers: the 2013 EU Statistics on Income and Living Conditions (EU-SILC) module on well-being included a variety of inter-personal and institutional trust questions, the former of which has once again been included in the 2018 version of that module. Individual countries within and beyond the OECD, including the United Kingdom, New Zealand, Australia, Canada, Poland, the Netherlands, Mexico, Peru, Ecuador, Chile, and Colombia have also occasionally collected data on different aspects of social capital, as well as trust in government.

The bulk of the literature on inter-personal trust has focused on trust in people that one does not know personally, as opposed to trust in relatives, family, or neigh-bors. In surveys, inter-personal trust is most often measured with the "generalised trust question," first introduced by Almond and Verba (1963) in their study of civil society in post-war Europe: "Generally speaking, would you say that most people can be trusted, or that you can't be too careful when dealing with others?" Possible answers are either "Most people can be trusted" or "Need to be very careful."

The same question is used in the European Social Survey (ESS), the US General Social Survey (GSS), the WVS, the Latinobarometer, and the Australian Community Survey. The ESS uses a more neutral wording with an answer on a 0–10 response scale rather than the binary answer where 1 = "Most people can be trusted" and 0 = "Can't be too careful." The *OECD Guidelines on Measuring Trust* (OECD, 2017) also recommend using this neutral wording, as there is evidence that the "Can't be too careful" phrasing may prime relatively vulnerable groups such as the elderly and women to report lower levels of trust compared with responses to a neutral wording. The *Guidelines* further suggest that a 0–10 response scale, in lieu of a binary one, allows for a greater degree of variance in responses and increases overall data quality and translatability, which is of particular concern for international comparability.

Surveys generally include other questions related to trust. For instance, the WVS asks the "fair question": "Do you think most people would try to take advantage of you if they got the chance, or would they try to be fair?" The GSS includes the trust question and the fair question, and adds the "help question": "Would you say that most of the time people try to be helpful, or that they are mostly just looking out for themselves?" These different questions are sometimes used to build indexes intended to provide alternative measures of trust or get an average indicator of moral values or civic capital (Tabellini, 2010; Guiso et al., 2011).

Although most of the surveys directly ask questions about generalized trust based on evaluations, there have also been attempts to measure trust with questions on expectations about what would happen in a given concrete situation. One of the most well-known examples is the "lost wallet" question used in the Gallup World Poll: "If you lost a wallet or a purse that contained items of great value to you, and it was found by a stranger, do you think it would be returned with its contents, or not?" However, this question is limited to a small number of surveys so far and the hypothetical nature of the question prevents it from being a real behavioral measure.

In the case of institutional trust, questions are traditionally formulated through a common heading: "Do you have confidence in your . . . ?" (The space is filled in with an entity taken from a list of institutions, such as "government" or "congress.") Possible answers are generally "yes/no/don't know," or a response on a scale from 0 to 10. The surveys generally ask questions about different, mainly public, institutions (e.g., the parliament, the courts, the government, the armed forces). Some questions also refer to those who are in charge of implementing the policies (e.g., civil servants, police officers, MPs). As noted by Delhey, Newton, and Welzel (2011), institutional trust can vary depending on the institution, and so it is recommended that questions are asked for each specific institution, rather than attempting to measure institutional trust as a single construct, or combine several questions into a trust index. Nevertheless, the *OECD Guidelines on Measuring Trust*, using a principal component analysis of different types of trust questions in the World Values Survey, find three main factors for institutional trust: trust in nongovernmental institutions (major companies, banks, universities, environmental organizations, women's organizations), trust in political institutions (government of the day, political parties, parliament, civil service), and trust in law and order institutions (armed forces, police, courts). While this analysis confirms the salience of distinct sub-dimensions of institutional trust, it also highlights that many of the finer distinctions often made between different categories of trust are not very informative empirically, and that a relatively narrow range of measures that covers these broad types of institutions will cover the most important aspects (OECD, 2017). Of course, depending on the needs of especially policy-makers, asking institution-specific questions can still be worthwhile.

Behavioral and Experimental Measures of Trust

Survey data supply subjective information—how people judge and feel—which requires caution in use and interpretation. Issues include how individuals interpret the question they are asked, and whether there are systematic differences between groups in that interpretation that might be misinterpreted as differences in the underlying level of trust. For example, individuals who respond that you "need to be very careful" to the trust question could be motivated by a strong aversion to risk (Fehr, 2009; Bohnet and Zeckhauser, 2004; Guiso, Sapienza, and Zingales, 2011). Surveys are generally unable to assess and disentangle the variety of social preferences that can be involved in inter-personal trust such as altruism, reciprocity, or social desirability and reputation, as discussed above.

For this reason, a revolution in experimental economics has led to the development of laboratory experiments designed to elicit a large variety of social behaviors, through protocols such as the "trust game" (described below) or the "public goods game." These carefully calibrated experiments, which measure the behavior and choices of people, with monetary incentives at stake, not only help disentangle different types of trust but also provide benchmarks against which survey questions can be compared, to determine whether survey questions are measuring actual behavior.

These games focus on a definition of trust that can be directly measured with experimental games, as shown by Fehr (2009). The trust that is measured in these experiments is best thought of as a behavior following Coleman's concept, according to whom "an individual trusts if he or she voluntarily places resources at the disposal of another party without any legal commitment from the latter, but with the expectation that the act of trust will pay off" (Coleman, 1990). This conception has two elements: a behavioral one, and an expectation that the act of trusting will be of benefit for the person granting it.

In general, these experiments use variants of the "investment game," also known as the "trust game," of Berg, Dickhaut, and McCabe (1995). In laboratory experiments, this game is played as follows. In stage 1, the subjects in rooms A and B are each given 10 dollars as a show-up fee. While subjects in room B pocket their show-up fee, subjects in room A must decide how much of their 10 dollars to send to an anonymous counterpart in room B. The amount sent, denoted by M, is tripled, resulting in a total return of 3M. In stage 2, a counterpart in room B is given the tripled money and must decide how much to return to the subject in room A. "Trust in others" is measured by the amount sent initially by the sender. Trustworthiness is measured by the amount sent back by the player in room B.

This framework can be adapted and supplemented with complementary experiments to measure trust as distinct from other attitudes, such as risk aversion, altruism, and reciprocal behaviors, and to distinguish between trusting behavior as a deep-seated preference, and trusting behavior as a function of one's beliefs about the trustworthiness of others (which can be quickly revised). For example, a positive correlation between the amount sent and the amount returned may reflect a preference for reciprocity. Disentangling altruism from reciprocity may be done by complementing the trust game with the dictator game, where one player has to decide what portion of a sum to share with another player who cannot react to the transfer and has no initial endowment of their own. Experiments along this line by Cox (2004) have demonstrated that reciprocity exists and that the trust motive exists separately from altruism. Other experiments have used measures of risk aversion alongside trust games.

Other studies have used neurobiological methods to measure the role of trust in comparison with preferences with greater precision. Oxytocin, a hormone released especially during breast-feeding and giving birth, is associated with sentiments of affinity and socialization. It is known for deactivating the transmission of feelings of anxiety related to the belief of being betrayed. Kosfeld et al. (2005) evaluated the effect of oxytocin on the pro-social behavior of individuals participating in trust games. The authors proposed additional experiments to distinguish pro-social preferences from risk-taking behavior and from the level of optimism of the participants. The participants in this study were randomly allocated into two groups. The first group inhaled oxytocin through a spray; the second inhaled a placebo and served as the control group. Results from this experiment show that individuals who received oxytocin displayed more trust, and that they continued to behave trustingly in the exchange with others even if the latter did not show any reciprocity. By contrast, other attitudes, such as prudence and risk-aversion, or even beliefs such as optimism in the actions of others, were not affected. Based on this evidence, Kosfeld et al. concluded that the trust game measures veritable preferences for cooperation, rather than risk aversion or anticipations of the others' actions (see Fehr, 2009, for a survey of experimental measures of trust).

Validity of Trust Measures

The OECD's *Guidelines on Measuring Trust* (OECD, 2017) distinguish several criteria for assessing the statistical quality of trust measures, in particular:

- Reliability: the degree to which the measures of trust produce consistent information over time and across different vehicles.
- Face validity: the degree to which a measure is intuitively plausible, measured by the nonresponse rate to the question.
- Convergent validity: whether a measure of trust correlates well with objective measures (e.g., whether self-reported trust correlates with behavioral trust).
- Construct validity: whether a measure behaves as common sense and theory dictate.

General Issues with Existing Survey-Based Measures

There are many practical issues with existing survey-based data on trust that are at least as important, and possibly more so, than the conceptual issues described above.

- Data generally come from nonofficial surveys with very small sample sizes, typically of around 1,000 per country, and sometimes low response rates. This raises concerns about noise-to-signal ratio and nonresponse bias in the sample. The lack of representative samples also makes it very difficult to get a comprehensive description of the level of trust at the local level and to analyze the economic, social, and policy determinants of trust.
- Data coverage is also relatively poor, particularly over time. As an illustration, one of the most used surveys in the literature, the WVS, provides waves only at irregular intervals (every 5 years on average) and the countries covered vary from wave to wave. Lack of time-series data makes it difficult to look at what drives changes in trust. In particular, these databases cannot be used to analyze how policy reforms affect the evolution of trust in others and in institutions.
- Different surveys are very heterogeneous in the question wordings, limiting comparability across surveys. In the case of institutional trust, for instance, questions sometimes refer to similar concepts but use different descriptions, such as "courts" or the "judicial system," "politicians" or "the government." Also, different surveys use different response scales. Some surveys rely primarily on a "yes/no/don't know" response format

(GWP), while others surveys such as the ESS and the WVS use longer numeric scales (0–10 or 1–4). This raises a real issue since researchers are forced to rely on different data sources for different groups of countries (WVS for developing countries, and ESS for European countries in the figures used in this chapter) to cope with the poor geographical and time coverage of each survey.

Validity of Survey-Based Measures of Inter-personal Trust

The *OECD Guidelines on Measuring Trust* (OECD, 2017) find strong evidence for the validity of measures of inter-personal trust: they are consistent across different data sources and over time, their nonresponse rates are relatively low, and they are highly correlated with a large variety of social and economic outcomes. Their policy relevance has also been supported by academic research, as discussed below.

Studies that have analyzed the relationship between survey answers from the generalized trust question and the amount sent in the trust game, an indication of convergent validity, found mixed results. Some studies found that the trust question predicted some aspect of trust behavior, either trustworthiness or trustfulness, but not always the same one (Glaeser et al., 2000; Fehr et al., 2002; Lazzarini et al., 2005; Ermisch et al., 2009). Other studies found differences in the relationship of the trust question to behavior in different countries (Holm and Danielson, 2005). However, differences between the conclusions of the studies may also be due to differences in experimental design, as the designs of the games are not identical between the different experiments. The recently launched TrustLab project, jointly launched by the OECD and France's Sciences-Po international research university, is the first international database on people's behaviors, social norms, and preferences, and collects information on trust via survey and experimental measures in a comparable way and on nationally representative samples in different OECD countries (see "TrustLab" sidebar). TrustLab analysis from the first set of countries has found that survey and experimental measures of trust are positively correlated, and that the survey measure of trust, when controlling for other factors, captures altruism and expected trustworthiness of others (Murtin et al., 2018). This confirms the argument that expected trustworthiness of others, rather than one's own trustworthiness, matters the most for evaluating trust in other people (Fehr, 2009).

Overall, the *OECD Guidelines* therefore conclude that survey questions on inter-personal trust provide valid and reliable information, and there is a strong case for including them in official statistical vehicles.

Validity of Survey-Based Measures of Institutional Trust

The validity of survey-based measures of institutional trust is more mixed, but still positive (OECD, 2017). Although their potential policy relevance is clear and they perform well in terms of construct validity, some interpretation and statistical issues still remain open. Nevertheless, although the evidence base on their validity is not as strong as for measures of inter-personal trust, the OECD recommendation is that these measures should also be collected by official statistics.

Differences in interpretation by respondents can be particularly important with respect to questions on institutional trust. People may interpret "How much do you trust the government?" in several different ways. Do they think the government is competent to deliver services? Do they think the government is honest? Do they think that the government will enact good policies? The answer to these questions may be very different depending on which interpretation the respondent uses. Questions on trust in institutions do not necessarily measure something structural about how well institutions work, since people might answer these questions by thinking about the government in power at the time or about the deep-seated traits of a political system.

In addition, statistics on institutional trust must be used with caution. Should these statistics be used as a measure of people's *perception* of institutional trustwor-thiness, or as a measure of the actual objective level of trustworthiness or transpar-ency? That is, should differences in measures of institutional trust across countries be taken as an indicator, for example, of different levels of corruption? It is diffi-cult to distinguish between beliefs and perceptions on the one hand, and objective measures on the other, especially when individuals are asked about the extent of transparency or corruption of various institutions (Charron, 2016).

So far there has been little evidence on the convergent validity of institutional trust measures. While for inter-personal trust there is a consensus on using general-ized trust as the preferred measure, institutional trust covers several dimensions, all of which are of interest (police, banks, and so on). Furthermore, with respect to experimental analyses (against which survey measures might be compared, as in the case of inter-personal trust), the standard trust game does not have an experimental counterpart for the analysis of trust in institutions. However, there are studies that rely on Implicit Association Tests, a method from experimental psychology, to validate institutional trust questions, with promising results (Intawan and Nicholson, 2017). The TrustLab project also includes an Implicit Association Test as experimental measure of institutional trust, and, encouragingly, finds that, controlling for a range of individual characteristics, experimental trust in government is significantly and positively related with survey data on trust in government and trust in the judicial system (Murtin et al., 2018).

Going forward, more consistent and harmonized data will increase the evidence base available and allow researchers to better understand and improve these measures.

TRUSTLAB: MEASURING TRUST AND SOCIAL NORMS THROUGH EXPERIMENTAL TECHNIQUES

TrustLab is an experimental platform developed by Sciences-Po and the OECD to:

- Produce new measures of trust and social norms using a range of techniques.
- Compare trust and social norms across countries and groups of people.
- Understand the drivers of trust at the individual level.

The platform combines experimental and nonexperimental techniques. As such, it overcomes some limitations of the experimental approaches used so far, in particular their very small sample sizes, the use of samples that are not nationally representative, and the fact that experimental findings are not linked to comparable survey data.

TrustLab relies on an integrated online platform developed by MediaLab

Table 10.1. Modules Featuring in TrustLab

Module	Focus	Technique
1. Behavioral games (trust game, public goods game, dictator game)	Generalized trust	Experimental
2. Implicit Association Tests	Trust in institutions	Quasi-experimental
3. Survey and demographic module	Generalized trust	Traditional self-reported survey questions
	Trust in institutions	
	Drivers of trust	

StatLink 2 http://dx.doi.org/10.1787/888933840076.

Sciences-Po. In every participating country, a representative national sample of 1,000 people answers a number of traditional survey questions and participates in experimental games providing both behavioral and self-reported information. Games are played with real resources at stake (mean value around 15 euros). Table 10.1 presents the different survey modules and instruments that are used in TrustLab.

Data from TrustLab provide a rich description of different social norms (trust in others, trustworthiness, altruism, cooperation, reciprocity) and of trust in different institutions (government, parliament, police, judicial system, media, and banks), in addition to some of the potential determinants of trust.

Following a pilot phase in 2016, TrustLab has now been implemented in France, Korea, Slovenia, the United States, Germany, Italy, and the United Kingdom, with a range of academic and governmental partners joining the effort.

Validity of Experimental Measures of Trust

We still know very little about whether and to what extent the experimental results established in the lab carry over to field situations. An investigation of the relationship between lab-based experimental measures and field outcomes is required if we are to rely on the experimental method to make inferences about the real world. Unfortunately, research has so far mainly focused on lab experiments with very small and nonrepresentative samples of students or other citizens, raising important concerns about external validity (see Henrich et al., 2001, for a comparison of social preferences across small-scale societies). This issue is all the more problematic since these samples are generally drawn from university students in Western countries. In the field of psychology, Arnett (2008) found that 96% of subjects in studies published in top journals were from "WEIRD" (Western, educated, industrialized, rich, and democratic) backgrounds. Researchers—often implicitly—assume that either there is little variation in experimental results across populations, or that these WEIRD subjects are as representative of the human species as any other population. This is not the case: WEIRD subjects are "among the least representative populations one could find for generalizing about humans," and there is substantial variability of results across countries (Heinrich et al., 2001).

Due to its lack of external validity, experimental economics leaves important questions unanswered. What is the heterogeneity of social preferences across populations, organizations, or countries, based on real and comparable behaviors? How does this heterogeneity explain economic and institutional development? How is this heterogeneity explained by economic and institutional factors? How well do behaviors exhibited in experimental games (which are often conducted in somewhat artificial environments) match behavior in the real world?

Karlan (2005) uses the trust game to obtain individual-level measures of taste for reciprocity, and shows that it can be used to predict loan repayment among participants, up to one year later, in a Peruvian microcredit program. De Oliveira, Croson, and Eckel (2014) elicit subjects' taste for cooperation in the lab using a traditional public goods game. They show that the results are correlated with subjects' contributions to local charities in a donation experiment, and with whether they self-report contributing time and/or money to local charitable causes. Similarly, Laury and Taylor (2008) and Benz and Meier (2008) use public goods games to elicit participants' taste for cooperation and show that it is associated with the probability to contribute to a public good in the field through a charitable donation. Algan et al. (2015) also show that trust is a good predictor of contributions in online economics communities. In particular, the emergence of large organizations based on cooperation and nonmonetary incentives, such as Wikipedia and open software, provides a perfect experiment to test the relationship between experimental measures and field behaviors.

The main concern with experimental measures of trust is related to the limited and nonrepresentative samples for the lab experiments. Survey questions, on the other hand, have representative samples if collected by National Statistical Offices, but they measure individual beliefs (about others and themselves) rather than how much people actually engage in trusting behavior.

Combining Experimental and Survey Data

Survey-based questions on trust are good predictors of macro-economic outcomes, but by themselves cannot disentangle the underlying mechanisms involved. Experimental measures of trust can do so, but they cannot be conducted on a wide scale. Experiments carried out on representative samples could shed light on the exact nature of social attitudes and on the extent of bilateral cooperation between individuals in the larger population, not only WEIRD subjects. In addition, with a few exceptions, identical experiments are not repeated in different countries, so it is difficult to understand if there is cross-country variation in the underlying mechanisms of trust. The TrustLab project has the potential to overcome these limitations. For the first time, researchers, civil society, and government can compare social preferences drawn from an identical experimental setup based on representative samples for different countries.

What Can We Say Based on Available Evidence?

International surveys have yielded evidence of large differences in trust levels across countries. In Norway, the country with the highest level of trust in the sample, more than 68% of the population are trusting others (Figure 10.4). At the opposite end of the ranking lies Trinidad and Tobago, where only 4% of the population report high levels of inter-personal trust. In general, Northern European countries lead the ranking with high-average levels of inter-personal trust, while populations in African and South American countries seem not to trust others very much. The United States ranks in the top quarter of countries, with an average trust level of more than 40%. The extent to which people trust others, however, varies not only across countries, but also across regions in the same country. Algan and Cahuc (2014) show that trust levels vary remarkably between regions across Europe, the United States, and in several other countries.

Figure 10.4. Average Trust in Others Across 109 Countries, 2014

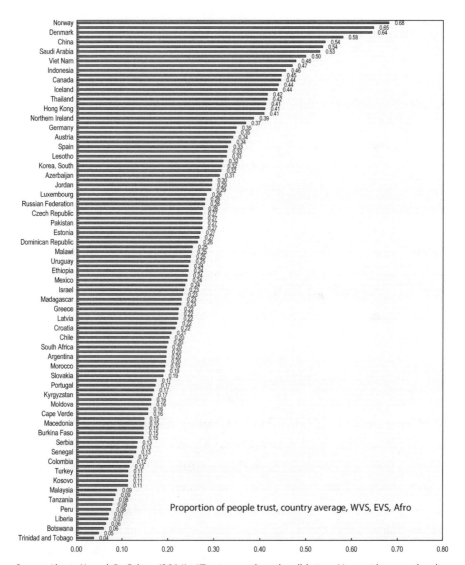

Source: Algan, Y. and P. Cahuc (2014), "Trust, growth and well-being: New evidence and policy implications," in Aghion, P. and S. Durlauf (eds.), *Handbook of Economic Growth*, Vol. 2, Elsevier, North-Holland, Amsterdam, pp. 49–120. StatLink 2 http://dx.doi.org/10.1787/888933840095.

In addition to better understanding the distribution of trust across countries, researchers have expanded the evidence base on the three observed relationships that justify interest in trust: its relationship with economic activity and GDP growth, with people's subjective well-being, and with governance and public policy. Research on each of these relations is described later on.

Trust Matters for Economic Activity and Growth

Trust in others is the only statistically significant predictor for the cross-country variation in income per capita and GDP growth after controlling for education, ethnic fractionalization (number, size, socio-economic, and geographical location of distinct cultural groups), legal origins, and political institutions (Algan and Cahuc, 2014). One concern has been that this correlation, first noted by Knack and Keefer (1997), could go the other way around, i.e., from income to trust. Alternatively, the trust variable could be picking up the deeper influence of time-invariant features such as legal origins, the quality of institutions, initial education, the extent of ethnic segmentation, and geography.

More light on this issue is provided by Algan and Cahuc (2010), who established a steady causal relationship going from trust to income by controlling for confounding factors and reverse causality. Algan and Cahuc used time variation in *inherited* trust of children of immigrants to the United States to explain GDP growth in the countries of their forebears—since children inherit some of their trusting nature from their parents, one can work backward to estimate their immigrant forebears' trust, and use this to estimate the level of trust in the origin country at the time the forebears left. Since the forebears left their home country at different times, one can estimate the level of trust in the home country at different times, obtaining a data set that traces changes in trust over time in different countries.[2] This structure of data—a panel data set—allows for the estimation of the impact of changes in generalized trust on income per capita in the countries of origin. By focusing on the inherited component of trust, the authors avoid reverse causality. By providing a time-varying measure of trust over long periods, they can control for both omitted time-invariant factors and other observed time-varying factors such as changes in the economic, political, cultural, and social environments.

Algan and Cahuc find a significant impact. Income per capita in 2000 would have been 546% higher in Africa if, all else being equal, the level of inherited trust had been the same as inherited trust from Sweden. Inherited trust also has a nonnegligible impact on GDP per capita in eastern European countries and Mexico. Income per capita would have increased by 69% in the Russian Federation, 59% in Mexico, 30% in Yugoslavia, 29% in the Czech Republic, and 9% in Hungary had these countries inherited the same level of inter-personal trust as Sweden. The effect, though less important, is also sizable in more developed countries. Income per capita would have been 17% higher in Italy, 11% in France, 7% in Germany, and 6% in the United Kingdom if these countries had had the same level of inherited trust as Sweden. The authors also compare the effect of trust on income per capita and of time-invariant factors such as geography and institutions. For countries in Africa or Latin America, initial economic development and invariant factors have a large impact on income per capita. In contrast, change in income per capita in developed countries is overwhelmingly explained by inherited trust.

Progress has been made not only in understanding the role of trust at a macro-economic level, but also at a micro-economic level. Trust in others shapes the capacity to achieve common goals through pooling of resources, reduced transaction costs and coordination failures during economic exchanges, and more generally the way people live together (OECD, 2015). Therefore, innovation, investment, and the functioning of financial and labor markets are contingent on trust (Algan and Cahuc, 2009). Algan and Cahuc (2014) show different channels through which generalized trust can affect economic growth. Trust plays a preponderant role for economic activities—investment and especially innovation—that are affected by uncertainty on account of moral hazard and the difficulties of contract enforcement. The effect of trust also acts through the organization of firms and the functioning of the labor market. By facilitating cooperation among anonymous persons, trust favors the emergence and growth of private and public organizations (Fukuyama, 1995; La Porta et al., 1997; Bertrand and Schoar, 2006). Trust favors the decentralization of decisions within organizations, allowing them to adapt better to alterations in the environment (Bloom, Sadun, and Van Reenen, 2012). Trust likewise influences the functioning of the labor market through several channels. For example, countries with higher generalized trust have higher levels of cooperative relations between labor and management (Aghion, Algan, and Cahuc, 2011);

in turn, the quality of employer-employee relations is associated with an array of factors that favor GDP growth and well-being.

Trust Matters for Subjective Well-Being

Trust and subjective well-being are positively correlated, and there is growing evidence for this in the literature. For example, Helliwell and Wang (2011) show that trust can mitigate the impact of bad shocks on individuals and is associated with lower suicide rates. Helliwell and Putnam (2004) and Helliwell and Wang (2011) provide cross-country micro-evidence on the positive relationship between trust and subjective well-being, and estimate how much this relationship is "worth" in terms of the effects on income. From the 2006 wave of the Gallup World Poll, they use the "lost wallet" trust question for 86 countries. Individuals are asked what is the likelihood of the respondent's lost wallet (with clear identification and $200 cash) being returned if found by a neighbor, a police officer, or a stranger. Helliwell and Wang estimate that an increase in income by two-thirds is necessary to compensate the welfare loss associated with thinking that no one will bring back your wallet and your documents. For example, to live in a country like Norway (highest mean expected wallet return of 80%) rather than in Tanzania (lowest mean expected wallet return of 27%) is equivalent to a 40% increase in household income. Boarini et al. (2012) take this analysis further, and show that average levels of inter-personal trust at the country level are strongly correlated with the life satisfaction of individuals living in these countries, independently of the individual's own trust, and after controlling for demographic and economic variables. A more general study on the country's endowment of relational capital, proxied by the share of the cooperative sector, finds that more cooperativeness is associated with more happiness, after controlling for countries' Human Development Index and other variables (Bruni and Ferri, 2016).

All these studies focus on cross-country correlations. But the same type of evidence holds within a given community, and changes in trust over time are associated with changes in subjective well-being over time. Helliwell et al. (2009) show that the same result holds in the workplace. Using micro-data from Canada (the 2003 wave of the Equality, Security and Community Survey) and the United States (the 2000 wave of the Social Capital Benchmark Survey), the authors find that the climate of trust in the workplace, in particular workers' trust in their managers, is strongly related to the subjective well-being of workers. On a 1–10 scale, an increase by one point of workers' trust in managers has the same effect on their life satisfaction as an increase in household income by 30%.

There is also evidence to suggest that generalized trust correlates positively with better health outcomes for individuals (Boreham, Samurçay, and Fischer, 2002; Arber and Ginn, 2004). For example, Hamano et al. (2010) studied around 200 neighborhoods in Japan and found that high levels of generalized trust (along with high levels of membership in associations) were linked with better mental health after controlling for age, sex, household income, and educational attainment. A study of Chicago neighborhoods showed that high levels of reciprocity, generalized trust, and civic participation were associated with lower death rates and rates of heart disease, after controlling for neighborhood material deprivation (Lochner et al., 2003).

However, the causal pathways between trust in others and well-being are still unclear. One possible explanation of the associations described above is that less-trusting individuals may have a tendency toward social isolation, thereby depriving themselves of many of the positive health benefits of supportive social networks (Glass and Balfour, 2003). Another possible explanation is that people living in higher-trust communities have lower levels of social anxiety, and thus lower levels of chronic stress (Wilkinson, 2000).

To get more causal evidence, recent research has looked at the physiological reaction and brain images of participants depending on their degree of cooperation in a trust game. Zack, Kursban, and Matzner (2004) show that when people cooperate with others in trust games, they increase production of oxytocin. The authors also tested a variant in which the receiver receives a monetary transfer not from a real person but from a lottery. In this variant, the level of oxytocin does not rise with the money received. This result illustrates that it is trust that is associated with sentiments of happiness, and not the mere fact of receiving money. These results have been confirmed by brain images: as soon as individuals do not cooperate in trust games, the insular cortex activates (Sanfey et al., 2003). This area of the brain is known for being active in states of pain and disgust. The main conclusion from this research is that the nonmonetary dimension of having trusting behavior with

others affects happiness by more than the monetary gains derived from cooperation. All in all, these results suggest that trust affects many dimensions of social
progress, including both economic development and life evaluations, and is a key
component of human development at large.

Trust in Institutions and Social and Economic Progress

There is also good evidence of a positive relationship between institutional trust
and citizen support for government policy (OECD, 2016). In one of the earli-
est studies on this subject, Knack and Keefer (1997) analyzed responses to World
Values Surveys across about 30 countries, finding a positive correlation between
measures of citizens' confidence in government and objective indicators of bureau-
cratic efficiency. In a cross-country analysis, Zhao and Kim (2011) highlight a positive correlation between institutional trust and levels of foreign direct investment.
Murphy, Tyler, and Curtis (2009) find a strong positive relationship between trust
in regulators and voluntary compliance in the area regulated, while Daude, Gutiérrez, and Melguizo (2012) find a strong relationship between institutional trust and
willingness to pay taxes. There is also a robust cross-country correlation between
people's trust in institutions and their perceptions of corruption (OECD, 2013).
These studies, based on the correlation between citizen support for government
and trust in institutions, need to be understood in a context where there is almost
certainly reverse causality, i.e., people are less likely to trust inept or corrupt institutions (highlighting the issue of interpretation of the institutional trust measure
discussed above). It should be stressed though that most of these studies are based
on correlations and the research still needs to make progress in establishing a causal
link between trust in institutions and economic progress.

Trust in institutions is also necessary to maintain democratic systems. The recent
trust crisis in Europe is a good illustration of the risks. Algan et al. (2017) show that
the financial crisis and Great Recession that followed it, and the inability of European institutions to cope, led to a sharp decline in trust in European and national
parliaments, associated with a rise in extreme votes and populism. Algan et al. find
a strong relationship between increases in unemployment and voting for nonmain-
stream, especially populist parties, and a decline in trust in national and European
political institutions. In an effort to advance on causation, the authors extract the

component of increases in unemployment stemming from the pre-crisis structure of the economy, and in particular the share of construction in regional GDP, which is strongly related both to the build-up and outbreak of the crisis. Crisis-driven economic insecurity is a substantial driver of populism and political distrust. An important policy implication from the European economic crisis is that national governments and the European Union should focus not only on structural reforms, but also on protecting the trust of their citizens from economic insecurity.

Trust in institutions is also directly related to subjective well-being. Figure 10.5 shows positive correlations between life satisfaction and trust in the judicial system (Panel A) and in the government (Panel B). This relationship can be explained if trusted institutions function better, and are therefore associated with better outcomes that raise people's life satisfaction. The causality can also go in the other direction though, with people trusting institutions that function better. But there is also evidence of a direct impact of trust in institutions on people's subjective well-being. Frey, Benz, and Stutzer (2004) and Frey and Stutzer (2005, 2006) show the importance of "procedural utility" (i.e., the process through which people are *involved* in making important collective decisions) for people's subjective well-being, independently of the actual outcome of the decision. In this perspective, although a policy decision might increase total income, the welfare effect could be reduced due to the losses resulting from a decision process perceived by people as unfair or nondemocratic. This literature may be important to understand the current rise in populism in much of the world.

Trust and Income Inequality

There is a strong negative correlation between generalized trust and Gini indexes of income inequality, both across countries (Figure 10.6, Panel A) and across US states (Panel B). High-trusting societies are more equal (they have lower Gini coefficients), while low-trusting societies typically show higher levels of income inequality. Cross-country and cross-US states regressions controlling for income, population, education, and ethnic fractionalization confirm this correlation (Algan and Cahuc, 2014).

Alesina and La Ferrara (2000) show that this negative relationship between trust and income inequality also holds at a more local level within US counties and

Figure 10.5. Institutional Trust and Life Satisfaction, 2006–15

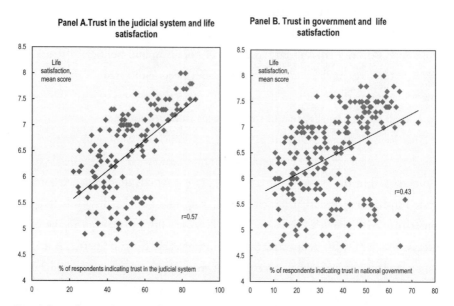

Panel A.Trust in the judicial system and life satisfaction

Panel B. Trust in government and life satisfaction

Note: Life satisfaction data comes from the Gallup World Poll. Data on trust in the judicial system and in government are sourced from the Eurobarometer.

Source: OECD (2017), *OECD Guidelines on Measuring Trust,* OECD Publishing, Paris. StatLink 2 http://dx .doi.org/10.1787/88933840114.

municipalities. Rothstein and Uslaner (2005) document a within-states correlation for the United States between the rise in income inequalities and the decline of trust over the last decades. A pending issue is that of causality. Inequality might correlate negatively with trust for several reasons. On the one hand, as suggested by Rothstein and Uslaner, high levels of trust and cooperation might go along with high preferences for redistribution and thereby contribute to lower inequality.[3] On the other hand, high inequality can make individuals perceive themselves as unfairly treated by people belonging to social classes different from their own, leading them to restrict cooperative action and trust to members of their own class (Rothstein and Uslaner, 2005). Kumlin and Rothstein (2005) also show that more universalist and egalitarian welfare state regimes are associated with higher levels of trust than corporatist welfare state systems that divide social benefits by status.

Research is still needed to nail down the causal effect of income inequality on

Figure 10.6. Income Inequality and Generalized Trust
Across Countries and US States

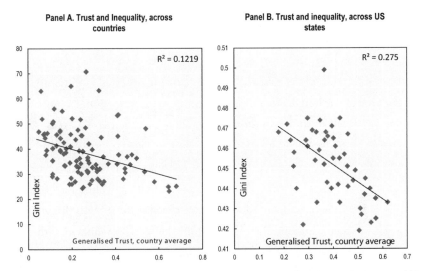

Panel A. Trust and Inequality, across countries

Panel B. Trust and inequality, across US states

Note: Inequality is measured by the average of the Gini index between 2005 and 2012 (World Bank). Generalized trust is measured as the country average from World Values Survey (1981–2009) and European Values Survey (1981–2008). For the United States, inequality is measured by the Gini index in 2010 (US Census Bureau). Generalized trust is taken from the General Social Survey (1973–2006). *Source:* Algan, Y. and P. Cahuc (2014), "Trust, growth and well-being: New evidence and policy implications," in Aghion, P. and S. Durlauf (eds.), *Handbook of Economic Growth*, Vol. 2, Elsevier, North-Holland, Amsterdam, pp. 49–120. StatLink 2 http://dx.doi.org/10.1787/888933840133.

generalized trust. The application of behavioral surveys looking at cooperation between individuals depending on their demographics, status, and income would improve the investigation of this causal relationship.

How Can Policy Affect Trust?

Trust varies significantly within countries, depending on income, education, employment status, and household type (OECD, 2017). Both generalized trust and trust in institutions are higher among higher-income groups and among more highly educated people, and lower among unemployed people and single-person households with at least one dependent child.

While these patterns hold true across the majority of OECD countries, it is important to study the drivers of trust in the context of countries' specific circumstances, and how policy-makers could develop such an important type of social capital. If trust plays a key role in explaining economic and social outcomes, it becomes urgent to identify the institutions and public policies needed for it to develop.

Research on this subject is still in its early stages, owing mainly to the lack of adequate behavioral measures across time and localities. Part of the literature considers trust to be a deeply rooted cultural component, whose determinants must be searched for in the long history of each country, with little room for immediate action. However, recent studies on immigrants show that their level of trust gradually converges to the average level of trust prevailing in their country of destination. This ambiguity is well illustrated by the two conflicting views of the evolution of trust given by Robert Putnam. According to "Putnam I" (Putnam, Leonardi, and Nanetti, 1993), social capital is largely determined by history. In this account, higher levels of social capital in the regions of northern Italy compared with those in the south originated in the free-city experience during the medieval period. On the other hand, according to "Putnam II" (Putnam, 2000), trust evolves from one generation to the next, and is strongly influenced by the environment. In *Bowling Alone*, Putnam shows that the levels of social capital, as measured by membership in associations and clubs, have starkly declined in the United States since World War II.

Depending on which perspective we take, "Putnam I" or "Putnam II," the room for policy intervention would be small or large. In fact, both approaches have an element of truth. Trust is partly inherited from past generations and shaped by historical shocks, as the underlying beliefs regarding the benefits of trust and cooperation are transmitted in communities through families (Bisin and Verdier, 2001; Benabou and Tirole, 2006; Tabellini, 2008; Guiso, Sapienza, and Zingales, 2008). But another part of trust is shaped by personal experience from the current environment, be it social, economic, or political. In Bisin and Verdier's terminology, both the vertical channel of transmission from parents to children and the oblique/horizontal channel from the contemporaneous environment are at play in building trust. This debate is also influenced by what generalized trust really measures. If trust consists of beliefs about the trustworthiness of others, it is likely that individuals update their beliefs depending on the environment where they live, the civic spirit of their fellow citizens, and the transparency of their institutions.

If trust consists of deep preferences and moral values, transmitted in early childhood and disconnected from personal experience, as suggested by Uslaner (2002), it might take more time to adjust. Another interpretation is that there are equilibria that persist and are hard to change, unless citizens are nudged with relevant public policy (Hoff and Stiglitz, 2016).

The Role of Education

The bulk of the existing policy-relevant evidence on the drivers of trust is on education programs. There is some evidence that more education is associated with higher social capital (Helliwell and Putnam, 2007; Glaeser, Ponzetto, and Shleifer, 2007). However, variation in the average years of education of the population across developed countries is too small to explain the observed cross-country differences in trust. Algan, Cahuc, and Shleifer (2013) propose a complementary explanation by looking at the relationship between how students are taught and students' beliefs in cooperation. They show that methods of teaching differ widely across countries, both between schools and within schools in a country. Some schools and teachers emphasize vertical teaching practices, whereby teachers primarily lecture, students take notes or read textbooks, and teachers ask students questions. In this model the central relationship in the classroom is between the teacher and the student. Other schools and teachers emphasize horizontal teaching practices, whereby students work in groups, do projects together, and ask teachers questions. In this model, the central relationship in the classroom is among students.

Consistent with the idea that beliefs underlying social capital are acquired through the practice of cooperation, and that social skills are acquired in early childhood, Algan, Cahuc, and Shleifer (2013) show that horizontal teaching practices can develop social capital. This evidence calls for adding questions on social capital and teaching methods in traditional cross-country educational surveys such as PISA.

Several studies provide justification for policy intervention in the form of early childhood programs aimed at developing children's social skills. Recent longitudinal studies suggest that much of the impact of programs that improve adult achievement (such as the Perry Preschool program or Project STAR in the United States) flows through some sort of noncognitive channel (Heckman and Kautz, 2012; and

Heckman et al., 2013). Algan et al. (2012) use data from a large and detailed longitudinal study following the social, cognitive, and emotional development of men who were kindergarteners in neighborhoods of low socio-economic status in Montreal in 1984. The study incorporates a randomized evaluation of an intensive two-year social skills training program at the beginning of elementary school for the most disruptive children. Those who participated in the training program had significantly more favorable social and economic outcomes upon reaching adult age. By distinguishing between the different cognitive and noncognitive channels through which this intervention operates, the authors conclude that noncognitive skills are the main channel shaping economic outcomes in adult life.

The Role of Institutions

This chapter has so far treated inter-personal trust and institutional trust separately. But as we have mentioned, a key ingredient of inter-personal trust is the belief that others will behave in a fair and cooperative way. The role of institutions is crucial to strengthen cooperation. This is a real policy lever to build trust in the short run by improving the integrity and transparency of institutions.

Figure 10.7 first shows a strong positive correlation between generalized inter-personal trust and the quality of the legal system for a sample of 100 countries. This robustly correlates to using different measures of institutional quality commonly used in the economic literature (such as the rule of law, the strength of property rights, and the enforcement of contracts, as well as government effectiveness, accountability, and corruption) and to controlling for other influences of institutional quality.

Several papers try to go beyond this correlation by showing a causal impact of legal enforcement on generalized inter-personal trust. Tabellini (2008) provides evidence that suggests that generalized morality is more widespread in European regions that used to be ruled by nondespotic political institutions in the distant past. Weak legal enforcement also forces citizens to rely on informal and local rules, and to develop limited trust as opposed to generalized trust. This pattern is well illustrated by the experience of the Italian Mafia. According to Gambetta (1993), feudalism was formally abolished in Sicily much later than in the rest of Europe, and the state was too weak to enforce private property rights concerning land.

The Mafia benefited from this institutional vacuum by offering local protection through informal patronage.

Other evidence shows that the transparency and integrity of institutions are important drivers of generalized trust not only in a cross-section of countries (Rothstein and Stolle, 2008), but also in an experimental context that isolates causality (Rothstein and Eek, 2009). The main theory behind this channel is that citizens who think that civil servants are corrupt extrapolate the same belief to others and to the population in general (Sønderskov and Dinesen, 2016).

Democratic institutions also have an impact on cooperative behavior. Bardhan (2000) finds that farmers are less likely to violate irrigation rules when they themselves have set up those rules. Frey (1998) shows that tax evasion in Swiss cantons is lower when democratic participation is greater. All these different works suggest an impact of democracy on cooperation.

An alternative approach for identifying the effect of institutions on cooperation is to mimic formal and legal rules in experimental games. Formal and legal rules implemented in experimental games obviously differ from real institutions. But this setting has the advantage of providing a controlled experiment to estimate how people change their cooperation and trust depending on exogenous variations in the rules of the games. Fehr and Gachter (2000) analyze cooperation in a public goods game, showing that free riders are heavily punished even if punishment is costly and does not provide any material benefits to the punisher. The opportunity for costly punishment causes a large increase in cooperation levels because potential free riders face a credible threat. In the presence of a costly punishment opportunity, almost complete cooperation can be achieved and maintained during the games. Herrmann, Thöni, and Gächter (2008) have used this setup to measure conditional cooperation in 16 different cities across the world. They find that cooperation for the funding of the public good is the highest in Boston and Melbourne and lowest in Athens and Muscat. This ordering is highly correlated with the rule of law and the transparency of institutions in the corresponding country. Similarly, Rothstein (2011) uses various experiments with students in Sweden and Romania that show their generalized trust and trust in civil servants decline substantially when students witness a police officer accepting a bribe. His interpretation is that the absence of transparency in institutions and of civic spirit by public officials can

Figure 10.7. Generalized Trust and Quality of Institutions

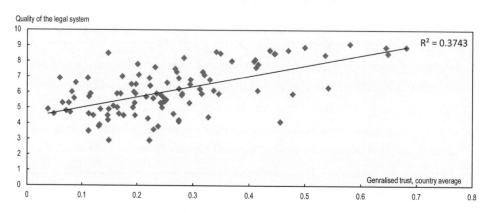

Note: Measures of the quality of the legal system are taken from the Economic Freedom of the World Index (2007). Generalized trust is measured as the country average from World Values Survey (1981–2009).
Source: Algan, Y. and P. Cahuc (2014), "Trust, growth and well-being: New evidence and policy implications," in Aghion, P. and S. Durlauf (eds.), *Handbook of Economic Growth*, Vol. 2, Elsevier, North-Holland, Amsterdam, pp. 49–120. StatLink 2 http://dx.doi.org/10.1787/888933840152.

have very large damaging effects on generalized trust: if public officials, who are expected to represent the law, are corrupt, people infer that most other people cannot be trusted either.

Conclusions

We propose three main recommendations to make progress on the measurement and analysis of inter-personal trust and institutional trust, and on how to reinforce the complementarities between survey measures and experimental measures.

Survey Measures of Trust

Survey measures will always out-perform experimental platforms in terms of sample size and coverage, but there is room for improvement, harmonization, and expansion. As discussed above, current survey measures have various shortcomings: their small sample size, which makes it impossible to get a comprehensive description of the level of trust at the local level and to analyze the economic, social, and policy determinants of trust; their relatively poor coverage, particularly over time, which makes it difficult to analyze how policy reforms affect the evolution of inter-personal trust and trust in institutions; and the heterogeneity across surveys in question wording and response scales.

We recommend two steps:

- Invest in research about methodological issues such as question wording, scale use, and priming effects (i.e., how memory of a preceding stimulus influences response to the question being asked) in trust questions; and move toward a common and integrated approach to measurement for data producers. Institutional trust in particular would benefit from additional methodological research. The *OECD Guidelines on Measuring Trust* are an important step in this direction and include a set of prototype question modules that cover both inter-personal and institutional trust and can be readily inserted in household surveys.

- Include trust measures, especially the generalized trust question, in official (and unofficial) surveys. As shown above, the validity of the questions about inter-personal trust has been firmly established, and this dimension is critical for social progress and well-being. To maximize the use of these data, we need larger sample sizes, more detailed geographic locations, and time variation to provide policy-makers with more useful conclusions about the impact of trust and how to best support it. More research should be done on institutional trust. In addition to the shortcomings in coverage shared by inter-personal trust, we lack a sufficiently deep theoretical understanding of what the construct of institutional trust is. While institutional trust measures based on self-reported surveys are still worth collecting, further developing experimental measures of trust in institutions (discussed below) will be an important part of this line of research.

Experimental Measures of Trust

The important value added of experimental measures is that they describe observed behaviors and provide a true sense of bilateral cooperation between different individuals and groups within a society. They are not better than survey measures in all respects, but they have a different and independent set of biases, so that we can learn something important from looking at the two approaches combined. We thus recommend expanding these measures, in particular TrustLab, which combines classical laboratory experiments with a more traditional internet-based questionnaire based on a representative sample. Progress in this field requires actions to improve the validity of these two approaches:

- Develop behavioral measures of trust in institutions. Implicit Association Tests are a promising step in this direction, because they allow for the measurement of attitudes difficult to capture through explicit self-reporting (Greenwald et al., 2002). Implicit Association Tests have been successfully applied to measure perceptions, stereotypes, and attitudes toward commonly stigmatized groups such as black people, women, and old people. The combination of these behavioral measures of institutional trust with survey questions and their application in different geographic contexts and over time will be of great help.
- Reinforce the complementarities between survey and experimental measures by harmonizing questionnaires. Falk et al. (2016) have conducted representative surveys with a few questions first validated from small experimental samples of students showing a consistency between behaviors in the lab and self-reported surveys. It would be important to enlarge the focus beyond trust by developing and refining a short survey module on norms and values and include such modules in official surveys. The *Guidelines on Measuring Trust* refer to some questions of Falk's Global Preference module in their prototype question modules.

Wrapping Up

If trust is so important for well-being and social progress, policy should focus not only on building it but also protecting it. Trust, and more generally social capital, is characterized by an important asymmetry: it is much more easily destroyed than built. And a negative shock to trust can have an enduring effect on the level of cooperation within communities, as illustrated by the persistent effect of the slave trade on contemporaneous trust in Africa (Nunn, 2009): slavery was a devastating shock, whose consequences lasted for centuries.

There are important lessons from this experience, for example on the response to more recent shocks such as the rapid deregulation of markets in transition economies and the financial crisis. As documented by Aghion et al. (2010), the sharp deregulation of markets in the 1990s in former communist countries, in the context of an initially low cooperative and trusting environment, led to a rise in noncooperative values and in distrust toward others, and to a demand for the return to higher regulation to correct the negative externalities generated by antisocial attitudes. This natural experiment also shows the importance of considering the initial level of trust between individuals and in institutions before recommending any policy reform.

The recent financial crisis provides another illustration of how rapidly the stock of trust can be depleted. As shown by Algan et al. (2017), the financial crisis and the inability of European institutions to cope with its devastating economic effects led to a sharp and dramatic decline in the level of trust in institutions in some countries, especially Southern European countries that previously were the most trusting of the European project.

Governments need the trust of their people to successfully address current and future policy challenges, and to be able to convince the public about the efficacy and necessity of certain—a priori unpopular—policy choices. Inter-personal trust is an important factor for economic growth and development. The loss of trust might then explain the enduring economic crisis in some parts of the world. Trust might well be damaged persistently for generations, even after economic recovery. Insufficient measurement of nonmonetized capital (such as human, social, and natural capital) will lead policy-makers to ignore it, and to invest insufficient resources to protect it. Inadequate investment to cushion shocks, for instance in social safety nets, means that the social capital and well-being of generations could be lost forever.

We need better measures of trust, at higher frequencies, with better geographic coverage and based on more representative samples in order to analyze how trust is affected by shocks, how it can be preserved, and how relevant policies can restore and reinforce it.

Notes

1. Coleman (1990) proposes a similar distinction between "strong ties," defined as the quality of the relationship among family members; and "weak ties," defined as the strength of social relationships outside the family circle.

2. For instance, by comparing Americans of Italian and German origin whose forebears migrated between 1950 and 1980, you can detect differences in trust inherited from these two source countries between 1950 and 1980. You can get time-varying measures of trust inherited from these two countries by running the same exercise for forebears who immigrated in other periods, for instance between 1920 and 1950.

3. This issue could be addressed in future research by looking at inequality in market income, i.e., before redistribution.

References

Acemoglu, D., J. Robinson, and S. Johnson (2001), "The colonial origins of comparative development: An empirical investigation," *American Economic Review*, Vol. 91, pp. 1369–1401.

Aghion, P. et al. (2010), "Regulation and distrust," *Quarterly Journal of Economics*, Vol. 125(3), pp. 1015–1049.

Aghion, P., Y. Algan, and P. Cahuc (2011), "Can policy affect culture? Minimum wage and the quality of labor relations," *Journal of the European Economic Association*, Vol. 9(1), pp. 3–42.

Alesina, A. and E. La Ferrara (2000), "Participation in heterogeneous communities," *Quarterly Journal of Economics*, Vol. 115(3), pp. 847–904.

Algan, Y. et al. (2017), "The European trust crisis and the rise of populism," *Brookings Papers on Economic Activity*.

Algan, Y. et al. (2015), "Social motives and the organization of production: Experimental evidence from open source software," *Sciences Po Working Paper*.

Algan, Y. et al. (2012), "The long-term impact of social skills training at school entry: A randomized controlled trial," working paper.

Algan, Y. and P. Cahuc (2014), "Trust, growth and well-being: New evidence and policy implications," in Aghion, P. and S. Durlauf (eds.), *Handbook of Economic Growth*, Vol. 2, Elsevier, North-Holland, Amsterdam, pp. 49–120.

Algan, Y. and P. Cahuc (2010), "Inherited trust and growth," *American Economic Review*, Vol. 100, pp. 2060–2092.

Algan, Y. and P. Cahuc (2009), "Civic culture and labor market institutions," *American Economic Journal: Macroeconomics*, Vol. 1(1), pp. 1–55.

Algan, Y., P. Cahuc, and A. Shleifer (2013), "Teaching practices and social capital," *American Economic Journal: Applied Economics*, Vol. 5(3), pp. 189–210.

Almond, G. and S. Verba (1989), *The Civic Culture: Political Attitudes and Democracy in Five Nations* (first published 1963), Sage Publications, London.

Anderson, S.P., J. Goeree, and C.A. Holt (1998), "A theoretical analysis of altruism and decision error in public goods games," *Journal of Public Economics*, Vol. 70(2), pp. 297–323.

Andreoni, J. (1989), "Giving with impure altruism: Applications to charity and Ricardian equivalence," *Journal of Political Economy*, Vol. 97(6), pp. 1447–1458.

Arber, S. and J. Ginn (2004), "Ageing and gender: Diversity and change," *Social Trends*, Vol. 34, Office for National Statistics, London, pp. 1–14.

Arnett, J.J. (2008), "The neglected 95%: Why American psychology needs to become less American," *American Psychologist*, Vol. 63(7), pp. 602–614.

Arrow, K.J. (1972), "Gifts and exchanges," *Philosophy & Public Affairs*, Vol. 1(4), pp. 343–362.

Banfield, E. (1958), *The Moral Basis of a Backward Society*, Free Press, New York.

Bardhan, P. (2000), "Irrigation and cooperation: An empirical analysis of 48 irrigation communities in South India," *Economic Development and Cultural Change*, Vol. 48(4), pp. 847–865.

Benabou, R. and J. Tirole (2006), "Incentives and prosocial behavior," *American Economic Review*, Vol. 96(5), pp. 1652–1678.

Benz, M. and S. Meier (2008), "Do people behave in experiments as in the field? Evidence from donations," *Experimental Economics*, Vol. 11(3), pp. 268–281.

Berg, J., J. Dickhaut, and K. McCabe (1995), "Trust, reciprocity and social history," *Games and Economic Behavior*, Vol. 10, pp. 122–142.

Bertrand, M. and A. Schoar (2006), "The role of family in family firms," *Journal of Economic Perspectives*, Vol. 20(2), pp. 73–96.

Beugelsdijk, S. (2006), "A note on the theory and measurement of trust in explaining differences in economic growth," *Cambridge Journal of Economics*, Vol. 30(3), pp. 371–387.

Bisin, A. and T. Verdier (2001), "The economics of cultural transmission and the dynamics of preferences," *Journal of Economic Theory*, Vol. 97, pp. 298–319.

Blind, P.K. (2007), "Building trust in government in the twenty-first century: Review of literature and emerging issues," 7th Global Forum on Reinventing Government—Building Trust in Government, pp. 26–29.

Bloom, N., R. Sadun, and J. van Reenen (2012), "The organization of firms across countries," *Quarterly Journal of Economics*, Vol. 127(4), pp. 1663–1705.

Boarini, R. et al. (2012), "What makes for a better life? The determinants of subjective well-being in OECD countries—evidence from the Gallup World Poll," *OECD Statistics Working Papers*, No. 2012/03, OECD Publishing, Paris, http://dx.doi.org/10.1787/k9b9ltjm937-en.

Bohnet, I. and R. Zeckhauser (2004), "Trust, risk and betrayal," *Journal of Economic Behavior & Organization*, Vol. 55, pp. 467–484.

Boreham, N.C., R. Samurçay, and M. Fischer (eds.) (2002), *Work Process Knowledge*, Routledge, London.

Bowles, S. and H. Gintis (2007), "Power," *University of Massachusetts–Amherst Economics Department Working Paper Series*, No. 2007-03.

Bowles, S. and S. Polania-Reyes (2012), "Economic incentives and social preferences: Substitutes or complements?," *Journal of Economic Literature*, Vol. 50(2), pp. 368–425.

Bruni, L. and G. Ferri (2016), "Does cooperativeness promote happiness? Cross-country evidence," Money and Finance Research group (Mo.Fi.R.), Marche Politecnica University, *Department of Economic and Social Sciences Working Paper*, No. 107.

Charron, N. (2016), "Do corruption measures have a perception problem? Assessing the relationship between experiences and perceptions of corruption among citizens and experts," *European Political Science Review*, Vol. 8(1), pp. 147–171.

Coleman, J.S. (1990), *Foundations of Social Theory*, Belknap Press of Harvard University Press, Cambridge, MA.

Coleman, J.S. (1974), *Power and the Structure of Society*, Norton, New York.

Cox, J., 2004, "How to identify trust and reciprocity," *Games and Economic Behavior*, Vol. 46, pp. 260–281.

Dasgupta, P. (2005), "The economics of social capital," *Economic Record*, Vol. 81, Issue supplement S1, pp. S2–S21.

Dasgupta, P. and I. Serageldin (eds.) (2000), *Social Capital: A Multifaceted Perspective*, World Bank, Washington, DC.

Daude, C., H. Gutiérrez, and Á. Melguizo (2012), "What drives tax morale?," *OECD Development Centre Working Papers*, No. 315, OECD Publishing, Paris, http://dx.doi.org/10.1787/k8zk8m61kzq-en (accessed on 7 June 2018).

Delhey, J., K. Newton, and C. Welzel (2011), "How general is trust in 'most people'? Solving the radius of trust problem," *American Sociological Review*, Vol. 76(5), pp. 786–807.

Dixit, A.K. (2004), *Lawlessness and Economics—Alternative Models of Governance*, Princeton University Press, Princeton.

Ermisch, J. and D. Gambetta (2010), "Do strong family ties inhibit trust?," *Journal of Economic Behavior and Organisation*, Vol. 75(3), pp. 365–376.

Ermisch, J. et al. (2009), "Measuring people's trust," *Journal of the Royal Statistical Society, Series A*, Vol. 172(4), pp. 749–769.

Falk, A. and U. Fischbacher (2006), "A theory of reciprocity," *Games and Economic Behavior*, Vol. 54, pp. 293–315.

Falk, A. et al. (2016), "The preference survey module: A validated instrument for measuring risk, time, and social preferences," *University of Bonn Working Paper*.

Farrell, H. (2009), *The Political Economy of Trust Institutions, Interests, and Inter-firm Cooperation in Italy and Germany*, Cambridge University Press, Cambridge, MA.

Fehr, E. (2009), "On the economics and biology of trust," Presidential address at the 2008 meeting of the European Economic Association, *Journal of the European Economic Association*, Vol. 7(2–3), pp. 235–266.

Fehr, E. and K.M. Schmidt (1999), "A theory of fairness, competition, and cooperation," *Quarterly Journal of Economics*, Vol. 114(3), pp. 817–868, https://doi.org/10.1162 /003355399556151 (accessed on June 7, 2018).

Fehr, E. and S. Gachter (2000), "Cooperation and punishment in public goods games," *American Economic Review*, Vol. 4, pp. 980–994.

Fehr, E. et al. (2002), "A nation-wide laboratory: Examining trust and trustworthiness by integrating behavioral experiments into representative surveys," *CESifo Working Paper*.

Frey, B. (1998), "Institutions and morale: The crowding-out effect," in Putterman, L. and A. Ben-Ner (eds.), *Economics, Values, and Organization*, pp. 437–460, Cambridge University Press, Cambridge.

Frey, B., M. Benz, and A. Stutzer (2004), "Introducing procedural utility: Not only what, but also how matters," *Journal of Institutional and Theoretical Economics (JITE) / Zeitschrift für die gesamte Staatswissenschaft*, Vol. 160(3), pp. 377–401.

Frey, B. and A. Stutzer (2006), "Does marriage make people happy, or do happy people get married?," *Journal of Behavioral and Experimental Economics*, Vol. 35(2), pp. 326–347.

Frey, B. and A. Stutzer (2005), "Happiness research: State and prospects," *Review of Social Economy*, Vol. 63, pp. 207–228.

Fukuyama, F. (1995), *Trust: The Social Virtues and the Creation of Prosperity*, Free Press, New York.

Gambetta, D. (1993), *The Sicilian Mafia: The Business of Private Protection*, Harvard University Press, Cambridge, MA.

Gintis, H. et al. (2005), *Moral Sentiments and Material Interests: The Foundations of Cooperation in Economic Life*, MIT Press, Cambridge, MA.

Glaeser, E.L. et al. (2004), "Do institutions cause growth?," *Journal of Economic Growth*, Vol. 9, pp. 271–303.

Glaeser, E.L. et al. (2000), "Measuring trust," *Quarterly Journal of Economics*, Vol. 115(3), pp. 811–846.

Glaeser, E.L., G. Ponzetto, and A. Shleifer (2007), "Why does democracy need education?," *Journal of Economic Growth*, Vol. 12, pp. 77–99.

Glass, T.A. and J.L. Balfour (2003), "Neighborhoods, aging and functional limitations," in Kawachi, I. and L.F. Berkman, *Neighborhoods and Health*, Oxford University Press, New York.

Greenwald, A.G. et al., (2002), "A unified theory of implicit attitudes, stereotypes, self-esteem, and self-concept," *Psychological Review*, Vol. 109, pp. 3–25.

Greif, A. (1994), "Theoretical reflection on collectivist and individualist societies," *Journal of Political Economy*, Vol. 102(5), pp. 912–950.

Greif, A. (1993), "Contract enforceability and economic institutions in early trade: The Maghribi traders' coalition," *American Economic Review*, Vol. 83(3), pp. 525–548.

Guiso, L., P. Sapienza, and L. Zingales (2011), "Civic capital as the missing link," in Benhabib, J., A. Bisin, and M.O. Jackson (eds.), *Handbook of Social Economics*, Vol. 1A, Elsevier Science, North-Holland, Amsterdam.

Guiso, L., P. Sapienza, and L. Zingales (2008), "Long-term persistence," *National Bureau of Economic Research Working Paper*, No. 14278.

Hamano, T. et al. (2010), "Social capital and mental health in Japan: A multilevel analysis," *PLoS ONE*, Vol. 5(10), https://doi.org/10.1371/journal.pone.0013214 (accessed on June 7, 2018).

Hardin, R. (2004), *Trust and trustworthiness*, Russell Sage Foundation, New York.

Heckman, J.J. and T.D. Kautz (2012), "Hard evidence on soft skills," *Labour Economics*, Vol. 19(4), pp. 451–464.

Heckman, J.J. et al. (2013), "Understanding the mechanisms through which an influential early childhood program boosted adult outcomes," *American Economic Review*, Vol. 103(6), pp. 2052–2086.

Helliwell, J. (2007), "Well-being and social capital: Does suicide pose a puzzle?," *Social Indicators Research*, Vol. 81(3), pp. 455–496.

Helliwell, J. and R. Putnam (2007), "Education and social capital," *Eastern Economics Journal*, Vol. 33(1), pp. 1–19.

Helliwell, J. and R. Putnam (2004), "The social context of well-being," *Philosophical Transactions of the Royal Society B: Biological Sciences*, Vol. 359(1449), pp. 1435–1446.

Helliwell, J. and S. Wang (2011), "Weekends and subjective well-being," *National Bureau of Economic Research Working Paper*, No. 17180.

Helliwell, J. et al. (2009), "International evidence on the social context of well-being," *National Bureau of Economic Research Working Paper*, No. 14720.

Henrich, J. et al. (2001), "In search of homo economicus: Behavioral experiments in 15 small-scale societies," *American Economic Review*.

Herrmann, B., C. Thöni, and S. Gächter (2008), "Antisocial punishment across societies," *Science*, Vol. 319(5868), pp. 1362–1367.

Hoff, K., M. Kshetramade, and E. Fehr (2011), "Caste and punishment: the legacy of caste culture in norm enforcement," *Economic Journal*, Vol. 121(556), pp. F449–F475, https://doi.org/10.1111/j.1468-0297.2011.02476.x.

Hoff, K. and J.E. Stiglitz (2016), "Striving for balance in economics: Towards a theory of the social determination of behavior," *Policy Research Working Paper Series 7537*, World Bank.

Holm, H. and A. Danielson (2005), "Tropic trust versus Nordic trust: Experimental evidence from Tanzania and Sweden," *Economic Journal*, Vol. 115, pp. 505–532.

Intawan, C. and S.P. Nicholson (2017), "My trust in government is implicit: Automatic trust in government and system support," unpublished manuscript.

Karlan, D. (2005), "Using experimental economics to measure social capital and predict financial decisions," *American Economic Review*, Vol. 95(5), pp. 1688–1699.

Klijn, E.H., J. Edelenbos, and B. Steijn (2010), "Trust in governance networks; its impact and outcomes," *Administration and Society*, Vol. 42(2), pp. 193–221.

Knack, S. and P. Keefer (1997), "Does social capital have an economic payoff? A cross-country investigation," *Quarterly Journal of Economics*, Vol. 112(4), pp. 1252–1288.

Kosfeld, M. et al. (2005), "Oxytocin increases trust in humans," *Nature*, Vol. 435, pp. 673–676.

Kumlin, S. and B. Rothstein (2005), "Making and breaking social capital: The impact of welfare state institutions," *Comparative Political Studies*.

La Porta, R. et al. (1997), "Trust in large organizations," *American Economic Review, Papers and Proceedings*, Vol. 87(2), pp. 333–338.

Laury, S.K. and L.O. Taylor (2008), "Altruism spillovers: Are behaviors in context-free experiments predictive of altruism toward a naturally occurring public good?," *Journal of Economic Behavior & Organization*, Vol. 65(1), pp. 9–29.

Lazzarini, S. et al. (2005), "Measuring trust: An experiment in Brazil," *Brazilian Journal of Applied Economics*, Vol. 9(2), pp. 153–169.

Lindström, M. (2005), "Social capital, the miniaturization of community and high alcohol consumption: A population-based study," *Alcohol and Alcoholism*, Vol. 40(6), pp. 556–562.

Lochner, K.A. et al. (2003), "Social capital and neighborhood mortality rates in Chicago," *Social Science & Medicine*, Vol. 56(8), pp. 1797–1805.

Marien, S. and M. Hooghe (2011), "Does political trust matter? An empirical investigation into the relation between political trust and support for law compliance," *European Journal of Political Research*, Vol. 50(2), pp. 267–291.

Murphy, K., T.R. Tyler, and A. Curtis (2009), "Nurturing regulatory compliance: Is procedural justice effective when people question the legitimacy of the law?," *Regulation & Governance*, Vol. 3, pp. 1–26.

Murtin, F. et al. (2018), "Trust and its determinants: Evidence from the Trustlab experiment," *OECD Statistics Working Papers*, No. 2018/02, OECD Publishing, Paris, https://doi.org/10.1787/869ef2ec-en.

Nooteboom, B. (2007), "Social capital, institutions and trust," *Review of Social Economy*, Vol. 65(1), pp. 29–53.

North, D.C. (1990), *Institutions, Institutional Change and Economic Performance*, Cambridge University Press, Cambridge, MA.

Nunn, N. (2009), "The importance of history for economic development," *Annual Review of Economics*, Vol. 1, pp. 65–92.

OECD (2017), *OECD Guidelines on Measuring Trust*, OECD Publishing, Paris, http://dx.doi.org/10.1787/-en.

OECD (2016), *Society at a Glance 2016: OECD Social Indicators*, OECD Publishing, Paris, http://dx.doi.org/10.1787/-en.

OECD (2015), "Trust in government," in *Government at a Glance 2015*, OECD Publishing, Paris, http://dx.doi.org/10.1787/_glance-2015-50-en.

OECD (2013a), "Trust in government," in *Government at a Glance 2013*, OECD Publishing, Paris, http://dx.doi.org/10.1787/_glance-2013-7-en.

OECD (2013b), *OECD Guidelines on Measuring Subjective Well-Being*, OECD Publishing, Paris, https://doi.org/10.1787/9789264191655-en.

OECD (2011), *How's Life? Measuring Well-Being*, OECD Publishing, Paris, http://dx.doi.org/10.1787/-en.

OECD (2001), *The Well-Being of Nations: The Role of Human and Social Capital*, OECD Publishing, Paris, http://dx.doi.org/10.1787/-en.

De Oliveira, A.C., R.T. Croson, and C. Eckel (2014), "One bad apple? Heterogeneity and information in public good provision," *Experimental Economics*, Vol. 18(1), pp. 116–135, https://doi.org/10.1007/s10683-014-9412-1 (accessed on June 7, 2018).

Petrou, S. and E. Kupek (2008), "Social capital and its relationship with measures of health status: Evidence from the Health Survey for England 2003," *Health Economics*, Vol. 17(1), pp. 127–143.

Poortinga, W. (2006), "Social relations or social capital? Individual and community health effects of bonding social capital," *Social Science & Medicine*, Vol. 63(1), pp. 255–270.

Putnam, R. (2000), *Bowling Alone: The Collapse and Revival of American Community*, Simon and Schuster, New York.

Putnam, R., R. Leonardi, and R.Y. Nanetti (1993), *Making Democracy Work: Civic Traditions in Modern Italy*, Princeton University Press, Princeton.

Rothstein, B. (2011), *The Quality of Government, Social Trust and Inequality in International Perspective*, University of Chicago Press, Chicago.

Rothstein, B. (2000), "Trust, social dilemmas and collective memory," *Journal of Theoretical Politics*, Vol. 12(4), pp. 477–501, https://doi.org/10.1177/0951692800012004007 (accessed on June 7, 2018).

Rothstein, B. and D. Eek (2009), "Political corruption and social trust—an experimental approach," *Rationality and Society*, Vol. 21(1), pp. 81–112.

Rothstein, B. and D. Stolle (2008), "The state and social capital: An institutional theory of generalized trust," *Comparative Politics*, Vol. 40, pp. 441–467.

Rothstein, B. and E.M. Uslaner (2005), "All for one: Equality, corruption, and social trust," *World Politics*, Vol. 58(1), pp. 41–72.

Sanfey, A.G. et al. (2003), "The neural basis of economic decision-making in the ultimatum game," *Science*, Vol. 300, pp. 1755–1758.

Scrivens, K. and C. Smith (2013), "Four interpretations of social capital: An agenda for measurement," *OECD Statistics Working Papers*, No. 2013/06, OECD Publishing, Paris, http://dx.doi.org/10.1787/jzbcx010wmt-en.

Sønderskov, K.M. and P. Dinesen (2016), "Trusting the state, trusting each other? The effect of institutional trust on social trust," *Political Behavior*, Vol. 38(1), pp. 179–202.

Stiglitz, J.E. and R. Arnott (1991), "Moral hazard and nonmarket institutions: Dysfunctional crowding out or peer monitoring?," *American Economic Review*, Vol. 81(1), pp. 179–190.

Stiglitz, J.E., A. Sen, and J.-P. Fitoussi (2009), *Report by the Commission on the Measurement of Economic and Social Progress*, http://ec.europa.eu/eurostat/documents/118025 /118123/Fitoussi+Commission+report.

Tabellini, G. (2010), "Culture and institutions: Economic development in the regions of Europe," *Journal of the European Economic Association*, Vol. 8(4), pp. 677–716.

Tabellini, G. (2008), "Institutions and Culture," *Journal of the European Economic Association*, Vol. 6(2–3), pp. 255–294, https://doi.org/10.1162/JEEA.2008.6.2-3.255 (accessed on June 7, 2018).

UNECE (2013), *Conference of European Statisticians Recommendations on Measuring Sus-*

tainable Development, Geneva, www.unece.org/fileadmin/DAM/stats/publications /2013/CES_SD_web.pdf.

Uslaner, E.M. (2008), "Trust as a moral value," in Castiglione, D., J. van Deth, and G. Wolleb (eds.), *The Handbook of Social Capital*, pp. 101–121, Oxford University Press, Oxford.

Uslaner, E.M. (2002), *The Moral Foundations of Trust*, Cambridge University Press, Cambridge.

Wilkinson, R.G. (2000), *Mind the Gap: Hierarchies, Health, and Human Evolution*, Yale University Press.

World Bank, (2002), *World Development Report 2002: Building Institutions for Markets*, Oxford University Press, New York.

Zack, P., R. Kursban, and W. Matzner (2004), "The neurobiology of trust," *Annals of the New York Academy of Sciences*, pp. 224–227.

Zhao, H. and S.H. Kim (2011), "An exploratory examination of the social capital and FDI linkage and the moderating role of regulatory quality: A cross-country study," *Thunderbird International Business Review*, Vol. 53(5), pp. 629–646.

HIGH-LEVEL EXPERT GROUP ON THE MEASUREMENT OF ECONOMIC PERFORMANCE AND SOCIAL PROGRESS

Chairs

Joseph E. Stiglitz, Professor of Economics, Business and International Affairs, Columbia University

Jean-Paul Fitoussi, Professor of Economics at Sciences-Po, Paris and Luiss University, Rome

Martine Durand, Chief Statistician, OECD

Members

Yann Algan, Professor of Economics, Sciences-Po, Paris

François Bourguignon, Paris School of Economics

Angus Deaton, Senior Scholar and Dwight D. Eisenhower Professor of Economics and International Affairs Emeritus, Woodrow Wilson School of Public and International Affairs and Economics Department, Princeton University

Enrico Giovannini, Professor of Economic Statistics, University of Rome Tor Vergata

Jacob Hacker, Director of the Institution for Social and Policy Studies, and Stanley B. Resor Professor of Political Science, Yale University

Geoffrey Heal, Garrett Professor of Public Policy and Corporate Responsibility, Professor of Economics and Finance, Columbia University Graduate School of Business; Director of the Earth Institute Center for Economy, Environment, and Society, Columbia University

Ravi Kanbur, T.H. Lee Professor of World Affairs, International Professor of Applied Economics and Management and Professor of Economics, Cornell University

Alan B. Krueger, Bendheim Professor of Economics and Public Affairs, Princeton University

Nora Lustig, Samuel Z. Stone Professor of Latin American Economics, Tulane University

Jil Matheson, Former United Kingdom National Statistician

Thomas Piketty, Professor, Paris School of Economics

Walter Radermacher, Former Director-General, Eurostat

Chiara Saraceno, Honorary fellow at the Collegio Carlo Alberto, Turin

Arthur Stone, Senior Behavioral Scientist, Professor of Psychology, University of Southern California

Yang Yao, Director of CCER and Dean of National School of Development, Peking University

Rapporteurs

Marco Mira d'Ercole, OECD

Elizabeth Beasley, CEPREMAP and Sciences-Po